discover
SAN
FRANCISCO

ALISON BING

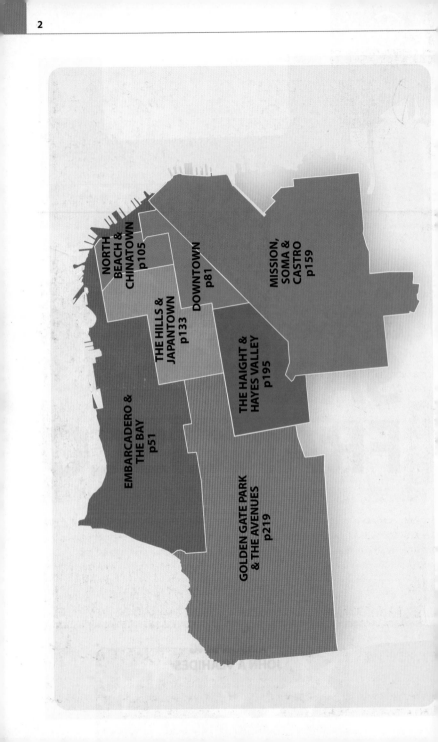

NORTH BEACH & CHINATOWN p105

THE HILLS & JAPANTOWN p133

DOWNTOWN p81

MISSION, SOMA & CASTRO p159

EMBARCADERO & THE BAY p51

THE HAIGHT & HAYES VALLEY p195

GOLDEN GATE PARK & THE AVENUES p219

DISCOVER SAN FRANCISCO

Embarcadero & the Bay (p51) Imitate the sea lions and go gourmet by the sparkling bay.

Downtown (p81) Grand buildings and great performances, plus dive bars and bargain Levis.

North Beach & Chinatown (p105) Duck into alleys named after poets for cappuccino and hot fortune cookies.

The Hills & Japantown (p133) Ride cable cars into the sunset, then rock and sushi-roll the night away.

Mission, SoMa & Castro (p159) Where the action is: clubs, skate parks, gallery openings and late-night burritos.

The Haight & Hayes Valley (p195) Fashion rebels, bookish anarchists and the occasional Zen monk troll the sidewalks.

Golden Gate Park & the Avenues (p219) Discover SF's wild streak alongside waddling penguins and charging bison.

Day Trips (p243) Sip your way across Wine Country, wander mighty redwoods or contemplate crashing surf.

⬆ CONTENTS

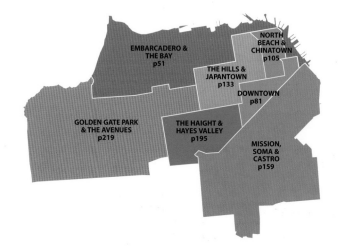

EMBARCADERO &
THE BAY
p51

NORTH
BEACH &
CHINATOWN
p105

THE HILLS &
JAPANTOWN
p133

DOWNTOWN
p81

GOLDEN GATE PARK
& THE AVENUES
p219

THE HAIGHT &
HAYES VALLEY
p195

MISSION,
SOMA &
CASTRO
p159

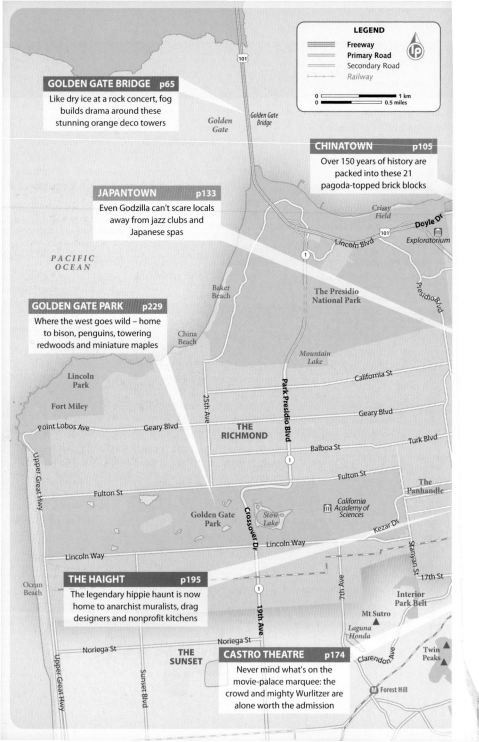

LEGEND

Freeway
Primary Road
Secondary Road
Railway

0 _____ 1 km
0 _____ 0.5 miles

GOLDEN GATE BRIDGE p65

Like dry ice at a rock concert, fog builds drama around these stunning orange deco towers

CHINATOWN p105

Over 150 years of history are packed into these 21 pagoda-topped brick blocks

JAPANTOWN p133

Even Godzilla can't scare locals away from jazz clubs and Japanese spas

GOLDEN GATE PARK p229

Where the west goes wild – home to bison, penguins, towering redwoods and miniature maples

THE HAIGHT p195

The legendary hippie haunt is now home to anarchist muralists, drag designers and nonprofit kitchens

CASTRO THEATRE p174

Never mind what's on the movie-palace marquee: the crowd and mighty Wurlitzer are alone worth the admission

Golden Gate

Golden Gate Bridge

Crissy Field

Doyle Dr

Lincoln Blvd

Exploratorium

PACIFIC OCEAN

Baker Beach

The Presidio National Park

Presidio Blvd

China Beach

Mountain Lake

Lincoln Park

Fort Miley

Point Lobos Ave

Geary Blvd

25th Ave

Park Presidio Blvd

California St

Geary Blvd

THE RICHMOND

Balboa St

Turk Blvd

Upper Great Hwy

Fulton St

Fulton St

The Panhandle

California Academy of Sciences

Golden Gate Park

Stow Lake

Kezar Dr

Crossover Dr

Lincoln Way

Stanyan St

Lincoln Way

Ocean Beach

17th St

7th Ave

Interior Park Belt

Mt Sutro

19th Ave

Laguna Honda

Noriega St

Noriega St

THE SUNSET

Sunset Blvd

Clarendon Ave

Twin Peaks

Forest Hill

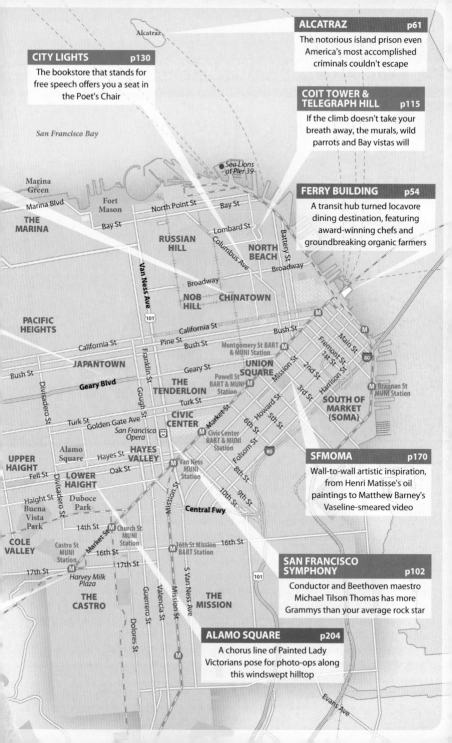

ALCATRAZ p61

The notorious island prison even America's most accomplished criminals couldn't escape

CITY LIGHTS p130

The bookstore that stands for free speech offers you a seat in the Poet's Chair

San Francisco Bay

COIT TOWER & TELEGRAPH HILL p115

If the climb doesn't take your breath away, the murals, wild parrots and Bay vistas will

FERRY BUILDING p54

A transit hub turned locavore dining destination, featuring award-winning chefs and groundbreaking organic farmers

Marina Green

Marina Blvd

Fort Mason

THE MARINA

North Point St

Bay St

Lombard St

Bay St

Sea Lions at Pier 39

RUSSIAN HILL

Columbus Ave

NORTH BEACH

Battery St

Broadway

Broadway

Van Ness Ave

NOB HILL

CHINATOWN

PACIFIC HEIGHTS

California St

Pine St

Bush St

101

Bush St

California St

JAPANTOWN

Franklin St

Geary St

Montgomery St BART & MUNI Station

UNION SQUARE

Fremont St

Main St

1st St

M

80

Bush St

Geary Blvd

Gough St

THE TENDERLOIN

Powell St BART & MUNI Station

Mission St

2nd St

Harrison St

M Brannan St MUNI Station

Divisadero St

Turk St

Turk St

Golden Gate Ave

Market St

6th St

Howard St

5th St

3rd St

SOUTH OF MARKET (SOMA)

CIVIC CENTER

San Francisco Opera

M Civic Center BART & MUNI Station

Folsom St

UPPER HAIGHT

Alamo Square

Hayes St

HAYES VALLEY

80

Fell St

Oak St

LOWER HAIGHT

M Van Ness MUNI Station

8th St

SFMOMA p170

Wall-to-wall artistic inspiration, from Henri Matisse's oil paintings to Matthew Barney's Vaseline-smeared video

Divisadero St

Haight St

Duboce Park

Mission St

9th St

10th St

Haight St

Buena Vista Park

14th St

Central Fwy

M Church St MUNI Station

COLE VALLEY

Castro St MUNI Station

Market St

16th St

M 16th St Mission BART Station

16th St

SAN FRANCISCO SYMPHONY p102

Conductor and Beethoven maestro Michael Tilson Thomas has more Grammys than your average rock star

17th St

M

Harvey Milk Plaza

17th St

S Van Ness Ave

101

THE CASTRO

Guerrero St

Valencia St

Mission St

THE MISSION

Dolores St

ALAMO SQUARE p204

A chorus line of Painted Lady Victorians pose for photo-ops along this windswept hilltop

M

Evans Ave

Alcatraz

↘ THIS IS SAN FRANCISCO

California is all about grand gestures, staggering sequoia trees and breathtaking coastline. But then there's San Francisco, that impertinent seven-by-seven-mile peninsula that sticks up into the Bay like a raised forefinger. Is it volunteering for parade duty, ordering sustainable sushi or just begging to differ?

As this is San Francisco, the answer is obvious: all of the above. Good times and social revolutions tend to start here, from manic gold rushes to blissful hippie Be-Ins. Spontaneity is practically a local rule of law. If there's a skateboard move yet to be busted, technology still unimagined, poems left unspoken or a green scheme untested, chances are it's about to happen here. Yes, right now: this town has lost almost everything in earthquakes and dot-com gambles, but never its nerve.

In this capital of radical reinvention, dinnertime may be the only tradition that's held sacred. Most meals begin with heads bowed, as San Franciscans seek menu suggestions from their social media networks on their smart phones – all invented in the Bay Area, of course. With an abundance of ultrafresh, locally grown ingredients and the most restaurants per capita anywhere in North America, San Francisco is spoiled for choice.

No wonder composting is mandatory citywide: it's the least this pack of picky eaters can do to give back to the many pioneering local, organic farms that keep them so well fed.

The city's population numbers under a million, yet everyone seems to converge on year-round farmers markets, same-sex weddings at City Hall or free concerts in Golden Gate Park – and no one waits for an excuse to throw on some glitter and start a parade. Never afraid to lose its shirt on the next big idea, this town makes a virtue of shirtlessness at frequent street fairs and the clothing-optional end of Baker Beach. So consider permission permanently granted to step up, strip down and go too far. Once you get outlandish, you've got the hang of San Francisco.

'this town has lost almost everything in earthquakes and dot-com gambles, but never its nerve'

↘ SAN FRANCISCO'S
TOP 25 EXPERIENCES

1

↘ GO WILD IN GOLDEN GATE PARK

The resident bison agree: civilization is overrated. Golden Gate Park (p229) lets San Franciscans do what comes naturally, whether that be roaming a rainforest dome, tickling tiny bonsai or sniffing carnivorous plants and squealing 'Eeewwww!' In their paddock, the bison just shake their shaggy heads, and carry on stampeding.

↘ GLIMPSE THE GOLDEN GATE BRIDGE 2

Sunny days suit most cities just fine, but San Francisco saves its most dramatic view of **Golden Gate Bridge** (p65) for lousy weather. When fog swirls around the towers, romantics and photographers rejoice – and you'll swear you see the ghost of Alfred Hitchcock at misty **Fort Point** (p68), rubbing his hands with glee at the noir-movie scenery.

3

↘ LOCKUP IN ALCATRAZ

Step into the cell, shut the iron door and listen carefully: beyond these bars and across the Bay, you can hear the murmur of everyday life. Now you appreciate how **Alcatraz** (p61) became America's most notorious prison, and why inmates risked rip tides to escape. On the boat back to San Francisco, freedom never felt so good.

1 Roller skaters, Golden Gate Park (p229); 2 Surfers beneath the Golden Gate Bridge (p65); 3 D-Block cells, Alcatraz (p61)

⬎ GRAZE AT THE FERRY BUILDING

4

Rock stars must envy **Ferry Building** (p62) farmers and sous-chefs. On market days, there's pandemonium for organic peach samples, an edible-wildflower fan club and complete Korean-taco hysteria; inside, foodies jockey for position for **Hog Island** (p73) oysters, **Mijita** (p73) fish tacos, and **Recchiuti** (p79) chocolate printed with limited-edition artwork.

5

⬎ CAREEN ON CABLE CARS

A firm grip on the brake seems to be the only thing between you and cruel fate as your **cable car** picks up speed downhill, and heads smack into a traffic jam. But Andrew Hallidie's 1873 contraptions have held up miraculously well on San Francisco's breakneck slopes, and creaking breaks just add to the carnival-like thrills.

↘ FIND YOUR FORTUNE IN CHINATOWN

Don't let the quaint deco pagodas fool you: these 21 blocks have made and lost fortunes, survived earthquakes and changed history. Bootleggers battled and revolutionaries plotted in these 150-year-old **alleyways** (p108), and fortunes are still made fresh daily at **Golden Gate Fortune Cookie Company** (p131).

6

4 SABRINA DALBESIO; 5 HOLGER LEUE; 6 ROBERTO GEROMETTA

4 Mijita, Ferry Building (p62); 5 Cable car, Hyde St; 6 Waverly Place (p118), Chinatown

↘ SEE SFMOMA SENSATIONS

With art-star discoveries such as Matthew Barney, the San Francisco Museum of Modern Art (SFMOMA; p170) seems audaciously gifted. But wait until you see what more the museum has in store: with the recent windfall of 1100 works donated by the Fisher family (founders of the Gap) and a $480 million expansion in the works, the museum is set to triple in size.

7

8

⬐ WAX POETIC IN NORTH BEACH

Get well-versed in the Poet's Chair at City Lights Bookstore (p130), then explore the Beat Museum (p116) and North Beach alleyways named for Beat Generation writers, from Kerouac to Kauffman (p113). If the haiku still won't come to you, try an espresso from Caffe Trieste (p128) – and check out the bathroom walls for literary inspiration.

⬐ CHEER 'ENCORE!' FOR MORE

9

Hearts skip beats to keep time with Beethoven and Rossini as performed by the Grammy-winning San Francisco Symphony (p102) and San Francisco Opera (p101). When the last note evaporates into thin air, the hushed crowd suddenly roars – SF knows its anthems and arias, and never takes conductor Michael Tilson Thomas or divas such as Renee Fleming for granted.

7 THOMAS WINZ; 8 DIANA MAYFIELD; 9 RICK GERHARTER

7 San Francisco Museum of Modern Art (SFMOMA; p170); 8 City Lights Bookstore (p130); 9 War Memorial Opera House

10

⬎ EXPLORE CALIFORNIA ACADEMY OF SCIENCES

Adorable tree frogs, flirty butterflies, and a giant, bashful pink octopus: even the most worldly visitor is sure to gasp at the **California Academy of Sciences** (p231). On Thursday nights, come for sunset cocktails on Renzo Piano's ingenious wildflower roof, just as the penguins are dozing off.

⬎ FLY YOUR RAINBOW FLAG

11

For everyone who left theirs at home – or in the closet – there's a giant rainbow flag greeting arrivals at **Harvey Milk Plaza** (p173). Head over the rainbow and into the Castro, where if party boys and political activists have their way, a good time and civil rights will be had by all.

↘ CONQUER TELEGRAPH HILL

Wild parrots may mock your progress every step of the way up Telegraph Hill's Filbert staircase and Greenwich St Stairway but, really, they can't expect to keep scenery like this to themselves. Hidden gardens, Bay vistas and rare birds in the trees reward you for taking the scenic route to **Coit Tower** (p115).

↘ DISCOVER YOUR SECRET MISSION

Bragging about Mission finds is a competitive sport in San Francisco, whether it's a mural in progress spotted in **Clarion Alley** (p168) or a desert-island-worthy disc from **Discolandia** (p193). But some secrets are meant to be shared: burritos from **La Taqueria** (p177) are too massive for one, and adults read their teenage journal entries onstage at the **Make-Out Room** (p185).

10 California Academy of Sciences (p231); 11 Harvey Milk Plaza (p173); 12 Filbert Street Steps (p115) leading up Telegraph Hill; 13 San Francisco Print Collective mural, Clarion Alley (p168)

14

↘ FLASHBACK IN THE HAIGHT

Groovy is a permanent state of mind in the Haight (p200), where hippies became rock stars and vintage stores (p213) keep suede fringe in fashion. The Summer of Love may be over, but anarchists still run a bookstore (p213), musicians perform free shows at Amoeba (p215), and volunteers (p203) dish free food for those in need.

⬊ SUNBATHE WITH SEA LIONS

Sea lions (p63) are living the dream at Pier 39: spending sunny days lolling on yacht docks, canoodling with harems and loudly digesting fresh, local seafood feasts. The city's unofficial mascots have been sunning their backsides at this marina since 1989, inspiring humans to follow suit along the wharf.

15

14 ANTHONY PIDGEON; 15 STEPHEN SAKS

14 Haight St (p203); 15 Sea lions, Pier 39 (p63)

↘ HIT THE ART SCENE

No white wall is safe in San Francisco: each month, artists take them by storm in **galleries** along Geary St (p87), Yerba Buena Arts District (p170), and the Mission (p167). Art schools keep the city supplied with fresh talent, so you'll never see what's coming next – and openings are the best parties in town, with freak fashion and free hooch.

16

⬏ MIND-BOGGLE AT THE EXPLORATORIUM

17

No theory is too far-out to test at the **Exploratorium** (p66). Can skateboards defy gravity? What can your eyes see in total darkness? Do puffy cheeks automatically make people cuter? The freaky hands-on displays here earned a MacArthur Genius Grant. If science class was always this cool we'd all have PhDs.

⬏ SCORE SF STYLE

18

Break out of the rut with fashion-forward finds in the Victorian storefront boutiques of **Hayes Valley** (p215), **Haight Street** (p213), **Fillmore Street** (p154) and the **Mission** (p190). Local designers and bold fashion statements win pride of place, and killer sale racks put mall mark-ups to shame.

16 SABRINA DALBESIO; 17 RICK GERHARTER; 18 SABRINA DALBESIO

16 Galería de la Raza (p170); 17 Exploratorium (p66); 18 Flight 001 (p218), Hayes Valley

↘ FROLIC IN THE PRESIDIO

Lollygagging and kite-flying on **Crissy Field** (p66) airstrip and public nudity at **Baker Beach** (p67): the behavior you'll see nowadays in the Presidio would've earned soldiers reprimands here a couple of decades ago, when this park was still a military base. Today the only commanding presence is the Yoda statue near the LucasArts offices, and he seems mildly amused.

19

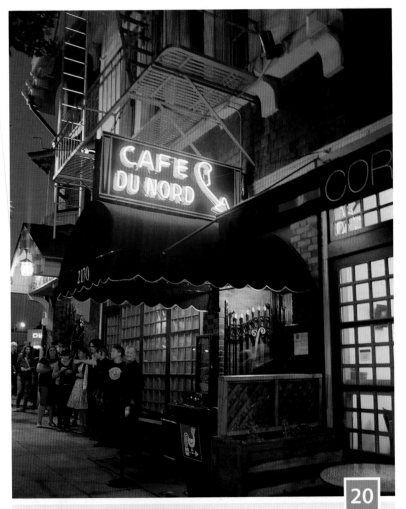

20

↘ DRINK IN SPEAKEASIES

A brief flirtation with respectability in 1906 convinced City Hall to ban dancing in bars, driving the action underground into speakeasies such as **Café du Nord** (p189) – and that's exactly how San Franciscans prefer it. In **SoMa** (p181), **Tenderloin** (p99) and **Mission** (p181) bars, expect speakeasy-style basement dance scenes, back-patio action and impromptu drag shows.

19 ANTHONY PIDGEON; 20 SABRINA DALBESIO

19 Crissy Field (p66); 20 Café du Nord (p189), the Castro

21

⬂ FIND NOVEL WAYS DOWN RUSSIAN HILL

Lombard Street (p142) gets all the attention, but shady stairway walks near **Sterling Park** (p141) and **Ina Coolbrith Park** (p144) are Russian Hill's saving graces. All that greenery prevented the 1906 fires from spreading to the area from Nob Hill, preserving quaint cottages for Jack Kerouac's marathon *On the Road* writing session and Macondray Lane for *Tales of the City* fame (see p144).

⬂ UNWIND IN JAPANTOWN **22**

Between tech booms, **Japantown** (p143) is where San Francisco spends its precious downtime. Lolita Goths in lacy pinafores raid the manga at **Kinokuniya** (p156), jazz cats bust air-piano moves at **Yoshi's** (p154), glowing grandmothers admire the ikebana at **Ikenobo** (p145) after visiting **Kabuki Springs & Spa** (p153) and black-clad film buffs debate the Brazilian dramas shown at **Sundance Kabuki Cinema** (p153).

↘ EAT YOUR VEGETABLES – GLADLY

23

Supermodels will quit nudging around lunch with their forks here – the Bay Area's fresh, organic produce makes even salads irresistible. At **Fleur de Lys** (p95), **Ubuntu** (p246) and **French Laundry** (p246), star chefs create lavish vegetarian tasting menus, and **Greens** (p74) and **Millennium** (p97) push vegetables from the sides to the center of the plate.

24

↘ GET SUNSET SHIVERS

When surfers clear out and fog rolls in, **Ocean Beach** (p229) will give you goosebumps. Ships fade into ghostly silhouettes, and an orange glow stretches across the horizon until you can't take it anymore. Head to join the shivering Sunset crowds warming up in **Mollusk** (p242) hoodies at **Trouble Coffee** (p236) and **Java Beach Café** (p238).

21 SABRINA DALBESIO; 22 SABRINA DALBESIO; 23 SABRINA DALBESIO; 24 ROBERTO GEROMETTA

21 Sterling Park (p141); 22 Japantown's Peace Pagoda (p143); 23 Fresh vegetables at a San Francisco eatery; 24 Ocean Beach (p229)

⬎ SHOUT FROM THE HILLTOPS

Gravity seems unkind as you scale SF's steepest hills, with calf muscles and cable-car wheels groaning in unison – but all grumbling ends once you hit the summit. With wind-sculpted trees, Victorian turrets and the world at your feet atop **Corona Heights Park** (p173), **Buena Vista Park** (p203) and 41 other peaks, one word comes to mind: wheeeeee!

25

25 SABRINA DALBESIO

View from Corona Heights Park (p173)

SAN FRANCISCO'S TOP ITINERARIES

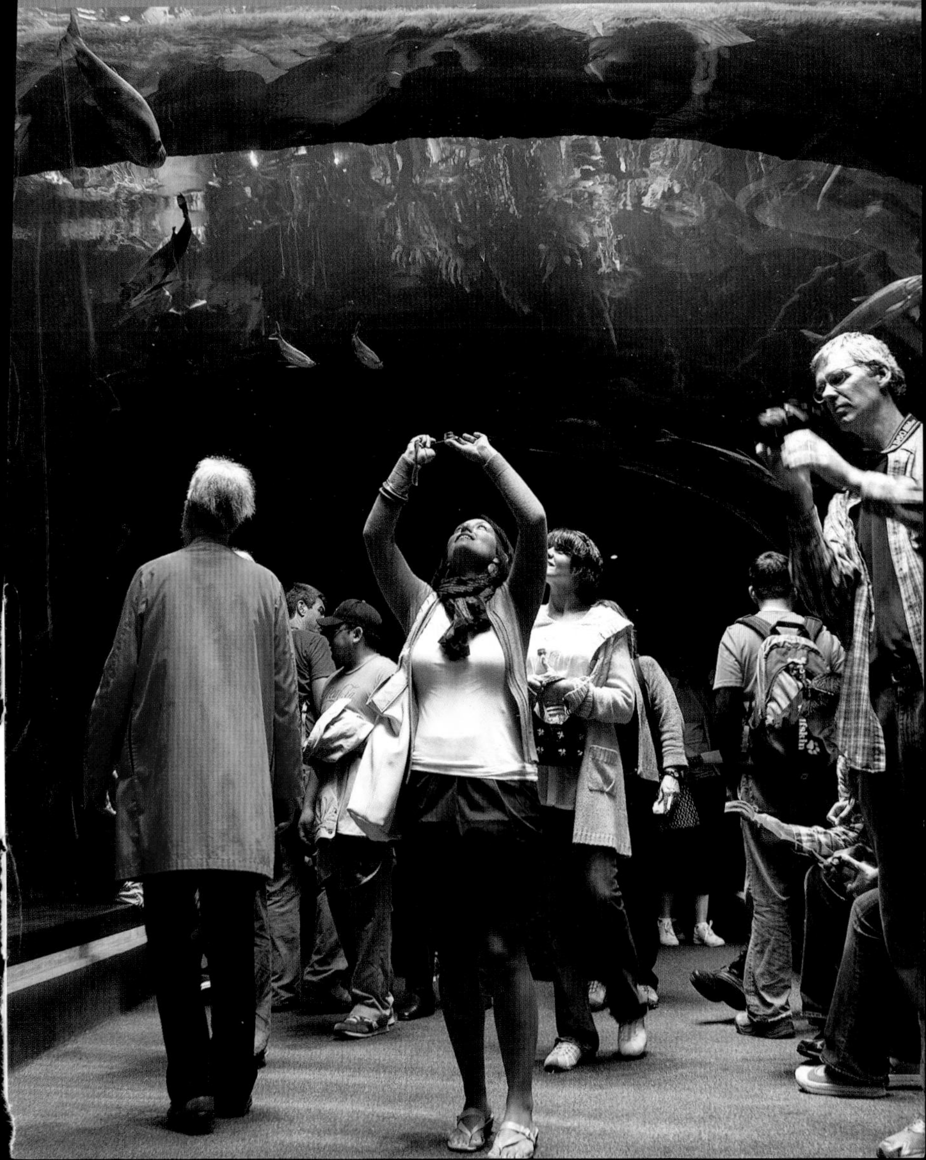

TOTALLY TRIPPY SF

FIVE HOURS GOLDEN GATE PARK TO THE FILLMORE AUDITORIUM

The psychedelic '60s may be over but San Francisco hasn't lost its surprise factor. Spend an afternoon in Golden Gate Park and the Haight, and enter a San Francisco state of mind.

❶ GOLDEN GATE PARK

Winter in Sharon Meadow was an unlikely setting for San Fran's clothing-optional Summer of Love – but strange things happen every day in Golden Gate Park (p229). Here you'll find pagan altars, a tiny bonsai forest in the Japanese Tea Garden (p232), giant carnivorous plants in the Conservatory of Flowers (p233) and Ruth Asawa's light-shattering sculptures in the MH de Young Memorial Museum (p231).

❷ CALIFORNIA ACADEMY OF SCIENCES

Dude, how'd they get poppies on the roof? Renzo Piano's LEED-certified California Academy of Sciences (p231) sprouts California wildflowers from its domed roof, but the scene only gets wilder inside the building. This place teems with wildlife, from the albino alligator that lives in the basement lagoon to the blue butterflies that rest on your shoulders inside the Rainforest Dome. From here, take a trip through outer space in the Planetarium, with SF native Whoopi Goldberg narrating – far out.

❸ THE HAIGHT

Even without supplies from its many head shops and legal 'herbal medicine' dispensaries, this historic hippie 'hood is a total trip. For a mind-bending time warp, take our Haight Flashbacks Walking Tour (p200) *backwards,* starting at Hippie Hill in Sharon Meadow and passing the candy-colored Victorians where rock and revolution was made.

California Academy of Sciences (p231)

SABRINA DALBESIO

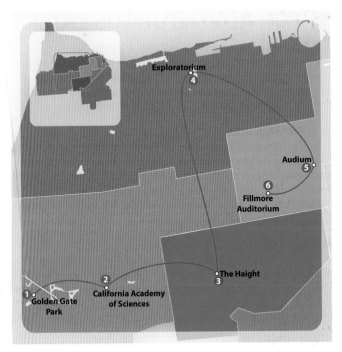

Follow the trail of homebrews and anarchist literature to **Buena Vista Park** (p203) to take in the view with your head in the clouds.

➍ EXPLORATORIUM

The 43 bus will whisk you from Haight and Masonic into another world, where the laws of physics bend and senses come alive inside the completely dark Tactile Dome at the **Exploratorium** (p66). Far-out scientific theories are put to the test with hands-on displays, and everything you think you know about music, skateboarding and adorability is stretched by the Exploratorium's MacArthur Genius inventors.

➎ AUDIUM

Listen closely and you'll hear the room breathing. No, really: the **Audium** (p147) was purpose-built to emit ambient sounds in free-form, hour-long 'room compositions.' Sit in the dark to hear this electronics-enabled music and try not to sneeze, lest you throw off the room's rhythm.

➏ FILLMORE AUDITORIUM

The 1960s happened at the **Fillmore** (p154), and it's got the DayGlo posters in the gallery upstairs to prove it: historic headliners included Janis Joplin, the Doors, Jefferson Airplane, Jimi Hendrix and, of course, the Grateful Dead. The auditorium is small, but still pulls in big names – everyone wants to play here and join the rock-god pantheon.

SF FOR ADVENTUROUS EATERS

THREE MEALS FERRY BUILDING TO KABUTO

Tell locals you're coming to town and they'll start debating about where you should have dinner. But why settle on one venue when you can dine your way across town? Begin with brunch Bayside, and graze westward to a dinner of Pacific Ocean oysters.

❶ FERRY BUILDING

One glimpse of the clock tower on the **Ferry Building** (p62), and San Franciscans start to salivate. Three days a week, the legendary year-round farmers market at the building's base overflows with organic produce, artisan cheeses and other gourmet goods. Graze the market's free samples, and don't miss the truffled eggs at **Boulette's Larder** (p73).

❷ THE MISSION

Hop on BART to 16th and Mission, and resume your foraging expedition along Valencia St to **Ritual Coffee Roasters** (p181) for cappuccino featuring locally roasted specialty beans and stiff foam. Lunch at **La Taqueria** (p177) explains what the SF burrito fuss is all about, and a stroll past the mural-covered 24th St bodegas takes you to **Humphry Slocombe** (p178) for the 'secret breakfast' sundae: bourbon ice cream with corn flakes and bittersweet hot fudge.

❸ THE SUNSET

Hungry yet? Well, maybe after the N Judah ride to 9th and Irving in the **Sunset** (p229) District, plus a tantalizing walk through the herb gardens at nearby **Strybing Arboretum** (p232). Cafes and budget bistros are

Fresh produce, Ferry Building (p62)

JERRY ALEXANDER

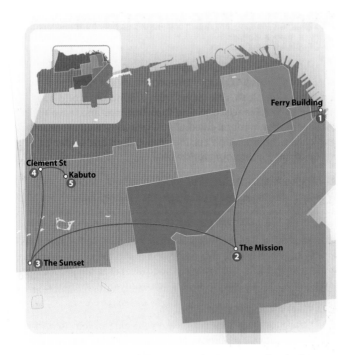

clustered around the N Judah stop, so take time to explore before you hop the 44 bus across the park to Clement St in the inner Richmond.

❹ CLEMENT ST

Mind your elbows as you join gourmet shoppers who sort expertly through towering displays of tropical durian fruit and an aisle's worth of chili sauces at **New May Wah** (p241), and browse the Japanese porcelain platters **Kamei Restaurant Supply** (p241). You may think you'll only be a minute in the cookbook section of **Green Apple Books** (p241), but when you see all the signed copies and remainders, you may need to rethink your dinner reservations.

❺ KABUTO

As you approach the outer Richmond, Geary St may not be much to look at – but wait until you get a whiff of what's cooking. Among the Russian delis and Korean barbecue, you'll run into fast and furious dim sum cart traffic at **Ton Kiang Restaurant** (p235), and bump into delectable organic Moroccan that needs no belly-dance introduction at **Aziza** (p234). For inspired California twists on sushi, you'll have to wait in line – even with reservations – at **Kabuto** (p234) – but the foie gras sushi drizzled with an olallieberry reduction, and '49er oyster with quail egg earn standing ovations and foodie bragging rights.

AROUND THE WORLD IN 48 HOURS

FORTY-EIGHT HOURS
MISSION MURALS TO GARY DANKO

Since the Gold Rush, risk-takers from around the world have headed to San Francisco to find their fortunes and leave their mark, whether in mural-filled alleys, treasure-filled museums or award-winning fusion cuisine. In two days and under 7 miles, SF may alter your worldview.

❶ MISSION MURALS

Wake up with an explosion of color in the Mission District by exploring backstreet **murals** (p162). Back in the 1970s, artists opposed to US policy in Latin America took to the streets, covering back-alley garage doors with vivid protests and moving memorials. Today *muralistas* have covered 24th St storefronts and community centers, mixing inspiration from Mexican muralist Diego Rivera's San Francisco work with graphic-art stylings from SF's homegrown skate culture.

❷ ASIAN ART MUSEUM

Take 24th St BART to Civic Center, where the old San Francisco library has been creatively repurposed by Italian architect Gae Aulenti to house the **Asian Art Museum** (p89). With masterworks gifted by collectors around the world, the pan-Asian collection outgrew its former home in Golden Gate Park, and these three floors of galleries are now constantly rotated to make way for new acquisitions – look for the blue 'Newly on View' sticker next to works such as Arpana Caur's modern

JERRY ALEXANDER

Asian Art Museum (p89)

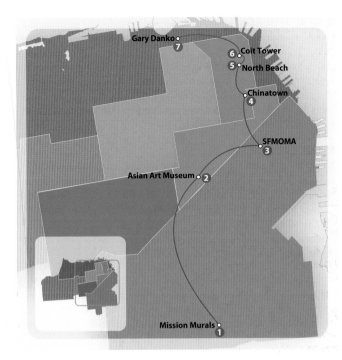

take on South Indian temple reliefs, and Masami Teraoka's geisha discovering Rocky Road ice cream.

❸ SFMOMA

Starting with masterpieces by Diego Rivera and Matisse in 1935, **San Francisco Museum of Modern Art** (SFMOMA; p170) expanded through the 1990s technology booms into its snazzy tuxedo-striped building by Italian modernist Mario Botta. It's set to triple in size by 2016, with an addition by Norwegian architecture firm Snøhetta. Explore the world-class collection from the top down, from the Alexander Calder mobile in the rooftop sculpture garden, downstairs past new media and San Francisco–born Matthew Barney's Vaseline-smeared videos, to Daido Moriyama's stray dog in the museum's photography collection.

❹ CHINATOWN

On your second day, enter Dragon's Gate to Chinatown. Grant St is purposefully picturesque, its pagoda-topped storefronts overflowing with bobble-headed Buddhas. But in its 41 **historic alleyways** (p108), Chinese revolutions were plotted, ladylike reputations were traded for a quarter, and temples stood their ground through earthquake, fire and political battles. These streets have mellowed since the Gold Rush – but you can still find your fortune at **Golden Gate Fortune Cookie Company** (p131).

❺ NORTH BEACH

Jack Kerouac Alley (p116) offers an inspired shortcut from Chinatown to North Beach past the City Lights Bookstore (p130), where Beat poetry and boundary-pushing ideas have filled the shelves since the 1950s. You'll know you've arrived in North Beach by the insistent aroma of espresso from Caffe Trieste (p128) and the soft, Tuscan accents of longtime North Beachers heading to Italian-language services at Saints Peter & Paul Church (p119).

❻ COIT TOWER

You may not be able to see the entire world from Coit Tower (p115), but you'll certainly feel on top of it once you reach the 360-degree viewing platform. The lobby is covered with Rivera-inspired 1930s murals showing ethnically diverse San Franciscans at work and play, reading books in Hebrew, Chinese and Russian – works once deemed dangerously subversive, but now protected as San Francisco landmarks.

❼ GARY DANKO

It may seem like a long way down Coit Tower, but if you have reservations at Gary Danko (p71) you don't have to return to earth just yet. Flights of fancy and Pacific Rim influences keep diners in suspense at this James Beard Award–winning bistro, where seasonal California cuisine ranges from Sonoma *panko*-crusted duck dumplings to crispy pork belly laced with jalapeño salsa.

THOMAS WINZ

Jack Kerouac Alley (p116)

↘PLANNING YOUR TRIP

ROBERTO GEROMETTA

➤ SAN FRANCISCO'S BEST...

⬊ DINING DISCOVERIES

- **Ferry Building** (p54) A historic port reinvented as a dining destination, with award-winning chefs and year-round farmers markets.
- **Ad Hoc** (p246) Thomas Keller's most inspired restaurant since French Laundry (p246) serves four courses for under $50 – no substitutions, no complaints.
- **Delfina** (p176) Maverick California cuisine takes on big, ultrafresh flavors with casual finesse.
- **Namu** (p234) How to make killer Korean tacos: combine organic ingredients and savory barbecue flavors with the expertise of chef Dennis Lee.

⬊ GIDDY VIEWS

- **Golden Gate Bridge** (p65) Fog sneaks between orange cables, tickles deco towers, then runs away.
- **Coit Tower** (p115) Step through Works Progress Administration (WPA) murals into the elevator, and head up for 360-degree SF views.
- **Alamo Square Park** (p204) Painted Lady Victorians pose for pictures with Downtown backdrops.
- **Sterling Park** (p141) Bay vistas to inspire poetry or tennis, whichever comes first.

⬊ ART TREASURES

- **SFMOMA** (p170) Discover priceless photography, ground-breaking installations and a windfall of modernist masterpieces.
- **Mission Murals** (p162) Alleys illuminated with works inspired by Mexican maestro Diego Rivera and homegrown skate culture.
- **Asian Art Museum** (p89) An epic afternoon's journey from Mogul miniatures to Japanese anime.
- **MH de Young Memorial Museum** (p231) Oceanic masks, Silk Rd carpets and Andy Goldworthy's earthquake sculptures.

SABRINA DALBESIO

Triweekly farmers market (p54), Ferry Building

URBAN WILDLIFE

- **Golden Gate Park** (p229) A home where the buffalo roam, carnivorous plants belch and goldfish chase paddleboats.
- **Crissy Field** (p66) Bow-legged pipers and contemplative herons model yoga poses on a reclaimed army airstrip.
- **Sea Lions at Pier 39** (p63) Sunning on yacht slips and consorting with harems: SF's mascots are the envy of rap stars.
- **California Academy of Sciences** (p231) A white alligator stalks downstairs, penguins cuddle upstairs and poppies run riot on the roof.

SHOWS

- **San Francisco Symphony** (p102) See why the Grammys keep coming for conductor Michael Tilson Thomas and his arrangements of Beethoven and Mahler.
- **San Francisco Opera** (p101) See Puccini and Verdi reinvented, plus world premieres of operas such as *Dead Man Walking* and *Harvey Milk*.
- **Castro Theatre** (p174) Show tunes on the mighty Wurlitzer introduce Fellini films and SF premieres at this deco movie palace.
- **American Conservatory Theater** (p100) Major playwrights, including Stoppard, Kushner and Mamet, launch provocative new works.

GAY/LESBIAN/BI/ TRANS LANDMARKS

- (p47) Crowds roar as 500,000 ers strut down Market St.

- **The Castro** (p184) The trailblazing, good-time gay neighborhood gives new meaning to party politics.
- **Human Rights Campaign Action Center** (p184) Features petitions and fashion statements for civil rights.
- **Women's Building** (p170) Inspiration inside and out: murals wrap around this landmark home to women's nonprofit organizations.

QUIRKS

- **826 Valencia** (p167) A Fish Theater and pirate supplies, for all your buccaneering needs.
- **Exploratorium** (p66) Hair-raising exhibits and a pitch-dark Tactile Dome.
- **Cartoon Art Museum** (p171) Where Batman hangs out with Fantastic Mr Fox and R Crumb.
- **Haight Flashbacks** (p200) Home to hippies and prime retail for rebels.

ESCAPES

- **Wine Country** (p244) Nine-course feasts, volcanic mud baths, and outdoor wine-tasting allows you to drink in the landscape.
- **Muir Woods** (p251) Nothing like a towering old-growth redwood grove to put modern life in perspective.
- **Point Reyes** (p234) Keep company with whales, seals and elk along protected coastal bluffs.
- **Alcatraz** (p61) Plot the ultimate getaway from behind bars at the notorious island prison.

THINGS YOU NEED TO KNOW

AT A GLANCE

- **ATMs** Ubiquitous; surcharges may apply
- **Credit cards** Widely accepted
- **Tipping** Minimum 15% restaurants and taxis, $1 per drink, $2 per night hotel maid service
- **Languages** English; Mandarin and Spanish widely spoken

ACCOMMODATIONS

- **Boutique hotels** Extensive Downtown options include literary posh (Rex; p92), designer cool (Palomar; p91) and live-in art installation (Hotel des Arts; p92).
- **B&Bs** Victorian mansion digs range from swanky (Inn San Francisco; p174) to psychedelic (Red Vic; p205); best selection is in Castro (p176) and the Haight (p204).
- **Motels** Retro 1950s classics line Lombard Street in the Marina (p70); centrally located options in Hayes Valley (p206).

- **Luxury hotels** Upgrade to historic Victorian swank (Palace Hotel; p91) or waterfront views (Hotel Vitale; p175).
- **Spa hotels** Unwind alongside SFMOMA (W; p175) or retreat to Wine Country (Carneros Inn; p246).

ADVANCE PLANNING

- **Three months before** Check visa requirements (p297); act fast for high-season hotels and French Laundry dining reservations (p246).
- **One month before** Reserve flights and accommodations; book tickets for Alcatraz (p62), Symphony (p102) or Opera (p101); reserve tours of Mission murals or Chinatown alleyways (p108); explore volunteering options (p45).
- **One week before** Nab tickets for totally wild cocktail hours at the California Academy of Sciences (p231); find out about hot SF shows and events (p45).

Golden Gate Bridge (p65), viewed from Crissy Field

- **One day before** From fashion shows to scavenger hunts, find SF activities to join at sfbay.craigslist.org/act; make dinner reservations in the Mission (p176).

BE FOREWARNED

- **Taxes** Factor SF taxes into dining, sleeping and shopping budgets (p296).
- **Overbooking** To avoid overbooking and high-season premiums, check the convention calendar at www.sfcvb.org/convention/calendar.asp and book around those dates.
- **Use street smarts** Especially in the Tenderloin and at night around parks.
- **Panhandling** Expect to be asked for spare change, but don't feel obliged – donations stretch further at organizations such as the nonprofit Haight Ashbury Food Program (p203).

COSTS

- **$100 per day** Motels and modest B&Bs; art gallery openings and free concerts; burritos and beer; cable cars into the sunset
- **$200 per day** Boutique hotels and spiffy B&Bs; symphonies and movie premieres; cocktails and casual California bistros; carshare to Sausalito
- **More than $200** Spa hotels and tower rooms with views; opera openings and headliners at the Fillmore; chef's menus and Napa wine tasting; convertible rentals for coastal getaways

EMERGENCY NUMBERS

- **Police, fire & ambulance** ☎ emergency 911, nonemergency 311
- **San Francisco General Hospital** ☎ emergency room 415-206-8111, main hospital 415-206-8000
- **Trauma Recovery** ☎ 415-437-3000
- **Drug Treatment** ☎ 415-362-3400

GETTING AROUND

- **Muni** Bus, streetcars, cable cars (p299).
- **BART** Transit around SF, to/from SFO airport and East Bay (p301).
- **Taxis** 24-hour dispatches (p301).
- **Carshare** For short trips around town (p300).

GETTING THERE & AWAY

- **Air** Three airports are near San Francisco (p297).
- **Train** Take the scenic route along the coast (p301).
- **Car** Rentals are handy for excursions, but parking's a hassle (p300).

TECH STUFF

- **Mobile phones** Operate on CDMA, not European-standard GSM
- **Social media** The Bay Area is HQ to Twitter, Facebook and Yelp; get online and mingle
- **Internet** More than 370 free wi-fi hot spots citywide; try hotel lobbies (free) and cafes (free with purchase); for computer terminals, see p295
- **Digital photos** Can be burned onto discs at Walgreens (p296)

⬂ TRAVEL SEASONS

- **Spring** March to May, SF dries off and warms up; reasonable room rates.
- **Summer** High season rates and foggy days run June to August; street fairs compensate.
- **Fall** SF summer happens September to October; November is cooler but dry.
- **Winter** Rainy season runs December to January, but temperatures don't dip below freezing and February gets freakishly warm; for forecasts, see www.sfgate.com/weather.

⬂ WHAT TO BRING

- **Coat** Expect 55–70˚F (12–21˚C) by day.
- **Dog** For SF hotels that allow dogs, see www.dogfriendly.com.
- **Camera** Have you see the Golden Gate Bridge (p65)? Enough said.
- **Thirst** Across the Golden Gate Bridge, Wine Country awaits (p244).
- **Hunger** San Francisco is foodie Nirvana (p40).

⬂ WHEN TO GO

- **For wildflowers & film festivals** Spring
- **For street fairs & farmers markets** Summer
- **For sunny days & free concerts** Fall
- **For seafood & symphonies** Winter

LEE FOSTER

Alamo Square (p204)

GET INSPIRED

BOOKS

- **The Maltese Falcon** (Dashiell Hammett, 1930) Sam Spade gumshoe caper best read aloud over martinis at John's Grill (p99).
- **Howl and Other Poems** (Allen Ginsberg, 1956) Free verse that trumped censors, inspiring 'angelheaded hipsters burning for the ancient heavenly connection.'
- **On the Road** (Jack Kerouac, 1957) The ultimate Beatnik road trip to San Francisco, written in a Russian Hill love shack (p144).
- **Slouching Toward Bethlehem** (Joan Didion, 1968) Revealing essays expose the itchy underside of the Summer of Love (p279).
- **Heartbreaking Work of Staggering Genius** (Dave Eggers, 2000) Gen X memoir of innocence lost and purpose found in SF, where Eggers founded 826 Valencia (p167).

FILMS

- **City Lights** (1931, directed by Charlie Chaplin) Chaplin's silent classic, filmed in SF, was the namesake for the City Lights Bookstore (p130).
- **Vertigo** (1958, directed by Alfred Hitchcock) The Golden Gate Bridge views from Fort Point (p68) stole scenes in this Hitchcock mystery.
- **Harold and Maude** (1971, directed by Hal Ashby) A May-to-December romance blooms in the Conservatory of Flowers (p233) and Sutro Baths (p228).
- **Milk** (2008, directed by Gus Van Sant) Oscar winner Sean Penn stars in this biopic. Real-life colleagues of Harvey Milk cameo.

MUSIC

- **Blue Rondo á la Turk** Turk St jazz pianist Dave Brubeck defined West Coast jazz with this virtuouso track from 1959's 'Take Five.'
- **Everyday People** The 1968 hit from SF band Sly and the Family Stone coined a catchphrase for San Francisco: 'Different strokes/for different folks.'
- **Lights** 'When the lights go down in the city/and the sun shines on the Bayayyy…' Journey's 1978 hit, 'When the Lights Go Down in the City,' is a SF karaoke staple.
- **San Francisco Anthem** San Quinn remixes The Mamas and Papas' 1967 hit 'San Francisco' with 2008 rap: 'roll in like fog/the battle's uphill…'
- **Right On** The Roots' 2010 riff on SF indie favorite Joanna Newsom loops the '50s jazz-cat phrase that has become SF's mantra.

WEBSITES

- **Craiglist** (sfbay.craigslist.org) The SF community site lists events, rentals, cooking classes and more.
- **7x7** (www.7x7.com) SF mag covers food, drink, shopping and fashion.
- **SFist** (sfist.com) Blog captures SF's definitive quirks; see the '7 Reasons to Love SF' photo essays.
- **VolunteerMatch** (www.volunteermatch.org) Matches your interests and skills to a Bay Area nonprofit.

⬇ CALENDAR   JAN   FEB   MAR   APR

⬇ JANUARY

DINE ABOUT TOWN
Forget resolutions: more than 100 top San Francisco restaurants offer set-price lunch and dinner specials all month, including seasonal Dungeness crab that'll make you wish winter lasted longer; see www.sfdineabouttown.com.

⬇ FEBRUARY–MARCH

LUNAR NEW YEAR PARADE
Party with a 200ft dragon and fierce toddler kung fu classes, and get showered with lucky red envelopes and tons of fireworks. Late February/early March; see www.chineseparade.com.

ST PATRICK'S DAY PARADE
Join the party that's brought luck and libations to San Francisco mid-March since 1851. Perfectly good beer gets dyed green, and boozer trolleys fill streets with spirited mispronunciations of 'Erin Go Bragh!'; see www.sfstpatricks dayparade.com.

⬇ APRIL

CHERRY BLOSSOM FESTIVAL
Flower power and *taiko* (drums) welcome spring to Japantown in mid-April. Hip-hop dancers storm the Bush St stage, the aroma of barbecued chicken yakitori fills the air, and flower arrangers show off their best ikebana; see www.nccbf.org.

SAN FRANCISCO INTERNATIONAL FILM FESTIVAL
Pace yourself throughout this two-week blitz of 325 films and premieres by 200 directors from all over the world. Shows

ROBERTO GEROMETTA

Lunar New Year Parade

happen daily from late April to early May at the Sundance Kabuki Cinema, where you'll spot stars in the Balcony Bar; see www.sfiff.org.

MAY

BAY TO BREAKERS
Many jog costumed, some go naked, and a handful of the 65,000 participants actually take this footrace seriously on the third Sunday in May. Runners dressed as salmon head upstream from the Ocean Beach finish line to the Embarcadero beginning; see www.baytobreakers.com.

CARNAVAL
Get head-dressed to impress, and head to the Mission to shake your tail feathers on the last weekend in May. Foggy morning parades bring out G-strings and goosebumps – bring layers; see www.carnavalsf.com.

JUNE

HAIGHT ASHBURY STREET FAIR
We've got the free music, you bring the free love. Battles of the jam bands and tie-dye T-shirts galore have revived the Summer of Love since 1978, when Harvey Milk got the party started. Mid-June; see www.haightashburystreetfair.org.

PRIDE
Come out wherever you are: SF shows GLBT pride with miles of rainbow flags and a half-million-strong parade, held on the last Sunday in June; see www.sfpride.org. If you're here, queer, and ready for a premiere, also don't miss the Gay & Lesbian Film Festival; see www.frameline.org.

RICK GERHARTER

Pride

↘ JULY

INDEPENDENCE DAY   JUL 4

July 4 explodes with fireworks despite summer fog, celebrating San Francisco's dedication to life, liberty and the pursuit of barbecue – no matter what the economic, political and meteorological climate.

AIDS WALK

Fancy footwork benefits 43 AIDS organizations in SF's pioneering 10km fundraiser, which heads through Golden Gate Park on the third Sunday in July. Since 1987, SF walkers have raised $74 million to fight the pandemic and support people living with HIV; see www .aidswalk.net/sanfran.

↘ SEPTEMBER

OPERA IN THE PARK

Divas sing grace notes gratis at Sharon Meadow in Golden Gate Park on the second Sunday in September. The outdoor showcase reprises the historic free opera shows that brought San Francisco back to its feet after the 1906 earthquake; see sfopera.com/park.

FOLSOM STREET FAIR

Enjoy watching public spankings in aid of local charities on the last weekend of September. Here you'll notice that yes, people do get pierced and tattooed down there – but don't stare unless you're prepared to compare; see www .folsomstreetfair.com.

SF SHAKESPEARE FESTIVAL

The play's the thing in the Presidio, outdoors and free of charge on sunny September weekends. The company also offers classes and performances for kids; see www.sfshakes.org.

↘ OCTOBER

LITQUAKE

Stranger-than-fiction literary events take over SF the second week of October, with bestselling and cult-hit authors spilling true stories and trade secrets over drinks at the legendary Lit Crawl; see litquake.org.

HARDLY STRICTLY BLUEGRASS FESTIVAL

The West goes wild for free concerts by bluegrass legends such as Emmylou Harris, Ralph Stanley and Earl Scruggs, and supporting headliners such as Billy Bragg, Aimee Mann and Elvis Costello. The three-day, three-stage lineup happens outside in Golden Gate Park; see www.strictlybluegrass.com.

SAN FRANCISCO JAZZ FESTIVAL

Horns and minds are blown from late September until November, as jazz greats and breakthrough talents improvise on stages across town. Big tickets such as Arturo Sandoval, Taj Mahal and Lila Downs sell fast, and festival favorites Marcus Shelby and Jon Jang always bring down the house; see www .sfjazz.org.

| MAY | JUN | JUL | AUG | SEP | OCT | NOV | DEC |

GREG GAWLOWSKI

Costumed runner, Bay to Breakers (p47)

⬐ NOVEMBER

DÍA DE LOS MUERTOS
(DAY OF THE DEAD)   NOV 2
Zombie brides, skeleton stilt-walkers, and feathered Aztec dancers dance to wake the dead from Balmy Alley to Mission Cultural Center, where respects are paid to the dearly departed at community altars; see www.dayofthe deadsf.org.

GREEN FESTIVAL
Never mind the low-watt fluorescents: the ideas are mighty bright at this showcase for green technology, cuisine and design. Crowds pack events featuring 150 eco-luminaries and 400 pioneering green businesses – especially those on sustainable wine tastings and benefit rap concerts; see www .greenfestivals.org.

⬐ DECEMBER

DANCE-ALONG NUTCRACKER
The nation's finest – OK, only – audience-performed version of the Tchaikovsky classic, with kids, comedians and the San Francisco Lesbian/Gay Freedom Band bouncing through early-December shows at Yerba Center for the Arts; see http://dancealongnutcracker.org.

↘ EMBARCADERO & THE BAY

EMBARCADERO & THE BAY

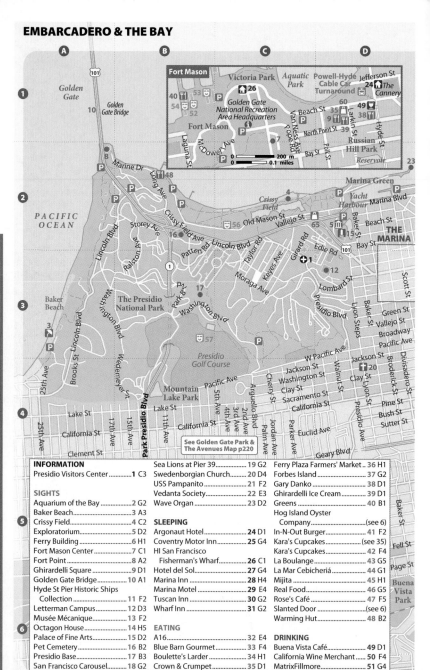

INFORMATION

Presidio Visitors Center **1** C3

SIGHTS

Aquarium of the Bay **2** G2
Baker Beach...................................**3** A3
Crissy Field....................................**4** C2
Exploratorium...............................**5** D2
Ferry Building...............................**6** H1
Fort Mason Center.......................**7** C1
Fort Point......................................**8** A2
Ghirardelli Square........................**9** D1
Golden Gate Bridge...................**10** A1
Hyde St Pier Historic Ships
   Collection..................................**11** F2
Letterman Campus.....................**12** D3
Musée Mécanique.......................**13** F2
Octagon House............................**14** H5
Palace of Fine Arts.....................**15** D2
Pet Cemetery...............................**16** B2
Presidio Base...............................**17** B3
San Francisco Carousel..............**18** G2

Sea Lions at Pier 39.....................**19** G2
Swedenborgian Church...............**20** D4
USS Pampanito.............................**21** F2
Vedanta Society............................**22** E3
Wave Organ...................................**23** D2

SLEEPING

Argonaut Hotel..............................**24** D1
Coventry Motor Inn......................**25** G4
HI San Francisco
   Fisherman's Wharf.....................**26** C1
Hotel del Sol..................................**27** G4
Marina Inn.....................................**28** H4
Marina Motel..................................**29** G4
Tuscan Inn......................................**30** G2
Wharf Inn.......................................**31** G2

EATING

A16...**32** E4
Blue Barn Gourmet.......................**33** F4
Boulette's Larder...........................**34** H1
Crown & Crumpet.........................**35** D1

Ferry Plaza Farmers' Market....**36** H1
Forbes Island **37** G2
Gary Danko **38** D1
Ghirardelli Ice Cream...............**39** D1
Greens..**40** B1
Hog Island Oyster
   Company..............................(see 6)
In-N-Out Burger.........................**41** F2
Kara's Cupcakes ....(see 35)
Kara's Cupcakes.........................**42** F4
La Boulange................................**43** G5
La Mar Cebicheriá.....................**44** G1
Mijita...**45** H1
Real Food....................................**46** G5
Rose's Café.................................**47** F5
Slanted Door........................(see 6)
Warming Hut...............................**48** B2

DRINKING

Buena Vista Café.........................**49** D1
California Wine Merchant **50** F4
MatrixFillmore.............................**51** G4

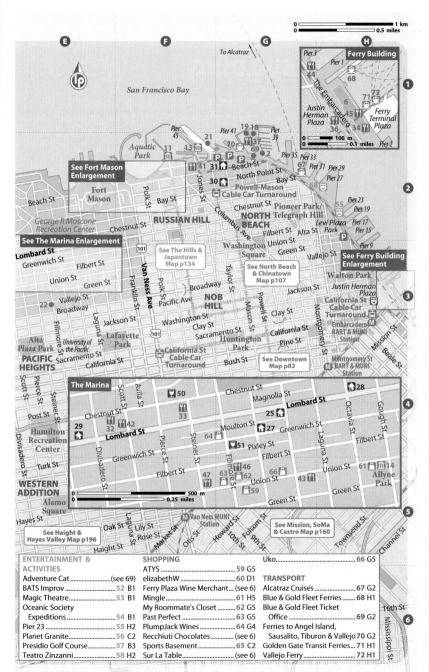

EMBARCADERO & THE BAY

HIGHLIGHTS

1 FERRY BUILDING

The towering achievement at the Ferry Building isn't the 19th-century clock tower, modeled after Seville's La Giralda: it's the 21st-century food, pioneered in the Bay Area. Award-winning chefs serve signature dishes with sparkling Bay views, and local vendors supply pristine ingredients so that you can take culinary inspiration home.

↘ OUR DON'T MISS LIST

❶ FERRY PLAZA FARMERS' MARKET

Ever wonder how the Bay Area produces so many top chefs? The secrets to their success are revealed on Tuesdays, Thursdays, and especially Saturdays year-round, with local vendors selling sustainable produce, artisan cheeses, and killer organic tamales. Up to 100 stalls wrap around the building, with ready-made foods on the south side, near the statue of a famished Gandhi.

❷ SLANTED DOOR

Shaking beef may not be part of your gourmet vocabulary yet, but you'll be shouting its name once you try the succulent, grass-fed Cali-Vietnamese version by award-winning chef Charles Phan. Reserve ahead for window seating, which features sweeping Bay views.

❸ GOURMET KIOSKS

Wild-crafted chanterelle mushrooms, boar bacon, fresh goat cheese wrapped in mint, and oh yes, **Recchiuti**

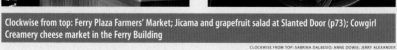

Clockwise from top: Ferry Plaza Farmers' Market; Jicama and grapefruit salad at Slanted Door (p73); Cowgirl Creamery cheese market in the Ferry Building

EMBARCADERO & THE BAY

HIGHLIGHTS

Chocolates (p79): there's clearly a conspiracy afoot among local producers inside the Ferry Building to spoil you for eating anywhere but San Francisco... and it just may work.

❶ Ferry Plaza Farmers' Market
❷ Slanted Door
❸ Gourmet Kiosks
❹ Hog Island Happy Hour
❺ Vallejo Ferry to Napa

0 ――――――――― 100 m
0 ――――――――― 0.05 miles

Pier 1/2
San Francisco Bay
Ferry Building
Ferry Terminal Plaza
The Embarcadero
Justin Herman Plaza

❹ HOG ISLAND HAPPY HOUR

The surefire cure for Mondayitis is sustainably farmed, succulent oysters still briny from nearby Tomales Bay, chased with bargain beer or local bubbly. Happy yet? Thought so.

❺ VALLEJO FERRY TO NAPA

For a change of foodie scene, you don't have to go far – just roll down the docks and catch the Vallejo Ferry to Napa, and indulge in wine tasting and comparative grazing at the town's rival to the Ferry Building: Oxbow Market.

↘ THINGS YOU NEED TO KNOW

Star power To rub elbows with top chefs, hit the farmers market before 8am Saturday **Good to go** When restaurants are packed, get yours boxed to enjoy on bayside benches **Transportation** Get off at Embarcadero BART/Muni station and head east **For full Ferry Building details, see p62**

HIGHLIGHTS

2

⬂ ALCATRAZ

Any mention of America's most notorious **prison** (p61) from 1933 to 1963 is mentally followed by ominous music: *duh dunh dunhhhh!* Tours of 'the Rock' include an audio tour with tales of solitary confinement, attempted prison breaks and visiting days told by former inmates and guards. Faded water tower graffiti reads 'This Is Indian Land,' a reminder of the 1969–71 Native American Alcatraz occupation.

3

⬂ GOLDEN GATE BRIDGE

Only one bridge in the world makes you wish for bad weather and a traffic jam. San Francisco fog saves all its best tricks for this **span** (p65), making the orange cables disappear and the deco towers appear to float on air. Late mornings are best for bike rides and sunny strolls, but late afternoons are ideal for maximum fog and an eerie red blur of brake lights – bundle up and bring a camera.

⇖ CRISSY FIELD

Once this **army base** (p66) was stained with leaked fuel, as planes transporting generals and world leaders zoomed in for a landing. A vast contrast to the present – now bow-legged herons perch meditatively while kids fly their first kites. If that's not heartwarming enough for you, try a fair-trade espresso at the cozy, denim-insulated **Warming Hut** (p75).

⇖ EXPLORATORIUM

Put your theories about the physiology of cuteness, the physics of skateboarding and the emotional life of robots to the test in this **hands-on discovery museum** (p66), with displays that earned Exploratorium designers a MacArthur Genius grant. Reserve ahead for the Tactile Dome, where you'll grope your way to enlightenment in total darkness.

⇖ MARINA BOUTIQUES

No one ever packs correctly for San Francisco – what with summer fog, day hikes and impromptu dinner party invites, you'd need a steamer trunk to cover your fashion needs here. Not to worry: **Union**, **Fillmore** and **Chestnut Sts** (p79) have your back stylishly covered with local designers, sporting gear, Napa wines and, yes, antique steamer trunks.

2 RAY LASKOWITZ; 3 ROBERTO GEROMETTA; 4 LEE FOSTER; 5 RICK GERHARTER; 6 SABRINA DALBESIO

2 Alcatraz (p61); 3 Crossing the Golden Gate Bridge (p65); 4 Cyclists in Crissy Field (p66); Exploratorium (p66); Union St, Marina district (p79)

WALKING TOUR: BARBARY COAST

Cover the waterfront in three hours, from historic piers where sailors abandoned ship during the Gold Rush, past Barbary Coast bars where fortunes were made and lost, and through a redwood grove that's taken root atop whaling ships. In 3 miles, you'll arrive at the transit depot foodies refuse to leave.

❶ HYDE ST PIER HISTORIC SHIPS COLLECTION

Start your tour of SF's waterfront just as a Gold Rush sailor pulling into port would have seen it: from the deck of a 19th-century ship.

❷ SEA LIONS

As you cover the waterfront, take a detour by Pier 39 to watch sea lions take over the yacht marina, canoodling and belching in public rather like sailors.

❸ LEVI'S PLAZA

This pleasant plaza would've been muddy sludge 150 years ago, when Levi Strauss began making his tough denim pants in San Francisco. Without his copper-riveted pockets, lucky miners would've had no-where to stash their gold nuggets – and Barbary Coast saloon-keepers would've fleeced them that much faster.

❹ OLD SHIP SALOON

Instead of abandoning the good ship *Arkansas* in 1851, enterprising Joseph Anthony built a bar around it at 298 Pacific Ave. Sailors drank here at their own risk, knowing this bar was notorious for drugging customers, who woke up miles from shore, shanghaied into service on a crew.

❺ GOLD ST

Prospectors who struck it rich during the Gold Rush headed directly to this brick-lined alleyway, where finds were evaluated at the assay office. Thieves, swindlers and pimps were never far behind.

❻ BARBARY COAST BOHEMIA

When the block of buildings at 708–720 Montgomery St was rebuilt after the 1906 fire, it became even more notorious than during its Barbary Coast days. In 1925, artists moved into studios here and stayed for 35 years; Diego Rivera worked here when he was in town. Housed at 710 Montgomery St was the Black Cat bar, which won a landmark 1951 California Supreme Court case that allowed gays to congregate in bars.

❼ REDWOOD PARK

Alongside the Transamerica Pyramid, the distinguishing feature of SF's skyline, is a grove of 80 redwood trees, where occasional free concerts

BARBARY COAST WALKING TOUR

are held and there are kitschy/creepy bronze statues of cackling children and frogs leaping from lily pads in the fountain.

❽ WHALESHIP PLAZA

Ships left to rot by prospecting sailors came in handy to shore up SF's waterfront; at least two whaling ships are underfoot here.

❾ JUSTIN HERMAN PLAZA

Daredevil skaters, crafts vendors and protesters do their best to distract visitors from a fountain that looks like an industrial accident.

❿ FERRY BUILDING

The long-vacant 1898 ferry hub was gutted and spiffed up in 2001 to become a gourmet-food emporium and upscale farmers market, with gourmet stalls and acclaimed restaurants such as Slanted Door.

EMBARCADERO & THE BAY

WALKING TOUR: BARBARY COAST

BEST...

⬏ DARES IN THE DARK

- **Alcatraz by night** (right) Spooky tours of the island prison.
- **Exploratorium Tactile Dome** (p67) Feel your way through exhibits.
- **Adventure Cat sunset cruise** (p76) Ride the trampoline between the catamaran's hulls.
- **BATS Improv** (p77) Get onstage and wing it.

⬏ SEAFARING ADVENTURES

- **USS Pampanito** (p64) Go below deck on a WWII submarine.
- **Oceanic Society whale-watching** (p78) Boat trips to spot breaching whales.
- **Aquarium of the Bay** (p64) Walk underwater for fish-eye Bay views.
- **Forbes Island** (p72) Dine on an eccentric millionaire's floating island.

⬏ BARGAINS GALORE

- **Musée Mécanique** (p63) Fifty cents saves the world from Space Invaders.
- **My Roommate's Closet** (p79) Year-round designer sample sale.
- **Wave Organ** (p70) Hear the tide give free concerts.
- **Kara's Cupcakes** (p75) Nostalgia trip gratis, with $2 mini cupcakes.

⬏ NATURAL WONDERS

- **Sea Lions at Pier 39** (p63) Beach bums take over the yacht marina.
- **Crissy Field** (p66) Army airstrip turned coastal sanctuary.
- **Swedenborgian Church** (p70) Secret garden and splendid landscapes.
- **Baker Beach** (p67) Windswept pines and locals au naturel.

STEPHEN SAKS

Sea lions at Pier 39, Fisherman's Wharf (p63)

DISCOVER EMBARCADERO & THE BAY

Back in 1849 when adventurers and miners arrived, most of the Embarcadero was under water. A steady buildup of sludge, debris, docks, saloons, and ships abandoned by crews with gold fever extended the waterfront east, and a retaining wall was built to keep the piers from drifting. Not many people wanted to be downwind from the Marina back in those early days, when inland breezes carried the stench of cattle, moonshine stills, drying fish and most of Northern California's dirty laundry. Now the Marina is strictly top-drawer and dry-cleaned, with sales reps and ad execs in all their front-office finery at happy hour.

San Francisco's official motto is still 'Oro en Paz, Fierro en Guerra' (Gold in Peace, Iron in War), but the wooded Presidio coastline is dotted with kites, surfers and nudists where once there were fighter planes, gunboats and cannons. For decades now, the only wars going on here have been of the interstellar variety, in George Lucas' Presidio screening room.

SIGHTS

EMBARCADERO & THE PIERS

ALCATRAZ

☎ Alcatraz Cruises 415-981-7625; ticket info http://alcatrazcruises.com, park info www.nps.gov/alcatraz; day tickets adult/child under 5yr/ child 5-11yr/senior/family (2 adults, 2 children) $26/free/16/24.50/79, night tours adult/child under 5yr/child 5-11yr/child 12-17yr/senior $33/free/19.50/30.50/32; ☽ call center 8am-7pm, ferries depart from Pier 33 every half hour 9am-3:55pm, night tours 6:10pm & 6:45pm; 🚋 F to Pier 33 for ferry

Alcatraz

Ferry Building
SABRINA DALBESIO

In 1859 a new post on Alcatraz became the first US West Coast fort, and soon proved handy as a holding pen for Civil War deserters, insubordinates and those who had been court-martialed. The army began building a new concrete military prison in 1909, but upkeep was expensive, and in 1934 the Federal Bureau of Prisons took over Alcatraz as a prominent showcase for its crime-fighting efforts.

A-list criminals doing time on Alcatraz included Chicago crime boss Al 'Scarface' Capone; dapper kidnapper George 'Machine Gun' Kelly; hot-headed Harlem mafioso and sometime poet 'Bumpy' Johnson; and Morton Sobell, the military contractor found guilty of Soviet espionage along with Julius and Ethel Rosenberg. Though Alcatraz was considered escape-proof, in 1962 the Anglin brothers and Frank Morris floated away on a makeshift raft and were never seen again. Security and upkeep proved prohibitively expensive, and finally the island prison was abandoned to the birds in 1963.

Native Americans claimed sovereignty over the island in the '60s, noting that Alcatraz had long been used by the Ohlone as a spiritual retreat, yet federal authorities refused their proposal to turn Alcatraz into a Native American study center. Then on the eve of Thanksgiving, 1969, 79 Native American activists broke a Coast Guard blockade to enforce their claim. Over the next 19 months, some 5600 Native Americans would visit the occupied island. Public support eventually pressured President Richard Nixon to restore Native territory and strengthen self-rule for Native nations in 1970.

After the government regained control of the island, it became a national park, and by 1973 had already become a major draw. Tickets should be booked two weeks or more in advance – especially for the popular night tour – so plan your escape now.

FERRY BUILDING
☎ 415-983-8000; www.ferrybuildingmarket place.com; Market St & the Embarcadero;

🕙 10am-6pm Mon-Fri, 9am-6pm Sat, 11am-5pm Sun; 🚌 2, 6, 9, 14, 21, 31, 66, 71, F; 🚌 & 🚇 Embarcadero

Like a grand salute, the Ferry Building's trademark 240ft tower greeted dozens of ferries daily after its inauguration in 1898. But once the Bay Bridge and Golden Gate Bridge provided more convenient ways to cross the bay in the 1930s, ferry traffic subsided. Then the overhead freeway obscured the building's grand facade and car fumes turned it ashen. Only after the 1989 earthquake did city planners come to their senses and notice what they'd been missing: with its grand halls and bay views, this was the perfect place to stop for a bite. You can still catch a ferry here (p296), and on that rare warm, sunny day, it might qualify as a highlight of your visit. Ferries go to Jack London Sq in Oakland and to Sausalito and Tiburon in Marin County (p249). To get to Napa (p244), hop on the Vallejo ferry here and transfer to the Napa Valley Vine bus at the Vallejo terminal.

SEA LIONS AT PIER 39

☎ California Welcome Center 415-981-1280; www.pier39.com; Pier 39, Beach St & the Embarcadero; 🕙 Jan-Jul & whenever else they feel like it; 🚌 15, 37, 49, F

Beach bums took over San Francisco's most coveted waterfront real estate in 1990 and have been making a public display of themselves ever since, canoodling, belching, scratching their naked backsides and gleefully shoving one another off the docks. Naturally these unkempt squatters became San Francisco's favorite mascots, and since California law requires boats to make way for marine mammals, yacht owners have to relinquish valuable slips to accommodate as many as 1300 sea lions who 'haul out' onto the docks between January and July, and whenever else they feel like sunbathing.

MUSÉE MÉCANIQUE

☎ 415-346-2000; www.museemecanique.org; Shed A, Pier 45; admission free; 🕙 10am-7pm Mon-Fri, to 8pm Sat, Sun & holidays; 🚌 47, F; 🚇 Powell-Mason, Powell-Hyde; ♿

Sinister, freckle-faced Laughing Sal has creeped out kiddies for more than a hundred years, but don't let this manic mannequin deter you from what is the best arcade west of Coney Island. A few quarters lets you start bar brawls in coin-operated Wild West saloons, peep at belly dancers through a vintage Mutoscope, feed the insatiable Ms Pac-Man and get your fortune told by an eerily lifelike wooden swami.

⬆ TRANSPORTATION: EMBARCADERO & THE PIERS

BART Embarcadero station.

Bus Most Market St Muni lines terminate near the Ferry Building. The 49 skirts the north shore along the Piers.

Streetcar F streetcars run down Market St to San Francisco Bay, then follow the northern curve of the Embarcadero to Fisherman's Wharf. The N-Judah line runs underground down Market St, then follows the Embarcadero south to AT&T Park. The T goes from the Embarcadero station past AT&T Park, down 3rd St past Dog Patch.

Parking There are parking lots south of the Ferry Building at Pier 3 and at Embarcadero Center.

↘ FAMILY FUN ALONG FISHERMAN'S WHARF

Sea lions laze the day away sunbathing and posing for photo ops on Pier 39, where an **aquarium**, **carousel** and carnival-style attractions keep little kids wide-eyed. Many of the ships you'll see docked on Pier 45 are actually museums, giving naval-gazers a chance to check out **tall ships**, **submarines** and **WWII warships**. Bring your quarters to consult the spooky mechanical fortune tellers and save the world from space invaders at **Musée Mécanique** (p63). Immediately to the west is **Ghirardelli Square**, a former chocolate factory with boutiques, sweet shops, and **Crown & Crumpet** (p72) tearoom.

USS PAMPANITO

☎ 415-775-1943; www.maritime.org/pamp home.htm; Pier 45; adult/child under 6yr/child over 6yr/senior/family (2 adults, 4 children) $10/free/4/6/20; ⏱ 9am-6pm Sun-Thu, to 8pm Fri & Sat Oct 14-May 23, 9am-8pm Thu-Tue, to 6pm Wed May 24-Oct 13; 🚌 19, 32, F; 🚃 Powell-Hyde

Talk about a survivor: this WWII-era US Navy submarine completed six wartime patrols, sunk six Japanese ships (including two carrying British and Australian POWs), battled three others and lived to tell the tale. Submariners' stories of tense moments in stealth mode will have you holding your breath – caution claustrophobics – and all those cool brass knobs and mysterious hydraulic valves make 21st-century technology seem overrated.

AQUARIUM OF THE BAY

☎ 415-623-5300, 888-732-3483; www.aquarium ofthebay.com; Pier 39; adult/senior & child $16.95/8; ⏱ 9am-8pm daily summer, 10am-6pm Mon-Fri, to 7pm Sat & Sun rest of year; 🚌 49, F; 🚹

Watch sharks circle overhead, manta rays skate shyly by and seaweed sway all around, as conveyer belts guide you through glass tubes right into the bay. Not for the claustrophobic, perhaps, but the thrilling fish-eye view of San Francisco leaves kids and parents wide-eyed and humming *Little Mermaid* tunes.

HYDE STREET PIER HISTORIC SHIPS COLLECTION

☎ 415-561-7100; www.nps.gov/safr; Pier 45, 499 Jefferson St at Hyde St; adult/child under 16yr $5/free; ⏱ 9:30am-5pm Oct-May, to 7pm Jun-Sep; 🚌 19, 32, F; 🚃 Powell-Hyde

'Aye, she's a beauty,' you'll growl like a true salty dog once you've visited any of the four historic Bay Area boats currently open as museums along Hyde St Pier – especially elegant 1891 schooner *Alma* and the steamboat *Eureka*, the world's largest ferry c 1890. For more mariner action, check out the toylike, steam-powered paddlewheel tugboat *Eppleton Hall* and the magnificent triple-masted, iron-hulled *Balclutha*, an 1886 British vessel that brought coal to San Francisco and took grain back to Europe via the dreaded Cape Horn.

SAN FRANCISCO CAROUSEL

☎ California Welcome Center 415-981-1280; www.pier39.com; Pier 39, Beach St & the Embarcadero; admission $3; ⏱ 11am-7pm; 🚌 F; 🚹

Your chariot awaits to whisk you and the kiddies past the Golden Gate Bridge, Alcatraz and other SF landmarks hand-painted on this Italian carousel twinkling with 1800 lights at the bayside end of Pier 39. The old-timey organ carnival music is loud enough to drown out the inevitable tiny tot clinging for dear life to a high-stepping horsey.

GHIRARDELLI SQUARE

☎ 415-775-5500; www.ghirardellisq.com; 900 North Point St; ☺ 10am-9pm daily summer, 10am-9pm Mon-Sat, to 6pm Sun rest of year; 🚌 19, 49; 🚋 Powell-Hyde; ♿

Willy Wonka would tip his hat to Domingo Ghirardelli (g*ear*-ar-deli), whose business became the West's largest chocolate factory in 1893. After the company moved to the East Bay, two sweet-talking developers reinvented the factory as a mall and landmark ice-cream parlor in 1964. Today, the square is looking spiffy, with local boutiques such as **elizabethW** (p78), along with the charming tearoom **Crown & Crumpet** (p72) and tempting branch of **Kara's Cupcakes** (p75).

THE MARINA & THE PRESIDIO

GOLDEN GATE BRIDGE

☎ Fri-Mon 415-556-1693; www.goldengate.org; Fort Point Lookout Marine Dr; southbound car $6, car pools (3 or more passengers) admission free btwn 5-9am & 4-6pm; 🚌 28, 29, Golden Gate Transit buses; ♿

Strange but true: the elegant suspension bridge painted a signature shade called 'International Orange' was almost nixed by the navy in favor of concrete pylons and yellow stripes. Joseph B Strauss correctly gets heaps of praise as the engineering mastermind behind this marvel, but without the aesthetic intervention of architects Gertrude and Irving Murrow and the incredibly quick work of daredevil workers, this 1937 landmark might have been just another traffic bottleneck.

The War Department didn't want to take any chances with the ships passing through the Golden Gate, so safety and solidity were its primary goals – but a green light was given to the counterproposal by Strauss and the Murrows for a subtler deco span and color that harmonized with the natural environment. Before the War Department could insist on an eyesore, laborers dove into the treacherous riptides of the bay and got the bridge underway in 1933.

Today, Brooklyn still tries to debate who has the more beautiful bridge, but

RICK GERHARTER

Aquarium of the Bay

EMBARCADERO & THE BAY

SIGHTS

for San Franciscans that argument was won 70 years ago, and the only debatable point is where to get the best vantage point on their beloved bridge. Cinema buffs believe Hitchcock had it right: seen from below at **Fort Point** (p68), the bridge induces a thrilling case of *Vertigo*. Fog aficionados prefer the lookout at Vista Point in Marin, on the north side of the bridge, to watch gusts rush through the bridge cables. **Crissy Field** (below) is a key spot to appreciate the whole span, with windsurfers and kite-fliers to add action to your snapshots. A German stunt man jumped from Golden Gate Bridge in 1980 with the intention of surviving, but didn't – suffice to say Tarzan swings are not among the best ways to cross the bridge (see boxed text, below).

CRISSY FIELD

☎ 415-561-7690; www.crissyfield.org; btwn Mason St & Golden Gate Promenade; 🚌 28, 30, 43, 76

Where military aircraft once zoomed in for a landing, bird-watchers now huddle in the silent rushes of a reclaimed tidal marsh. Joggers pound beachside trails that were once oil-stained asphalt, and the only security alerts are raised by puppies suspiciously sniffing surfers. On foggy days, stop by the certified-green **Warming Hut** (p75) to browse regional nature books and thaw out over fair-trade coffee.

EXPLORATORIUM

☎ 415-561-0360, 415-563-7337; www.explora torium.edu; 3601 Lyon St; adult/child under 4yr/ child 4-12yr/senior & student $15/free/10/12, 1st Wed of month free; 🕙 10am-5pm Tue-Sun; 🚌 28, 30, 43, 76; ♿

Is there a science to skateboarding, do robots have feelings, and do toilets really flush counterclockwise in Australia? Head to the Exploratorium to get fascinating scientific answers to all those questions you always wanted to ask in science class. Try

↘ THREE WAYS TO CROSS THE BRIDGE

- Bike it – follow the 49-Mile Dr signs along Lincoln Blvd through the Presidio to the parking lot right before the toll plaza. Beyond the lot is a paved bike path, which begins just past a sign showing a map of Fort Point; it takes you under the bridge and around to the sidewalk on the westbound side, which is reserved for bikes only. You can cross on bikes 24 hours a day.
- Hoof it – from the Fort Point Lookout a pathway leads up to the toll plaza, then it's 1.7 miles across. Go during off-peak hours to minimize your exhaust intake, and bus it back if the 3.4-mile round-trip seems too much. Note: pedestrian access in summer is open 5am to 9pm, shorter in winter.
- Catch the bus – skip the $6 car toll and take a bus instead. The 29 Muni bus runs from the Sunset to the Fort Point Lookout and the toll plaza (which is on the SF side); the 28 Muni runs from 19th Ave just to the toll plaza; and the 76 Muni (Sundays only) runs into the Marin Headlands (p250). The fastest, most comfortable way to reach the bridge from Downtown is to take any Marin County–bound Golden Gate Transit bus (routes 70 and 80 run frequently) and get off at the toll plaza.

ANTHONY PIDGEON

Palace of Fine Arts

out a punk hairdo courtesy of the static-electricity station, and crawl, climb and feel your way – in pitch-black darkness – through the maze of the highly recommended **Tactile Dome** (☎ 415-561-0362; incl general admission $20); visitors must be over seven years old, and reservations are required.

PALACE OF FINE ARTS
Palace Dr; 🚌 28, 30, 43, 76
Like a fossilized party favor, this romantic, fake Greco-Roman ruin is the memento San Francisco decided to keep from the 1915 Panama-Pacific International Exposition. The original was built in wood, burlap and plaster by celebrated Berkeley architect Bernard Maybeck as a picturesque backdrop, and by the 1960s was beginning to crumble. The structure was recast in concrete, so that future generations could gaze up at the rotunda relief to glimpse 'Art Under Attack by Materialists, with Idealists Leaping to her Rescue.'

BAKER BEACH
🕑 sunrise-sunset; 🚌 28, 29
Picnic amid the sheltering pines, fish among the rocks or frolic nude – you know, all the usual stuff you do on a military base. Spectacular views of Golden Gate Bridge and the Lincoln Golf Course

↘ TRANSPORTATION: THE MARINA & THE PRESIDIO

Bus Bus 30 gets you to Fort Mason and the Marina from Union Square. Buses 42, 47 and 49 serve Fort Mason from Van Ness Ave. The 28 bus goes from the Marina to the Presidio and Golden Gate Bridge.
Cable car The Powell-Hyde line terminates three blocks from Fort Mason.
Parking Ample parking in the Presidio, especially Crissy Field. There are two lots in Fort Mason and one at Marina Green.

remind you you're still in the city, but don't let that make you self-conscious – out here, among locals, no one's going to notice a few tan lines. The all-gay local beach is further north, at Marshall's Beach (aka Marcia's Beach), immediately before the bridge. (Ask around for directions, but *never* climb the dangerous rugged cliffs north from Baker to reach it.) Mind the currents and the c-c-cold water.

PRESIDIO BASE
☎ 415-561-4323; www.nps.gov/prsf; ✆ center 9am-5pm, park dawn-dusk; 🚌 43, 76

What started out as a Spanish fort built by conscripted Ohlone in 1776 is now a treasure hunt of oddities. Begin your adventures by heading across the parade grounds at Moraga to get a trail map at the **visitors center (Moraga Ave near Arguello Blvd)** in the old Officers' Club (verify location ahead of time; it's slated to move). Fans of the maudlin and macabre hike directly to the **Pet Cemetery** off Crissy Field Ave, where handmade tombstones mark the final resting places of military hamsters who've completed their final tour of duty.

Head east of the parade grounds toward the Palace of Fine Arts and you'll come across the **Letterman Campus**, home to nonprofits and *Star Wars* filmmaker George Lucas, whose offices require a special pass – but you can pay your respects to the Yoda statue out front.

FORT POINT
☎ 415-556-1693; Marine Dr; admission free; ✆ 10am-5pm Fri-Sun; 🚌 28

The fort was completed with 126 cannons in 1861, just in time to protect the bay against certain invasion by Confederate soldiers during the Civil War…or not, as it turned out. Without firing a single shot, Fort Point was abandoned in 1900 and became neglected once the Golden Gate Bridge was built over it. Alfred Hitchcock saw deadly potential in Fort Point, and shot the trademark scene from *Vertigo* of Kim Novak leaping from the lookout to certain death into the bay…or not, as it turned out. Fort Point has since given up all pretense of being deadly, and now provides a gift center, Civil War displays and panoramic viewing decks.

↘ THE PRESIDIO GIVES PEACE A CHANCE

The Presidio is a quintessentially San Franciscan playland of nude beaches, free Shakespeare and spectacular views of the Golden Gate Bridge, but it wasn't always so welcoming. After it became a Spanish military harbor in 1776, any boat entering the San Francisco Bay would have to pass the Presidio's trigger-happy cannons and gunboats.

Relics from the Civil War can be seen at Fort Point, the three-story fort that took eight years to build and had 126 cannons that saw not one day of military action. A key base of operations for the Allied Pacific campaign in World War II, the Presidio was used during the Cold War as a bulwark against communism across the Pacific in China, Korea and Vietnam.

In 1996 the Presidio was repurposed as public parkland, and most of the military buildings have since been turned over to nonprofits, low-income housing and *Star Wars* filmmaker George Lucas, whose Presidio offices are presided over by a bronze Yoda statue.

Fort Point passage

RAY LASKOWITZ

FORT MASON CENTER
☎ 415-441-3400; www.fortmason.org; Bay & Franklin Sts; 🚍 22, 28, 30, 43, 47, 49
San Francisco takes subversive glee in turning military installations into venues for nature, fine dining and out-there experimental art – evidence, Fort Mason. The military mess halls are gone, replaced by vegan-friendly **Greens** (p74), a restaurant run by a Zen community. Warehouses now host cutting-edge theater at **Magic Theatre** (p77) and improvised comedy workshops at **BATS** (p77), and the dockside Herbst Pavilion has art fairs and craft fairs in its arsenal – see the website for upcoming performances and events.

SLEEPING
EMBARCADERO & THE PIERS
ARGONAUT HOTEL   Hotel $$$
☎ 415-563-0800, 866-415-0704; www.argonaut hotel.com; 495 Jefferson St; r $205-325; 🚍 F; 🛜 🛗

The top hotel at Fisherman's Wharf was built as a cannery in 1908, and has century-old wooden beams and exposed brick walls. Rooms sport an over-the-top nautical theme, with porthole-shaped mirrors and plush deep-blue carpets. Though it has amenities of an upper-end hotel – ultracomfy beds, stereo CD players – some rooms are tiny and get limited sunlight. Pay extra and you'll get light and a mesmerizing bay view.

TUSCAN INN   Hotel $$
☎ 415-561-1100, 800-648-4626; www.tuscan inn.com; 425 North Point St; r $169-229; 🚍 47; 🛜 🛗
Just because you want to stay at touristy Fisherman's Wharf, it doesn't mean you have to settle for a plain-Jane chain, such as the nearby Marriott or Hilton. The Tuscan Inn – managed by fashion-forward Kimpton Hotels – is just as comfortable, but has way more character, with spacious rooms done in bold colors and mixed patterns. Kids love the in-room Nintendo; parents love the afternoon wine hour.

WHARF INN   Motel $$

☎ 415-673-7411, 800-548-9918; www.wharfinn
.com; 2601 Mason St; r $139-189; 🚌 F;
ⓟ 🛜 ♿

This standard-issue, two-story motor
lodge has clean, simple rooms, ideal for
kids who make a mess. Rates fluctuate
wildly with the tourist tide. Free parking.

THE MARINA & THE PRESIDIO

HOTEL DEL SOL   Theme Hotel $$

☎ 415-921-5520, 877-433-5765; www.thehotel
delsol.com; 3100 Webster St; d $149-199; 🚌 28,
43; ⓟ 🛜 🏊 ♿

The kid-friendly del Sol is a riot of color
with its tropical-themed decor. A quiet, re-
vamped 1950s motor lodge with a palm-
lined central courtyard, it's also one of the
few San Francisco hotels with a heated
outdoor pool. Family suites have bunks
and board games.

MARINA MOTEL   Motel $$

☎ 415-921-9406, 800-346-6118; www.marina
motel.com; 2576 Lombard St; r $105-145; 🚌 76;
ⓟ 🛜

Established in 1939 to accommodate
visitors arriving via the new Golden Gate
Bridge, the Marina has an inviting, vintage
Spanish-Mediterranean look, with a quiet
bougainvillea-lined courtyard. Rooms
are homey, simple and well maintained
(never mind the occasional scuff mark);

⬂ IF YOU LIKE...

If you like the **Golden Gate Bridge**, check out these other only-in-SF structures:

- **Wave Organ** Built right into the tip of the Marina Boat Harbor jetty by Exploratorium engineers, this experimental sound system is made of PVC tubes, concrete pipes and marble from San Francisco's old cemetery. Depending on the waves, winds and tide, the tones emitted can sound like nervous humming or spooky horror-movie heavy breathing. The Organ is open and free to all during daylight hours; take bus 28, 43 or 76 to Marina Harbor and walk to the jetty's end.

- **Swedenborgian Church** (☎ 415-346-6466; www.sfswedenborgian.org; 2107 Lyon St; admission free; 🕐 hours vary; 🚌 1, 24, 43) Hidden behind a modest brick archway is this 1894 landmark to the glories of nature, the collaborative effort of naturalist John Muir, California Arts and Crafts pioneer Bernard Maybeck and architect Arthur Page Brown. Beyond a secret garden of trees from around the world is a chapel supported by mighty madrone trunks, graced with murals of Northern California landscapes that took William Keith 40 years to complete.

- **Vedanta Society** At 2963 Webster St, there's no mistaking this psychedelic 1905 mashup of Victorian and Eastern architecture. The Vedanta Society's red turrets represent major world religions and its Hindu-inspired organizing principle: 'the oneness of existence.'

- **Octagon House** (☎ 415-441-7512; 2645 Gough St; admission $3; 🕐 noon-3pm on 2nd & 4th Thu & 2nd Sun of month, closed Jan; 🚌 45) According to an 1860s San Francisco superstition, eight-sided houses are good for your health. Test the theory by visiting architect William C McElroy's eccentric structure .

Argonaut Hotel (p69)

DAVID PHELPS

some have full kitchens (an extra $10). Rooms on Lombard Street are loud; request one in back.

COVENTRY MOTOR INN   Motel $
☎ 415-567-1200; www.coventrymotorinn.com; 1901 Lombard St; r $95-145; 🚌 76; P 🛜 ♿
Of the scores of motels lining Lombard Street (Hwy 101), the generic Coventry has the highest overall quality-to-value ratio, with spacious, well-maintained (if plain) rooms and extras such as air-con (good for quiet sleeps) and covered parking. Parents: there's plenty of floor space to unpack the kids' toys, but no pool.

MARINA INN   Inn $
☎ 415-928-1000, 800-274-1420; www.marinainn .com; 3110 Octavia Blvd; r $69-99; 🚌 28, 30; 🛜
A good deal in the Marina, this pretty, white turn-of-the-century inn has a little parlor lobby and 40 clean, straightforward and comfortable rooms with cabbage-rose decor, offering a cozier alternative to a generic motel. Rooms facing Lombard Street are loud, and there's no onsite park-

ing, but the inn is close to Union St shopping and bars.

HI SAN FRANCISCO
FISHERMAN'S WHARF   Hostel $
☎ 415-771-7277; www.hihostels.com; Bldg 240, Fort Mason; dm $26-30, r $75-125; 🚌 30, 47, 49; P 🛜
The hostel trades Downtown convenience for a lush, parklike setting just spitting distance from the bay. Dorms range from a manageable four beds to a whopping 24 beds; some are coed. There's no curfew, but daytime access to dorms is limited. Groups of three or four should opt for a private room. There's limited free parking.

EATING
EMBARCADERO & THE PIERS
FISHERMAN'S WHARF
GARY DANKO   Californian $$$
☎ 415-749-2060; www.garydanko.com; 800 North Point St; 🕑 dinner; 🚌 10, 19, 30, 47; 🚃 Powell-Hyde

Smoked-glass windows prevent passersby from tripping over their tongues at the sight of exquisite roasted lobster with trumpet mushrooms, blushing duck breast with rhubarb compote, trios of crème brûlée and the lavish cheese cart. Take your server's seasonal recommendations of two to six small courses for $44 to $98, and prepare to be impressed. Gary Danko has won multiple James Beard Awards for providing an impeccable dining experience, from inventive salad courses such as oysters with caviar and lettuce cream to the casually charming server who hands you tiny chocolate cakes as a parting gift.

FORBES ISLAND   Grill $$$
☎ 415-951-4900; www.forbesisland.com; Pier 41; ⏰ 5-10pm Wed-Sun; 🚌 15, 37, 49, F; ♿

No man is an island, except for an eccentric millionaire named Forbes Thor Kiddoo. A miniature lighthouse, thatched hut, waterfall, sandy beach and swaying palms transformed his moored houseboat into the Hearst Castle of the bay. Today this bizarre domicile is a restaurant strong on grilled meats and atmosphere. Reserve in advance and catch boat shuttles from Pier 39; landlubbers dining below deck should bring their motion-sickness meds.

CROWN & CRUMPET   Cafe $$
☎ 415-771-4252; www.crownandcrumpet.com; 207 Ghirardelli Sq; ⏰ 10am-6pm Mon-Thu, 10am-9pm Fri, 9am-9pm Sat, 9am-6pm Sun; 🚌 10, 19, 30, 47; 🚋 Powell-Hyde; ♿

Designer style and rosy cheer usher teatime into the 21st century: girlfriends rehash hot dates over scones with strawberries and champagne, and dads and daughters clink porcelain teacups with crooked pinkies and 38 kinds of tea. Reservations recommended on weekends.

GHIRARDELLI ICE CREAM   Ice Cream $
☎ 415-474-3938; www.ghirardellisq.com; 900 North Point St, West Plaza; ⏰ 10am-11pm Sun-Thu, to midnight Fri & Sat; 🚌 10, 19, 30, 47; 🚋 Powell-Hyde; ♿

Gee, Mr Ghirardelli, you sure make a swell sundae. Chocolate milkshakes are

ROBERTO GEROMETTA

Boulette's Larder

for sharing and making moony eyes over, and the legendary Cable Car comes with Rocky Road ice cream, marshmallow topping and enough hot fudge to pave Jack Kerouac Alley.

IN-N-OUT BURGER   Burgers $

☎ 800-786-1000; www.in-n-out.com; 333 Jefferson St; ⏰ 10:30am-1am Sun-Thu, to 1:30am Fri & Sat; 🚌 10, 30, 47, J; 🚃 Powell-Hyde; ♿

Gourmet burgers have taken SF by storm, but In-N-Out has had a good thing going for 60 years: prime chuck beef it processes itself, plus fries and shakes made with ingredients you can pronounce, all served by employees paid a living wage. Ask for yours off the menu 'wild style,' cooked in mustard with grilled onions.

EMBARCADERO & FERRY BUILDING

LA MAR CEBICHERIÁ   Peruvian, Seafood $$$

☎ 415-397-8880; www.lamarcebicheria.com; Pier 1.5 Embarcadero; ⏰ 11:30am-2:30pm Mon-Fri, noon-2:30pm Sat & Sun, 5:30-10pm Mon-Thu, 5:30-10:30pm Fri & Sat, 5:30-9pm Sun; 🚌 21, 71, F, J, K, L, M, N; 🚌 & 🚃 Embarcadero

Business lunches here could lead to some very untoward office behavior: the key ingredient in these collaged plates of Peruvian ceviche is *leche de tigre,* the 'milk of the tiger,' a marinade of lime, chili and brine that 'cooks' the fish without a fire, and is said to have aphrodisiac properties.

SLANTED DOOR   Vietnamese $$

☎ 415-861-8032; 1 Ferry Bldg; ⏰ lunch & dinner; 🚌 2, 21, 71, F, J, K, L, M, N; 🚌 & 🚃 Embarcadero

San Francisco's most effortlessly elegant restaurant harmonizes California ingredients, Continental influences and Vietnamese flair. Owner/chef Charles Phan enhances top-notch ingredients with bright flavors, heaping local

Dungeness crab atop cellophane noodles and garlicky Meyer Ranch 'shaking beef' on watercress. The wildly successful venture is still a family establishment, with 20 Phan family members serving multistar meals for here and to go at Out the Door.

HOG ISLAND OYSTER COMPANY   Seafood $$

☎ 415-391-7117; www.hogislandoysters.com; 1 Ferry Bldg; ⏰ 11:30am-8pm Mon-Fri, 11am-6pm Sat & Sun; 🚌 2, 21, 71, F, J, K, L, M, N; 🚌 & 🚃 Embarcadero

Slurp down the bounty of the North Bay with a view of the East Bay. Take yours au naturel, with caper beurre blanc, spiked with bacon and paprika, or perhaps classic lemon and shallots… Oh, go on, try some of each. Mondays and Thursdays between 5pm and 7pm are happy hours indeed for shellfish fans, with $1 oysters and $3.50 beer.

BOULETTE'S LARDER   Californian $$

☎ 415-399-1155; www.bouletteslarder.com; 1 Ferry Bldg; ⏰ 8-10:30am & 11:30am-2:30pm Mon-Fri, 10am-2:30pm Sun; 🚌 2, 21, 71, F, J, K, L, M, N; 🚌 & 🚃 Embarcadero

Dinner theater doesn't get better than brunch here at the communal table, strategically placed inside a working kitchen, amid a swirl of chefs preparing for dinner service. Inspired by their truffled eggs and beignets? Get spices and mixes to go at the pantry counter.

MIJITA   Mexican $

☎ 415-399-0814; www.mijitasf.com; 1 Ferry Bldg; ⏰ 10am-7pm Mon-Thu, 10am-8pm Fri, 9am-8pm Sat, 10am-4pm Sun; 🚌 2, 21, 71, F, J, K, L, M, N; 🚌 & 🚃 Embarcadero; 🅥 ♿

Owner/chef Traci Des Jardins puts her signature twist on her Mexican grandmother's standbys, using fresh local produce for tangy-savory jicama and grapefruit salad with pumpkin seeds, and sustainably harvested fish cooked with the minimum of oil in seriously addictive Baja fish tacos. Wash it all down with melon *agua frescas* (fruit-flavored drinks) bayside, with envious seagulls circling overhead.

THE MARINA & THE PRESIDIO

The usual Marina dining destinations are on Chestnut St from Fillmore to Divisadero Sts, and Union St between Fillmore St and Van Ness Ave, but some fun, funky fare is found on Lombard Street, and Greens makes the hike to Fort Mason worthwhile.

A16   Italian $$
☎ 415-771-2216; www.a16sf.com; 2355 Chestnut St; ☽ 11:30am-2:30pm Wed-Fri, 5-10pm Sun-Thu, 5-11pm Fri & Sat; 🚌 2, 3, 4, 22, 38

Like a high-maintenance date, this Neapolitan pizzeria demands reservations and then haughtily makes you wait in the foyer for chewy-but-not-too-thick-crust pizza. Skip the spotty desserts and concentrate on adventurous house-cured

salumi platters, including the delectably spicy pig's ear terrine (no, really).

GREENS   Vegetarian, Californian $$
☎ 415-771-6222; www.greensrestaurant.com; Fort Mason Center, Bldg A; ☽ restaurant lunch Tue-Sat, dinner Mon-Sat, brunch Sun; take-out 8am-8pm Mon-Thu, 8am-5pm Fri & Sat, 9am-4pm Sun; 🚌 22, 28, 30; Ⓥ ♿

Career carnivores won't realize there's no meat in the hearty black bean chili with crème fraîche and pickled jalapeños, or that roasted eggplant *panino* (sandwich), packed with hearty flavor from ingredients mostly grown on a Zen farm in Marin. On sunny days, get yours to go so you can enjoy it on a wharfside bench, but if you're planning a sit-down weekend dinner or Sunday brunch you'll need reservations.

ROSE'S CAFÉ   Californian $$
☎ 415-775-2200; www.rosescafesf.com; 2298 Union St; ☽ 7am-10pm Mon-Thu, 8am-10pm Fri & Sat, 8am-9:30pm Sun; 🚌 22, 41, 45; Ⓥ ♿

Follow your salads and housemade soups with rich organic polenta with gorgon-

Slanted Door (p73)

SABRINA DALBESIO

zola and thyme, then linger over your espresso or grenadine-and-vanilla Monk's Blend tea. Shop if you must, but return to this corner cafe from 4pm to 6pm for half-price wine by the glass.

BLUE BARN GOURMET
Sandwiches, Salads $

☎ 415-441-3232; www.bluebarngourmet.com; 2105 Chestnut St; 🕑 11am-8:30pm Sun-Thu, to 7pm Fri & Sat; 🚍 22, 28, 30, 43, 76, 91

Toss aside thoughts of ordinary salads. Here for $8.50 you can build a mighty mound of organic produce from Sonoma's Oak Hill Farm, topped with your choice of six fixings: artisan cheeses, caramelized Copra onions, heirloom tomatoes, candied pecans, pomegranate seeds, even Meyer grilled sirloin. For a hot meal, try the toasted panini oozing with Manchego cheese, fig jam and chorizo.

WARMING HUT
Cafe, Sandwiches $

☎ 415-561-3040; 983 Marine Dr; 🕑 9am-5pm; 🚍 29

Wetsuited windsurfers and Crissy Field kite fliers thaw out with fair-trade coffee, organic pastries and organic hot dogs at the Warming Hut, while browsing an excellent selection of field guides and sampling honey made by Presidio honeybees. This eco-shack below the Golden Gate Bridge has walls ingeniously insulated with recycled denim and a heartwarming concept: all purchases fund Crissy Field's ongoing conversion from US Army air strip to wildlife preserve.

LA BOULANGE
Sandwiches, Bakery $

☎ 415-440-4450; www.baybread.com; 1909 Union St; 🕑 7am-6pm; 🚍 22, 41, 45, 47, 49, 76; Ⓥ ♿

La Combo is a $7 lunchtime deal to justify your next Union St boutique purchase: half a tartine (open-faced sandwich) with

SABRINA DALBESIO
Greens

soup or salad, plus all the Nutella and pickled cornichons (gherkins) you desire from the condiment bar.

KARA'S CUPCAKES
Bakery, Dessert $

☎ 415-563-2253; www.karascupcakes.com; 3249 Scott St; 🕑 10am-8pm Mon-Thu, 10am-10pm Fri-Sat, 10am-7pm Sun; 🚍 22, 28, 30, 43, 76, 91

Stand back and watch Proustian nostalgia wash over fully grown adults as they bite into the carrot cake with cream-cheese frosting, or babble excitedly about magician birthday parties over the chocolate-marshmallow.

REAL FOOD
Groceries $

☎ 415-567-6900; www.realfoodco.com; 3060 Fillmore St; 🕑 8am-9pm; 🚍 22, 41, 45

Head to the deli for respectable *nigiri* sushi, freshly roasted eggplant and tomato salad, free-range herb turkey on focaccia, organic gingerbread and fair-trade coffee, and on less windy days, grab a seat on the front patio.

DRINKING
EMBARCADERO & THE PIERS

BUENA VISTA CAFÉ   Bar
☎ 415-474-5044; www.thebuenavista.com; 2765 Hyde St; ⏱ 9am-2am Mon-Fri, 8am-2am Sat & Sun; 🚋 Powell-Hyde

Warm your cockles with a prim little goblet of bitter-creamy Irish coffee, introduced to the US at this destination bar that once served sailors and cannery workers. The creaky Victorian floor manages to hold up carousers and families alike, served community-style at round tables overlooking the wharf.

THE MARINA & THE PRESIDIO

CALIFORNIA WINE MERCHANT   Bar
☎ 415-567-0646; www.californiawinemerchant. com; 2113 Chestnut St; ⏱ 10am-midnight Mon-Wed, 10am-1:30am Thu-Sat, 11am-11pm Sun; 🚍 30

Part wine store, part wine bar, this little shop on busy Chestnut St caters to grey-at-the-temples professionals and neighborhood wine aficionados, and serves half-glasses as well as flights. Arrive early to score a table, or stand and gab with the locals.

MATRIXFILLMORE   Bar
☎ 415-563-4180; www.matrixfillmore.com; 3138 Fillmore St; ⏱ 6pm-2am; 🚍 22, 45

The neighborhood's most notorious up-market pick-up joint provides a fascinating glimpse into the lives of single, white Marina swankers. Treat it as a comic sociological study, while enjoying the stellar cocktails, blazing fireplace and sexy lounge beats. Bring your credit card.

ENTERTAINMENT & ACTIVITIES
EMBARCADERO & THE PIERS

TEATRO ZINZANNI   Comedy
☎ 415-438-2668; http://zinzanni.org; Pier 29, Embarcadero; admission $117-195; ⏱ 7:30-11pm; 🚍 F

Inside a 19th-century Spiegeltent (an opulent Belgian traveling-circus tent), top circus talent flies overhead, a celeb-diva croons, and clowns pull wacky stunts as you dig into a surprisingly good five-course dinner. Former stars have included Joan Baez and Broadway's Liliane Montevecchi. Be prepared for audience participation – especially if you're a looker.

PIER 23   Jazz, Blues & Funk
☎ 415-362-5125; www.pier23cafe.com; Pier 23; admission free-$10; ⏱ shows 5-7pm Tue, 6-8pm Wed, 7-10pm Thu, 10pm-midnight Fri & Sat, 4-8pm Sun; 🚍 F

It looks like a surf shack, but this old waterfront restaurant on Pier 23 regularly features R & B, reggae, Latin bands, mellow rock and the occasional jazz pianist. The dinner menu features pier-worthy options such as batter-fried oysters and whole roasted crab.

ADVENTURE CAT   Sailing & Windsurfing
☎ 415-777-1630; www.adventurecat.com; Pier 39; cruises from $30; 🚍 F; ♿

There's no better view of San Francisco than from the water, especially at twilight on a fogless evening aboard a sunset cruise. Adventure Cat uses catamarans, with a windless indoor cabin for grand-mums and a trampoline between the hulls for bouncy kids.

THE MARINA & THE PRESIDIO

BATS IMPROV   Comedy

Bay Area Theatersports; ☎ 415-474-8935; www.improv.org; 3rd fl, bldg B, Fort Mason Center; shows usually $15, admission depends on class/event; ⊙ weekend shows 8pm; 🚌 22, 28, 30

Bay Area Theatersports explores all things improv, from audience-inspired themes to wacked-out musicals at completely improvised weekend shows. Or take center stage yourself at an improv-comedy workshop (held on weekday nights and weekend afternoons). Think fast: classes fill quickly.

PRESIDIO GOLF COURSE   Golf

☎ 415-561-4661; www.presidiogolf.com; Arguello Blvd & Finley Rd; Mon-Thu resident/nonresident $69/125, Fri $85/145, Sat & Sun $99/145; ⊙ sunrise-sunset; 🚌 28

Whack balls with military-style precision on the course once reserved exclusively for US forces. You can book up to 30 days in advance on the website, where you can sometimes find rate specials, too. Cart is included in the price.

PLANET GRANITE   Rock Climbing

☎ 415-692-3434; www.planetgranite.com; Glass Palace, 924 Old Mason St, Crissy Field; day use adult/child $18/10; ⊙ 6am-11pm Mon-Fri, 8am-8pm Sat, 8am-6pm Sun; 🚌 29

Take in spectacular bay views through a wall of glass as you ascend false-rock structures in this kick-ass 25,000-sq-ft climbing center – the ideal place to train for a hiking expedition to Yosemite. Check the web for class schedules.

MAGIC THEATRE   Theater

☎ 415-441-8822; www.magictheatre.org; 3rd fl, Bldg D, Fort Mason Center; 🚌 22, 28, 30

The Magic Theatre is well known for taking risks and staging provocative plays by such playwrights as Bill Pullman, Terrence McNally, Edna O'Brien, David Mamet and longtime playwright-in-residence Sam Shepard. Watch the next generation

EMBARCADERO & THE BAY

ENTERTAINMENT & ACTIVITIES

JUDY BELLAH

Mijita (p73)

of playwrights and provocateurs break through in professionally staged works written by teenagers as part of the Young California Writers Project.

OCEANIC SOCIETY EXPEDITIONS
Whale-Watching

☎ 415-474-3385; www.oceanic-society.org; Bldg A, Fort Mason Center; per person $100-120; ✆ office 9am-5pm Fri-Mon, trips Sat & Sun; 🚌 22, 28, 30

The Oceanic Society runs ocean-going boat trips – sometimes to the Farallon Islands – during both whale-migration seasons, with top-notch naturalists providing keen insight. Cruises depart from Fort Mason and last all day. Kids must be 10 years or older. Reservations required.

SHOPPING
EMBARCADERO & THE PIERS

ELIZABETHW Beauty Products, Local Maker

☎ 415-351-2800; www.elizabethw.com; 900 North Point St; ✆ 10am-6pm Mon-Thu & Sun,

to 8:30pm Fri & Sat; 🚌 2, 21, 71, F, J, K, L, M, N; 🚋 & 🚈 Embarcadero

Thermometers permanently hover around 70°F in San Francisco, but local scent-maker elizabethW supplies the tantalizing aromas of changing seasons without the sweaty brows or frozen toes. Sweet Tea smells like a Georgia porch in summertime, Vetiver like autumn in Maine. For a true SF fragrance, Leaves is as audaciously green as Golden Gate Park in January.

FERRY PLAZA
WINE MERCHANT Food & Drink

☎ 415-391-9400; www.fpwm.com; 1 Ferry Plaza; ✆ 11am-8pm Mon, 10am-8pm Tue-Wed, 10am-9pm Thu-Fri, 8am-9pm Sat, 10am-7pm Sun; 🚌 2, 21, 71, F, J, K, L, M, N; 🚋 & 🚈 Embarcadero

Stock up on California wines after you've sipped a few – start with viogniers, work your way to cabs, and swish and spit when you only want to taste. The bar is jammed on Saturdays, but otherwise staff will take the time to suggest pairings and exciting new releases.

SABRINA DALBESIO

Ferry Plaza Wine Merchant

RECCHIUTI CHOCOLATES
Food & Drink, Local Maker

☎ 415-834-9494; www.recchiuticonfections. com; 1 Ferry Bldg; ⏱ 10am-7pm Mon-Fri, 8am-6pm Sat, 10am-5pm Sun; 🚌 2, 21, 71, F, J, K, L, M, N; 🚌 & 🚋 Embarcadero

No San Franciscan can resist Recchiuti: Pacific Heights parts with old money for its *fleur de sel* caramels; Noe Valley's child foodie prodigies prefer S'more Bites to the campground variety; and the Mission splurges on chocolates designed by developmentally disabled artists from **Creativity Explored** (p168) – part of the proceeds benefit the nonprofit gallery.

SUR LA TABLE
Housewares

☎ 415-262-9970; www.surlatable.com; 1 Ferry Bldg, most classes at 77 Maiden Lane; ⏱ 9am-7pm Mon-Fri, 8am-7pm Sat, 10am-6pm Sun; 🚌 2, 21, 71, F, J, K, L, M, N; 🚌 & 🚋 Embarcadero

Can't fathom life without an espresso maker and citrus reamer? You'll never need to, thanks to these understanding salespeople. The Ferry Building location features free demos; evening classes at the Maiden Lane store on knife skills, seasonal California cuisine and more cost $79 to $89.

THE MARINA & THE PRESIDIO

PAST PERFECT
Antiques & Collectibles

☎ 415-929-7651; 2230 Union St; ⏱ 11am-7pm; 🚌 22, 41, 45

So this is how Pacific Heights eccentrics fill up those mansions: Fornasetti face plates, Danish teak credenzas and Lucite champagne buckets. The store is a collective, so prices are all over the place – some sellers apparently believe their belongings owe them back rent, while others are happy just to unload their ex's mother's prized spoon collection.

MINGLE
Clothing & Accessories, Local Designer

☎ 415-674-8811; www.mingleshop.com; 1815 Union St; ⏱ 11am-7pm Mon-Fri & Sun, 10:30am-7pm Sat; 🚌 41, 45, 47, 49, 76

Local designers keep this boutique stocked with hot Cleopatra-collar dresses, mod ring-buckled bags and plaid necklaces, all for less than you'd pay for Marc Jacobs on mega-sale. Men emerge from Mingle date-ready in dark tailored denim and black Western shirts with white piping – the SF version of a tux.

MY ROOMMATE'S CLOSET
Clothing & Accessories

☎ 415-447-7703; www.myroommatescloset. com; 3044 Fillmore St; ⏱ 11am-6:30pm Mon-Fri, 11am-6pm Sat, noon-5pm Sun; 🚌 22, 28, 41, 43, 45

All the half-off bargains and none of the clawing dangers of a sample sale. You'll find cloudlike Catherine Malandrino chiffon party dresses, executive-office Diane Von Furstenburg wrap dresses, and designer denim at prices approaching reality.

UKO
Clothing & Accessories

☎ 415-563-0330; 2070 Union St; ⏱ 11am-6:30pm Mon-Sat, noon-5:30pm Sun; 🚌 22, 28, 41, 43, 45

Get bonus fashion IQ points for clever jackets with hidden pockets-within-pockets, Cop-Copine wrap skirts with oddly flattering flaps, and silver drop earrings that add an exclamation point to your look.

PLUMPJACK WINES
Food & Drink, Local Makers

☎ 415-346-9870; www.plumpjack.com; 3201 Fillmore St; ⏱ 11am-8pm Mon-Sat, to 6pm Sun; 🚌 22, 28, 41, 43, 45

Discover a new favorite organically grown California vintage under $30 at

LEE FOSTER

Gourmet cheeses, Ferry Building (p73)

the distinctive wine boutique that won former owner Mayor Gavin Newsom respect from even Green Party gourmets. A more knowledgeable staff is hard to find anywhere in SF, and they'll set you up with the right bottles to cross party lines.

ATYS   Housewares
☎ 415-441-9220; www.atysdesign.com; 2149b Union St; ⏰ 11am-6:30pm Mon-Sat, noon-6pm Sun; 🚌 22, 41, 45

Tucked away in a courtyard, this design showcase offers version 2.0 of essential household items: a mirrored coat rack, a rechargeable flashlight, and a zero-emissions solar-powered toy airplane.

SPORTS BASEMENT   Sporting Goods
☎ 415-437-0100; www.sportsbasement.com; 610 Old Mason St; ⏰ 9am-9pm Mon-Fri, 8am-8pm Sat & Sun; 🚌 15

This 70,000 sq ft of sports and camping equipment was once a US Army Post Exchange, which is why you'll find hiking boots near the Fresh Produce sign.

DOWNTOWN

INFORMATION
Apple Store................................**1** E4
Bank of America......................**2** E4
Civic Center Post Office..........**3** C5
French Consulate **4** E2
Irish Consulate **5** G2
New Zealand Consulate...........**6** G1
San Francisco Visitor
  Information Center................**7** E4
UK Consulate **8** G3
US Post Office **9** E3

SIGHTS
49 Geary **10** F3
77 Geary **11** F3
AP Hotaling Warehouse........**12** F1
Asian Art Museum.................**13** C5
Bohemian Club **14** D3
City Hall..................................**15** B6
Gallery Paule Anglim.............**16** F3
Glide Memorial United
  Methodist Church...............**17** D4
Luggage Store Gallery...........**18** D5
Powell St Cable Car
  Turnaround.........................**19** E4
San Francisco Main
  Library.................................**20** C6

Transamerica Pyramid &
  Redwood Park.....................**21** F1
United Nations Plaza.............**22** D5

SLEEPING
Adelaide Hostel......................**23** D3
Golden Gate Hotel **24** D3
Hotel Adagio..........................**25** D3
Hotel California **26** D3
Hotel des Arts **27** F3
Hotel Diva **28** D3
Hotel Frank.............................**29** E3
Hotel Palomar........................**30** E4
Hotel Rex **31** E3
Hotel Triton **32** E3
Hotel Union Square **33** E3
Hotel Vertigo..........................**34** C3
Mandarin Oriental Hotel **35** G2
Orchard Garden Hotel **36** F2
Palace Hotel **37** F3
Petite Auberge **38** D3
Phoenix Hotel.........................**39** C5
Stratford Hotel **40** E3
Warwick Regis **41** D3

Westin St Francis Hotel..........**42** E3
White Swan Inn.......................**43** D3

EATING
Bocadillos...............................**44** F1
Boxed Foods............................**45** F3
Dottie's True Blue Café **46** D4
farmerbrown...........................**47** E4
Fish & Farm.............................**48** D4
Fleur de Lys **49** D3
Gitane......................................**50** F3
Jardinière **51** B6
Kokkari....................................**52** G1
Millennium **53** C5
Muracci's Curry.......................**54** F2
Restaurant Michael Mina......**55** E3
Saigon Sandwich Shop..........**56** C4
Shalimar..................................**57** D4

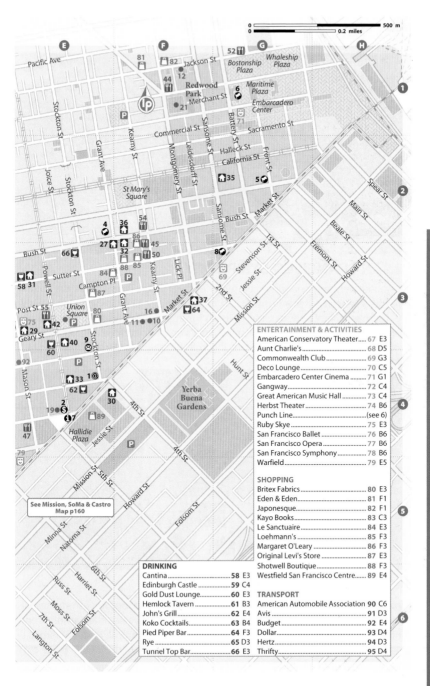

ENTERTAINMENT & ACTIVITIES

American Conservatory Theater.....	67 E3
Aunt Charlie's...............................	68 D5
Commonwealth Club........................	69 G3
Deco Lounge....................................	70 C5
Embarcadero Center Cinema	71 G1
Gangway..	72 C4
Great American Music Hall	73 C4
Herbst Theater...............................	74 B6
Punch Line.................................(see 6)
Ruby Skye..	75 E3
San Francisco Ballet	76 B6
San Francisco Opera	77 B6
San Francisco Symphony.................	78 B6
Warfield..	79 E5

SHOPPING

Britex Fabrics.................................	80 E3
Eden & Eden...................................	81 F1
Japonesque.....................................	82 F1
Kayo Books.....................................	83 C3
Le Sanctuaire..................................	84 E3
Loehmann's.....................................	85 F3
Margaret O'Leary	86 F3
Original Levi's Store........................	87 E3
Shotwell Boutique...........................	88 F3
Westfield San Francisco Centre.......	89 E4

TRANSPORT

American Automobile Association	90 C6
Avis..	91 D3
Budget..	92 E4
Dollar..	93 D4
Hertz...	94 D3
Thrifty...	95 D4

DRINKING

Cantina **58** E3
Edinburgh Castle......................**59** C4
Gold Dust Lounge....................**60** E3
Hemlock Tavern **61** B3
John's Grill...............................**62** E4
Koko Cocktails..........................**63** B4
Pied Piper Bar..........................**64** F3
Rye **65** D3
Tunnel Top Bar.........................**66** E3

See Mission, SoMa & Castro
Map p160

HIGHLIGHTS

DOWNTOWN

HIGHLIGHTS

↘ SAN FRANCISCO SYMPHONY

Talk about a supergroup: since conductor Michael Tilson Thomas took the baton, the San Francisco Symphony (p102) has racked up 13 Grammys. Arrive early for Thomas' insights about what to listen for in each composition, and pick up last-minute tickets for $20 – never mind what's on. From summer Mozart through stormy winter Berlioz, this is heart-racing, mind-expanding classical music.

↘ ASIAN ART MUSEUM

When San Francisco's Pacific Ocean panoramas are lost in fog, you can still see all the way across Asia here. The Asian (p89) brings 6000 years of art history from China, Taiwan, Tibet, Japan, Korea, Pakistan, India and more, all under one roof – and common themes and uncommon talents emerge from the 17,000-piece collection. Don't miss ground-floor contemporary shows.

↘ RIDING CABLE CARS

Take a leap onto the baseboard and grab a strap: you're in for the ultimate urban carnival ride. Burly operators work that handbrake and bell as though their lives depend on it and, well, little else prevents these 1870s contraptions from careening downhill into traffic. When climbs yield glimpses of the Golden Gate, public transit never seemed so poetic.

↘ SAN FRANCISCO OPERA

Divas have been bringing down the house in SF since the Gold Rush – and when the 1906 earthquake leveled the city's opera houses, they sang in the streets to keep spirits high. Mega-talents such as Renee Fleming and Nina Stemme command the **stage** (p101) in celebrated productions, plus free Stern Grove performances.

↘ TRANSAMERICA PYRAMID & REDWOOD PARK

'Spacey' is a fair way to describe many San Franciscans – and the defining feature of their downtown skyline. William Pereira's **pyramid** (p87) cleverly maximizes sunshine in the streets below, drawing lunchtime lollygaggers to the redwood grove that thrives in its pointy shadow.

1 MARK & AUDREY GIBSON; 2 RICK GERHARTER; 3 SABRINA DALBESIO; 4 ANTHONY PIDGEON; 5 LEE FOSTER

1 San Francisco Symphony (p102); 2 Asian Art Museum (p89); 3 Downtown cable car; 4 War Memorial Opera House; 5 Transamerica Pyramid (p87)

BEST...

↘ EDGE-OF-SEAT PERFORMANCES

- **American Conservatory Theater** (p100) Hit shows before they storm Broadway.
- **Great American Music Hall** (p101) Bands rock a former bordello.
- **San Francisco Ballet** (p101) *En pointe* 100 shows a year.
- **Punch Line** (p99) Here comes comedy, fast and fearless.
- **City Arts & Lectures** (p101) Q&A with top intellects.

↘ BIZARRE BAR SCENES

- **Edinburgh Castle** (p99) Where Scots and authors get lit.
- **Hemlock Tavern** (p99) A blur of peanut shells and postpunk.
- **Gold Dust Lounge** (p98) Rickety rockabilly saloon.
- **Aunt Charlie's** (p100) Drag/dance/dive bar.
- **Pied Piper Bar** (p98) Cautionary mural shows children led astray... Drink, anyone?

↘ AVANT-GARDE ART GALLERIES

- **49 Geary** (opposite) Photography, assemblage, even land art.
- **Gallery Paule Anglim** (p88) High concepts, big names.
- **77 Geary** (p88) Subversive ideas, carefully executed.
- **Luggage Store Gallery** (p90) Where street art gets poetic.

↘ FOODIE FINDS

- **Jardinière** (p96) Traci des Jardins makes bold with local flavors.
- **Farmerbrown** (p95) Soul food with organic attitude.
- **Le Sanctuaire** (p104) Molecular gastronomy creations.
- **UN Plaza farmers market** (p90) Local ingredients and foodie fare.
- **Saigon Sandwich Shop** (p96) Stuffed baguette bargains.

RACHAEL NUSBAUM

Luggage Store Gallery (p90)

DOWNTOWN

Downtown was once a notorious dock area, where saloon owner Shanghai Kelly and madam Miss Piggot conked new arrivals on the head and delivered them to ships in need of crew. The seductive spirit of yore is kept alive in Jackson Square's designer showrooms, Geary Street art galleries, and Union Square department store sales that will coax the last dollar out of you. Where once sailors abandoned their ships in search of gold, Financial District stock brokers now speculate on Asian markets.

Few Downtown establishments tempt San Franciscans to stick around after work, but Civic Center restaurants crowds chatter with the thrill of great performances at Davies Symphony Hall (p102) and the War Memorial Opera House (p101). Upscale lounge-bars in the neighboring Tenderloin seem oddly placed, since the seedy sidewalk scene is a rather ominous cautionary tale for casual girls-night-out cocktails. Bright spots on the horizon include the landmark Asian Art Museum (p89), the nonprofit Luggage Store Gallery (p90) and an excellent farmers market (p90).

SIGHTS

DOWNTOWN

TRANSAMERICA PYRAMID & REDWOOD PARK

600 Montgomery St; admission to park free; ☾ park 9am-6pm; 🚌 1, 15, 41; 🚋 & Ⓔ Embarcadero

The defining feature of San Francisco's skyline was built during the Jet Age, atop the wreck of a whaling ship abandoned in the 1849 Gold Rush, on the site of a saloon frequented by Mark Twain and the newspaper office where Sun Yat-sen drafted his Proclamation of the Republic of China. Even those who still love to hate the 1972 building adore Redwood Park, the half-acre stand of redwood trees at its base. Since September 11, the viewing platform at the tip of the pyramid has been closed to visitors 'for security reasons.'

⚓ TRANSPORTATION: DOWNTOWN

BART Montgomery St station serves the Financial District; Powell St serves Union Square.

Bus Market St Muni lines serve Downtown, as does the 38 Geary bus.

Cable car All lines run through Downtown. The Powell St lines link Union Square to Chinatown, North Beach, Russian Hill and Fisherman's Wharf. The California St line links the Financial District with Nob Hill.

Metro The J, K, L, M and N metro lines run under Market St.

Streetcar F streetcars run above Market St.

Parking Street parking is difficult. The lot at Stockton and Sutter Sts is convenient to the Financial District and Union Square. The lot at 5th and Mission Sts is convenient to Union Square.

DOWNTOWN

SABRINA DALBESIO

Union Square

SIGHTS

49 GEARY

☎ San Francisco Art Dealers Association 415-788-9818; www.sfada.com; 49 Geary St; admission free; ⏲ galleries 10:30am-5:30pm Tue-Fri, 11am-5pm Sat; ⊜ 5, 6, 15, 21, 31, 38, 71, F, J, K, L, M, N; ⊜ & ⊕ Montgomery St

Four floors of galleries feature standout international and local works including eclectic, eye-popping photography ranging from the 19th to 21st centuries at **Fraenkel Gallery** to sculptor Seth Koen's crocheted minimalist pieces at **Gregory Lind**. Don't miss Andy Goldsworthy installations at **Haines Gallery** (for more top gallery picks, see the boxed text, p173) or Todd Hido's haunted suburban landscapes at **Stephen Wirtz**.

77 GEARY

77 Geary St; admission free; ⏲ 10:30am-5:30pm Tue-Fri, 11am-5pm Sat; ⊜ 5, 6, 15, 21, 31, 38, 71, F, J, K, L, M, N; ⊕ Montgomery St

The most intriguing art in San Francisco usually appears in what appears like the wrong place, and 77 Geary's unmarked entryway is definitely no exception. See **Marx & Zavattero** (www.marxzav.com) for David Hevel's neo-baroque, middle-America-meets-Hollywood taxidermy sculptures, and **Rena Bransten Gallery** (www.renabranstengallery.com).

GALLERY PAULE ANGLIM

☎ 415-433-2710; www.gallerypauleanglim.com; 14 Geary St; admission free; ⏲ 10am-5:30pm Tue-Fri, to 5pm Sat; ⊜ 5, 6, 15, 21, 31, 38, 71, F, J, K, L, M, N; ⊜ & ⊕ Montgomery St

Here you'll find marquee names such as Tony Oursler, whose video projections of distorted faces grumble and squeak in the corner. But works by local upstarts threaten to steal the show, including Ala Ebtekar's paintings of soldiers and storm clouds gathering on ancient Iranian scriptures.

POWELL STREET CABLE CAR TURNAROUND

cnr Powell & Market Sts; ⊜ & ⊕ Powell St; ♿ 'Wire-rope railway' was a name that didn't inspire confidence in Andrew Hallidie's invention in the 1870s, when crowds steered clear of his rickety wooden trolleys on their early downhill runs. More than a century later, the two cable car lines from this terminus seem more like carnival rides than commuter transport – and therein lies the appeal.

UNION SQUARE

cnr Geary, Powell, Post & Stockton Sts; 🚌 5, 6, 21, 31, 38, 71, F, J, K, L, M, N; 🚇 & Ⓟ Powell St; 🚋 Powell-Mason, Powell-Hyde

Louis Vuitton is more top-of-mind than the Emancipation Proclamation, but this plaza, bordered by brand-name retailers, was named after pro-Union Civil War rallies held here 150 years ago. Redeeming features include Emporio Rulli Caffè and a half-price theater-ticket booth.

CIVIC CENTER & THE TENDERLOIN

ASIAN ART MUSEUM

☎ 415-581-3500; www.asianart.org; 200 Larkin St; adult/child under 12yr/student & child 13-17yr/senior $12/free/7/8, 1st Sun of month free, after 5pm Thu $5; 🕙 10am-5pm Tue-Sun, to 9pm Thu Feb-Sep; 🚌 5, 6, 21, 31, 71, F, J, K, L, M, N; 🚇 & Ⓟ Civic Center; 🚶

The largest collection of Asian art outside Asia covers 6000 years and thousands of miles of terrain. A trip through the galleries is a treasure-hunting expedition, from racy Rajasthan palace miniatures to the largest collection of Japanese sculptural baskets outside Japan to the jewel-box gallery of Chinese lustrous jade – just don't bump into those priceless Ming vases. As if the constantly rotating collection wasn't enough, the Asian also emphasizes educational programs that keep pan-generational crowds thronging the place. Think DJs spinning Japanese hip-hop, sake-makers pouring tastings and crafty types making Chinese paper lanterns to ward off hungry ghosts.

CITY HALL

☎ 415-554-4000, tour info 415-554-6023, art exhibit line 415-554-6080; www.ci.sf.ca.us/cityhall; 400 Van Ness Ave; admission free; 🕙 8am-8pm Mon-Fri, tours 10am, noon & 2pm; 🚌 5, 19, 21, 49; 🚇 & Ⓟ Civic Center; 🚶

That mighty beaux-arts dome pretty much covers San Francisco's grandest ambitions and fundamental flaws. Anti-McCarthy sit-in protesters were hosed off the grand staircase in 1960, but finally ran McCarthy out of town; Harvey Milk was assassinated here in 1978; and the cheers heard around the world in 2004 were from families and friends of the 4037 same-sex couples who celebrated their marriages here, thanks to Mayor Newsom's short-lived challenge to California state marriage law. If you want insight into how San Francisco government works – or doesn't, as the case

DOWNTOWN

SIGHTS

⤴ TRANSPORTATION: CIVIC CENTER & THE TENDERLOIN

BART Civic Center is the main BART stop for both areas; Powell St station also serves the Tenderloin.

Bus All Market St Muni lines stop at Civic Center and at various points in the Tenderloin; the northern end of the Tenderloin is also accessed by buses 1, 2, 3, 4, 5, 19, 38, 47 and 49; Civic Center is accessible via Van Ness Ave buses 47 and 49.

Streetcar The aboveground F streetcar makes stops at Civic Center and in the Tenderloin, and underground streetcars J, K, L, M and N all stop at Civic Center and Van Ness Ave (along the western edge of Civic Center).

Parking Public parking is available at the garage at 5th and Mission Sts.

DOWNTOWN

may be – the Board of Supervisors meets Tuesdays at 2pm in City Hall; check the agenda and minutes online.

LUGGAGE STORE GALLERY

☎ 415-255-5971; www.luggagestoregallery. org; 1007 Market St; admission free; ☉ noon-5pm Wed-Sat; 🚌 5, 6, 21, 31, 71, F, J, K, L, M, N; 🚇 & Ⓒ Civic Center

A dandelion pushing through cracks in the sidewalk, this plucky nonprofit gallery has brought signs of life to one of the toughest blocks in the Tenderloin for more than 20 years. Two Luggage Store regulars you might recognize around town are Rigo, who did the 'One Tree' mural that looks like a one-way sign by the 101

Fwy on-ramp in SoMa, and Brazilian duo Ogemeos, who did the mural of a defiant kid holding a lit firecracker atop the gallery building.

UNITED NATIONS PLAZA

Market St btwn Hyde & Leavenworth Sts; ☉ 6am-midnight; 🚌 5, 6, 14, 21, 31, 71, F, J, K, L, M, N; 🚇 & Ⓒ Civic Center

This vast brick-paved triangle commemorates the signing of the UN charter in San Francisco. It offers a clear view of City Hall, sundry Scientologists drumming up converts, and the odd drug deal in progress. Thankfully, a wonderful **farmers market** (☎ 415-558-9455) provides a fresher perspective on the Tenderloin,

SIGHTS

↘ IF YOU LIKE...

If you like **City Hall**, you might want to check out these other history-making San Francisco institutions:

- **AP Hotaling Warehouse** (451-455 Jackson St; 🚌 10, 12, 15) 'If, as they say, God spanked the town/For being over-frisky/Why did He burn His churches down/And spare Hotaling's whiskey?' After Hotaling's 1866 whiskey warehouse survived the 1906 earthquake and fire, this snappy comeback was captured in a bronze plaque that still graces the resilient Italianate building.

- **Bohemian Club** (624 Taylor St; 🚋 Powell-Mason, Powell-Hyde) America's most eccentric, secretive men's club has a roster ranging from the power elite to famous artists: apparently both George W Bush and Bob Weir are current members. On the ivy-covered brick wall on Post St, note the plaque honoring Gold Rush–era author Bret Harte.

- **Glide Memorial United Methodist Church** (☎ 415-674-6090; www.glide.org; 330 Ellis St; ☉ celebrations 9am & 11am Sun; 🚌 & Ⓒ Powell St) The 1500-strong congregation sings along to a rainbow-robed gospel choir, provides housing for 52 formerly homeless families and dishes out a million free meals a year .

- **San Francisco Main Library** (☎ 415-557-4400; sfpl.lib.ca.us; 100 Larkin St; ☉ 10am-6pm Mon & Sat, 9am-8pm Tue-Thu, noon-6pm Fri, noon-5pm Sun; 🚌 & Ⓒ Civic Center; ☏ ♿)Besides its eclectic collection of San Franciscans and their favorite books, the library hosts high-profile lecture series, excellent historical exhibits, and artist Ann Chamberlain's 2nd-floor wallpaper made of cards from the old card catalog .

HOTEL VERTIGO

Hotel Vertigo (p94)

every Wednesday and Sunday from about 7am to 5pm.

SLEEPING
DOWNTOWN

MANDARIN ORIENTAL Hotel $$$

☎ 415-276-9888, 800-622-0404; www.mandarin oriental.com; 222 Sansome St; r $295-375, ste from $875; 🚌 1; 🚌 & Ⓜ Montgomery St; Ⓐ California; 🛜

Occupying the top 11 floors of the third-tallest building in SF, the Mandarin has sweeping, unobstructed views from every room. If you can swing it, book a 'Mandarin King' room (from $500), which has an oversized bathtub surrounded by floor-to-ceiling windows with views of either the Golden Gate or Bay Bridge.

PALACE HOTEL Historic Hotel $$$

☎ 415-512-1111, 800-325-3535; www.sfpalace .com; 2 New Montgomery St; r $199-329; 🚌 & Ⓜ Montgomery St; 🛜 💺

The 1906 landmark Palace stands as a monument to turn-of-the-20th-century grandeur, aglow with century-old Austrian crystal chandeliers. The cushy (if staid) accommodations cater to expense-account travelers, but prices drop on weekends. There's also an onsite spa; kids love the big indoor pool.

HOTEL PALOMAR Boutique Hotel $$$

☎ 415-348-1111, 866-373-4941; www.hotel palomar-sf.com; 12 4th St; r $199-299; 🚌 & Ⓜ Powell St; 🛜

The chic and stylin' Hotel Palomar is decked out with crocodile-print carpets, stripy persimmon-red chairs, chocolate-brown wood and cheetah-print robes in the closet. Beds are sumptuous, with feather-light down comforters and Frette linens, and there's plenty of floor space to stretch out for in-room yoga (ask at the front desk for a mat and yoga DVD).

HOTEL ADAGIO Boutique Hotel $$

☎ 415-775-5000, 800-228-8830; www.thehotel adagio.com; 550 Geary St; r $149-229; 🚌 38; 🛜

Huge rooms and a super-snappy aesthetic set the Adagio apart. The hotel's designers placed a premium on style, blending chocolate-brown and off-white leather furnishings with bright-orange splashes. Beds have Egyptian-cotton sheets and feather pillows; great bar downstairs.

ORCHARD GARDEN HOTEL   Eco Hotel $$
☎ 415-399-9807, 888-717-2881; www.theorchard gardenhotel.com; 466 Bush St; r $179-249; 🚌 2, 3, 4, 30, 45; 🛜

San Francisco's first all-green-practices hotel opened in 2006, and uses sustainably grown wood, chemical-free cleaning products and recycled fabrics in its soothingly quiet rooms. Don't think you'll be trading comfort for conscience: rooms have unexpectedly luxe touches such as flat-screen TVs, iPod docking stations, high-end down pillows and Egyptian-cotton sheets.

HOTEL REX   Boutique Hotel $$
☎ 415-433-4434, 800-433-4434; www.jdvhospi tality.com; 562 Sutter St; r $149-279; 🚌 2, 3, 4; 🚋 Powell St; 🛜

Strains of French gramophone music fill the intimate lobby and the adjoining dimly lit lounge, intended to conjure New York's Algonquin in the 1920s. The Rex exudes a sexy broodiness: rooms are done in chocolate-brown and brick-red, with antique rotary telephones, hand-painted lampshades and works by local artists. Great beds, too, with top-notch mattresses, crisp linens and down pillows.

HOTEL DES ARTS   Art Hotel $$
☎ 415-956-3232, 800-956-4322; www.sfhotel desarts.com; 447 Bush St; r $139-199, without bathroom $99-149; 🚌 & Ⓜ Montgomery St; 🛜

Finally a midbudget hotel for art freaks. Specialty rooms are painted with jaw-dropping murals by underground street artists. Standard rooms are less exciting but are clean and great value, with a few smart design touches.

HOTEL CALIFORNIA   Boutique Hotel $$
☎ 415-441-2700, 800-227-4223; www.thesavoy hotel.com; 580 Geary St; r $149-169; 🚌 38; 🛜

SABRINA DALBESIO

Hotel des Arts

Alas, no pink champagne on ice, but it does provide frosted tequila shots upon check-in. This bay-windowed vintage-1920s mainstay of the theater district has fresh-looking rooms with cheery yellow walls, hardwood floors, flat-screen TVs, fluffy beds, and double-pane windows that are great for blocking street noise (request a quiet room).

WARWICK REGIS — Boutique Hotel $$

☎ 415-928-7900, 800-203-3232; www.warwick sf.com; 490 Geary St; r $149-249; 🚇 38; 🛜

Conveying discreet tastefulness, with European antiques and Chinese porcelain, it's an ideal choice for debutantes and royalty on a budget. Beds are remarkably comfortable, and even have triple-sheeting, but you'll have to request feather pillows.

WESTIN ST FRANCIS HOTEL — Historic Hotel $$$

☎ 415-397-7000, 800-228-3000; www.westin. com; 335 Powell St; r $209-369; 🚇 & 🚈 Powell St; 🚋 Powell-Mason & Powell-Hyde; 🛜

This is one of SF's most storied hotels – Gerald Ford was shot right outside. We prefer the original building's old-fashioned charm, with its high ceilings and crown moldings. Don't miss the glass elevators, even if you're not staying here.

HOTEL FRANK — Boutique Hotel $$

☎ 415-986-2000, 800-553-1900; www.hotel franksf.com; 386 Geary St; r $169-269; 🚇 38; 🛜

Redone in 2008, the Frank (formerly the Maxwell) has a snappy, vaguely Austin Powers black-and-white design aesthetic, with big houndstooth checks and faux-alligator headboards. The bathrooms are tight and few have tubs (request one, if it matters), but extras such as plasma-screen TVs and the just-off Union Square location compensate.

WHITE SWAN INN — Inn $$

☎ 415-775-1755, 800-999-9570; www.jdv hotels.com; 845 Bush St; r $159-199; 🚇 27; 🛜

In the tradition of English country inns, the romantic White Swan is styled with cabbage-rose wallpaper, red-plaid flannel bedspreads and polished Colonial-style furniture. Each oversized room has a gas fireplace – a cozy touch on a foggy night.

HOTEL UNION SQUARE — Hotel $$

☎ 415-397-3000, 800-553-1900; www.hotel unionsquare.com; 114 Powell St; r $160-220; 🚇 & 🚈 Powell St; 🛜

Renovated in 2008, the Hotel Union Square looks sharp, with swank design touches complementing the original brick walls. The main drawbacks are lack of sunlight and small rooms, but designers compensated with cleverly concealed lighting, mirrored walls and plush fabrics.

GOLDEN GATE HOTEL — Hotel $$

☎ 415-392-3702, 800-835-1118; www.golden gatehotel.com; 775 Bush St; r with/without bathroom $165/105; 🚇 2, 3, 4; 🚋 Powell St

Like an old-fashioned pensione, the Golden Gate has kindly owners and simple rooms with mismatched furniture, inside a 1913 Edwardian hotel safely up the hill from the Tenderloin. Enormous croissants, homemade cookies and a resident kitty-cat provide TLC after a long day's sightseeing.

HOTEL TRITON — Boutique Hotel $$

☎ 415-394-0500, 800-800-1299; www.hotel -tritonsf.com; 342 Grant Ave; r $169-239; 🚇 & 🚈 Montgomery St; 🛜

This was one of SF's first boutique hotels, and every room is different. Suites are decorated in honor of celebs such as Carlos Santana and Jerry Garcia. Don't miss the tarot-card readings and chair massages during the nightly wine hour.

DOWNTOWN

SLEEPING

Orchard Garden Hotel (p92)

PETITE AUBERGE   Inn $$
☎ 415-928-6000, 800-365-3004; www.jdvhospi
tality.com; 863 Bush St; r $169-219; ☒ 27
Petite Auberge feels like a French country
inn, with floral-print fabrics, a sunny yel-
low color scheme, and fireplaces in many
rooms. Breakfast and afternoon wine are
served fireside in the cozy salon.

HOTEL DIVA   Boutique Hotel $$
☎ 415-885-0200, 800-553-1900; www.hotel
diva.com; 440 Geary St; r $159-229; ☒ 38; ☞
Favored by midbudget fashionistas and
traveling club kids, the industrial-chic
Diva's stainless-steel and black-granite
design aesthetic feels like a dot-com-era
holdover, but still conveys a sexy urban
look.

STRATFORD HOTEL   Hotel $
☎ 415-397-7080, 888-504-6835; www.ctwo
hotels.com; 242 Powell St; r incl breakfast $89-
149; ☒ & ◉ Powell St; ☞
A great value at Union Square, the eight-
story Stratford has clean, simple and
smallish rooms. Bathrooms are gleaming

and have thirsty towels and rainfall showerheads, but no tubs. Rooms on Powell St
are loud; book a room in back.

ADELAIDE HOSTEL   Hostel $
☎ 415-359-1915, 877-359-1915; www.adelaide
hostel.com; 5 Isadora Duncan Lane; dm $31, r
$55-90, incl breakfast; ☒ 38; ☞
Down a mysterious little alley, the 18-
room Adelaide sets the standard for San
Francisco hostels, with personal service,
surprisingly well-done decor, thick carpeting, up-to-date furnishings and sparkling
bathrooms with shiny chrome fixtures.
The big kitchen even has granite counter-
tops, and the place is blissfully quiet.

CIVIC CENTER & THE TENDERLOIN

HOTEL VERTIGO   Boutique Hotel $$
☎ 415-885-6800, 800-553-1900; www.hotel
vertigosf.com; 940 Sutter St; r $169-219; ☒ 2, 3,
4, 19, 27; ☞
Scenes from Hitchcock's *Vertigo* were
shot here, and the refurb of the former
York Hotel (the Empire Hotel, in the film)

nods to the master with Spirograph-like artwork reminiscent of the opening sequence. The snappy aesthetic mixes burnt-orange, cocoa-brown and bright-white, with low-slung wingchairs beside platform beds with down duvets.

PHOENIX HOTEL   Motel $$

☎ 415-776-1380, 800-248-9466; www.jdvhospitality.com; 601 Eddy St; r incl breakfast $119-169; 🚍 5, 19, 31, 38; 🅿 🛜 🚇

The city's rocker crash pad draws minor celebs and Dionysian revelers to a vintage-1950s motor lodge with basic rooms dolled up with tropical decor. Check out the cool shrine to actor-director Vincent Gallo, opposite room 43. One complaint: noise. Bring earplugs.

EATING

The Financial District can seem desolate at night and Union Square can get rough around the peripheries west of Powell St and south of Sutter St, but as always in San Francisco, superior dining rewards the adventurous.

DOWNTOWN

RESTAURANT MICHAEL MINA   American $$$

☎ 415-397-9222; www.michaelmina.net; 335 Powell St; 🕑 5:30-9:30pm Tue-Thu, 5:30-10pm Fri & Sat; 🚍 38, F, J, K, L, M, N; 🚇 & Ⓟ Powell St

Though the signature triple tuna tartare starter and lobster pot pie mains have inspired raves and legions of copycats, the seasonal menu showcases innovation and ripe flavors – butter-poached lobster with melon laced with red curry, or foie gras terrine with pickled strawberries. Consultations with your well-versed servers and sommelier to navigate the complex menu options should come with a certificate of completion, especially

at $105 to $135 for a full three-course menu, or $60 for three smaller plates in the lounge.

FLEUR DE LYS   French $$$

☎ 415-673-7779; www.fleurdelyssf.com; 777 Sutter St; 🕑 6-9:30pm Tue-Thu, 5:30-10:30pm Fri, 5-10:30pm Sat; 🚍 38, F, J, K, L, M, N; 🚇 & Ⓟ Powell St

Long before celebrity chef Hubert Keller took his show on the road to Vegas and *Top Chef Masters,* this was the ultimate over-the-top SF destination. There's nothing subtle about the swanky sultan's tent interiors, but it's oddly suited to princely repasts involving gnocchi graced with chanterelles and hazelnut-encrusted scallops, halibut crowned with rhubarb coulis and truffle, as well as a king's ransom of foie gras on every other dish.

KOKKARI   Greek $$$

☎ 415-981-0983; www.kokkari.com; 200 Jackson St; 🕑 lunch Mon-Fri, 5:30-10pm Mon-Thu, 5:30-11pm Fri, 5-11pm Sat, 5-10pm Sun; 🚍 41, 45, F; Ⓥ

This is one Greek restaurant where you'll want to lick your plate instead of break it, with starters such as grilled octopus with a zing of lemon and oregano, and a signature lamb, eggplant and yogurt moussaka as rich as the Pacific Stock Exchange. Reserve ahead to avoid waits, or make a meal of hearty Mediterranean apps at the bar.

FARMERBROWN   New American $$

☎ 415-409-3276; www.farmerbrownsf.com; 25 Mason St; 🕑 lunch Mon-Fri, 5-10pm Sun-Wed, to 11pm Thu-Sat, 9am-2:30pm Sat & Sun; 🚍 5, 6, 21, 31, F, J, K, L, M, N; 🚇 & Ⓟ Powell St

Half of SF has a crush on this rebel from the wrong side of the block, which dishes up a mean seasonal watermelon

DOWNTOWN

EATING

⤵ GOURMET GRUB TO GO

When lunch gets squeezed between shopping and sightseeing, head here for prime takeaway:

- **Boxed Foods** (☎ 415-981-9376; www.boxedfoodscompany.com; 245 Kearny St; ☯ 8am-3pm Mon-Fri; 🚌 1, 15; 🚋 California; V) Offers organic, local, seasonal options such as strawberry salad with walnuts and goat cheese, plus the classic Boxed BLT.
- **Muracci's Curry** (☎ 415-773-1101; www.muraccis.com; 307 Kearny St; ☯ 11am-6pm Mon-Thu, to 5pm Fri; 🚌 1, 15; 🚋 California; V) Muracci's dishes out steaming curry-topped *katsu* (breaded cutlet) or Japanese grilled chicken atop rice or noodles.
- **Saigon Sandwich Shop** (☎ 415-474-5698; 560 Larkin St; ☯ 6:30am-5:30pm; 🚌 5, 19, 31) Will make you a believer in $3.50 *banh mi* – baguettes piled high with your choice of Vietnamese roast pork, chicken, pâté, meatballs and/or tofu, plus pickled carrots, cilantro, jalapeño and slivered onion.

margarita with a cayenne salt rim (genius), ribs that stick to yours, and coleslaw with a kick that'll leave your lips buzzing like an everlasting game of spin the bottle. Chef-owner Jay Foster works with local organic and African American farmers to provide food with actual soul, in a setting that's rusted and cleverly repurposed as a shotgun shack, with harried service (it's always busy) and a band banging away in a corner some nights.

GITANE   Basque, Mediterranean $$
☎ 415-788-6686; www.gitanerestaurant.com; 6 Claude Lane; ☯ 5:30pm-midnight Tue-Sat, bar to 1am; 🚌 1, 15; 🚋 California; V

The decor and menu wink at Basque, Spanish and Moroccan traditions, but pure decadence is the real draw, with flirting co-workers in the bar feeding one another bacon bon-bons (goat-cheese-stuffed prunes wrapped in bacon and doused in cinnamon-port sauce). Serious canoodlers should get a room in the restaurant upstairs to share fragrant free-range chicken *tagines* (stews) on low divans.

BOCADILLOS   Basque $
☎ 415-982-2622; www.bocasf.com; 710 Montgomery St; ☯ 7am-10pm Mon-Fri, 5-10pm Sat; 🚌 15, 30, 41, 45

Forget the suburban sprawl of multipage menus and SUV-sized portions, and tuck into a North-Beach-studio-sized choice of two small sandwiches on dinner rolls served with a green salad for $7 to $9. The juicy lamb-burgers, snapper ceviche with Asian pears, and Catalan sausages are just-right Basque bites with wine by the glass.

CIVIC CENTER & THE TENDERLOIN

JARDINIÈRE   Californian $$$
☎ 415-861-5555; www.jardiniere.com; 300 Grove St; ☯ 5-10:30pm Tue-Sat, to 10pm Sun & Mon; 🚌 5, 21, 42, 47, 49

Iron Chef and James Beard Award–winner Traci Des Jardins has a way with organic vegetables, free-range meats and sustainably caught seafood that's slightly naughty, topping succulent octopus with crispy pork belly, and drizzling Sonoma lavender honey over squash blossoms bursting with molten sheep's cheese. Go Mondays, when $45 scores three decadent courses with wine pairings.

MILLENNIUM — Vegetarian $$$

☎ 415-345-3900; www.millenniumrestaurant.com; 580 Geary St; ⏱ 5:30-9:30pm Sun-Thu, 5-10pm Fri & Sat; 🚌 38; 🚌 & ◐ Powell St; 🚋 Powell-Hyde; Ⓥ

If all vegan food could be this satisfying and opulent, there could be cattle roaming the streets of SF and no one would give them a second glance. Seasonal first courses include grilled semolina flatbread topped with caramelized onions, wilted spinach and a flourish of almond romesco, followed by a peppery pastry roulade that opens with a fork's touch to reveal a creamy center of golden potatoes and smoky achiote (chili) chard, and a saffron-scented rice pudding with mango sorbet.

FISH & FARM — Californian $$

☎ 415-474-3474; www.fishandfarmsf.com; 339 Taylor St; ⏱ 5-10pm Tue & Wed, to 11pm Thu-Sat; 🚌 38; 🚋 Powell-Mason

Eco comfort food bound to improve your mood and the planet, featuring organic produce, sustainable seafood and humanely raised meats sourced within 100 miles of San Francisco. White Brentwood corn and organic sweet onions make a silky, sensational soup, while local cod gets soused on Liberty Ale batter, and fried, and topped with malted salt for fish and chips that would make an Englishman weep.

DOTTIE'S TRUE BLUE CAFÉ — American $

☎ 415-885-2767; 522 Jones St; ⏱ 7:30am-3pm Wed-Mon; 🚌 19, 38; 🚌 & ◐ Powell St; 🚋 Powell-Hyde

Consider yourself lucky if you stand in line less than an hour and get hit up for change only once – but fresh baked goods come to those who wait at Dottie's. Cinnamon pancakes, grilled cornbread, scrambles with whiskey fennel sausage and anything else off the griddle are tried and true blue.

SABRINA DALBESIO

Jardinière

DOWNTOWN

SHALIMAR   Indian $
☎ 415-928-0333; www.shalimarsf.com; 532
Jones St; ☺ noon-midnight; ☐ 2, 3, 4, 27, 38
Follow your nose to tandoori chicken
straight off the skewer and naan bread
still bubbling from the oven; vegetables
are leaden, so don't hold back on the succulent tandoori chicken that started the
fluorescent-lit Pakistani restaurant scene.

DRINKING
DOWNTOWN

DRINKING

CANTINA   Bar
☎ 415-398-0195; www.cantinasf.com; 580 Sutter St; ☺ 5pm-2am Mon-Sat; ☐ 2, 3, 4
All the Latin-inspired cocktails (think tequila, *cachaça* and pisco) are made with
fresh juice – there's not even a soda gun
behind the bar – at this mixologist's dream
bar that's mellow enough on weeknights
for conversation. DJs spin on weekends.

PIED PIPER BAR   Bar
☎ 415-512-1111; www.sfpalace.com; 2
New Montgomery St; ☺ 11:30am-11pm;
☐ & ⊕ Montgomery St

Deep within the opulent Palace Hotel,
the Pied Piper's mahogany walls and
plush seating up the swank factor, but
what sets it apart is the creepy-gorgeous
1909 Maxfield Parrish mural behind
the bar. Prices are steep but include
munchies.

TUNNEL TOP BAR   Bar
☎ 415-722-6620; www.tunneltop.com; 601 Bush
St; ☺ 5pm-2am Mon-Sat; ☐ 1, 2, 3, 4, 30, 45
You can't tell who's local and who's not
in this happening, chill two-story bar with
exposed beams, beer-bottle chandelier,
and rickety balcony that always seems
about ready to give out. Cash only.

GOLD DUST LOUNGE   Bar
☎ 415-397-1695; 247 Powell St; ☺ 7am-2am;
☐ & ⊕ Powell St
Precarious Victorian brass chandeliers
hover over a bar full of visitors and a
twangy rockabilly band at this Union
Square anachronism, with swinging
doors, coat stands and nude paintings –
you almost expect someone to beckon
you to a brothel upstairs.

SABRINA DALBESIO

Hemlock Tavern

JOHN'S GRILL
Bar

☎ 415-986-0069; 63 Ellis St; ⏱ 11am-10pm Mon-Sat, noon-10pm Sun; 🚇 & 🔵 Powell St; 🚋 Powell-Mason, Powell-Hyde

It could be the martinis, the low lighting, or the *Maltese Falcon* statuette upstairs, but something about Dashiell Hammett's favorite bar lends itself to hard-boiled tales of lost love and true crimes, confessed while chewing toothpicks.

CIVIC CENTER & THE TENDERLOIN

EDINBURGH CASTLE
Bar

☎ 415-885-4074; www.castlenews.com; 950 Geary St; ⏱ 5pm-2am; 🚇 19, 38, 47, 49

SF's finest old-school monument to drink comes complete with dart boards, pool tables, rock bands, occasional literary readings and locals acting out (as is our habit). Photos of bagpipers, the *Trainspotting* soundtrack on the jukebox and a service delivering vinegary fish and chips in newspaper are all the Scottish authenticity you could ask for, short of haggis.

HEMLOCK TAVERN
Bar

☎ 415-923-0923; www.hemlocktavern.com; 1131 Polk St; ⏱ 4pm-2am; 🚇 2, 3, 4, 19, 38, 47, 49

When you wake up tomorrow with peanut shells in your hair (weren't they all over the floor?), a stiff neck from rocking entirely too hard to the Family Curse (weren't they good?) and someone else's mascara on your armpit (should we even ask?), you'll know it was another successful night at the Hemlock.

KOKO COCKTAILS
Bar

☎ 415-885-4788; www.kokococktails.com; 1060 Geary St; ⏱ 5pm-2am; 🚇 2, 3, 4, 19, 38, 47, 49

Our favorite place to start a Polk St pub crawl is a retro-cool cocktail lounge that looks like a gussied-up rumpus room from the 1970s. Seven bucks gets you a fancy, hand-muddled cocktail, which you can sip at handmade tables of reclaimed oak.

RYE
Bar

☎ 415-474-4448; www.ryesf.com; 688 Geary St; ⏱ 5:30pm-2am Mon-Fri, 7pm-2am Sat & Sun; 🚇 27, 38

Rye's high-style design mixes concrete, steel and polished wood, and its leather sofas are a sexy spot for a basil gimlet or anything else made with herb-infused spirits or fresh-squeezed juice. It packs after 10pm; arrive early.

ENTERTAINMENT & ACTIVITIES

DOWNTOWN

RUBY SKYE
Clubbing

☎ 415-693-0777; www.rubyskye.com; 420 Mason St; admission $10-25; ⏱ 9pm-late Fri & Sat, sometimes Thu & Sun; 🚇 2, 3, 4, 38; 🚇 & 🔵 Powell St

The city's premier-name nightclub occupies a vintage theater reminiscent of classic NY clubs, with reserveable balcony boxes above the floor. The who's-who of the world's DJs play here – think Danny Tenaglia, Dimitri from Paris, Christopher Lawrence and Paul Van Dyk.

PUNCH LINE
Comedy

☎ 415-397-4337; www.punchlinecomedyclub. com; 444 Battery St; admission $12-23 plus 2-drink minimum; ⏱ shows 8pm Sun & Tue-Thu, 8pm & 10pm Fri & Sat; 🚇 1, 2, F, J, K, L, M, N; 🚇 & 🔵 Embarcadero

Known for launching promising talent (think Robin Williams, Chris Rock, Ellen DeGeneres and David Cross), this historic stand-up venue is small enough for you to see into performers' eyes.

DOWNTOWN

ENTERTAINMENT & ACTIVITIES

↘ DOWNTOWN'S GAY & LESBIAN SCENE

San Francisco's oldest openly gay scene isn't the Castro or SoMa: it's the Tenderloin around Polk and Larkin Sts, where historic dives still cater to a specific subset of sailors on shore leave. Here's where to go on Saturday night:

- **Gangway** (☎ 415-776-6828; 841 Larkin St; ☷ 8am-2am; ▣ 19, 38) Tenderloin's longest-running gay dive, drawing toothless drunks and merry hipsters with gritty authenticity and rare opportunities to meet old-guard drag performers out of face.
- **Aunt Charlie's** (☎ 415-441-2922; www.auntcharlieslounge.com; 133 Turk St; admission $3; ☷ 9am-2am; ▣ 31; ⊕ Powell St) It may be on one of the city's worst blocks, but divey-chic Aunt Charlie's brings vintage pulp-fiction covers to life with the Hot Boxxx Girls, the city's best classic drag show, Friday and Saturday nights at 10pm (call for reservations).
- **Deco Lounge** (☎ 415-346-2025; www.decosf.com; 510 Larkin St; ☷ 10am-2am Sun-Thu, to 4am Fri & Sat; ▣ 5, 19, 31) A wildly indecorous all-male dive, featuring disco-queen extravaganzas, shirtless-bear nights, and wet-jockstrap contests.

EMBARCADERO CENTER CINEMA　　　　　　　　　Film

☎ 415-267-4893; www.landmarktheatres.com; top fl, 1 Embarcadero Center; adult/senior, child & matinee $10.50/8; ▣ & ⊕ Embarcadero

Blockbusters do nothing for the cinephile crowds at the Embarcadero – instead, people queue up for the latest Almodóvar film and whatever won best foreign film at the Oscars. The snack bar caters to discerning tastes with good local coffee, fair-trade chocolate and popcorn with real butter.

COMMONWEALTH CLUB　　　Readings

☎ 415-597-6700; www.commonwealthclub.org; 595 Market St; ▣ 71, F; ▣ & ⊕ Montgomery St

Every US president since Teddy Roosevelt has spoken at the club, the longest-running, most-influential public-affairs forum in the US. Intellectual luminaries and other important figures speak at more than 400 annual events. Topics range from politics and economics to culture and society.

WARFIELD　　　　　　　　　　　Rock

☎ 415-775-7722; tickets www.livenation.com; 982 Market St; cover varies; ☷ box office at the Fillmore 10am-4pm Sun, show nights 7:30-10pm; ▣ 6, F; ▣ & ⊕ Powell St

Uber-famous names have played this former vaudeville theater, including the Beastie Boys, PJ Harvey and the Grateful Dead.

AMERICAN CONSERVATORY THEATER　　　　　　　　　Theater

☎ 415-749-2228; www.act-sf.org; 415 Geary St; ▣ 2, 3, 4, 27, 38; ▣ Powell-Mason, Powell-Hyde

Breakthrough shows that are destined for the big time in London or New York sometimes pass muster at the turn-of-the-century Geary Theater, which has hosted the American Conservatory Theater's landmark productions of Tony Kushner's *Angels in America* and Robert Wilson's *Black Rider,* with a libretto by William S Burroughs and music by the Bay Area's very own Mr Tom Waits.

CIVIC CENTER & THE TENDERLOIN

SAN FRANCISCO BALLET   Dance

☎ 415-861-5600, tickets 415-865-2000; www.sfballet.org; War Memorial Opera House, 301 Van Ness Ave; tickets $10-120; 🚌 21, 47, 49; 🚌 & Ⓜ Civic Center

The San Francisco Ballet is the USA's oldest ballet company, and the first to premier the *Nutcracker*, which it performs annually. In San Francisco, its home is the War Memorial Opera House, but it also appears at other venues now and then; check the website.

SAN FRANCISCO OPERA   Opera, Classical Music

☎ 415-864-3330; www.sfopera.com; War Memorial Opera House, 301 Van Ness Ave; tickets $10-350; 🚌 21, 47, 49; 🚌 & Ⓜ Civic Center

The gorgeous 1932 hall is cavernous and echoey, but there's no more glamorous seat in SF than the velvet-curtained boxes, complete with champagne service. The best midrange seats for sightlines and sound are in the front section of the dress circle. Hang in the back of the hall with die-hard opera buffs with standing-room-only tickets: starting at 10am, the box office sells 150 standing-room spots ($10, cash only); two hours before curtain, they release 50 more. Snag an empty seat after intermission, when somnambulant seniors go home – though all bets are off for Rossini and Mozart.

CITY ARTS & LECTURES   Readings

☎ box office 415-392-4400; www.cityarts.net; Herbst Theater, 401 Van Ness Ave; 🚌 21, 47, 49; 🚌 & Ⓜ Civic Center

The city's foremost lecture series hosts an all-star lineup of today's most celebrated artists, writers and intellectuals, from Joan Didion to David Sedaris and Madeline Albright to Michael J Fox.

GREAT AMERICAN MUSIC HALL   Rock

☎ 415-885-0750; www.musichallsf.com; 859 O'Farrell St; admission $12-35; ⏱ box office 10:30am-6pm Mon-Fri & on show nights; 🚌 19, 38

RICHARD CUMMINS

Mural by Johanna Poethig, Great American Music Hall

JOSEPH SOHM/ALAMY

Davies Symphony Hall and Henry Moore's 1973 sculpture, *Large Four Piece Reclining Figure*

◤ SAN FRANCISCO SYMPHONY

The SF Symphony often wins Grammys, thanks to celeb-conductor and musical-director Michael Tilson Thomas, the world's foremost Mahler impresario. The best sound is in the cheap seats in the center terrace, but the loge is most comfy and glam and has the best sightlines. Call the **rush-ticket hotline** after 6:30pm to find out whether the box office has released $20 next-day tickets, which you must pick up in person the day of performance: choose the side terrace over the front orchestra – unless you want to be 10ft from the strings, but the sound is uneven so close to the stage.

Things you need to know: ☎ 415-864-6000, rush-ticket hotline 415-503-5577; www.sfsymphony.org; tickets $30-125; Davies Symphony Hall, 201 Van Ness Ave; 🚌 21, 47, 49; 🚇 & Ⓜ Civic Center

Once a bordello, the rococo Great American Music Hall is one of SF's coolest places for shows. A balcony with table seating rims the main standing-room floor area, the sound system is top-notch, and there are food and drinks.

SHOPPING
DOWNTOWN
EDEN & EDEN
Clothing & Accessories, Housewares
☎ 415-983-0490; www.edenandeden.com; 560 Jackson St; ☽ 10am-7pm Mon-Fri, 10am-6pm Sat, noon-6pm Sun; 🚌 15, 30, 41, 45

Quirkiness is an SF style trademark that can either be achieved through an MFA program or a quick stop at Eden & Eden. Everything you might dream up after diligent study of pop art is already here: a necklace that looks like a giant zipper shaggy-haired orange tea cozies, a cushion that says 'blahblahblah,' and hideous apartment buildings on bone-china plates.

SHOTWELL BOUTIQUE
Clothing & Accessories
☎ 415-399-9898; www.shotwellsf.com; 320 Grant Ave; ☽ 11am-5pm Mon-Sat, noon-6pm Sun; 🚌 1, 15, 30; 🚋 California

SF fashion vanguardians could shop for decades for a look achieved in an afternoon at Shotwell: purple-rimmed '80s sunglasses, Surface to Air low-tops, a '70s fedora, draped tank from Society for Rational Dress over Cheap Monday jeans, and locally designed bling.

LOEHMANN'S   Clothing & Accessories
☎ 415-982-3215; www.loehmanns.com; 222 Sutter St; ☽ 9am-8pm Mon-Sat, 11am-7pm Sun; 🚍 15, 30, 41, 45

North Beach artists drift to the middle floor for almost-free Free People smocks; Pacific Heights charity fundraisers hit the top floor for discounted Prada shirtdresses; and gift shoppers converge around 40%-off red-tagged Kate Spade clutches in main-floor accessories.

MARGARET O'LEARY
Clothing & Accessories, Local Designer
☎ 415-391-1010; www.margaretoleary.com; 1 Claude Lane; ☽ 10am-5pm Tue-Sat; 🚍 1, 15, 30; 🚋 California

Ignorance of the fog is no excuse in San Francisco, but should you confuse SF for LA (the horror!) and neglect to pack the obligatory sweater, Margaret O'Leary will sheathe you in knitwear, no questions asked. The San Francisco designer's specialties are warm, whisper-light cardigans in cashmere, organic cotton or eco-minded bamboo yarn.

ORIGINAL LEVI'S STORE   Clothing & Accessories
☎ 415-501-0100; www.us.levi.com; 300 Post St; ☽ 10am-9pm Mon-Sat, to 6:30pm Sun; 🚍 2, 3, 4, 30, 38, 45; 🚍 & Ⓜ Powell St; 🚋 Powell-Mason & Powell-Hyde

The flagship store in Levi Strauss' hometown sells classic jeans that fit without fail, plus limited-edition pairs made of tough Japanese selvage and eco-organic cotton denim.

WESTFIELD SAN FRANCISCO CENTRE   Department Store
☎ 415-512-6776; http://westfield.com/sanfrancisco; 865 Market St; ☽ most shops 10am-8:30pm Mon-Sat, 11am-7pm Sun; 🚍 5, 6, 21, 31, 71, F, J, K, L, M, N; 🚍 & Ⓜ Powell St; 🚋 Powell-Mason & Powell-Hyde; ♿

DOWNTOWN

SHOPPING

RICK GERHARTER

Westfield San Francisco Centre

DOWNTOWN

SHOPPING

SABRINA DALBESIO

Britex Fabrics

Best/only reasons to brave this behemoth: postholiday sales, H&M's Spanish cousin Mango, bathrooms (including lounges with changing tables for women and families) and a respectable basement food court.

BRITEX FABRICS   DIY
☎ 415-392-2910; www.britexfabrics.com; 146 Geary St; ☽ 10am-6pm Mon-Sat; ⊞ 2, 3, 4, 30, 38, 45; ⊞ & ⊙ Powell St; ⊠ Powell-Mason & Powell-Hyde

First floor: designers bicker over who gets first dibs on caution-orange chiffon. Second floor: glam rockers dig through a velvet goldmine. Third floor: Hollywood stylists squeal 'To die for!' over '60s Lucite buttons. Top floor: fake fur flies and remnants roll as costumers prepare for Burning Man, Halloween and your average SF weekend.

LE SANCTUAIRE   Food & Drink
☎ 415-986-4216; www.le-sanctuaire.com; 5th fl, 315 Sutter St; ☽ by appointment 10:30am-4:30pm Mon-Fri; ⊞ 2, 3, 4, 30, 38, 45; ⊠ Powell-Mason & Powell-Hyde

Mad scientists, thrill seekers and professional chefs are buzzed in speakeasy-style to this culinary curiosity shop selling anchovy juice, spherifiers to turn fruit into caviar, salt for curing meats, and of course that hallmark of molecular gastronomy: foaming agents.

JAPONESQUE   Housewares, Arts & Crafts
☎ 415-391-8860; 824 Montgomery St; ☽ 10:30am-5:30pm Tue-Sat, 11am-5pm Sun; ⊞ 10, 12, 15

Owner Koichi Hara stocks antique Japanese bamboo baskets and raku ceramics alongside Ruth Rhoten's molten silver vases and Hiromichi Iwashita's graphite-coated, chiseled-wood panels that look like bonfire embers.

CIVIC CENTER & THE TENDERLOIN

KAYO BOOKS   Books
☎ 415-749-0554; www.kayobooks.com; 814 Post St; ☽ 11am-6pm Thu-Sat; ⊞ 2, 3, 4, 27, 38, 76

Juvenile delinquents will find an entire section dedicated to their life stories here, where vintage pulp fiction, true crime and erotica titles ending in exclamation points (including the succinct *Wench!*) induced John Waters to endorse this place on National Public Radio.

ROBERTO GEROMETTA

Ross Alley (p121), Chinatown

NORTH BEACH & CHINATOWN

NORTH BEACH & CHINATOWN

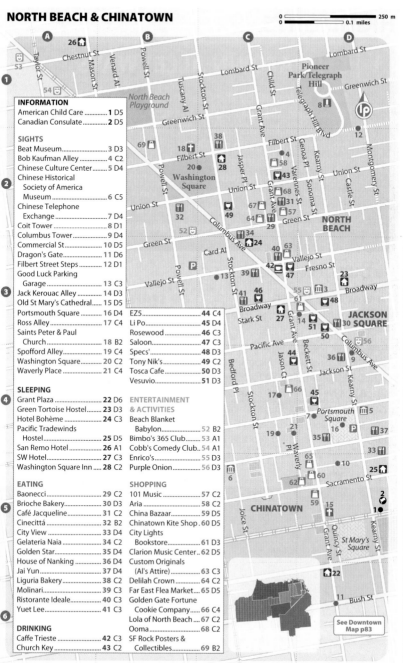

INFORMATION
American Child Care **1** D5
Canadian Consulate **2** D5

SIGHTS
Beat Museum **3** D3
Bob Kaufman Alley **4** C2
Chinese Culture Center **5** D4
Chinese Historical
 Society of America
 Museum **6** C5
Chinese Telephone
 Exchange **7** D4
Coit Tower **8** D1
Columbus Tower **9** D4
Commercial St **10** D5
Dragon's Gate **11** D6
Filbert Street Steps **12** D1
Good Luck Parking
 Garage **13** C3
Jack Kerouac Alley **14** D3
Old St Mary's Cathedral **15** D5
Portsmouth Square **16** D4
Ross Alley **17** C4
Saints Peter & Paul
 Church **18** B2
Spofford Alley **19** C4
Washington Square **20** C2
Waverly Place **21** C4

SLEEPING
Grant Plaza **22** D6
Green Tortoise Hostel **23** D3
Hotel Bohème **24** C3
Pacific Tradewinds
 Hostel **25** D5
San Remo Hotel **26** A1
SW Hotel **27** C3
Washington Square Inn **28** C2

EATING
Baonecci **29** C2
Brioche Bakery **30** D3
Café Jacqueline **31** C2
Cinecittá **32** B2
City View **33** D4
Gelateria Naia **34** C2
Golden Star **35** D4
House of Nanking **36** D4
Jai Yun **37** D4
Liguria Bakery **38** C2
Molinari **39** C3
Ristorante Ideale **40** C3
Yuet Lee **41** C3

DRINKING
Caffe Trieste **42** C3
Church Key **43** C2

EZ5 .... **44** C4
Li Po **45** D4
Rosewood **46** C3
Saloon **47** C3
Specs' **48** D3
Tony Nik's **49** C2
Tosca Cafe **50** D3
Vesuvio **51** D3

**ENTERTAINMENT
& ACTIVITIES**
Beach Blanket
 Babylon **52** B2
Bimbo's 365 Club **53** A1
Cobb's Comedy Club **54** A1
Enrico's **55** D3
Purple Onion **56** D3

SHOPPING
101 Music **57** C2
Aria **58** C2
China Bazaar **59** D5
Chinatown Kite Shop **60** D5
City Lights
 Bookstore **61** D3
Clarion Music Center **62** D5
Custom Originals
 (Al's Attire) **63** C3
Delilah Crown **64** C2
Far East Flea Market **65** D5
Golden Gate Fortune
 Cookie Company **66** C4
Lola of North Beach **67** C2
Ooma **68** C2
SF Rock Posters &
 Collectibles **69** B2

HIGHLIGHTS

1 CHINATOWN ALLEYWAYS

Don't be fooled by the late-afternoon mellow that fills these 41 historic alleyways, packed into Chinatown's 22 blocks. If these brick walls could talk, they'd make a racket: here madams and opium den-masters hawked their services to 49ers, Sun Yat-sen plotted revolution, and gun battles erupted over Prohibition bootlegging operations. Today in these byways you'll hear mah jong tiles clicking and Chinese orchestras warming up – the hard-won peace of a community that has survived against unimaginable odds.

⬂ OUR DON'T MISS LIST

❶ WAVERLY PLACE
Off Sacramento St are the flag-festooned balconies of Chinatown's historic temples, which survived the 1906 earthquake and fire and corrupt politicians, who attempted to forcibly relocate Chinese San Franciscans outside city limits and cash in on Chinatown real estate. Defying relocation orders, Waverly Pl temples held services in the smoldering ruins, and have stayed put to this day.

❷ SPOFFORD ALLEY
On a byway where beauticians gossip indiscreetly over blow-dryers, you might once have overheard the whispers of Sun Yat-sen and his conspirators at No 36 plotting the 1911 overthrow of China's last dynasty.

❸ GOLDEN GATE FORTUNE COOKIE COMPANY
Once mural-lined Ross Alley was notorious for its back-parlor brothels, but today the only sign of its past is the

Clockwise from top left: Waverly Place (p118); Golden Gate Fortune Cookie Company (p131); Spofford Alley (p119)

CLOCKWISE FROM TOP LEFT: ROBERTO GEROMETTA; HANNAH LEVY; JUDY BELLAH

rated-R fortunes in the 'French' cookies here on vintage machines.

❶ Waverly Place
❷ Spofford Alley
❸ Golden Gate Fortune Cookie Company
❹ City View
❺ EZ5

0 ———— 100 m
0 ———— 0.04 miles

Fresno St
NORTH BEACH
Broadway
Columbus Ave
Montgomery St
Pacific Ave
JACKSON SQUARE
Jackson St
Grant Ave
Kearny St
❸
Old Chinatown La
Stockton St
CHINATOWN
Washington St
Portsmouth Square P
Mark Twain St
❷
Waverly Pl
Clay St
❺❹
❶
Commercial St
Sacramento St

❹ CITY VIEW

Feast on plump dumplings shaped like Chinese gold ingots and you'll feel like you struck it rich in Chinatown. From the picture windows, imagine the view here during the Gold Rush: red lights lured sailors to Commercial St's houses of ill repute, while ships were abandoned to rot at piers.

❺ EZ5

A peep into the commerce being conducted along Commercial St back in the 19th century could run you $10. Today you can witness tech deals sealed at EZ5's happy hour, and start some Ms PacMan action for a buck.

↘ THINGS YOU NEED TO KNOW

Lunar new year Usually January/February (p46), with fireworks, markets and dancing **Parking** Good Luck Parking Garage (p121) is aptly named – try parking below Portsmouth Sq instead **Transportation** Walk up Grant, or take the Powell-Mason cable car **For full Chinatown alley details, see p118**

HIGHLIGHTS

2

⬎ COIT TOWER & TELEGRAPH HILL

The exclamation point on San Francisco's skyline is **Coit Tower** (p115), the stark white deco tower eccentric heiress Ms Lillie Hancock Coit left a fortune to build as a monument to San Francisco firefighters. Over the years, this concrete projectile has been a lightning rod for controversy for the radical 1930s Works Projects Administration (WPA) murals inside – but there's no debating the 360-degree panoramas from Coit Tower's viewing platform, 210ft above San Francisco.

3

POETRY ROOM

⬎ CITY LIGHTS

Unlike its namesake – a Charlie Chaplin movie shot in San Francisco – this **bookstore** (p130) just wouldn't stay silent. After his arrest for 'willfully and lewdly' publishing Allen Ginsberg's epic *Howl and Other Poems,* founder and Beat poet Lawrence Ferlinghetti fought the law and won the right to free speech. These three floors are a literary landmark, creatively organized into sections such as Muckraking and Stolen Continents.

⬆ CHINESE HISTORICAL SOCIETY

Taking a breather from her work on Hearst Castle, architect Julia Morgan built this building in 1932 to house the Chinatown YWCA. Today it's the landmark home of the Chinese Historical Society (p118), and hosts contemporary art shows and exhibits of personal artifacts that provide tangible insights to life in Chinatown.

⬆ FILBERT STREET STEPS

In the 19th century, a ruthless entrepreneur began quarrying Telegraph Hill and blasting away roads – much to the distress of his neighbors – and this boardwalk became the main uphill route. City Hall eventually stopped the quarrying of Telegraph Hill, but the view from Filbert Street Steps (p115) is still (wait for it) dynamite.

⬆ GRANT AVENUE

Looking from Chinatown's Dragon's Gate at the streetlamps that illuminate souvenir shops, it's hard to picture this avenue (p120) a century ago, when it was called DuPont and lined with brothels. Led by businessman Look Tin Ely, forward-thinking Chinatown leaders reinvented this bordello byway into a family-friendly tourist attraction.

2 ANTHONY PIDGEON; 3 SABRINA DALBESIO; 4 SABRINA DALBESIO; 5 SABRINA DALBESIO; 6 LEE FOSTER

2 Coit Tower, Telegraph Hill (p115); 3 City Lights Bookstore (p130); 4 Chinese Historical Society of America Museum (p118); 5 Filbert Street Steps (p115); 6 Dragon's Gate (p120), Grant Avenue

WALKING TOUR: NORTH BEACH BEAT

Poetry is in the air and on the sidewalk on this literary tour of North Beach, starting with the legendary City Lights Bookstore. It's an easy 1.5-mile walk, but you'll want at least a couple of hours to see the neighborhood as *On the Road* author Jack Kerouac did – with drinks at the beginning, middle and end.

❶ CITY LIGHTS BOOKSTORE

At the home of Beat poetry and free speech, get some lit to inspire your journey into the heart of literary North Beach – Lawrence Ferlinghetti's *San Francisco Poems* is a good bet.

❷ CAFFE TRIESTE

Order a potent espresso, check out the opera on the jukebox and slide into the back booth where Francis Ford Coppola allegedly wrote his first draft of *The Godfather*. This place has been beloved since 1956, with the local characters and bathroom wall poetry to prove it.

❸ WASHINGTON SQUARE

Pause to admire parrots in the treetops and octogenarians' smooth tai chi moves below: pure poetry in motion.

❹ LIGURIA BAKERY

Focaccia hot from a hundred-year-old oven makes a worthy pit stop for ravenous readers.

ANTHONY PIDGEON

Caffe Trieste (p128)

❺ BOB KAUFMAN ALLEY

This quiet alley renamed for the legendary street-corner poet, who broke a 12-year vow of silence when he walked into a North Beach cafe and recited his poem 'All Those Ships That Never Sailed': 'Today I bring them back/Huge and transitory/And let them sail/Forever.'

❻ BEAT MUSEUM

Don't be surprised to hear a Dylan jam session by the front door, or see Allen Ginsberg naked in documentary footage screened inside the museum: the Beat goes on here in rare form.

NORTH BEACH BEAT

❼ SPECS'

Begin your literary bar crawl here amid merchant-marine memorabilia, tall tales, choice words worthy of a sailor and a glass of (what else?) Anchor Steam.

❽ VESUVIO

Jack Kerouac once blew off Henry Miller to go on a bender here; try the house brew and see if you have the will to continue this walking tour…

❾ JACK KEROUAC ALLEY

It's poetic justice that this mural-covered byway is named for the Beat Generation's most famous author, since this is where he was tossed after a raucous night at Vesuvio. Kerouac's words from *On the Road*, embedded in the alley, seem to sum up North Beach nights: 'The air was soft, the stars so fine, the promise of every cobbled alley so great…'

❿ LI PO

Follow the literary lead of Kerouac and Ginsberg and end your night in a vinyl booth at Li Po, with another beer beneath the gold Buddha's forgiving gaze.

BEST...

⬈ TASTE SENSATIONS

- **Molinari** (p124) House-cured salami sandwiches.
- **Jai Yun** (p125) Creates abalone and jellyfish cravings.
- **Café Jacqueline** (p123) Chocolate soufflé for two...or maybe one.
- **Gelateria Naia** (p125) East-meets-West black sesame gelato.
- **Golden Star** (p126) Noteworthy noodle soup – *pho* real.

⬈ BOHEMIAN STYLE UPGRADES

- **Al's Attire** (p130) Skinny-lapel suits, made to measure.
- **Clarion Music Center** (p132) Bongos, obviously.
- **Delilah Crown** (p130) Silkscreened artists' smocks.
- **Aria** (p129) Antique butterfly hair pins.
- **City Lights** (p130) Faraway expression (free with poetry purchase).

⬈ CHEAP & MODERATELY PRICED LAUGHS

- **Beach Blanket Babylon** (p128) Wigs and satire that go way over the top.
- **Cobb's Comedy Club** (p128) Two words of warning: audience participation.
- **Purple Onion** (p128) Where Woody Allen and Robin Williams cracked wise.
- **Chinatown Kite Shop** (p131) Go fly a paper pink flamingo.

⬈ MEDITATIVE MOMENTS

- **Bob Kaufman Alley** (p117) Borrow a page from this street's silent poet.
- **Tien Hou Temple** (p118) Light incense on the historic altar.
- **Filbert Street Steps** (opposite) Catch your breath with the views.
- **Good Luck Parking Garage** (p121) Find your fortune in the asphalt.
- **Li Po** (p128) Beer with a big gold Buddha.

RICK GERHARTER

Ralph Stackpole's 1934 mural, *Industries of California*, Coit Tower

DISCOVER NORTH BEACH & CHINATOWN

Back in the 19th century, Columbus Ave was a dividing line between San Francisco's most historic Chinese and Italian neighborhoods: now it's everyone's favorite spot for lunar new year parades and Beat poetry readings, tai chi classes and jukebox opera, chrysanthemum tea and cappuccino. The Chinese railroad workers and Italian fishermen who originally settled the area are gone now, but wild parrots and hawks have moved in, circling above the area as though waiting, as Beat poet Lawrence Ferlinghetti once put it in his poem 'I Am Waiting,' 'for a rebirth of wonder.'

Or maybe they're just looking for a parking spot. Yet there is poetry here, even in perpetual parking misfortune. Explore quiet side streets off Columbus, and you'll hear heartstring-plucking Chinese orchestras and the soft consonants of Tuscan-accented Italian. You'll notice North Beach alleyways named after Beat writers, and in Chinatown's aptly named Good Luck Parking Garage, each spot is labeled with a fortune-cookie prediction. Staircases and garden-lined boardwalks up steep Telegraph Hill yield great rewards: historic murals and 360-degree views from Coit Tower.

SIGHTS

NORTH BEACH

COIT TOWER & TELEGRAPH HILL

☎ 415-362-0808; Telegraph Hill Blvd; adult/child 12-17yr & senior/under 12yr $5/3/1.50; ☿ 10am-6:30pm; 🚍 39

Go ahead and snicker at the wacky hose-shaped concrete projectile that eccentric Ms Lillie Hancock Coit left a third of her considerable fortune to build – everyone does – but the climb here is no joke, the tower's dedication to firefighters is heart-felt and the views inside the tower will win you over to Lillie's point of view.

The heiress had some radical ideas (see the boxed text, p116), and the tower built in her name in 1934 has plenty of its own, as seen in the worker-glorifying **WPA murals** that line the lobby. For decades after their completion, the murals and the 25 artists who worked on them were denounced as communist. But the red-baiting backfired: for the controversy they ignited as well as the artistic effort involved, San Franciscans embraced the tower and its murals as a beloved city landmark.

After climbing the Greenwich St or Filbert St Steps to get here, the wait for the elevator is well worth it. From the top of the tower, you can take in panoramic views and spot colorful flocks of parrots turning the treetops red and blue.

FILBERT STREET STEPS

Telegraph Hill Blvd from Sansome St or Washington Sq; 🚍 39

Somewhere in the middle of the steep climb up Filbert Street Steps to Coit Tower, you might begin to wonder if it's worth the trouble. Well, take a breather and look around. Already you're passing hidden cottages along a wooden boardwalk called Napier Lane, sculpture tucked in among gardens flowering year-round, and sweeping vistas of the Bay Bridge. If you need a few words of encouragement, the wild parrots in the trees have been known to interject a few choice words that your gym instructor would probably get sued for using.

JACK KEROUAC ALLEY

btwn Grant & Columbus Aves; 🚌 15, 30, 41
Fans of *On the Road* and *Dharma Bums* will appreciate how fitting it is that Kerouac's namesake alleyway offers a poetic and slightly seedy shortcut between Chinatown and North Beach via favorite Kerouac haunts **City Lights Bookstore** (p130) and **Vesuvio** (p127) – Kerouac took his books, Buddhism and drink to heart.

BEAT MUSEUM

☎ 1-800-537-6822 (1-800-KER-OUAC); www. thebeatmuseum.org; 540 Broadway; admission $5; ⏱ 10am-7pm; 🚌 15, 30, 41, 45
The Beat goes on, and on – OK, so it rambles a little – at this truly obsessive collection of SF literary-scene ephemera c 1950–69. The banned edition of Allen Ginsberg's *Howl* is the ultimate free- speech trophy, and the 1961 check

Jack Kerouac wrote to a liquor store has a certain dark humor, but some items are head-shakers: did those Kerouac bobble-head dolls and yo-yos ever really go into mass production?

Enter the museum through a turnstile in the back of the store, grab a ramshackle reclaimed theater seat redolent with the accumulated odors of pot and pets, and watch fascinating films about the Beat era's leading musicians, artists, writers, politicos and undefinable characters. Upstairs there are shrines to individual Beats with first-hand remembrances and artifacts, and 1st editions of books that expanded the American outlook to include the margins.

WASHINGTON SQUARE

Columbus Ave & Union St; 🚌 15, 30, 41, 45
Wild parrots, tai chi masters, nonagenarian churchgoing *nonnas* (grandmothers) and Ben Franklin are the company you'll keep on this lively patch of lawn. The parrots keep their distance in the treetops, but like anyone else in North Beach, they can probably be bribed into friendship with focaccia from **Liguria Bakery** (p125) on the square's northeast corner. The 1897 statue of Ben Franklin

---

⬎ THE FIERY, FEISTY HEIRESS

In 19th-century San Francisco, fire engines were usually pulled by horses, but they had to be pushed up steep inclines by firefighters, who until 1866 were well-to-do volunteers. There were some 16 squads in all, and No 5 had the advantage of being urged on by its mascot, the self-appointed fire cheerleader and eccentric heiress Lillie Hancock Coit. She was the ultimate groupie: she could drink, smoke and play cards as well as any off-duty firefighter, rarely missed a fire or a firefighter's funeral, and even had the firehouse emblem embroidered on her bedsheets. Eventually she split town to join the bohemian scene in Paris, but she left $5000 (about $50,000 today) in her will to each firefighter in the No 5 company, and funds to construct the monument to the city's firefighters now known as **Coit Tower** (p115).

is a non sequitur, and the taps below his feet falsely advertise mineral water from Vichy, France – yet another example of a puzzling public artwork courtesy of a certifiable SF eccentric, Henry D Cogswell, who made his fortune fitting miners with gold fillings.

BOB KAUFMAN ALLEY
off Grant Ave near Filbert St; 🚌 15, 30, 41, 45
What, you mean your hometown doesn't have a street named after an African American Catholic-Jewish-voodoo an-archist Beat poet who refused to speak for 12 years? The man revered in France as the 'American Rimbaud' was a major poet who helped found the legendary *Beatitudes* magazine in 1959 and a spoken-word bebop jazz artist who was never at a loss for words, yet he felt com-pelled to take a Buddhist vow of silence after John F Kennedy's assassination that he kept until the end of the Vietnam War.

Kaufman's life was hardly pure poetry: he was a teenage runaway, periodically found himself homeless, was occasionally

> ### ↘ TRANSPORTATION: NORTH BEACH
>
> **Bus** Lines 30 and 45 run up Stockton St from Union Square; buses 15 and 41 run along Columbus Ave.
> **Cable car** The Powell-Mason St line skirts the top of North Beach – get off at Vallejo or Green Sts and walk about three blocks to Columbus Ave.
> **Parking** Street parking is remotely possible, but a waste of time. Try your luck first at the public Good Luck Parking Garage (p121), on Vallejo St between Powell and Stockton Sts.

jailed for picking fights in poetry with po-lice, battled methamphetamine addiction with varying success and once claimed his goal was to be forgotten. Yet like the man himself, this hidden alleyway in his honor is offbeat, streetwise and often pro-foundly silent.

RICK GERHARTER

Beat Museum

Tien Hou Temple on Waverly Place

JUDY BELLAH

CHINATOWN
WAVERLY PLACE

🚌 1, 30, 45; 🚋 California, Powell-Mason, Powell-Hyde; ♿

There was no place to go but up in Chinatown after 1870, when local laws limited where Chinese San Franciscans could live and work. Temples were built atop the barber shops, laundries and neighborhood associations lining Waverly Pl, making their presence known with brightly painted balconies festooned with flags and lanterns.

Tien Hou Temple (🕐 hours vary) atop 125 Waverly Pl was built in 1852, and the altar miraculously survived the 1906 earthquake and fire to become a symbol of community endurance. Drop by and pay your respects; entry is free, but it's customary to leave an offering for temple upkeep.

↘ TRANSPORTATION: CHINATOWN

Bus Lines 30 and 45 run up Stockton St from Union Square; bus 15 runs along Kearny St, while bus 1 runs along California St.

Cable car The Powell-Mason St line links Union Square to Chinatown; the California St line runs through Chinatown on its ascent to Nob Hill.

Parking Street parking is impossible; try your luck at the public Good Luck Parking Garage (p121).

CHINESE HISTORICAL SOCIETY OF AMERICA MUSEUM

☎ 415-391-1188; www.chsa.org; 965 Clay St; adult/senior/child 6-17yr $3/2/1, 1st Thu of month free; 🕐 noon-5pm Tue-Fri; 🚌 1, 30, 45; 🚋 California, Powell-Mason, Powell-Hyde; ♿

Picture what it was like to be Chinese in America during the Gold Rush, transcontinental railroad construction or the Beat heyday at the nation's largest Chinese American historical institute. Intimate vintage photos, an 1880 temple altar and personal artifacts are seen alongside the Daniel KE Ching collection of thousands of vintage advertisements, toys and post-cards conveying Chinese stereotypes. Temporary art shows are across the court-yard in this graceful 1932 landmark build-ing, built as Chinatown's YWCA by Julia Morgan of Hearst Castle fame.

SPOFFORD ALLEY

🚌 1, 15, 30, 45; 🚋 California, Powell-Mason, Powell-Hyde; 🚹

Sun Yat-sen once plotted the overthrow of China's Manchu dynasty here at No 36, and during Prohibition, this was the site of turf battles over local bootlegging and protection rackets. Spofford has mel-lowed with age; it's now lined with senior community centers. But the action still starts around sundown, when a Chinese orchestra strikes up a tune, the clicking of a mah jong game begins, and beauty par-lor owners and florists use the pretense of sweeping their doorsteps to gossip.

PORTSMOUTH SQUARE

733 Kearny St; 🚌 1, 15, 41, 45; 🚋 California; 🚹

Since apartments in Chinatown's old brick buildings are small, Portsmouth Sq is the neighborhood's living room. The square is named after John B Montgomery's

---

➰ IF YOU LIKE...

If you like **Coit Tower** (p115), you might enjoy these other towering monu-ments to San Francisco's checkered past:

- **Columbus Tower** (**916 Kearny St;** 🚌 **15, 30, 41**) This tower was built by shady political boss Abe Ruef in 1905 – just in time to be reduced to its steel skel-eton in the 1906 earthquake and fire. The Grammy-winning folk group the Kingston Trio bought the copper-clad tower in the 1960s, and the Grateful Dead recorded in the basement. Since the 1970s it has been owned by Francis Ford Coppola, and film history has been made here by Coppola's American Zoetrope, *The Joy Luck Club* director Wayne Wang and Academy Award–winning actor/director Sean Penn.
- **Chinese Telephone Exchange** (**743 Washington St;** 🚌 **1, 15, 30, 45;** 🚋 **California**) The exchange was built in1894 and staffed by live-in switchboard operators who spoke fluent English and five Chinese dialects, and knew at least 1500 Chinatown residents by name, residence and occupation. Since anyone born in China was prohibited by law from visiting San Francisco through-out the 1882–1943 Chinese Exclusion era, this switchboard was the main means of contact with family and business partners in China. The exchange operated until 1949, and the landmark was bought and restored by Bank of Canton in 1960.
- **Saints Peter & Paul Church** (☎ **415-421-0809; www.stspeterpaul.san-francisco.ca.us; 666 Filbert St; admission free;** 🕒 **7:30am-4pm;** 🚌 **15, 30, 41, 45**) This lacy 1924 triple-decker white cathedral that looks like a wedding cake offers services in Italian and Chinese, and pulls a triple wedding shift on Saturdays. Joe DiM-aggio and Marilyn Monroe had their wedding photos taken here, though they weren't permitted to marry in the church because both had been divorced.

sloop, which pulled up near here in 1846 to stake the US claim on San Francisco, but the presiding deity at this park is the Goddess of Democracy, a bronze replica of the statue made by Tiananmen Square protesters in 1989.

First light is met with outstretched arms by tai-chi practitioners. By afternoon toddlers rush the playground slides, and tea crowds collect at the kiosk under the pedestrian bridge to joke and dissect the day's news. The checkers and chess played on concrete tables in gazebos late into the evening aren't mere games, but 365-day obsessions, come rain or shine. Bronze plaques dot the perimeter of the historic square, noting the site of San Francisco's first bookshop and elementary school and the bawdy Jenny Lind Theater, which with a few modifications became San Francisco's first City Hall.

CHINESE CULTURE CENTER

☎ 415-986-1822; www.c-c-c.org; 3rd fl, Hilton Hotel, 750 Kearny St; gallery free (donation requested), tours adult/child $25/20; ⏰ 10am-4pm Tue-Sat; 🚌 1, 15, 41
You can see all the way to China on the 3rd floor of the Hilton inside this cultural center, which hosts exhibits of traditional Chinese arts and such breakthrough contemporary shows as the Present Tense Biennial. Kid-friendly, docent-led Chinese Heritage Walks guide visitors through the living history and mythology of Chinatown in two hours; tours are available by reservation with a two-person minimum. For more first-hand experiences of Chinese culture, check the center's schedule of Mandarin classes, poetry readings, movies and genealogy services.

OLD ST MARY'S CATHEDRAL

☎ 415-288-3800; www.oldsaintmarys.org; 660 California St; ⏰ 11am-6pm Mon-Tue, 11am-7pm Wed-Fri, 9am-6:30pm Sat, 9am-4:30pm Sun; 🚌 1, 15, 30, 45; 🚋 California, Powell-Mason, Powell-Hyde; ♿
Many thought it a lost cause, but California's first cathedral, inaugurated in 1854, tried for decades to give San Francisco some religion – despite its location in brothel central. Hence the stern admonition on the church's brick clock tower: 'Son, observe the time and fly from evil.'

Eventually the archdiocese abandoned attempts to convert Dupont St whoremongers and handed the church over to a Chinese community mission run by the activism-oriented Paulists. During WWII, the church served the US military as a recreation center and cafeteria. The 1906 fire destroyed one of the district's biggest bordellos directly across from the church, making room for **St Mary's Square**. Today, skateboarders do tricks of a different sort on the park's rails and benches, under the watchful eye of Beniamino Bufano's 1929 pink granite and steel **statue of Sun Yat-sen**.

DRAGON'S GATE

cnr Grant Ave & Bush St; 🚌 1, 15, 30, 45; 🚋 California; ♿
Enter the Dragon archway and you'll find yourself on the once-notorious street known as Dupont in its red-light heyday. Sixty years before the family-friendly overhaul of the Las Vegas Strip, Look Tin Eli and a group of forward-thinking Chinatown businessmen pioneered the approach here in Chinatown, replacing seedy attractions with more tourist-friendly ones.

After consultation with architects and community groups, Dupont was transformed into Grant Ave, with Deco-Chinoiserie dragon lamps and tiled pagoda rooftops, and police were reluctantly persuaded to enforce the 1914 Red Light Abatement Act in Chinatown. By the time this gate was donated by Taiwan in 1970 grandly proclaiming that 'everything in the world is in just proportions,' Chinatown finally had a main street that did the community greater justice.

ROSS ALLEY

🚌 1, 30, 45; 🚋 Powell-Mason, Powell-Hyde; 🚶
The colorful murals lining Ross Alley hint at the colorful characters that once roamed SF's oldest alleyway, which has been known variously as Mexico, Spanish and Manila St after the ladies who once staffed its notorious back-parlor brothels. More recently, Ross Alley has been occasionally pimped out to Hollywood production companies as the picturesque backdrop for sequels such as *Karate Kid II* and *Indiana Jones and the Temple of Doom*.

GOOD LUCK PARKING GARAGE

735 Vallejo St; 🚌 1, 15, 30, 45; 🚋 California, Powell-Mason, Powell-Hyde
Each parking spot at this garage comes with fortune-cookie wisdom stenciled onto the asphalt: 'You have already found your true love. Stop looking.' These omens are brought to you by artist Harrell Fletcher and co-conspirator Jon Rubin, who also gathered the vintage photographs of local residents' Chinese and Italian ancestors that grace the entry tiles like heraldic emblems.

COMMERCIAL ST

742 Commercial St; 🚌 1, 15, 41, 45; 🚋 California; 🚶
Back when the red lights of Commercial St could be seen down by the waterfront, this strip provided many provocative answers to the age-old question: what do you do with a drunken sailor? Conveniently located across Portsmouth Sq from San Francisco's City Hall, this hot spot caught fire in 1906. The city banned its 25¢ Chinese brothels in favor of white-run 'parlor houses,' where basic services were raised to $3 – watching cost $10 at the faux-French Parisian Mansion. Today that much gets you a couple of hot dishes – of dumplings, that is, at **City View** (p126).

RICK GERHARTER

Dragon's Gate, Chinatown

Hotel Bohème

SABRINA DALBESIO

SLEEPING
NORTH BEACH

WASHINGTON SQUARE INN   Inn $$$

☎ 415-981-4220, 800-388-0220; www.wsisf.com; 1660 Stockton St; r incl breakfast $179-329; 🚌 30, 45; 🛜

On leafy, sun-dappled Washington Square, the inn looks decidedly European and caters to the over-40 set, with tasteful rooms and a few choice antiques, including carved-wooden armoires. The least expensive rooms are tiny, but what a stellar address. Wine and cheese each evening, and optional breakfast in bed sweeten the deal.

HOTEL BOHÈME   Boutique Hotel $$

☎ 415-433-9111; www.hotelboheme.com; 444 Columbus Ave; r $174-194; 🚌 30, 45; 🛜

Our favorite boutique hotel is a love letter to the jazz era, with moody orange, black and sage-green color schemes that nod to the 1950s. Inverted Chinese umbrellas hang from the ceiling, and photos from the Beat years decorate the walls. Rooms are smallish, and some front onto noisy Columbus Ave (the quietest are in back), but the hotel is smack in the middle of North Beach's vibrant street scene.

SAN REMO HOTEL   Hotel $

☎ 415-776-8688, 800-352-7366; www.sanremo hotel.com; 2237 Mason St; d $55-85; 🚌 30, 45; 🛜

One of the city's best values, the San Remo dates to 1906 and is long on old-fashioned charm. Rooms are simply done, with mismatched turn-of-the-century furnishings, and all share bathrooms. Think reputable, vintage boarding house. Note: the least-expensive rooms have windows onto the corridor, not the outdoors.

GREEN TORTOISE HOSTEL   Hostel $

☎ 415-834-1000; www.greentortoise.com; 494 Broadway; dm/d incl breakfast $29/70; 🚌 15; 🛜

An international crowd of young party-scene backpackers flocks to the Green Tortoise. It's on Broadway, North Beach's seedy (though safe) strip-joint strip. If you're into rowdy hostels, look no further. Bars, restaurants and cafes are right around the corner. No curfew.

CHINATOWN
SW HOTEL   Hotel $$
☎ 415-362-2999, 888-595-9188; www.swhotel.com; 615 Broadway; r $109-149; 🚇 45; Ⓟ 🛜
The legendary flophouse known as the Sam Wong underwent a late-'90s overhaul that included earthquake retrofitting and updated decor. Now it's simple and respectable, with bland pastel decor. Parking is first-come, first-served and not always available. The hotel's number-one selling point is location – on the Broadway axis dividing North Beach and Chinatown.

GRANT PLAZA   Hotel $
☎ 415-434-3883, 800-472-6899; www.grantplaza.com; 465 Grant Ave; r $69-129; 🚇 California; 🛜
Many rooms overlook the blinking neon and exotic street scene of Grant Ave, which is the best reason to stay here. Rooms are generally clean (never mind the heavy air-freshener), but blandly decorated with generic furniture. If you want to be in the heart of Chinatown, this is the place.

PACIFIC TRADEWINDS
HOSTEL   Hostel $
☎ 415-433-7970, 888-734-6783; www.san-francisco-hostel.com; 680 Sacramento St; dm $24-26; 🚇 1; 🛜
San Francisco's smartest-looking all-dorm hostel has a blue-and-white nautical theme, fully equipped kitchen and spotless glass-brick showers. The nearest BART station is Embarcadero. Alas, you'll have to haul your bags up three flights, but it's worth it. Great service, fun staff.

EATING
NORTH BEACH
When choosing an Italian restaurant in North Beach, use this rule of thumb: if a host has to lure you in with 'Ciao bella!' on the sidewalk, keep walking. Try smaller neighborhood Italian American restaurants on side streets off Grant Ave and Washington St, where staff are gossiping in Italian.

CAFÉ JACQUELINE   French $$$
☎ 415-981-5565; 1454 Grant Ave; 🕐 5:30-11pm Wed-Sun; 🚇 20, 30, 39, 41, 45, 91
The secret terror of top chefs is the classic French soufflé: only when the ingredients are in golden-mean proportions, whipped into perfect peaks, baked at the right temperature and removed from the oven not a second too early or late will a soufflé rise to the occasion. Chef Jacqueline's soufflés float across the tongue like the fog over the Golden Gate Bridge, and with the right person across the tiny wooden table to share that seafood soufflé, dinner could hardly get more romantic – until you order the chocolate for dessert.

RISTORANTE IDEALE   Italian $$
☎ 415-391-4129; 1309 Grant Ave; 🕐 dinner; 🚇 15, 30, 41, 45
Italian regulars are stunned that a restaurant this authentic borders the Pacific, with *bucatini ammatriciana* (Roman tube pasta with savory tomato-pancetta-pecorino sauce) served properly al dente, creamy seafood risotto made with superior Canaroli rice, and a well-priced selection of robust Italian wines, served by wisecracking Tuscan waitstaff and a Roman chef. The portions are lavishly American, but seafood and meat preparations remain strictly Italian to highlight flavors released in cooking – unlike North Beach's many goat-cheese-and-sundried-tomato-pesto-on-everything imposters.

Molinari

SABRINA DALBESIO

MOLINARI
Italian, Deli $

☎ 415-421-2337; 373 Columbus Ave; ⏱ 9am-5:30pm Mon-Sat; 🚌 15, 30, 41, 45

Grab a number and a crusty roll, and when your number rolls around, the guys behind the counter will stuff it with translucent sheets of prosciutto di Parma, milky buffalo mozzarella, tender marinated artichokes or slabs of the legendary house-cured salami (the city's best). While you wait, load up on essential Italian groceries for later, such as truffle-filled gnocchi, seasoned *pecorino* (sheep's cheese) and aged balsamic vinegar.

CINECITTÁ
Pizza $

☎ 415-291-8830; 663 Union St; ⏱ noon-10pm Sun-Thu, to 11pm Fri & Sat; 🚌 15, 30, 41, 45; 🚋 Powell-Mason; Ⓥ ♿

That tantalizing aroma you followed from down the block into this 18-seat eatery is thin-crust Roman pizza, probably the crowd-pleasing Capricciosa: artichoke hearts, olives, fresh mozzarella, prosciutto and egg. Vegetarians prefer Funghi Selvatici, with wild mushrooms,

zucchini and sundried tomato, but that saliva-prompting aroma escaping the wood-fired oven is the ever-popular Travestere (fresh mozzarella, arugula and prosciutto), served with sass and a generous pint of draft Anchor Steam by Roman owner Romina. Save room for housemade tiramisu, hands down the best in North Beach.

BRIOCHE BAKERY
Bakery $

☎ 415-765-0412; 210 Columbus Ave; ⏱ 7am-8pm Mon-Sat; 🚌 15, 30, 41, 45

When Gold Rush miners found gold, they treated themselves to 'Frenchy food' here on what was once San Francisco's Barbary Coast – and now you too can start your day striking it rich with flaky cinnamon twists, not-too-sweet *pain au chocolat* (chocolate croissants), and namesake brioches golden with butter.

BAONECCI
Sandwiches, Bakery $

☎ 415-989-1806; www.caffebaonecci.com; 516 Green St; ⏱ noon-9:30pm Tue-Sat, 11am-3:30pm Sun; 🚌 20, 30, 39, 41, 45, 91

Recharge for the Coit Tower climb with panini turbo-loaded with bold Southern Italian flavors on house-baked ciabatta or focaccia. Tastebuds sit up and pay attention to the Studente, a ham and cheese sandwich slathered with hot Calabrese red-pepper paste and green olive spread for $6.50.

LIGURIA BAKERY   Italian $
☎ 415-421-3786; 1700 Stockton St; ◷ 8am-2pm Mon-Fri, 7am-2pm Sat, 7am-noon Sun; ◻ 15, 30, 41, 45; ◙ Powell-Mason
Bleary-eyed art students and Italian grandmothers are in line by 8am for the cinnamon-raisin focaccia hot out of the 100-year-old oven, leaving 9am dawdlers a choice of tomato or classic rosemary, and 10am stragglers out of luck. Take what you can get, and don't kid yourself that you're going to save it for lunch.

GELATERIA NAIA   Ice Cream $
☎ 415-677-9280; www.gelaterianaia.com; 520 Columbus Ave; ◷ 11am-11pm Sun-Thu, to midnight Fri & Sat; ◻ 15, 30, 41, 45
Chinatown and North Beach cross-pollinate with creamy concoctions that improve on the ordinary, elevating the usual Chinese green tea or Italian pistachio ice cream options to a decadent choice of Kyoto maccha tea or locally roasted California pistachio gelato. Local, seasonal flavors and constant experimentation introduce entirely new sorbet and gelato obsessions with flavors ranging from white peach to black sesame.

CHINATOWN
Ordering off the menu is overrated in Chinatown, where the best dishes are pushed past your table on a dim sum cart or listed in Chinese. Try out the dim sum places and noodle joints along Stockton St, and wander along side streets off Grant

Ave to find basement eateries where starving artists can afford to order in bulk, just like Jack Kerouac, Allen Ginsberg and the Beats did. But it's worth splashing out on local delicacies too – a feast in the Hong Kong indie-film atmosphere of Jai Yun, House of Nanking or Yuet Lee could be the highlight of your trip.

JAI YUN   Shanghai-Style Chinese $$$
☎ 415-981-7438; www.menuscan.com/jaiyun; 680 Clay St; ◷ lunch Mon-Fri, dinner daily by reservation only; ◻ 30; ◙ California, Powell-Mason, Powell-Hyde
'Hello? When? How many? $55, $65, $75 per person? OK, see you!' That's how the reservation system works at Jai Yun, where chef Nei serves 15- to 20-course Shanghai-style market-fresh feasts by reservation only. There's no menu, since the chef creates the bill of fare based on what's fresh that day – but fingers crossed, your menu will include tender abalone that drifts across the tongue like a San Francisco fog, housemade rice noodles with cured pancetta, and seemingly lowly yet truly opulent mung beans with sesame oil. Never mind that the restaurant has more mirrors than a Bruce Lee movie and Christmas tinsel wrapped around dining-room surveillance cameras – the sophisticated, fascinating flavors will leave you smugly assured in your impeccable taste.

HOUSE OF
NANKING   Shanghai-Style Chinese $$
☎ 415-421-1429; 919 Kearny St; ◷ 11am-10pm Mon-Fri, noon-10pm Sat, noon-9pm Sun; ◻ 15
Meekly suggest an interest in seafood, nothing deep-fried, perhaps some greens, and your no-nonsense server nods, snatches the menu and, within minutes, returns with meltaway scallops,

fragrant sautéed pea shoots, minced squab lettuce cups, and a tea ball that blossoms in hot water. For bright, clean flavors at a price you'd expect to pay for food half this good, you can put up with bossy service, a strict cash-only policy and the inevitable wait for a table.

YUET LEE   Chinese, Seafood $$

☎ 415-982-6020; 1300 Stockton St; ⏰ 11am-3am Wed-Mon; 🚌 1, 9, 15, 30, 45; 🚃 Powell-Mason, Powell-Hyde; Ⓥ ♿

With a radioactive green paint job and merciless fluorescent lighting, this so-hideous-it's-cool seafood diner isn't for first dates, but for drinking buddies and committed couples who have nothing to hide and are willing to share outstanding batter-dipped salt-and-pepper calamari and tender roast duck.

CITY VIEW   Dim Sum $

☎ 415-398-2838; 662 Commercial St; ⏰ 11am-2:30pm Mon-Fri, 10am-2:30pm Sat & Sun; 🚌 1, 10, 15, 30; 🚃 California

Dim sum aficionados used to cramped quarters and surly service are wowed by impeccable shrimp and leek dumplings; tangy, tender asparagus; and crisp Peking duck, all dished up from carts with a flourish in a spacious, sunny room. Try to come on the early or late side of lunch, when your server has the time to recommend that day's best dishes and you don't have to sit in the downstairs dining area contemplating the surreal Astroturf Zen garden beneath the stairs.

GOLDEN STAR   Vietnamese $

☎ 415-398-1215; 11 Walter Lum Pl; ⏰ 10am-9pm; 🚌 1, 9, 30, 45

Elementary school cafeterias could outclass the Golden Star for atmosphere – but if you know pho, you know this is the place to go. Five-spice chicken *pho* is the house specialty that warms the bones on a foggy day, but on a hot day, branch out and get the *bun* (rice vermicelli) topped with thinly sliced grilled beef, imperial rolls, mint and ground peanuts. Except in

SABRINA DALBESIO

Vesuvio

understandable cases of extreme noodle gluttony, your bill will be under $8.

DRINKING
NORTH BEACH

SPECS'   Bar
☎ 415-421-4112; 12 William Saroyan Pl; ☽ 5pm-2am; ☐ 1, 20

Hidden on a tiny pedestrian alley, cave-like Specs' draws barflies in the afternoon and hipsters, literary radicals and other colorful local characters in the evening. It's also a sort of museum, packed with weird ephemera culled from ports around the globe – nobody's sure which species' desiccated penis hangs behind the bar, but everyone agrees it's from a marine mammal.

TOSCA CAFE   Bar
☎ 415-391-1244; 242 Columbus Ave; ☽ 5pm-2am Tue-Sun; ☐ 1, 20

If Francis Ford Coppola had filmed *The Godfather* in San Francisco, he would surely have set an operatic bloodbath or quiet strangling in Tosca. Coppola, Sean Penn, Robert DeNiro or Bono might be lurking in the VIP room, but we'd rather hang at one of the round red-vinyl booths, Irish coffee or retro-classic cocktail in hand. The place has that self-assured Italian American brusqueness, with a smoke-stained ceiling, a worn linoleum floor and an all-opera jukebox (with genuine 45rpm platters).

VESUVIO   Bar
☎ 415-362-3370; 255 Columbus Ave; ☽ 6am-2am; ☐ 1, 20

Guy walks into a bar, roars and leaves. Without missing a beat, the bartender says to the next customer, 'Welcome to Vesuvio, honey – what can I get you?' It takes a lot more than a barbaric yawp to

get Vesuvio's regulars to glance up from their microbrewed beers. Kerouac blew off Henry Miller to go on a bender here, and after knocking back a couple with neighborhood characters, you'll get why.

ROSEWOOD   Bar
☎ 415-951-4886; 732 Broadway; ☽ 5:30pm-2am Wed-Fri, 7pm-2am Sat; ☐ 12, 30, 45

This unmarked bar delivers on its name with sleek floor-to-ceiling rosewood-paneled walls, dim lighting and low-slung tufted black-leather sofas. It's a cool first-drink spot and there's a bamboo-enclosed smokers' patio, but too many hard surfaces make conversation nearly impossible once crowds arrive and the music amps up.

SALOON   Bar
☎ 415-989-7666; 1232 Grant Ave; weekend cover $2-5; ☽ noon-2am; ☐ 20, 30, 45

A stalwart North Beach dive, the Saloon survived the 1906 fire when its loyal patrons brandished buckets of beer and wine to quench the flames. Today it's the oldest bar in SF, dating from 1861, and hasn't had a coat of paint in decades, which is exactly why disheveled old-timers and local hipsters love it. Blues and rock bands perform nightly and from 4pm weekend afternoons.

CHURCH KEY   Bar
☎ 415-986-3511; 1402 Grant Ave; ☽ 5pm-2am; ☐ 20, 30, 41, 45

If there's a connoisseur's beer from Belgium, Japan, Canada or New Zealand that you've been dying to try, chances are you'll find it at this sparsely furnished hole-in-the-wall, with a little upstairs mezzanine, off North Beach's main strip. The local crowd means good conversation about all things SF. Beer, wine and cash only.

TONY NIK'S
Bar

☎ 415-693-0990; 1534 Stockton St; ☾ 4pm-2am; ☒ 30, 45

Think Rat Pack lounge, c 1956, and you'll conjure retro-cool Tony Nik's, a tiny cocktail lounge with glass bricks, vintage granite floors and period wood-paneling. Good acoustics make for easy conversation. Aim for the cocktail tables in back, or hang with old-timers at the bar.

CAFFE TRIESTE
Cafe

☎ 415-392-6739; 601 Vallejo St; ☾ 6:30am-11pm Sun-Thu, to midnight Fri & Sat; ☒ 20, 30, 41, 45; ☞

Poetry on the bathroom walls, opera on the jukebox, monthly Saturday accordion concerts and occasional sightings of poet laureate Lawrence Ferlinghetti: this is North Beach at its best, as it's been since the 1950s. Linger over a legendary espresso, join aging anarchists debating how best to bring down the government, or just sit with your sketchpad and watch the world go by outside.

CHINATOWN

LI PO
Bar

☎ 415-982-0072; 916 Grant Ave; ☾ 2pm-2am; ☒ 45

A fave of the Beat poets, Li Po's fake-grotto decor comes with lurid 1960s-era plush red booths, bartenders shouting in Cantonese and an unexpected Chinese-meets-hipster clientele. On slow nights, it may be just you and the barkeep watching TV.

EZ5
Bar

☎ 415-362-9321; www.ez5bar.com; 682 Commercial St; ☾ 4pm-2am Mon-Fri, 6pm-2am Sat; ☒ 1, 10, 41

Don't worry if you're not looking your best – EZ5's lighting is dim, with blue and red strings of Christmas lights that are reminiscent of a long-since-over New Year's Eve party. But the '80s-ish cherry-red vinyl seating isn't sticky, the disco ball still turns, and crowds show up at happy hour and on weekends after 11pm for DJ beats (house and hip-hop) to kick-start the otherwise dead room. If nobody's here, console yourself with Ms Pac Man.

ENTERTAINMENT & ACTIVITIES

NORTH BEACH

BEACH BLANKET BABYLON
Comedy

☎ 415-421-4222; www.beachblanketbabylon.com; 678 Green St; admission $25-80; ☾ shows 8pm Wed & Thu, 6:30pm & 9:30pm Fri & Sat, 2pm & 5pm Sun; ☒ 45

San Francisco's longest-running musical-cabaret spoofs current events with content that changes so often that stagehands giggle along with the audience. Some personalities seem a little dated (Richard Simmons?), but they're in and out so fast the overall effect is hilarious. And oh! those hats – legendary. Reservations essential; arrive one hour early for best seats. Under-21s admitted only at matinees.

COBB'S COMEDY CLUB
Comedy

☎ 415-928-4320; www.cobbscomedyclub.com; 915 Columbus Ave; admission $10-35 plus 2-drink minimum; ☾ shows 8pm & 10pm; ☒ 15, 45; ☒ Powell-Mason

There's no room to be shy at Cobb's, where bumper-to-bumper shared tables make for an intimate (and vulnerable) audience. The comfy little club loves its local talent, but sometimes hosts big-name national acts. Check the website for shows.

PURPLE ONION
Comedy

☎ 415-956-1653; www.thepurpleonion.viviti.com; 140 Columbus Ave; admission $10-15; ☾ call for show times; ☒ 15, 30, 41, 45

RICK GERHARTER
Comedian Will Durst at the Purple Onion

Such legendary comics as Woody Allen and Phyllis Diller clawed their way up from underground at this grotto nightclub. Recently, comics took back the stage from lackluster lounge acts, and the club's been rejuvenated – Robin Williams has even stopped by to test material. Bookings are sporadic; call ahead.

ENRICO'S
Jazz, Blues & Funk
☎ 415-982-6223; www.enricossf.com; 504 Broadway; admission free; �ും music 7:30-10:30pm; ☐ 12, 20, 30, 45
The last old-school swank joint on Broadway has a big, heated sidewalk patio (ideal for smokers) opening into a white-tablecloth restaurant and bar with swoop-back booths, high cocktail tables, and a baby grand piano. Musical bookings run the gamut from classical guitar to R & B, with local chanteuses singing the Great American Songbook other nights. Shine your shoes.

BIMBO'S 365 CLUB
Rock
☎ 415-474-0365; www.bimbos365club.com; 1025 Columbus Ave; tickets from $20; �ും check calendar; ☐ 30; ☐ Powell-Mason

Rita Hayworth (aka Rita Casino) kicked up her heels in the chorus line at this vintage-1931 club, and Bimbo's still plays it fast and loose with strong drink and live shows by the likes of Zap Mama and Sandra Bernhard. It's not always open, so check the calendar.

SHOPPING
NORTH BEACH
ARIA
Antiques & Collectibles
☎ 415-433-0219; 1522 Grant Ave; �ും 11am-6pm Mon-Sat, noon-5pm Sun; ☐ 15, 30, 41, 45
This shop has all the makings of a Tom Waits song: wartime French love letters returned to senders, anatomical drawings of the heart, castle keys lost in gutters a century ago, a wax mannequin arm raised in ghostly salute. Hours are erratic whenever owner/chief scavenger Bill is out treasure-hunting.

SF ROCK POSTERS & COLLECTIBLES
Antiques & Collectibles
☎ 415-956-6749; www.rockposters.com; 1851 Powell St; �ും 10am-6pm Tue-Sat; ☐ 15, 30; ☐ Powell-Mason

Anyone who hazily remembers the '60s may recall long-lost bands (and brain cells) in this trippy temple to the rock gods. Nostalgia isn't cheap, so expect to pay hundreds or even thousands for first-run psychedelic Fillmore concert posters featuring Big Brother and the Holding Company or the Grateful Dead, but you can still find deals on handbills for the Dead Kennedys and Talking Heads.

Hepcats and slick chicks get their duds at Al's, where vintage styles are reinvented in rocker gabardine, noir-novel twill and philosophical tweeds. Prices aren't exactly bohemian, but recent finds in the sales rack include men's thin-lapel jackets and halter dresses that would make Marilyn Monroe gnash her teeth in envy. Ask about custom orders for weddings and other shindigs.

CUSTOM ORIGINALS (AL'S ATTIRE)
Clothing & Accessories, Local Designer
☎ 415-693-9900; www.alsattire.com; 1314 Grant Ave; ⏰ 11am-7pm Mon-Sat, noon-6pm Sun; 🚌 15, 30, 41, 45

DELILAH CROWN
Clothing & Accessories, Local Designer
☎ 415-765-9060; www.delilahcrown.com; 524 Green St; ⏰ 11am-6:30pm Tue-Sat, noon-5pm Sun; 🚌 15, 30, 41, 45

ANTHONY PIDGEON

Customers browse the City Lights Bookstore

⬊ CITY LIGHTS BOOKSTORE

'Abandon all despair, all ye who enter,' orders the sign by the door to City Lights written by founder and San Francisco poet laureate Lawrence Ferlinghetti. This commandment is easy to follow upstairs in the sunny Poetry Room, with its piles of freshly published verse, a designated Poet's Chair, and literary views of laundry strung across Jack Kerouac Alley. Poetic justice has been served here since 1957, when City Lights won a landmark ruling against book banning, and went on to publish Lenny Bruce, William S Burroughs, Angela Davis and Tahar Ben Jelloun, among others. When you abandon despair, you make more room for books.
Things you need to know: Map p107; ☎ 415-362-8193; http://citylights.com; 261 Columbus Ave; ⏰ 10am-midnight; 🚌 15, 30, 41, 45

The crowning touches to SF style are the screen-printing, pin-tucking and vintage fabrics used in owner Kristina De Pizzol's silver-crown-label designs: patch-pocket skirts with contrasting stitching, yellow shifts with vintage orange buttons, and mushroom-silkscreened T-shirts. Baby minitunics and gypsy skirts make tiny tots look like the charming end results of the Summer of Love.

OOMA Clothing & Accessories, Local Designer
☎ 415-627-6963; www.ooma.net; 1422 Grant Ave; ⏰ 11am-7pm Tue-Sat, noon-5pm Sun; 🚌 15, 30, 41, 45
Feel-good style is what Objects of My Affection is all about: ticklish coral waterfall earrings; springy Poetic License wedges; and locally made, sweatshop-free Del Forte organic denim. Better still, most items are in the affordable double-digit range, including laser-cut wood bubble earrings by local designer Molly M.

LOLA OF NORTH BEACH Gifts, Stationery
☎ 415-781-1817; www.lolaofnorthbeach.com; 1415 Grant Ave; ⏰ 11am-6:30pm Mon-Sat, to 5:30pm Sun; 🚌 15, 30; 🚃 Powell-Mason
Answers to all your SF gifting quandries, from creative souvenirs (ticket stub album for all those cool-looking SF museum tickets) to Silicon Valley baby showers ('my dad's a geek' onesies), plus California-made soy candles that smell like sunshine.

101 MUSIC Music
☎ 415-392-6369; 1414 Grant Ave; ⏰ 10am-8pm Tue-Sat, noon-8pm Sun; 🚌 15, 30, 41, 45
You'll have to bend over those bins to let DJs and hardcore collectors pass (and, hey, wasn't that Carlos Santana?!), but among the $5 to $10 discs are obscure releases (*Songs for Greek Lovers*) and original recordings by Oscar Peterson, Janis Joplin

and, oh yes, Pat Benatar. At the sister shop at 513 Green St, don't bonk your head on the vintage Les Pauls, and check out the sweet turntables that must've cost some kid a year's worth of burger-flipping c 1978.

CHINATOWN

GOLDEN GATE FORTUNE COOKIE COMPANY Food & Drink
☎ 415-781-3956; 56 Ross Alley; admission free; ⏰ 8am-7pm; 🚌 30, 45; 🚃 Powell-Mason, Powell-Hyde
You too can say you made a fortune in San Francisco after visiting this bakery, where cookies are stamped out on old-fashioned presses and folded while hot – just as they were back in 1909, when they were invented in San Francisco for the **Japanese Tea Garden** (p232). You can make your own customized cookies, or pick up a bag of the risqué 'French' fortune cookies – no need to add 'in bed' at the end to make these interesting.

CHINA BAZAAR Gifts
☎ 415-391-6369; 667 Grant Ave; ⏰ 10am-10pm; 🚌 1, 9, 30, 45; 🚃 California, Powell-Mason, Powell-Hyde
Wire racks are perilously overloaded with bargain novelty items in no discernible order, except for the tiki section, which will add some aloha to your home bar. Just when you thought home decor couldn't get any cheaper, check out the ceramics sale section downstairs.

CHINATOWN KITE SHOP Gifts
☎ 415-989-5182; www.chinatownkite.com; 717 Grant Ave; ⏰ 10am-6pm; 🚌 1, 9, 30, 41, 45; 🚃 California, Powell-Mason, Powell-Hyde
Be the star of Crissy Field and wow any kids in your life with a fierce 6ft-long flying shark, a flying panda bear that looks understandably stunned, or 'Pink Floyd,' the goofy pink flamingo (shouldn't that

NORTH BEACH & CHINATOWN

SHOPPING

101 Music (p131)

SABRINA DALBESIO

be a pig, really?). Pick up a papier-mâché two-person lion dance costume, and invite a date to bust some ferocious moves with you next lunar new year.

FAR EAST FLEA MARKET Gifts
☎ 415-989-8588; 729 Grant Ave; ☽ 10am-10pm; ⊟ 1, 9, 30, 45; ⊡ California, Powell-Mason, Powell-Hyde; ⚐

The shopping equivalent of crack, this bottomless store is dangerously cheap and certain to make you giddy and delusional. Of course you can get that sale samurai sword through airport security! There's no such thing as too many bath toys, paper lanterns and bobble-headed Edgar Allen Poe action figures! Step away from the dollar Golden Gate snow globes while there's still time…

CLARION MUSIC CENTER Music
☎ 415-391-1317; www.clarionmusic.com; 816 Sacramento St; ☽ 11am-6pm Mon-Fri, 9am-5pm Sat; ⊟ 1, 9, 30, 45; ⊡ California, Powell-Mason, Powell-Hyde

The minor chords of the *erhu* (Chinese string instrument) will pluck at your heartstrings as you walk through Chinatown's alleyways, and here you can try your hand at the bow yourself with a superior student model. With the impressive range of African congas and Central American marimbas and gongs, you could become your own multiculti one-man band. Check the website for concerts, workshops and demonstrations by masters.

THE HILLS & JAPANTOWN

A   **B**   **C**   **D**

INFORMATION
German Consulate **1** D4

SIGHTS
Anthony Meier Fine Arts **2** D5
Audium **3** E5
Cable Car Museum **4** G4
Cathedral of St Mary of the
   Assumption **5** D6
Cottage Row **6** C5
Diego Rivera Gallery **7** F2
First Unitarian Church **8** E6
Grace Cathedral **9** F4
Haas-Lilienthal House **10** D4
Ikenobo Ikebana Society **11** C6
Ina Coolbrith Park **12** F3
Jack Kerouac's Love Shack **13** E3
Japan Center **14** D6
Konko Temple **15** D5
Lombard Street **16** E2
Macondray Lane **17** F3
Masonic Auditorium **18** G4
Pacific-Union Club **19** G4
Peace Pagoda .... (see 14)
Ruth Asawa Fountains **20** D5
Sterling Park **21** E2

SLEEPING
Fairmont San Francisco **22** G4
Hotel Majestic **23** D5
Hotel Tomo **24** D5
Kabuki Hotel **25** D6
Mark Hopkins Intercontinental .. **26** G4

Nob Hill Hotel **27** F5
Nob Hill Inn **28** G5
Queen Anne Hotel **29** D5

EATING
Acquerello **30** E4
Benkyodo **31** D5
Cheese Plus **32** E4
Nijiya Supermarket **33** C6
Swan Oyster Depot **34** E4
Swensen's **35** E3
Tataki **36** B5
Za **37** E3

DRINKING
Bigfoot Lodge **38** E4
Butterfly Bar .... (see 23)
Cinch **39** E4
Dosa **40** C6
Harry's Bar **41** C5
Top of the Mark **42** G4

ENTERTAINMENT &
ACTIVITIES
Blazing Saddles **43** F2
Boom Boom Room **44** C6
Clay Theater **45** C5
Fillmore Auditorium **46** C6
Kabuki Springs & Spa **47** C6
Lumiere Theater **48** E4
Sundance Kabuki Cinema **49** C6
Yoshi's **50** C6

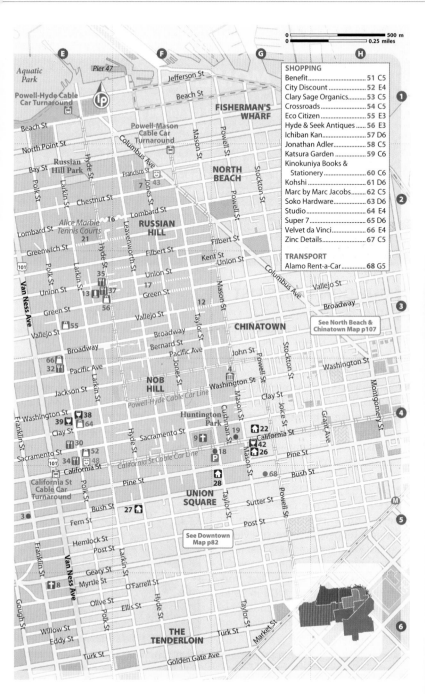

SHOPPING

Benefit	51 C5
City Discount	52 E4
Clary Sage Organics	53 C5
Crossroads	54 C5
Eco Citizen	55 E3
Hyde & Seek Antiques	56 E3
Ichiban Kan	57 D6
Jonathan Adler	58 C5
Katsura Garden	59 C6
Kinokuniya Books & Stationery	60 C6
Kohshi	61 D6
Marc by Marc Jacobs	62 C5
Soko Hardware	63 D6
Studio	64 E4
Super 7	65 D6
Velvet da Vinci	66 E4
Zinc Details	67 C5

TRANSPORT

Alamo Rent-a-Car	68 G5

THE HILLS & JAPANTOWN

HIGHLIGHTS

HIGHLIGHTS

1 HILLTOP MOMENTS

Despite what geologists will try to tell you, the defining feature of San Francisco isn't its 43 distinct hills: it's all the people atop them, gently panting. If the climb doesn't take your breath away on Russian and Nob Hills, the Golden Gate vistas surely will. Nature has been kind to San Francisco, but it takes San Franciscans to make hilltop moments happen, with waltzes, tennis matches, ice cream, art masterpieces and quiet moments of grace.

⤷ OUR DON'T MISS LIST

❶ STERLING PARK

Drivers gunning down Lombard miss spectacular photo-ops of the Golden Gate Bridge through Sterling Park's wind-swept pines. Uphill is the adjacent public court named after San Francisco's Alice Marble, the 1930s tennis champ who recovered from tuberculosis to win Wimbledon and serve as a US secret agent among the Nazis during WWII.

❷ GRACE CATHEDRAL

Grace's staid French Gothic exterior doesn't quite prepare you for its soaring interiors or progressive views. Look for Keith Haring's AIDS Memorial altar of angels taking flight – powerful imagery, since this was his last work before his death from AIDS in 1990. Events held at Grace's indoor labyrinth include meditation services and yoga.

❸ DIEGO RIVERA GALLERY

Master muralist Rivera was a regular in San Francisco from 1930 to 1940, returning to paint several murals, dine in Chinatown and rekindle his romance with Frida Kahlo. Here he paints himself as a hulking figure at the center of the San Francisco scene, which is fair enough – in the decades since, his works have inspired hundreds of murals around town.

Clockwise from top: Grace Cathedral (p141); Lombard Street (p142)

CLOCKWISE FROM TOP: ROBERTO GEROMETTA; ORIEN HARVEY

❹ TOP OF THE MARK

Never mind the menu that features 100 different martinis, or the couples who blissfully waltz past the grand piano: it's the view that'll make you misty. Servers are on standby for proposals and the prenup package: a quiet table and martinis for the happy couple and their lawyers. No wonder this is *Playboy* magazine's favorite bar in San Francisco.

❺ HYDE-POWELL CABLE CAR

Once you've had your fill of downtown destination dining, hop the cable car to the real deal: pizza by the slice (p150) and old-fashioned root-beer floats (p150) with Sterling sunsets.

❶ Sterling Park	❹ Top of the Mark
❷ Grace Cathedral	❺ Hyde-Powell Cable Car
❸ Diego Rivera Gallery	0 ▬▬▬ 200 m
	0 ▬▬▬ 0.1 miles

↘ THINGS YOU NEED TO KNOW

Lombard traffic jams To avoid them, go late morning – or on foot **Garden shortcuts** Flower-lined stairways lead from Hyde & Greenwich to Hyde & Leavenworth and from Macondray Lane to Taylor St **Transportation** To reach Nob Hill, take the Powell-Mason cable car **For full Russian & Nob Hill details, see** p141

HIGHLIGHTS

↘ LOMBARD STREET

Leave it to San Francisco to turn a traffic bottleneck into a joy ride. Model Ts careened down the steep slide of **Lombard** (p142) down Russian Hill until 1922, when eight hairpin turns were added to slow speeders. Now drivers patiently wait their turn to slooooowly round these flower-lined turns – saving reckless moves on Lombard for video games such as Tony Hawk's Pro Skater and Grand Theft Auto.

↘ KABUKI SPRINGS & SPA

Summer and winter aren't so different in San Francisco, but at **Kabuki's communal baths** (p153), you can change seasons yourself, alternating between 170˚F saunas and 55˚F cold plunges. Take your time and your choice of free teas and bath products, and relax, already. Summer fog is no match for treatments including ginger scrubs, private soaking tubs and steam massages.

↘ TATAKI

Satisfy your sushi cravings and your conscience at this trailblazing sustainable **sushi bar** (p151), with skipjack sashimi instead of endangered bluefin and innovative offerings such as 'sea-change salad' (daikon with jellyfish). Get the signature seared, lemon-zested scallops tataki, but don't overlook the vegetarian menu – especially the eggplant ratatouille roll.

↘ PEACE PAGODA

Peace pagodas were raised around the world in the 1960s, commemorating Gandhi in India and victims of war in Hiroshima, but Yoshiro Taniguchi's is a space-age standout. When the 100ft **tower** (p143) was unveiled, the naked concrete seemed shocking. Now it's recognized as a landmark, and commands center stage during the Cherry Blossom Festival (p46).

↘ SUNDANCE KABUKI CINEMA

Robert Redford's **Sundance Institute** (p153) is reinventing movie night, with reserved seating for opening-night blockbusters and year-round film-festival programming. Dinner and a movie means Hawaiian slow-roasted pork sandwiches and craft beer at the balcony bar inside Auditorium 1 – and the popcorn's not bad either.

2 SHANIA SHEGEDYN; 3 FRANKIE FRANKENY; 4 RACHAEL NUSBAUM; 5 SABRINA DALBESIO; 6 RAY LASKOWITZ

2 Lombard Street (p142); 3 Kabuki Springs & Spa (p153); 4 Tataki (p151); 5 Japantown's Peace Pagoda (p143); 6 Sundance Kabuki Cinema (p153)

BEST...

⇲ MUSICAL SENSATIONS

- **Fillmore Auditorium** (p154) Psychedelic rock powerhouse.
- **Yoshi's** (p154) Jazz greats get up close and personal.
- **African Orthodox Church of St John Coltrane** (p146) 'A Love Supreme' kicks off Sunday services.
- **Boom Boom Room** (p154) Blues, no chaser.
- **Audium** (p147) The entire room is an instrument.

⇲ HOME DECOR

- **Kohshi** (p157) Crumpled-paper teacups.
- **Katsura garden** (p157) Tiny, tempest-tossed pines.
- **Super7** (p156) Godzilla galore.
- **Zinc Details** (p158) Ogre pepper mills.
- **Jonathan Adler** (p158) Ceramic Quaalude jars.

⇲ UPLIFTING EXPERIENCES

- **Konko Temple** (p146) High-modernist shrine.
- **Ina Coolbrith Park** (p144) Flowers, panoramas, poetry.
- **Swensen's** (p150) Sundaes atop Russian Hill.
- **Benefit** (p155) Insta-glam eyebrow makeovers.
- **Masonic Auditorium** (p142) Balcony seats at foot-stomping concerts.

⇲ ECO-CONSCIOUS GIFTS

- **Crossroads** (p158) Vintage designer handbags.
- **Studio** (p154) Bookshelves made of classic books.
- **Eco Citizen** (p154) Recycled-gold earrings, made in SF.
- **Velvet da Vinci** (p155) Found-object statement jewelry.
- **Clary Sage Organics** (p156) Yoga tunics in organic California cotton.

ANTHONY PIDGEON

Fillmore Auditorium (p154)

DISCOVER THE HILLS & JAPANTOWN

Hilltop views are the pride of San Francisco, but until the 1870s, only hermits inhabited the windswept 338ft crag of Nob Hill. Once Andrew Hallidie's cable car provided easy summit access, it became prime real estate. But without a windbreak between Nob Hill's mansions, almost all were destroyed in the 1906 earthquake and fire.

Luckily, more greenery was kept intact between Russian Hill's comparatively modest homes. Russian Hill's garden stairway walks remain lined with minuscule playgrounds and hidden cottages with literary merits.

After the Great Quake, many Japanese San Franciscans relocated west of Van Ness to Nihonjinmachi, or 'Japanese people's town.' Following government-mandated internment during WWII, many Japanese Americans were resettled in makeshift Japantown apartments, downhill from Victorian homes they'd once owned. Yet 'Little Osaka' persevered, and today you wouldn't guess Japantown's historic hardships from relentlessly cheerful sushi bar *maneki-neko* (waving-kitty figurines).

Uphill from Japantown, Pacific Heights leads a charmed existence in Victorians the 1906 quake spared. But behind those stately doors are needlepoint Quaalude pillows, tape-art installations, soundscape concerts and classic SF eccentricity.

SIGHTS
RUSSIAN & NOB HILLS
STERLING PARK
www.rhn.org/pointofinterestparks.html; Greenwich & Hyde Sts; 🚌 19, 41, 45, 47, 49, 76; 🚋 Powell-Hyde; ♿

'Homeward into the sunset/Still unwearied we go/Till the northern hills are misty/With the amber of afterglow.' Poet George Sterling's 'City by the Sea' is almost maudlin – that is, until you watch the sunset over the Golden Gate from the hilltop park named in his honor.

Sterling was a great romancer of all San Francisco had to offer, including nature, idealism, free love and occasionally opium, and was frequently broke. But as the toast of the secretive, elite **Bohemian Club** (p90), San Francisco's high society indulged the poet in all his eccentricities, including carrying a lethal dose of cyanide as a reminder of life's transience. Broken by his ex-wife's suicide and the loss of his best friend, novelist Jack London, the 'King of Bohemia' apparently took this bitter dose in 1926 inside his apartment in the club. Within two years his influential friends had this park – with zigzagging paths and stirring, Sterling views – named after him.

GRACE CATHEDRAL
☎ 415-749-6300; www.gracecathedral.org; 1100 California St; except for services, suggested donation for adult/child $3/2; 🕐 7am-6pm Mon-Fri, 8am-6pm Sat, 8am-7pm Sun, services 8:30am & 11am (with choir) Sun; 🚌 1, 27; 🚋 California

This Episcopal church has been rebuilt three times since the Gold Rush, and the current French-inspired, reinforced concrete cathedral took 40 years to complete. But Grace keeps pace with the times. Its commitment to pressing social issues is embodied in its AIDS Memorial Chapel, which has a bronze altarpiece by artist-activist Keith Haring. Grace's spectacular stained-glass windows include a series dedicated to human endeavor, including one of Albert Einstein uplifted in a swirl of nuclear particles. Day and night you'll notice people absorbed in thought while walking the outdoor stone labyrinth, meant to guide restless souls through three stages: releasing, receiving and returning.

DIEGO RIVERA GALLERY
☎ 415-771-7020; www.sfai.edu; 800 Chestnut St; admission free; 🕑 9am-7:30pm; 🚌 30; 🚋 Powell-Mason

---

↘ TRANSPORTATION: RUSSIAN & NOB HILLS

Bus Bus 45 runs along Union St in Russian Hill. Bus 1 runs along Clay and Sacramento Sts in Nob Hill. Polk Gulch is accessible via bus 19, and is one block from Van Ness Ave buses 47 and 49.

Cable car The Powell-Hyde St line skirts the downtown side of Nob Hill, then doglegs to Hyde St, which takes it up Russian Hill. The Powell-Mason St line traces the Downtown side of Nob and Russian Hills. The California St line scales Nob Hill through the heart of the neighborhood.

Parking Street parking can be found by diligently circulating and then pouncing on the first available spot. There's a public lot on Taylor St, opposite the Huntington Hotel.

No, you're not seeing double: Diego Rivera's 1931 *The Making of a Fresco Showing a Building of a City* is a trompe l'oeil fresco within a fresco, showing the artist himself as he pauses to admire his work, as well as the work in progress that is San Francisco. The fresco takes up an entire wall in the Diego Rivera Gallery at the San Francisco Art Institute, on your left through the entryway courtyard. For a memorable 3-D San Francisco vista, head down the corridor to the terrace cafe for espresso and panoramic bay views.

LOMBARD STREET
1000 block btwn Hyde & Leavenworth Sts; 🚋 Powell-Hyde; 🚶
You've seen its eight switchbacks in a thousand photographs. The tourist board has dubbed this 'the world's crookedest street,' which is factually incorrect. Vermont St in Potrero Hill deserves this street cred, but Lombard is (much) more scenic, with its red-brick pavement and lovingly tended flowerbeds. It wasn't always so bent; before the automobile it lunged straight down the hill.

MASONIC AUDITORIUM
☎ 415-776-4702; www.masonicauditorium. com; 1111 California St; 🕑 10am-3pm Mon-Fri; 🚌 1; 🚋 California
Conspiracy theorists, jazz aficionados and anyone exploring immigrant roots should know about Masonic Auditorium. Built as a temple to freemasonry in 1958, the building regularly hosts top jazz acts, such as Wynton Marsalis and the Lincoln Center Jazz Orchestra, and the Preservation Hall Jazz Band. And every other Tuesday morning it hosts mass US-citizenship swearing-in ceremonies.

The modernist stained-glass windows supposedly depict founders of freemasonry in California and their accom-

SABRINA DALBESIO

Diego Rivera Gallery

plishments – that is, if you can decipher the enigmatic symbols and snippets of fabric embedded in the glass. The frieze below the windows has soil and gravel samples from all 58 California counties, plus Hawaii for some reason known only to those in on the secret handshake. Downstairs, a visitors center and art displays reveal some of the society's intriguing secrets.

CABLE CAR MUSEUM

☎ 415-474-1887; www.cablecarmuseum.org; 1201 Mason St; admission free; ⏱ 10am-6pm Apr-Sep, to 5pm Oct-Mar; 🚋 Powell-Mason, Powell-Hyde; ♿

Grips, engines, braking mechanisms… if terms like these warm your gearhead heart, you will be completely besotted with the Cable Car Museum, housed in the city's still-functioning cable-car barn. See three original 1870s cable cars and watch as cables glide over huge bull wheels – as awesome a feat of physics now as when the mechanism was invented by Andrew Hallidie in 1873.

PACIFIC-UNION CLUB

1000 California St; 🚌 1; 🚋 California

The only Nob Hill mansion to survive the 1906 earthquake and fire is a squat neoclassical brownstone, which is a private men's club. The exclusive membership roster lists newspaper magnates, both Hewlett and Packard of Hewlett-Packard, several US secretaries of defense and government contractors (insert conspiracy theory here). Democrats, people of color and anyone under 45 are scarce on the published list, but little else is known about the 800-odd, all-male membership: members can be expelled for leaking information.

JAPANTOWN & PACIFIC HEIGHTS
PEACE PAGODA

Peace Plaza, Japan Center; 🚌 2, 3, 4, 22, 38

When San Francisco's sister city of Osaka, Japan, made a gift of Yoshiro Taniguchi's five-tiered concrete stupa to the people of San Francisco in 1968, the city seemed stupa-fied what to do with the minimalist

THE HILLS & JAPANTOWN

SIGHTS

↘ IF YOU LIKE...

If you like waxing poetic over the views from **Sterling Park** (p141), check out these other hilltop literary locations:

■ **Ina Coolbrith Park** (Vallejo St; ⬚ Powell-Mason) On the San Francisco literary scene, all roads eventually lead to Ina Coolbrith, California's first poet laureate; colleague of Mark Twain and Ansel Adams; mentor of Jack London, Isadora Duncan, George Sterling and Charlotte Perkins Gilman; and lapsed Mormon (she kept secret from her bohemian posse that her uncle was Mormon prophet Joseph Smith). The tiny park is a fitting honor, long on romance and exclamation-inspiring vistas.

■ **Macondry Lane** (btwn Taylor & Leavenworth Sts; ⬚ 41, 45; ⬚ Powell-Mason) This scenic route down from Ina Coolbrith Park via a steep stairway and gravity-defying wooden cottages is so charming that it looks like something out of a novel. And so it is: Armistead Maupin used this as the model for Barbary Lane in his *Tales of the City* series.

■ **Jack Kerouac's Love Shack** (29 Russell St; ⬚ 19, 41, 45, 47, 49, 76; ⬚ Powell-Hyde) This modest house on a quiet alley was the source of major literature and major drama from 1951 to 1952, when Jack Kerouac shacked up with Neal and Carolyn Cassady and their baby daughter to pound out his 120ft-long scroll draft of *On the Road*. Jack and Carolyn became lovers at her husband Neal's suggestion, but Carolyn frequently kicked them both out – though Neal was allowed to move back for the birth of their son John Allen Cassady (named for Jack, and Allen Ginsberg).

monument, and kept clustering boxed shrubs around its stark nakedness. But with some well-placed cherry trees and low, hewn-rock benches in the plaza, the pagoda is finally in its element au naturel.

JAPAN CENTER
www.sfjapantown.org; 1625 Post St; ⊙ 10am-midnight; ⬚ 2, 3, 4, 22, 38
Entering this oddly charming mall is like walking onto a 1960s Japanese movie set – the fake-rock waterfall, indoor wooden pedestrian bridges, rock gardens and curtained wooden restaurant entryways have hardly aged a day since the mall's grand opening in 1968.

RUTH ASAWA FOUNTAINS
Buchanan Pedestrian St; ⬚ 2, 3, 4, 22, 38

Sit inside the fountain, splash around and stay awhile: celebrated sculptor and former WWII internee Ruth Asawa designed these fountains to be lived in, not observed from a polite distance. Bronze origami dandelions sprout from polished-pebble pools, with benches built right in for *bento*-box picnics.

ANTHONY MEIER FINE ARTS
☎ 415-351-1400; www.anthonymeierfinearts.com; 1969 California St; ⊙ 10am-5pm Tue-Fri; ⬚ 1, 2, 3, 4, 22
The toast of international art fairs, Anthony Meier specializes in abstract thinking from major museum artists and emerging talents, from Richard Tuttle's shape-shifting abstract assemblages to lacy, ethereal collages made of transpar-

ent office tape by San Francisco's own Rosana Castrillo Diaz.

IKENOBO IKEBANA SOCIETY

☎ 415-567-1011; Japan Center, 1625 Post St; 🚌 2, 3, 4, 22, 38

Even shoppers hell-bent on iron teapots and *maneki-neko* figurines stop and stare at the arrangements in the windows here. This is the oldest and largest society outside Japan for ikebana, the Japanese art of flower arranging, and has the displays to prove it: a curly willow branch tickling a narcissus under its chin in an abstract *jiyubana* (freestyle) arrangement, and a traditional seven-part Rikka landscape featuring pine and iris.

COTTAGE ROW

off Bush St btwn Webster & Fillmore Sts; 🚌 2, 3, 4, 22, 38

Take a detour to days of yore when San Francisco was a sleepy seaside fishing village, before houses got all uptight, upright and Victorian. Easygoing 19th-century California clapboard cottages hang back along a brick-paved pedestrian promenade and let plum trees and bonsai take center stage. The homes are private, but the minipark is public and ideal for a sushi picnic.

↘ TRANSPORTATION: JAPANTOWN & PACIFIC HEIGHTS

Bus The 38 follows Geary St from Downtown to Japantown. Bus 1 runs up California St to Pacific Heights. Bus 22 runs the length of Fillmore St on its way from the Mission to the Marina.

Cable car The California St line terminates at Van Ness Ave, from where you can take a strenuous seven-block trek up to Fillmore St.

Parking Street parking, while limited, can usually be found on quieter residential streets. There's a parking garage at Japan Center.

SABRINA DALBESIO

Architecture of Cottage Row

KONKO TEMPLE

☎ 415-931-0453; www.konkofaith.org; 1909 Bush St; ⏱ 8am-6pm Mon-Sat, to 3pm Sun; 🚌 2, 3, 4, 22

Inside the low-roofed, high-modernist temple, you'll find a handsome blond-wood sanctuary with a lofty beamed ceiling, vintage photographs of Konko events dating back 70 years, and friendly Reverend Joanne Tolosa, who'll greet you, answer any questions about the temple or its Shinto-based beliefs, and then leave you to your contemplation.

HAAS-LILIENTHAL HOUSE

☎ 415-441-3004; www.sfheritage.org/house .html; 2007 Franklin St; adult/senior & child $8/5; ⏱ noon-3pm Wed & Sat, 11am-4pm Sun; 🚌 1, 12, 19, 27, 47, 49

A grand Queen Anne–style Victorian with its original period splendor c 1882, this family mansion looks like a Clue game come to life – Colonel Mustard could definitely have committed murder with a rope in the dark-wood ballroom, or Miss Scarlet with a candlestick in the red-velvet parlor. One-hour tours are led by volunteer

↘ SAN FRANCISCO'S UNORTHODOX RELIGIOUS ARCHITECTURE

- **First Unitarian Church** (☎ 415-776-4580; www.uusf.org; 1187 Franklin St; ⏱ services 11am Sun; 🚌 38, 49) Low-down and rough around the edges aren't usually meant as compliments, and they're not usually applied to a church. But George Percy's down-to-earth 1888 design for a cathedral in rough-hewn stone was approved by the progressive Universalists, whose current church committees include a pagan interest group and gay marriage advocacy. The 1970-74 annex built by Callister Payne & Rosse is a modernist eye-catcher: a low, concrete-slab building that owes an obvious debt to Frank Lloyd Wright's Unity Temple in Oak Park, Illinois, as well as local Japanese influences appropriate to its location at the edge of Japantown.
- **Cathedral of St Mary of the Assumption** (☎ 415-567-2020; www.stmarycathe dralsf.org; 1111 Gough St; admission free; ⏱ 6:45am-12:10pm Mon-Fri, 6:45am-5:30pm Sat, 7:30am-1pm Sun; 🚌 38, 49) You might assume from afar that this 1971 concrete cathedral is a ship's prow or flying nun's habit. This behemoth started out as a modest proposal by a local architecture firm, but the archbishop read architectural criticism in his spare time and hired MIT guru Pietro Belluschi and Italian engineer Pier-Luigi Nervi to construct this sci-fi Catholic land-mark. Say what you will about the exterior, but the honeycomb ceiling has great acoustics for organ recitals.
- **African Orthodox Church of St John Coltrane** (☎ 415-673-7144; www. coltranechurch.org; 1286 Fillmore St; hmass noon-3pm Sun; 🚌 21, 22, 24) Cymbals shud-der, and the bassist plucks the opening notes of 'A Love Supreme.' The liturgy has begun just as it has every Sunday since 1971, and the entire congregation joins in the three-hour devotional jam session. Overseeing the celebration from mesmerizing icons on the wall is the musician vener-ated here as St John Will-I-Am Coltrane, shown with flames leaping from his saxophone.

docents whose devotion to Victoriana is almost cultish.

AUDIUM

☎ 415-771-1616; www.audium.org; 1616 Bush St; admission $15; ⏳ performances 8:30pm Fri & Sat, arrive by 8:15pm; ☒ 1, 2, 3, 4, 22

Sit in total darkness as Stan Shaff plays his hour-long compositions of sounds emitted by his sound chamber, which sometimes degenerate into 1970s sci-fi sound effects before resolving into oddly endearing Moog synthesizer wheezes. The Audium was specifically sculpted in 1962 to produce bizarre acoustic effects and eerie soundscapes that only a true stoner could enjoy for an hour in the dark – you know who you are.

SLEEPING
RUSSIAN & NOB HILLS

FAIRMONT
SAN FRANCISCO   Historic Hotel $$$

☎ 415-772-5000, 800-441-1414; www.fairmont.com; 950 Mason St; r $199-329; 🚗 California; 🛜

One of the city's most storied hotels, the Fairmont's enormous lobby is decked out with crystal chandeliers, marble floors and towering yellow-marble columns. Rooms sport traditional business-class furnishings, but lack the finer details of a top-end luxury hotel. For maximum character, book a room in the original 1906 building. Tower rooms have great views, but look generic.

MARK HOPKINS
INTERCONTINENTAL   Historic Hotel $$

☎ 415-392-3434, 800-327-0200; www.markhopkins.net; 999 California St; r $169-319; 🚗 California; 🛜

Glistening marble floors reflect glowing crystal chandeliers in the lobby of the 1926 Mark Hopkins, a San Francisco landmark. Detractors call it staid, but its timeless elegance is precisely why others love it. Rooms are done with tasteful furnishings and fabulous beds with Frette linens.

NOB HILL INN   Inn $$

☎ 415-673-6080; www.nobhillinn.com; 1000 Pine St; r $125-165, ste $195-275; 🚗 California; 🛜

Queen Anne Hotel (p148)

ROBERTO GEROMETTA

Situated in a genteel old Edwardian house one block below the top of Nob Hill, the 21 rooms at this inn are classically decorated with antiques, armoires and (some) four-poster beds. It's predominantly a timeshare-hotel, popular with an older crowd (read: quiet). Web specials drop rates as low as $99. Suites sleep four to six and have kitchenettes.

NOB HILL HOTEL Hotel $

☎ 415-885-2987; www.nobhillhotel.com; 835 Hyde St; r $95-135; 🚌 2, 3, 4; 🛜

Rooms in this 1906 hotel have been dressed up in Victorian style, with brass beds and floral-print carpet. The look borders on grandma-lives-here, but it's

Fairmont San Francisco (p147)

RICK GERHARTER

definitely not cookie cutter and service is warm and personable. Rooms on Hyde St are loud; book in back. Wi-fi in lobby.

JAPANTOWN & PACIFIC HEIGHTS

KABUKI HOTEL Theme Hotel $$

☎ 415-922-3200, 800-333-3333; www.jdvhotels .com/hotels/kabuki; 1625 Post St; r $129-249; 🚌 4; 🛜

The Kabuki nods to Japan, with shoji (rice-paper) screens on the windows and bright-orange silk dust ruffles beneath platform beds. The boxy 1960s architecture is plain, but rooms are spacious and we love the deep Japanese soaking tubs and adjoining showers – perfect for a classic Nippon bathing ritual with your lover. Don't miss the lovely bonsai garden off the '60s-modern glass lobby.

HOTEL TOMO Theme Hotel $$

☎ 415-922-3200, 800-333-3333; www.jdvhotels .com/tomo; 1800 Sutter St; r $109-179; 🚌 4; 🛜 ♿

Japanese pop culture informs the look of the Tomo, with big-eyed anime characters blinking on the lobby's TV screens. The blond minimalist room furniture and fatboy beanbags make it feel a bit like a college dorm, but it's great fun for families and anime nuts – if not high-heeled sophisticates.

QUEEN ANNE HOTEL Historic Hotel $$

☎ 415-441-2828, 800-227-3970; www.queen anne.com; 1590 Sutter St; r $99-179, ste $145-229; 🚌 4; 🛜

The Queen Anne occupies a lovely 1890 Victorian mansion, formerly a girls' boarding school. Rooms are comfy (some are tiny) and have a mishmash of antiques; some have romantic wood-burning fireplaces. There's wi-fi in the lobby.

CESAR RUBINO

Hotel Tomo

HOTEL MAJESTIC   Historic Hotel $
☎ 415-441-1100, 800-869-8966; www.thehotel
majestic.com; 1500 Sutter St; r $95-125;
🚌 2, 3, 4; 🛜
The 1902 Hotel Majestic holds a torch for
traditional elegance – even if its edges
are fraying. Rooms are done in dusty-
rose and sage-green, with Chinese porcelain lamps beside triple-sheeted beds,
and while they're showing signs of wear,
we like the stalwart old-school vibe. The
lobby has wi-fi, and the clubby lobby bar
is ideal for a clandestine meeting with
your paramour.

EATING
RUSSIAN & NOB HILLS
Along Hyde and Polk Sts, at the western
edge of Russian and Nob Hills, you'll be
glad you made the climb to prime picnic
spots and neighborhood bistros. These
hilltops add romantic views to the bill of
fare – and if the walk afterwards seems an-
ticlimactic, try leaping aboard a cable car.

RUSSIAN HILL
ACQUERELLO   Californian, Italian $$$
☎ 415-567-5432; www.acquerello.com; 1722
Sacramento St; 🕙 5:30-9:30pm Tue-Sat;
🚌 1, 19, 47, 49, 76; 🚋 California
A converted chapel is a fitting location
for a meal that'll turn Italian culinary
purists into true believers in Cal-Italian
cuisine. 'Oh…my…God…' is the obvious reaction to chef Suzette Gresham's
generous pastas and ingenious seasonal meat dishes, including heavenly
quail salad, devilish lobster *panzerotti*
(stuffed dough pockets in a spicy seafood broth) and venison loin chops. An
anteroom where brides once steadied
their nerves is now lined with limited-
production Italian vintages, which the
sommelier will pair by the glass.

SWAN OYSTER DEPOT   Seafood $$
☎ 415-673-1101; 1517 Polk St; 🕙 8am-5:30pm
Mon-Sat; 🚌 1, 19, 27, 47, 49; 🚋 California
Superior flavor without the superior
attitude of most seafood restaurants.

Tataki

RACHAEL NUSBAUM

The downside is an inevitable wait for the few counter seats, but the upside of the high turnover is unbelievably fresh seafood. On sunny days, place an order to go, browse Polk St boutiques, then breeze past the line to pick up your crab salad with Louie dressing and the obligatory top-grade oysters with mignonette sauce. Hike or take a bus up to the top of Sterling Park for superlative seafood with ocean views.

CHEESE PLUS   Deli $

☎ 415-921-2001; www.cheeseplus.com; 2001 Polk St; 🕑 10am-7:30pm Mon-Sat, to 7pm Sun; 🚌 12, 19, 27, 47, 49, 76, 90

Foodies, rejoice: here's one deli where they won't blink an eye if you say you'd rather have the aged, drunken goat cheese than the plastic provolone on your sandwich. For $8, you can get a salad loaded with oven-roasted turkey and sustainable Niman Ranch bacon, but the specialty is the classic $7 grilled cheese, made with the artisan cheese du jour.

NOB HILL

ZA   Pizza $

☎ 415-771-3100; www.zapizzasf.com; 1919 Hyde St; 🕑 noon-10pm Sun-Wed, to 11pm Thu-Sat; 🚌 41, 45; 🚋 Powell-Hyde

Sit down and savor that slice, already. You don't get a gourmet, cornmeal-dusted, thin-crust slice like this every day. Pizza lovers brave the uphill climb for pizza slices piled with fresh ingredients, a pint of Anchor Steam and a cozy bar setting with flirtatious pizza-slingers – all for under 10 bucks.

SWENSEN'S   Ice Cream $

☎ 415-775-6818; www.swensensicecream.com; 1999 Hyde St; 🕑 noon-10pm Tue-Thu, to 11pm Fri-Sun; 🚌 41, 45; 🚋 Powell-Hyde

Bite into your ice-cream cone, and you'll get instant brain-freeze and a hit of nostalgia besides. Oooh-ouch, that peppermint stick really takes you back, doesn't it? The 16oz root beer floats are the 1950s version of Prozac, but the classic hot fudge sundae is pure serotonin with sprinkles on top.

JAPANTOWN & PACIFIC HEIGHTS

The Japan Center is packed with restaurants, but some of the more intriguing Japanese restaurants can be found along Post St and in the Buchanan Mall, across Post St. Nearby Fillmore St is lined with restaurants that emphasize style over flavor – it's a nice place to shop, but you wouldn't necessarily want to eat there.

TATAKI   Japanese, Sushi $$

☎ 415-931-1182; www.tatakisushibar.com; 2815 California St; ☷ 11:30am-2pm & 5:30-10:30pm Mon-Thu, 11:30am-2pm & 5:30-11:30pm Fri, 5:30-11:30pm Sat, 5-9:30pm Sun; ☐ 1, 2, 4, 24

Pioneering sustainable-sushi chefs Kin Lui and Raymond Ho rescue dinner and the oceans with sustainable delicacies: silky Arctic char drizzled with yuzu-citrus and capers happily replaces at-risk wild salmon, and the Golden State Roll is a local hero, featuring spicy, line-caught scallop, Pacific tuna, organic-apple slivers and edible 24-karat gold leaf.

BENKYODO   Japanese $

☎ 415-922-1244; www.benkyodocompany.com; 1747 Buchanan St; ☷ 8am-5pm Mon-Sat; ☐ 2, 3, 4, 22, 38

Everything you really need in life is within reach of your stool at Benkyodo. The perfect retro lunch counter cheerfully serves an old-school egg-salad sandwich or pastrami for $3.50. Across the aisle are glass cases featuring teriyaki-flavored pretzels and $1 *mochi* (chewy Japanese rice-paste cakes) made in-house daily – come early for popular green tea and chocolate-filled strawberry varieties, but don't be deterred by the savory, nutty lima bean paste.

NIJIYA SUPERMARKET   Japanese, Sushi $

☎ 415-563-1901; www.nijiya.com; 1737 Post St; ☷ 10am-8pm; ☐ 2, 3, 4, 22, 38

Picnic under the Peace Pagoda with sushi or teriyaki *bento* boxes fresh from the deli counter and a swig of Berkeley-brewed Takara Sierra Cold sake from the drinks aisle, and you'll have change from a $20 for mango-ice-cream-filled *mochi*.

RICK GERHARTER

Clay Theater (p153)

DRINKING
RUSSIAN & NOB HILLS

BIGFOOT LODGE   Bar
☎ 415-440-2355; www.bigfootlodge.com; 1750 Polk St; 🕙 3pm-2am; 🚌 1, 19; 🚋 California
Log-cabin walls, antler chandeliers, taxidermy animals everywhere you look – you'd swear you were at a state-park visitors center, but for all the giggly-drunk 20-somethings. If you're looking for your gay boyfriend, he's wandered across the street to the Cinch.

TOP OF THE MARK   Bar
☎ 415-616-6916; www.topofthemark.com; 999 California St; cover $5-10; 🕙 5pm-midnight Sun-Thu, 4pm-1am Fri & Sat; 🚋 California
So what if it's touristy? Nothing beats twirling in the clouds to a full jazz orchestra in your best cocktail dress on the city's highest dance floor. Check the online calendar to ensure a band is playing the night you're coming. Expect $15 drinks.

CINCH   Bar
☎ 415-776-4162; www.thecinch.com; 1723 Polk St; 🕙 9am-2am Mon-Fri, 6am-2am Sat & Sun; 🚌 19, 47, 49
The last of the old-guard Polk St bars is best on Friday nights, when Anna Conda hosts Charlie Horse, the every-mess-was-there drag party. Pool, pinball and free popcorn lure locals from surrounding 'hoods other nights. Smokers patio.

JAPANTOWN & PACIFIC HEIGHTS

BUTTERFLY BAR   Bar
☎ 415-441-1280; www.cafemajesticsf.com; 1500 Sutter St; 🕙 5-11pm, sometimes later weekends; 🚌 2, 3, 4
The Hotel Majestic's intimate 20-seat lounge resembles an elegant library bar in an English manor house, with a gorgeous collection of rare butterflies adorning the walls. Great martinis. Bring a date.

DOSA   Bar
☎ 415-441-3672; http://dosasf.com; 1700 Fillmore St; 🕙 5:30pm-midnight; 🚌 2, 3, 4, 22, 38
Baubled glittering chandeliers hang from high ceilings at Dosa, an otherwise overpriced Indian restaurant with a happening bar scene of sexy, nonsnooty locals.

HARRY'S BAR   Bar
☎ 415-921-1000; 2020 Fillmore St; 🕙 11:30am-2am Mon-Fri, 10am-2am Sat & Sun; 🚌 1, 2
Cap off your upper Fillmore St shopping raid at Harry's mahogany bar with kick-ass Bloody Marys (made properly with horseradish) or freshly muddled *mojitos*.

ENTERTAINMENT & ACTIVITIES
RUSSIAN & NOB HILLS

BLAZING SADDLES   Cycling
☎ 415-202-8888; www.blazingsaddles.com; 1096 Columbus Ave; bikes per hr $7-11, per day $28-68; 🕙 8am-sunset; 🚌 30; 🚋 Powell-Mason; 🚴
Blazing Saddles is tailored to visitors, with a main shop on Columbus Ave and rental stands along Fisherman's Wharf. You can reserve a bike online for a 10% discount, and it includes all the extras (bungee cords, packs etc). But beware the after-hours return: it's a hassle to find the locker Downtown in the dark, and return instructions are complicated.

LUMIERE THEATER   Film
☎ 415-267-4893; www.landmarktheatres.com; 1572 California St; adult/senior, child & matinee $10.50/8; 🚌 19; 🚋 California
Right off Polk St, the rough-at-the-edges Lumiere has one large screening room

HOLGER LEUE

Blazing Saddles

and two smaller rooms, all with seats that need replacing. But we love the programming – a mix of first-run art-house, foreign and documentary films.

JAPANTOWN & PACIFIC HEIGHTS

CLAY THEATER   Film

☎ 415-267-4893; www.landmarktheatres.com; 2261 Fillmore St; adult/senior, child & matinee $10.50/8; 🚌 22

In business since 1913, the single-screen Clay regularly screens a mix of both independent and foreign films. On Saturdays (and occasionally Fridays) at midnight, look for classics such as *Rocky Horror Picture Show*.

SUNDANCE KABUKI CINEMA   Film

☎ 415-929-4650; www.sundancecinemas.com /kabuki.html; 1881 Post St; adult/child/senior $11/8/8.75; 🚌 22, 38

Cinema-going at its best. Reserve a stadium seat, belly up to the bar, and order from the bistro, which serves everything from rib-eye steak to mac 'n' cheese. A

multiplex initiative by Robert Redford's Sundance Institute, Kabuki features bigname flicks, festivals and exclusives – and it's a green venture, with recycled-fiber seating, reclaimed-wood decor and local chocolates and booze. Note: expect a $1 to $3 surcharge for the privilege of seeing a movie not preceded by commercials. Validated parking available.

KABUKI SPRINGS & SPA   Health & Beauty

☎ 415-922-6000; 1750 Geary Blvd; admission Mon-Fri $22, Sat & Sun $25; ⏱ 10am-9:45pm, coed Tue, women only Sun, Wed & Fri, men only Mon, Thu & Sat; 🚌 2, 3, 4, 22, 38

Our favorite urban retreat is a spin on communal Japanese baths. Scrub yourself down with salt in the giant steam room or sauna, then soak in the lovely hot pool before taking a cold plunge. Afterwards, doze off on wooden chaise longues. Quiet is the order of the day: if people get chatty, you need only tap the gong on the water-and-tea table, and all will fall silent. The look is sleek and modern, with wood, tile and low lighting that's sooth-ing after a stressful day. Men and women alternate days, except on Tuesday, when bathing suits are required. Plan two hours minimum; expect a 30 to 60-minute wait at peak times.

BOOM BOOM ROOM   Jazz, Blues & Funk
☎ 415-673-8000; www.boomboomblues.com; 1601 Fillmore St; admission $5-15; ⏱ 4pm-2am Tue-Sun; 🚌 22, 38

Cooking continuously since the '30s, the Boom Boom Room is an authentic relic from the jumping post-WWII years of Fillmore St. Blues, soul and New Orleans funk (and sometimes even gospel) are performed six nights a week, and top touring talent makes frequent stops here. A large dance floor, killer cocktails and cool old photos lining the walls may encourage lingering until 2am. Shows usually start at 9pm.

YOSHI'S   Jazz, Blues & Funk
☎ 415-655-5600; www.yoshis.com; 1300 Fillmore St; ⏱ shows 8pm & sometimes 10pm; 🚌 22, 38

San Francisco's definitive jazz club draws the world's top talent and hosts occa-sional rare appearances by the likes of Nancy Wilson. We suggest advance tick-ets – if you're with a group, we like the round, high-back booths (table numbers 30 to 40), but there's not a bad seat in the house. Make a night of it by show-ing up early for pretty good sushi in the adjoining restaurant.

FILLMORE AUDITORIUM   Rock
☎ 415-346-6000; www.thefillmore.com; 1805 Geary Blvd; admission $20-40; ⏱ box office 10am-4pm Sun, 7:30-10pm show nights; 🚌 2, 3, 4, 22, 38

Jimi Hendrix, Janis Joplin, the Doors – they all played the Fillmore. Now you

might catch the Indigo Girls, Duran Duran or Tracy Chapman in the historic 1250-capacity standing-room theater (if you're polite and lead with the hip, you might squeeze up to the stage). Don't miss the priceless collection of psych-edelic posters in the upstairs gallery.

SHOPPING
RUSSIAN & NOB HILLS
HYDE & SEEK ANTIQUES   Antiques & Collectibles
☎ 415-776-8865; 1913 Hyde St; ⏱ noon-6pm Tue-Sat; 🚌 19, 41, 45; 🚋 Powell-Hyde

Like the home of a long-lost eccentric aunt, this tiny storefront is full of surprises: a briefcase that opens to reveal a full tar-tan bar, a Danish-design silver calla lily, a Native basket more tightly wound than your boss – all at reasonable prices.

ECO CITIZEN   Clothing & Accessories
☎ 415-614-0100; www.ecocitizenonline.com; 1488 Vallejo St; ⏱ 11am-7pm Mon-Sat, noon-6pm Sun; 🚌 1, 19, 47, 49

Idealism meets street chic in this bou-tique of ecofriendly, fair-traded fabulous-ness, from ultraglam gold hemp jeans to Vivienne Westwood T-strap heels made of nontoxic PVC (recyclable onsite). Prices are reasonable and sales a steal – $50 could get you a fair-trade cashmere dress or SF-made Turk+Taylor organic cotton jacket.

STUDIO   Gifts, Local Designer
☎ 415-931-3130; www.studiogallerysf.com; 1815 Polk St; ⏱ 11am-8pm Wed-Fri, to 6pm Sat & Sun; 🚌 1, 19, 47, 49, 76; 🚋 California

Maybe shopping is a substitute for Prozac after all – especially that silver necklace in the shape of a serotonin molecule. Spiff up your pad with locally made arts and crafts at bargain prices, such as Mike Farruggia's altered street sign that cautions 'Beware the Pompitous,' Chiami Sekine's collages of birds tweeting instead of bloggers and Monique Tse's fat-free cupcakes made of blown glass.

CITY DISCOUNT   Housewares

☎ 415-771-4649; 1542 Polk St; ◷ 10am-6pm; 🚍 1, 19, 47, 49, 76; 🚋 California

Bargains never tasted so sweet: heart-shaped Le Creuset casseroles, frighteningly effective Microplane graters, Brika espresso makers and other specialty gourmet gear, all at 30% to 50% off the prices you'd pay Downtown. Hard-to-find appliance replacement parts, parchment paper and cooking tips are all readily available from dedicated foodie counter staff.

VELVET DA VINCI   Jewelry

☎ 415-441-0109; www.velvetdavinci.com; 2015 Polk St; ◷ noon-6pm Tue-Sat, to 4pm Sun; 🚍 12, 19, 47, 49, 76; 🚋 Powell-Hyde

You can actually see the ideas behind these handcrafted gems: Lynn Christiansen puts her food obsessions into a purse that looks like whipped cream, and Enric Majoral's Mediterranean meditations yield rings that appear to be made of sand. Shows here reveal brilliance behind the baubles; during the Ethical Metalsmiths' 'Radical Jewelry Makeover,' the public was invited to bring broken trinkets to be recycled into new jewelry, with sales supporting a campaign for responsible sourcing practices.

JAPANTOWN & PACIFIC HEIGHTS

BENEFIT   Beauty Products, Local Maker

☎ 415-567-0242; 2117 Fillmore St; ◷ 10am-7pm Mon-Wed, 9:30am-7pm Thu & Fri, 9am-6:30pm Sat, 10am-6pm Sun; 🚍 1, 2, 3, 4, 22

Get cheeky with BeneTint, the dab-on liquid blush made from roses, or raise some eyebrows with Brow Zings tinted brow wax – they're two of Benefit's signature products invented in San Francisco by the twin-sister team. Surgery is so LA: in SF, overnight Angelinas swear by LipPlump and Lindsay Lohan dark-eye-circles are cured with Ooh La Lift.

RACHAEL NUSBAUM

Velvet da Vinci

SABRINA DALBESIO

Super7

CLARY SAGE ORGANICS
Beauty Products, Clothing & Accessories
☎ 415-673-7300; www.clarysageorganics.com;
2241 Fillmore St; 🕙 10am-7pm Mon-Sat, 11am-
6pm Sun; 🚍 1, 3, 12, 22, 24
To top off your spa day at **Kabuki Springs
& Spa** (p153), Clary Sage will outfit you
with effortlessly flattering tunics made
from organic Californian cotton; organic
plant-based cleansers and lotions with
light, delectable scents; and homeopathic
flower-essence stress remedies.

KINOKUNIYA BOOKS
& STATIONERY   Books, Stationery
☎ 415-567-7625; 1581 Webster St; 🕙 10:30am-
8pm; 🚍 2, 3, 4, 22, 38
Like warriors in a showdown, the bookstore, stationery and manga divisions of
Kinokuniya compete for your attention.
Only you can decide where your loyalties
lie: with stunning photography books and
Harajuku fashion mags upstairs; vampire
comics downstairs; or the stationery department's *washi* paper, supersmooth
Sakura gel pens and pig notebooks with

the motto 'what lovely friends*they will
bring happy.'

SUPER7   Clothing & Accessories, Local Designer
☎ 415-409-4701; www.super7store.com; 1628
Post St; 🕙 noon-7pm Mon-Thu, noon-8:30pm Fri,
11am-8:30pm Sat, 11am-7pm Sun; 🚍 2, 3, 4, 38
After tiresome T-shirt trends of self-
promotion ('Porn Star') and retro-irony
('Virginia is for Lovers'), it's a shock to
find piles of limited-edition T-shirts this
original. 'Superterrific Animal Friendlies'
announces one Super7 T-shirt with an unlikely superhero team of cuddly owls, bats
and monkeys; 'Martial Art Garfunkel' pro-
claims another, with the 'Mrs Robinson'
crooner striking a karate pose. Godzilla
fans cannot miss the selection of rare action figures here.

MARC BY
MARC JACOBS   Clothing & Accessories
☎ 415-447-9322; www.marcjacobs.com; 2142
Fillmore St; 🕙 11am-7pm; 🚍 1, 2, 3, 4, 22
The USA's hippest designer usually
charges prices to match, but here along-

THE HILLS & JAPANTOWN

SHOPPING

side the $800 satchels and $300 flip-flops are bins of accessories under $25: $6 chunky resin bangles, $14 yellow belts and limited-edition $24 clutches with funky designs by SF's own **Creativity Explored** (p168).

SOKO HARDWARE
DIY, Housewares

☎ 415-931-5510; 1698 Post St; ☺ 9am-5:30pm Mon-Sat; 🚌 2, 3, 4, 22, 38

Cover all your San Francisco contingencies: window wipes (for fog), duct tape (for earthquakes), paper lanterns (to disguise those awkward Victorian chandeliers) and a rice cooker (because soggy rice is a culinary crime in SF). Ikebana, bonsai, tea ceremony and Zen rock-garden supplies are all here at fair prices.

KATSURA GARDEN
Flowers & Gardens

☎ 415-931-6209; 1581 Webster St; ☺ 10am-5:30pm Mon-Sat, 11am-5pm Sun; 🚌 2, 3, 4, 22, 38

When you're in the mood for a little something special, try a bonsai. Katsura Garden can set you up with a miniature juniper that looks like it grew on a windswept molehill, or a stunted maple that will shed five tiny, perfect red leaves this autumn.

ICHIBAN KAN
Gifts

☎ 415-409-0472; 22 Peace Plaza, Suite 540; ☺ 10:30am-8pm; 🚌 2, 3, 4, 22, 38

Really, it's a wonder you got this far in life without penguin soy-sauce dispensers, chocolate-covered pretzel 'Men's Pocky,' extra-spiky Japanese hair wax, soap dishes with feet, and the ultimate in gay gag gifts, the handy 'Closet Case' – all for under $5.

KOHSHI
Gifts

☎ 415-931-2002; www.kohshisf.com; 1737 Post St, Suite 335; ☺ 11am-7pm Tue-Sun

Let's be honest: San Francisco fog smells better when gently scented by Japanese incense. Here you'll find fragrant sticks for every purpose, from long-burning sandalwood for meditation to cinnamon-tinged Gentle Smile to atone for laundry left too long, plus lovely gift ideas: gentle charcoal soap, cups that look like crumpled paper, and purple Daruma figurines for making wishes.

RICK GERHARTER

Zinc Details (p158)

JONATHAN ADLER   Housewares

☎ 415-563-9500; www.jonathanadler.com;
2133 Fillmore St; ⏰ 11am-7pm Mon-Sat, noon-
6pm Sun; 🚌 1, 2, 3, 4, 22

Vases with handlebar mustaches and
cookie jars labeled 'Quaaludes' may seem
like holdovers from a Big Sur bachelor pad
c 1974, but they're the latest snappy interior inspirations from California pop potter
Jonathan Adler. Don't worry whether that
leather pig footstool matches your mid-
century couch – as Adler says, 'Minimalism
is a bummer.'

ZINC DETAILS   Housewares

☎ 415-776-2100; www.zincdetails.com; 1905
Fillmore St; ⏰ 11am-7pm Mon-Sat, noon-6pm
Sun; 🚌 2, 3, 4, 22, 38

Pacific Heights chic meets Japantown mod
at Zinc Details, with orange lacquerware

salad-tossers, a Rondo sake dispenser that
looks like a Zen garden boulder and bird-
shaped Alessi soy dispensers. If you can't
find what you need here, try up the street
at Zinc's 2410 California St location.

CROSSROADS   Vintage Clothing & Accessories

☎ 415-775-8885; www.crossroadstrading.com;
1901 Fillmore St; ⏰ 11am-7pm Mon-Thu, 11am-
8pm Fri & Sat, noon-7pm Sun; 🚌 1, 2, 3, 4, 22

Pssst, fashionistas: you know those designers you see lining Fillmore St? Many
of their creations can be found used at
Crossroads for a fraction of retail, thanks
to Pacific Heights clotheshorses who tire
of clothes fast and can't be bothered to
hang onto receipts. For even better deals,
trade in your own old stuff and browse
the half-price rack.

MISSION, SOMA & CASTRO

INFORMATION

American Express	1	E1
Australian Consulate	2	E1
Japanese Consulate	3	E1
Lyon-Martin Women's Health Services	4	B4
Mexican Consulate	5	E2
San Francisco General Hospital	6	D6

SIGHTS

Balmy Alley	7	C7
Cartoon Art Museum	8	E2
Catharine Clark Gallery	9	E2
Contemporary Jewish Museum	10	D2
Corona Heights Park	11	A5
Eleanor Harwood Gallery	12	D7
Electric Works	13	C3
Galería de la Raza	14	D6
Golden Gate Model Railroad Club	(see 19)	
Hosfelt Gallery	15	D3
Museum of Craft and Folk Art	16	D2
Museum of the African Diaspora	17	D2
Potrero del Sol/La Raza Skatepark	18	D7
Randall Junior Museum	19	A5
Ratio 3	20	B4
SFMOMA (San Francisco Museum of Modern Art)	21	E2
Zeum	22	D2

SLEEPING

Americania Hotel	23	D3
Hotel Vitale	24	E1
Inn San Francisco	25	C6
Mosser Hotel	26	D2
St Regis Hotel	(see 9)	
W Hotel	27	E2

EATING

Boulevard	28	E1
Butler & the Chef	29	E3
Home	30	B4
Humphry Slocombe	31	C6
Mission Beach Cafe	32	B4
Rainbow Grocery	33	C4
Salt House	34	E2
Sentinel	35	D2
Tropisueño	36	D2
Tu Lan	37	D3

Waterbar	38	F1

DRINKING

Blackbird	39	B5
Bloodhound	40	D3
Brainwash	41	D3
Butter	42	C4
Farley's	43	E5
Wild Side West	44	C8
Zeitgeist	45	B4

HIGHLIGHTS

1   MISSION MURALS

Diego Rivera has no idea what he started. Inspired by murals by the Mexican maestro's Depression-era works in San Francisco, generations of Mission muralists have covered neighborhood alleys and community institutions with protest, pride, angst and bad-ass graffiti attitude. Barflys can be merciless in these streets, relieving themselves even on notable works by muralists who've gone on to become art stars – but when historic Balmy Alley works are tagged, muralists carefully restore them.

↘ OUR DON'T MISS LIST

❶ BALMY ALLEY
When 1970s *muralistas* disagreed with US foreign policy in Latin America they took to the streets with paintbrushes in hand – beginning with Balmy Alley garage doors. You can still see original works in Balmy Alley dating as far back 1971, thanks to careful upkeep by **Precita Eyes** (p294).

❷ GALERÍA DE LA RAZA DIGITAL MURAL PROJECT
Instead of the usual cigarette advertisements, the billboard at 24th and

Bryant is reserved for provocative non-commercial messages such as 'Trust Your Struggle,' and stop-and-think imagery such as Artemio Rodriguez' *El Muerto* lowrider, tricked out to honor those lost to Hurricane Katrina and war.

❸ WOMEN'S BUILDING MAESTRA-PEACE
An all-star team of *muralistas* covered this home of women's community nonprofits with icons of female strength, from Mayan and Chinese goddesses to modern trailblazers:

Clockwise from top: Edythe Boone's 1995 mural *Those We Love, We Remember*, Balmy Alley (p167); Clarion Alley (p168)

CLOCKWISE FROM TOP: ANTHONY PIDGEON; SABRINA DALBESIO

you'll spot Rigoberta Menchu on the front, and Hanaan Ashrawi and former US Surgeon-General Dr Jocelyn Elders on the building's left flank.

❹ CHRIS WARE AT 826 VALENCIA

The literary nonprofit and Pirate Supply Store is fittingly topped with bookish booty: a gold-leafed mural celebrating human attempts (and the occasional failure) to communicate. You might recognize Ware's meticulous style from his graphic novel *Jimmy Corrigan, Smartest Kid on Earth*, which helped make him the first comics artist included in the Whitney Biennial.

❺ CLARION ALLEY

Incontinent art critics have taken over the east end; the less aromatic, more intricate murals are on the west.

❶ Balmy Alley
❷ Galería de la Raza Digital Mural Project
❸ Women's Building
❹ Chris Ware at 826 Valencia
❺ Clarion Alley

0 ———— 400m
0 ———— 0.1 miles

☚ THINGS YOU NEED TO KNOW

More murals Local muralists lead tours of 50-plus Mission murals by foot or bike through Precita Eyes Mission Mural Tours (p294) **Día de los Muertos** Parade starts from Balmy Alley each November 2 (p49) **Transportation** BART to Mission & 16th or 24th Sts **For full Mission mural details, see** p167

HIGHLIGHTS

2

↘ SFMOMA

The **San Francisco Museum of Modern Art** (SFMOMA; p170) moved into its showplace in 1995, and began featuring new-media art right from the beginning of the tech boom. Now, with a donation of 1100 modern works from the founders of the Gap and a $480 million expansion underway, the SFMOMA can finally accommodate all its riches and emerging niches.

3

↘ CASTRO THEATRE

Arrive early, because the show at the **Castro** (p174) begins even before the red velvet curtains part. As you gape at the chinoiserie deco dome, the mighty Wurlitzer suddenly rises from the orchestra pit below and strikes up classic show tunes. The crowd hums along, but bursts into hoots and roars at the anthem that signals the start of every movie: the theme from the movie *San Francisco*.

4

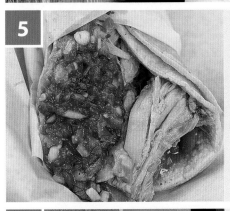

↘ YERBA BUENA CENTER FOR THE ARTS

San Francisco loves its spectacles, and **YBCA** (p187) keeps them coming in vast galleries and theaters built for big thinking and grand gestures – indoor Ferris wheels, video art and acrobatic dance are all on the bill. At openings and fundraisers here, San Francisco freak levels hit new highs.

5

↘ BURRITOS

This is the real deal. Your choice of beans (pinto, black or refried), meats (grilled or stewed) and salsas (fresh chopped *pico de gallo*, tangy green tomatillo, smoky mesquite or spicy mango) are loaded onto a flour tortilla and rolled into an enormous, tasty package at dozens of taquerias in the Mission.

6

↘ CARTOON ART MUSEUM

Introducing this **museum** (p171) to comics fans would be an insult – please, like you don't already know about its Batman retrospectives, or shows of original puppets from *Fantastic Mr. Fox*. But even fanboys will learn something from lectures about 1930s efforts to unionize overworked animators, and shows on underground comics legends.

2 RAY LASKOWITZ; 3 CHRISTIAN ASLUND; 4 RICHARD CUMMINS; 5 SABRINA DALBESIO; 6 SABRINA DALBESIO

2 Interior of SFMOMA (p170); 3 Castro Theatre (p174); 4 View from Yerba Buena Center for the Arts (p187); 5 Chicken taco from La Taqueria (p177); 6 Lobby of the Cartoon Art Museum (p171)

BEST...

➘ FOOD WITH CULT FOLLOWINGS

- **La Taqueria** (p177) Burritos for purists.
- **Delfina** (p176) Organic chicken and olive-oil mashed potatoes.
- **Bi-Rite** (p177) Salted caramel ice cream.
- **Sentinel** (p178) Corned beef and cabbage sandwiches with Russian dressing.
- **Hot Cookie** (p181) Food porn, literally: note signed porn-star underwear.

➘ BREAKOUT PERFORMANCES

- **Slim's** (p188) Small venue, big names.
- **Yerba Buena Center for the Arts** (p187) Dance and performance art.
- **Marsh** (p185) True stories, one-acts and solo shows.
- **Bottom of the Hill** (p185) Alt-rockers get the room bouncing.

➘ THEME NIGHTS

- **El Rio** (p182) Hard French Saturdays: soul on vinyl and backyard barbecue.
- **Make-Out Room** (p185) Mortifying: actual teen journals are read aloud.
- **Verdi Club** (p186) Tango Thursdays.
- **QBar** (p184) Wednesday is Booty Call for the boys: truth in advertising.

➘ PLACES TO WATCH & LEARN

- **Oberlin Dance Collective** (p183) Polished modern dance and classes.
- **Zeum** (p172) DIY videos, animation and technology.
- **Potrero del Sol/La Raza Skatepark** (p170) Grind, grab, kick-flip…or just watch.
- **Yoga Tree** (p185) From downward dog to arms-free headstands.
- **Roccapulco Supper Club** (p186) Features salsa with big-band backing.

SABRINA DALBESIO

La Taqueria (p177), Mission District

DISCOVER MISSION, SOMA & CASTRO

San Franciscans love to show off the Mission District as proof of their hipness, and are itching for you to ask: what kind of neighborhood is this, anyway? This is a trick question. Latinos, lesbians, star chefs, street artists, designers, activists, punks and suits all play featured roles in the Mission's avant-garde ensemble act.

Wander *South* of *Ma*rket St (hence the acronym) to find a neighborhood that's enjoying a rowdy, experimental second adolescence. If cutting-edge art shows in Yerba Buena Arts District strike you as risqué, wait until you check out the nightlife around Folsom St.

The Castro is where the Mission ends, SoMa club kids settle down, and the giant rainbow flag flies over Harvey Milk Plaza – named for the Castro entrepreneur who became the first openly gay man elected to US public office. Today there's no better place than the Castro to be out, proud and thirsty: landmark Gay/Lesbian/Bi/Trans (GLBT) bars and cafes line Castro, 18th and Market Sts.

SIGHTS
THE MISSION
BALMY ALLEY Map p160
btwn 24th & 25th Sts; 🚌 9, 27, 33, 48; 🚇 24th St Mission

Balmy Alley features historic early works by muralist groups such as the Mujeres Muralistas (Women Muralists) and Placa (meaning 'mark-making') transforming fences and garages into artistic statements. On November 2, the annual Mission parade **Día de los Muertos** (Day of the Dead; p49) begins here.

826 VALENCIA Map p168
☎ 415-642-5905; www.826valencia.com; 826 Valencia St; 🕑 noon-6pm; 🚌 14, 26, 33, 49; ♿
'No buccaneers! No geriatrics!' warns the sign above the vat of sand where kids gleefully rummage for buried pirates' booty. This eccentric nonprofit Pirate Supply Store selling eye patches, scoops from an actual tub o' lard, and

McSweeney's literary magazines is the front for a nonprofit offering free writing workshops and tutoring for youth, plus the occasional adult program on starting a magazine and scripting video games (check website for listings).

MISSION DOLORES Map p168
☎ 415-621-8203; www.missiondolores.org; 3321 16th St; adult/senior & child $5/3, audio tour $5; 🕑 9am-4pm Nov-Apr, to 4:30pm May-Oct; 🚌 14, 22, 33, 49, J; 🚇 16th St Mission

The city's oldest building and its namesake, the Misión San Francisco de Asis, was founded in 1776 and rebuilt in 1782 with conscripted Ohlone labor in exchange for a meal a day – note the ceiling patterned after Native baskets. With harsh living conditions and little resistance to introduced diseases, some 5000 Ohlone died in Mission measles epidemics in 1814 and 1826.

Today, the modest adobe mission is overshadowed by the adjoining ornate

MISSION, SOMA & CASTRO

SIGHTS

Churriguera-esque basilica, built in 1913 after an 1876 brick Gothic cathedral collapsed in the 1906 earthquake. The choir windows show St Francis beaming beatifically against an orange background, and lower windows along the nave feature the 21 California missions from Santa Cruz to San Diego and mission builders Father Junípero Serra and Father Francisco Palou.

CLARION ALLEY Map p168

btwn 17th & 18th Sts, off Valencia St; ▣ 14, 22, 26, 33, 49; ◉ 16th St Mission

Trial by fire is nothing compared with Clarion Alley's street-art test: unless a piece is truly inspired, it's going to get peed on or painted over. Very few pieces survive for years – Andrew Schoultz' mural of gentrifying elephants displacing scraggly birds, a silhouette of kung-fu-fighting female anarchists that makes Charlie's Angels look like chumps, and a trompe l'oeil escalator.

CREATIVITY EXPLORED Map p168

☎ 415-863-2108; www.creativityexplored.org; 3245 16th St; donations welcome; ⏱ 10am-

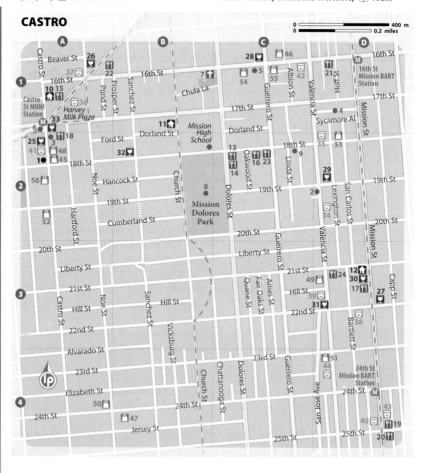

CASTRO

0   400 m
0   0.2 miles

3pm Mon-Fri, until 7pm Thu, 1-6pm Sat; 🚌 14, 22, 33, 49, J; 🚇 16th St Mission

Brave new worlds are captured in celebrated artworks that have appeared in museum retrospectives, major collections, even on Marc Jacobs clutches (see p156) – all by local developmentally disabled artists. Intriguing themed shows reveal fresh perspectives on themes ranging from jazz to alien life forms, and openings are joyous celebrations with the artists and their families.

MISSION DOLORES PARK Map p168

Dolores St, btwn 18th & 20th Sts; 🚌 14, 22, 33, 49, J; 🚇 16th St Mission; ♿

The site of quasi-professional Castro tanning contests, a small kids' playground, free theater and movies in summer and a Hunky Jesus Contest every Easter, this sloping park is also beloved for its year-round political protests and tennis courts and its basketball hoops that are open to all.

↘ TRANSPORTATION: THE MISSION & POTRERO HILL

BART Stations at 16th and 24th Sts serve the Mission.

Bus Line 14 runs along Mission St from Downtown. Bus 49 follows Van Ness Ave and Mission St, while the 33 links Potrero and the Mission to the Castro, the Haight, Golden Gate Park and the Richmond. The 22 connects Potrero Hill and the Mission to the Haight, Japantown, Pacific Heights and the Marina.

Streetcar The J streetcar passes through the Mission, stopping at Mission Dolores Park on its way from Downtown to Noe Valley. The T Muni line from Downtown via SoMa stops along 3rd St between 16th and 22nd, in Potrero's Dogpatch district.

CASTRO

INFORMATION
Walgreens **1** A2

SIGHTS
826 Valencia **2** D2
Castro Theatre **3** A2
Clarion Alley **4** D1
Creativity Explored **5** C1
Harvey Milk Plaza **6** A1
Mission Dolores **7** B1
Mission Dolores Park **8** B2
Women's Building **9** C2

SLEEPING
Inn on Castro **10** A1
Parker Guest House **11** B1
San Francisco Elements **12** D3

EATING
Bi-Rite **13** C2
Bi-Rite Creamery **14** C2
Catch **15** A1
Delfina **16** C2
Foreign Cinema **17** D3
Hot Cookie **18** A2
La Taqueria **19** D4

Mission Pie **20** D4
Pancho Villa **21** D1
Range .... (see 2)
Sushi Time **22** A1
Tartine **23** C2
Udupi Palace **24** D3

DRINKING
440 Castro **25** A2
Cafe Flore **26** A1
Doc's Clock **27** D3
Elixir **28** C1
Lexington Club **29** D2
Medjool Sky Terrace **30** D3
Ritual Coffee Roasters **31** D3
Samovar Tea Lounge **32** B2
Twin Peaks Tavern **33** A1

ENTERTAINMENT & ACTIVITIES
Amnesia **34** D2
Elbo Room **35** D2
Gold's Gym **36** A1
Lookout **37** A1
Make-Out Room **38** D3
Marsh **39** D3

Mission Cultural Center for
   Latino Arts **40** D4
Qbar **41** A2
Roxie Cinema **42** C1
Savanna Jazz **43** D4
Yoga Tree **44** D4

SHOPPING
A Different Light Bookstore **45** A2
Adobe Books & Backroom
   Gallery **46** C1
Ambiance **47** B4
Cliff's Variety **48** A2
Dema **49** D3
Global Exchange Fair Trade
   Craft Center **50** A4
Good Vibrations **51** D4
Human Rights Campaign
   Action Center **52** A2
Mission Statement **53** D2
Needles & Pens **54** C1
Paxton Gate .... (see 2)
Sunhee Moon **55** C1
Under One Roof **56** A2

WOMEN'S BUILDING Map p168

☎ 415-431-1180; www.womensbuilding.org; 3543 18th St; ☒ 14, 26, 33, 49, J; ⊕ 16th St Mission

The nation's first female-owned-and-operated community center has been quietly doing good work with 170 women's organizations since 1979, but the 1994 addition of the *Maestra-peace* mural showed this building for the landmark that it truly is.

POTRERO DEL SOL/
LA RAZA SKATEPARK Map p160

www.sfgov.org; 25th & Utah Sts; ☒ 9, 27, 33, 48; ⊕ 24th St Mission

An isolated, scrubby park that had been abandoned to gangs became NorCal's hottest urban skatepark in 2008 with support from the city's Park and Rec department. Day and night under strategically placed lights, newbies and pros blast ollies off the hip of these concrete bowls. For gear, hit up **Mission Skateboards** (p191).

GALERÍA DE LA RAZA Map p160

☎ 415-826-8009; www.galeriadelaraza.org; 2857 24th St; admission free; ☽ noon-6pm Wed-Sat, to 7pm Tue; ☒ 9, 27, 33, 48; ⊕ 24th St Mission

Art never forgets its roots at this showcase for Latino art since 1970. Witness Salvadoran Victor Cartagena's *Invisible Nation* installation of found ID photos, a group show exploring SF's Latin gay culture and David Bacon's portraits of indigenous Mexican migrant laborers.

SOMA

SFMOMA Map p160

☎ 415-357-4000; www.sfmoma.org; 151 3rd St; adult/child under 13yr/student & senior $18/free/9, 6-8:45pm Thu half-price, 1st Tue of month free; ☽ 11am-5:45pm Mon-Tue & Fri-Sun, to 8:45pm Thu, from 10am Jun-Sep; ☒ 6, 14, 21, 31, 71, F, J, K, L, M, N; ☒ & ⊕ Montgomery St

San Francisco Museum of Modern Art (SFMOMA) was destined from the start in 1935 to be an eclectic, unconventional

SABRINA DALBESIO

Galería de la Raza

⤵ TRANSPORTATION: SOMA

Bus Buses run up and down most streets. The 30 and 45 lines run down 4th St from Union Square. The 14 runs to the Mission District along Mission St.

Cable car The Powell St turnaround is at Market St, just two blocks from Yerba Buena Gardens.

Streetcar All of the Market St streetcars serve the upper part of SoMa. The N and T lines head south along the Embarcadero.

Parking The garage at 5th and Mission Sts is one block from Yerba Buena Gardens. Street parking can be surprisingly difficult, especially near nightclubs.

museum. But when it moved into architect Mario Botta's light-filled brick box in 1995, it became clear just how far this museum was prepared to push the art world. The new museum showed its backside to New York and leaned full-tilt toward the western horizon, taking risks on then-unknowns such as Matthew Barney and his poetic videos involving industrial quantities of Vaseline, and Olafur Eliasson's outer-space installations that distort all sense of reality.

But one constant is SFMOMA's standout photography collection, which got the jump-start on other museums with works by Ansel Adams, Edward Weston, Robert Frank, Dorothea Lange and William Klein, and has continued acquiring compelling contemporary works to keep the collection fresh. The 3rd-floor photography galleries are the place to begin, then up through the 4th- and 5th-floor major-contemporary exhibits, catching your breath outdoors at the 5th-floor rooftop sculpture garden. Tack on additional time for the excellent SFMOMA shop.

CARTOON ART MUSEUM Map p160
☎ 415-227-8666; www.cartoonart.org; 655 Mission St; adult/child under 6yr/child 6-12yr/student & senior $7/free/3/5, 1st Tue of month is 'pay what you wish' day; 🕙 11am-5pm Tue-Sun; 🚌 6, 14, 21, 31, 71, F, J, K, L, M, N; 🚇 & 🅼 Montgomery St

Comics fans need no introduction to the permanent collection here – think John Romita's amazing *Spiderman* cover drawings, or Edward Gorey's sketches for *Gashlycrumb Tinies,* starting with 'A is for Amy who fell down the stairs/B is for Basil assaulted by bears…' Founded on a grant from Bay Area cartoon legend Charles M Schultz of *Peanuts* fame, this bold museum isn't afraid of the dark, racy or political, including R Crumb drawings from the '70s and a show not so long ago featuring painfully funny cartoon satires of the US from Middle Eastern newspapers. Lectures and openings are rare opportunities to mingle with comic legends, Pixar studio heads and obsessively knowledgeable collectors.

CONTEMPORARY JEWISH MUSEUM
Map p160

☎ 415-344-8800; www.thecjm.org; 736 Mission St; adult/child under 18yr/senior & student $10/free/8, after 5pm Thu $5; 🕙 11am-5pm Fri-Tue, 1-8pm Thu; 🚌 6, 14, 21, 31, 71, F, J, K, L, M, N; 🚇 & 🅼 Montgomery St

Before Daniel Libeskind signed on to design New York's much-debated September 11 memorial, his design for this museum was already causing a stir in SF, with its blue-steel cladding and shape drawn from the Hebrew word *l'chaim,* 'to life' – a fine idea in theory, but one best appreciated

MISSION, SOMA & CASTRO

SIGHTS

Museum of the African Diaspora

RICK GERHARTER

from a helicopter. The steel structure incorporates the brick facade of the Jesse St Power substation, an 1881 industrial structure rather oddly ornamented with cream-colored cherubs and garlands. The exhibits inside are impeccably curated, compelling and heavy-hitting. Recent shows have included Warhol's Jews: Ten Portraits Reconsidered – their West Coast premier – and vintage Russian Jewish theater posters from 1919 to 1949, the years when Marc Chagall joined forces with theater people in the former Soviet Union.

MUSEUM OF CRAFT AND
FOLK ART Map p160
☎ 415-227-4888; www.mocfa.org; 51 Yerba Buena Lane; adult/under 18yr/senior $5/free/4; ☽ 11am-6pm Mon, Tue, Thu, Fri, to 5pm Sat

& Sun; 🚌 6, 14, 21, 31, 71, F, J, K, L, M, N; 🚈 & 🅜 Montgomery St
Vicarious hand cramps are to be expected from a trip to this museum, where amazing handiwork comes with fascinating backstories. Recent shows explored historic handmade ukuleles, four generations of African American quilt makers, and parallel lines in Scandinavian and Californian modernist furniture.

MUSEUM OF THE
AFRICAN DIASPORA Map p160
☎ 415-358-7200; www.moadsf.org; 685 Mission St; adult/child under 12yr/student & senior $10/free/5, Tue admission free; ☽ 11am-6pm Wed-Sat; 🚌 6, 14, 21, 31, 71, F, J, K, L, M, N; 🚈 & 🅜 Montgomery St
A three-faced divinity by Ethiopian icon painter Qes Adamu Tesfaw, a stereotype in silhouette by American Kara Walker, a regal couple by British sensation Chris Ofili: this museum has assembled a standout international cast of characters to tell the epic story of diaspora. Memorable recent shows include selections from the Bamako photography biennial and 'Africa .Dot.Com,' a show of digital technology in traditional African arts.

ZEUM Map p160
☎ 415-820-3320; www.zeum.org; 221 4th St; adult/child under 2yr/student & child $10/free/8; ☽ 1-5pm Wed-Fri, 11am-5pm Sat & Sun, 11am-5pm daily summer; 🚌 30, 45; 🚈 & 🅜 Powell St; ♿
No velvet ropes or hands off here: kids have the run of the place, with high-tech displays that double dare them to make their own music videos, claymation movies and soundtracks. Jump right into a live-action video game, and sign up for workshops with the Bay Area's superstar animators, techno-whizzes, robotbuilders and belly dancers.

THE CASTRO & NOE VALLEY

HARVEY MILK PLAZA Map p168

Market & Castro Sts; 🚌 24, 33, F, Castro St

The first thing you'll notice as you emerge from the Castro St Muni station is a huge, irrepressibly cheerful rainbow flag. Gay kids too young for the bars sit on the wall beneath; look closer and you'll notice a plaque honoring the man whose lasting legacy to the Castro is civic pride and political clout.

CORONA HEIGHTS PARK Map p160

bounded by 16th St & Roosevelt Way; 🚌 24, 37, F, Castro St

Urban hikers scramble up the rocky, 520ft summit of Corona Heights (aka Museum Hill or Red Rocks) for jaw-dropping eastward 180-degree views. Near the summit is the family-ready **Randall Junior Museum** (Map p160; ☎ 415-554-9600; www. randallmuseum.org; admission free; ⏰ 10am-5pm Tue-Sat; ♿), with live-animal exhibits and hands-on workshops (check the web);

⬇ IF YOU LIKE...

If you like seeing ahead of the art curve at **SFMOMA** (p170), check out the artistic breakthroughs at these SF galleries:

- **Catharine Clark Gallery** (Map p160; ☎ 415-399-1439; www.cclarkgallery.com; 150 Minna St; admission free; ⏰ noon-6pm Tue-Sat; 🚌 & Ⓜ Montgomery St) This gallery shows fearless, risqué visions, including Travis Somerville's altered class photos of California high-school students in Ku Klux Klan hoods, or Masami Teraoka's paintings of geisha superheroines fending off wayward priests.

- **Hosfelt Gallery** (Map p160; ☎ 415-495-5454; 430 Clementina St; admission free; ⏰ 11am-5:30pm Tue-Sat; 🚌 & Ⓜ Powell St) Induces trancelike states with meticulously detailed interior worlds, including Russell Crotty's giant orbs painstakingly sketched with a Bic pen and Marco Maggi's minutely carved stacks of office paper.

- **Electric Works** (Map p160; ☎ 415-626-5496; www.sfelectricworks.com; 130 8th St; admission free; ⏰ 11am-6pm Tue-Fri, to 5pm Sat; 🚌 & Ⓜ Civic Center) A working printmaking studio bringing unlikely visions to life, including Marcel Dzama's gangs of vampire toddlers and Sandow Birk's modern take on Dante's *Inferno;* sales from some print editions go to benefit local nonprofit organizations.

- **Eleanor Harwood Gallery** (Map p160; ☎ 415-867-7770; www.eleanorharwood.com; 1295 Alabama St; admission free; ⏰ 1-5pm Thu-Sat; 🚌 9, 27, 33, 48; Ⓜ 24th St Mission) Showcases Bay Area talents, from James Chronister's oil portraits painted tattoo-style with a tiny brush to Venice Biennale artist Emily Prince's obsessive daily drawings of lost hats and fallen soldiers.

- **Ratio 3** (Map p160; ☎ 415-821-3371; www.ratio3.org; 1447 Stevenson St; admission free; ⏰ 11am-6pm Wed-Sat; 🚌 14, 22, 33, 49; Ⓜ 16th St Mission) 'Brings vastness to mind' with Mission garage shows destined for international art fairs by graffiti auteur Barry McGee and sublime works in feathers by artist Jose Alvarez.

MISSION, SOMA & CASTRO

SLEEPING

downstairs is the **Golden Gate Model Railroad Club** (Map p160; ☎ 415-346-3303; www.ggmrc.org; ☉ 10am-4pm Sat; ♿), an elaborate collection of vintage Lionel trains.

SLEEPING
THE MISSION

INN SAN FRANCISCO Map p160   Inn $$
☎ 415-641-0188, 800-359-0913; www.innsf .com; 943 S Van Ness Ave; r $175-285, with shared bathroom $120-145, cottage $335, all incl breakfast; 🚌 49; 🛜

The stately Inn San Francisco occupies an elegant 1872 Italianate Victorian mansion, impeccably maintained and packed with period antiques. All rooms have fresh-cut flowers and sumptuous beds with fluffy featherbeds; some have Jacuzzi tubs. Outside there's an English garden and redwood hot tub open 24 hours (a rarity).

SAN FRANCISCO ELEMENTS
Map p168   Hostel $
☎ 415-647-4100, 866-327-8407; www.elements sf.com; 2524 Mission St; dm/d $29/60; 🚌 14; 🛜
At the heart of the nightlife scene, Elements has clean, up-to-date, good-looking (if institutional) rooms with noise-blocking double-pane windows. Dorms are coed or segregated, and all have bathrooms.

Castro Theatre
CURTIS MARTIN

⬊ CASTRO THEATRE

The city's grandest cinema since 1922 still has its landmark marquee, and a mighty Wurlitzer organ that rises from the orchestra pit before evening performances. The audience roars and whistles as the organ plays the opening bars of the theme from the 1936 silver-screen classic *San Francisco,* starring Clark Gable: 'San Francisco/Open your Golden Gate/You let no stranger wait/ Outside your door…' If there's a cult classic on the bill, such as *Whatever Happened to Baby Jane,* expect full audience participation. As Bette Davis says, 'Fasten your seatbelts; it's going to be a bumpy night.'

Things you need to know: Map p168; ☎ 415-621-6120; www.thecastrotheatre.com; 429 Castro St; adult/senior, child & matinee $9.50/7; 🚌 24, 33, K, L, M, Castro St

⬊ TRANSPORTATION: THE CASTRO & NOE VALLEY

Bus The 24 passes through the Castro on its way from Pacific Heights and the Haight to Noe Valley. The 33 links the Castro to the Mission, the Haight, Golden Gate Park and the Richmond.

Streetcar The K, L and M lines run under Market St, with stops at Castro St. The F streetcar does the same on the surface of Market St. The J line runs from Downtown and stops on the edge of the Castro at Church and Market Sts.

SOMA

ST REGIS HOTEL Map p160   Hotel $$$

☎ 415-284-4000, 877-787-3447; www.stregis
.com/sanfrancisco; 125 3rd St; r from $399;
🚌 30, 45; 🚇 & Ⓜ Montgomery St; 🛜 🖾
The pinnacle of luxury, the St Regis is one of SF's three five-star hotels (the others are Four Seasons and Ritz-Carlton), and it's our favorite for its art collection, which nods to the neighboring SFMOMA. Rooms have all the latest bells and whistles, including magnificent beds dressed with Pratesi linens.

HOTEL VITALE Map p160   Design Hotel $$$

☎ 415-278-3700, 888-890-8688; www.hotel
vitale.com; 8 Mission St; d $239-339, ste $669-
799; 🚇 & Ⓜ Embarcadero; 🛜
The ugly exterior disguises a fashion-forward shagadelic-chic hotel, with echoes of midcentury-modern design enhanced by up-to-the-minute luxuries and a soothing spa theme. Suites have extras such as waterfall showerheads, limestone-tile bathrooms, two-person soaking tubs, and – best of all – semicircular glass walls with stunning bay views.

W HOTEL Map p160   Hotel $$$

☎ 415-777-5300, 877-946-8357; www.whotel.
com; 181 3rd St; r from $259; 🚇 & Ⓜ
Montgomery St; 🛜 🖾
Every room in the 31-story tower has unobstructed city views (request a Bay Bridge view), upholstered window seats, stereos with chill music and sumptuous beds.

AMERICANIA HOTEL

Map p160   Design Motel $$
☎ 415-626-0200; www.jdvhotels.com; 121 7th
St; r $129-169; 🚇 & Ⓜ Civic Center; 🛜 🖾 ♿
Rooms at this restyled motor lodge face a central courtyard and look sharp, with

SABRINA DALBESIO

San Francisco Elements

a retro-'70s aesthetic incorporating black-and-teal-checked carpeting, white-vinyl headboards, pop art and playful extras such as Yahtzee dice.

MOSSER HOTEL Map p160 Hotel $
☎ 415-986-4400, 800-227-3804; www.themosser.com; 54 4th St; r $109-149, with shared bathroom $69-89; 🚇 & 🚊 Powell St; 🛜
A tourist-class hotel with stylish details, the Mosser has tiny rooms and tinier bathrooms, but rates are a bargain and it's close to Union Square shops, Yerba Buena museums and the Moscone Convention Center.

THE CASTRO & NOE VALLEY

PARKER GUEST HOUSE
Map p168 B&B $$
☎ 415-621-3222, 888-520-7275; www.parkerguesthouse.com; 520 Church St; r $139-229; 🚊 J; 🛜
The Castro's most stately digs occupy two side-by-side hundred-year-old Edwardian mansions. Rooms feel more like a swanky

hotel than a B&B, with super-comfortable beds and down comforters. Bathroom fixtures gleam.

INN ON CASTRO Map p168 B&B $$
☎ 415-861-0321; www.innoncastro.com; 321 Castro St; ste $155-185, r incl breakfast $135-165, without bathroom $115-125; 🚊 24, F; 🛜
A portal to the Castro's disco heyday, this Edwardian is decked out with top-end '70s-mod furnishings. Rooms are retro-cool and spotlessly kept. Exceptional breakfasts – the owner is a chef.

EATING
THE MISSION

DELFINA Map p168 Californian $$$
☎ 415-552-4055; www.delfinasf.com; 3621 18th St; 🕐 dinner; 🚊 14, 26, 33, 49, J; 🚇 16th St Mission; Ⓥ
Simple yet sensational seasonal California cuisine: Sonoma duck with Barolo-roasted cherries, wild nettle tagliatelle pasta, profiteroles with coffee gelato and candied

A chef at La Taqueria

SABRINA DALBESIO

almonds. Since this is the one California-cuisine restaurant all of SF's picky eaters agree on, it's always packed; make reservations and arrive prepared to wait, or settle for next-best Delfina Pizza next door.

FOREIGN CINEMA

Map p168   Californian $$$

☎ 415-648-7600; www.foreigncinema.com; 2534 Mission St; ☽ dinner nightly, brunch Sat & Sun, bar to 2am; 🚌 14, 26, 48, 49; ⊕ 24th St Mission; Ⓥ

Tasty dishes such as seared scallops with pancetta or pork tenderloin with tart cherries and olives are the main attractions, but Luis Buñuel and François Truffaut provide an entertaining backdrop with movies screened in the courtyard, and subtitles you can follow when the conversation lags.

RANGE Map p168   Californian $$

☎ 415-282-8283; www.rangesf.com; 842 Valencia St; ☽ dinner; 🚌 14, 26, 33, 49, J; ⊕ 16th St Mission; Ⓥ

Lowly pork shoulder becomes an eye-opener rubbed with coffee and served with bafflingly smooth grits, and bread pudding becomes a main event baked to velvety perfection with local radish sprouts and gooey Gruyère. Although the beer fridge is a repurposed medical cabinet ominously emblazoned with the words 'Blood Bank,' no resuscitation will be necessary after you get the check – mains are priced around $20, with desserts and drinks under $10.

MISSION

BEACH CAFE Map p160   Californian $$

☎ 415-861-0198; www.missionbeachcafesf.com; 198 Guerrero St; ☽ 7am-10pm Mon-Thu, 7am-11pm Fri, 9am-11pm Sat, 9am-6pm Sun; 🚌 22, 26, 37, 53, J, F

Brunch gets an upgrade to first class, with soufflé pancakes, *huevos rancheros* (ranch-style eggs) with sustainably raised pulled pork, eggs with caramelized onions and English muffins made by the in-house chef – all whipped up with organic ingredients.

LA TAQUERIA Map p168   Mexican $

☎ 415-285-7117; 2889 Mission St; ☽ 11am-9pm Mon-Sat, to 8pm Sun; 🚌 14, 26, 48, 49; ⊕ 24th St Mission; Ⓥ ♿

There's no debatable saffron rice, spinach tortilla or mango salsa here – just perfectly grilled meats, flavorful beans and classic tomatillo or mesquite salsa wrapped in a flour tortilla.

BI-RITE Map p168   Groceries $

☎ 415-241-9760; www.biritemarket.com; 3639 18th St; ☽ 9am-9pm; 🚌 14, 26, 33, 49, J; ⊕ 16th St Mission

Local artisan cheeses and chocolates, organic, seasonal dishes whipped up on the premises, and organic local fruit are displayed like jewels, and the selection of Californian wines is downright dazzling. Across the street is organic **Bi-Rite Creamery** (Map p168; ☎ 415-626-5600; 3692 18th St; ☽ 9am-9pm), where the salted caramel ice cream and housemade hot fudge are worth the wait in line.

UDUPI PALACE Map p168   Indian $

☎ 415-970-8000; www.udupipalaceca.com; 1007 Valencia St; ☽ 11:30am-10pm Mon-Thu, to 10:30pm Fri-Sun; 🚌 14, 26, 33, 49; ⊕ 24th St Mission

Tandoori in the Tenderloin is for novices – SF foodies swoon over the bright, clean flavors of South Indian *dosa*, a light, crispy pancake made with lentil flour dipped in mildly spicy vegetable *sambar* (soup) and coconut chutney. Don't miss the *medhu vada* (savory lentil donuts with *sambar* and chutney) or *bagala bhath* (yogurt rice with cucumber and nutty toasted mustard seeds).

HUMPHRY SLOCOMBE Map p160   Ice Cream $

☎ 415-550-6971; www.humphryslocombe. com; 2790 Harrison St; ⊙ noon-9pm; ⊚ 24th St Mission

Indie-rock ice cream may permanently spoil you for Top 40 flavors: once balsamic-vinegar caramel and olive oil have rocked your tastebuds, cookie dough seems so obvious, and ice cream sandwiches can't compare for decadence to foie gras ice cream between ginger snaps.

TARTINE Map p168   Bakery $

☎ 415-487-2600; www.tartinebakery.com; 600 Guerrero St; ⊙ breakfast, lunch & dinner; 🚍 14, 26, 33, 49, J; ⊚ 16th St Mission; Ⓥ

Riches beyond your wildest dreams: butter-intensive *pain au chocolat,* cappuccino with dense foam, and *croque monsieurs* turbo-loaded with ham, two kinds of cheese and béchamel.

PANCHO VILLA Map p168   Mexican $

☎ 415-864-8840; www.panchovillasf.com; 3071 16th St; ⊙ 10am-midnight; 🚍 14, 26, 33, 49; ⊚ 16th St Mission

The hero of the downtrodden and burrito-deprived, delivering a worthy condiments bar and tinfoil-wrapped meals the girth of your forearm. The line moves fast, and as you leave, the door is held open for you and your newly acquired Pancho's paunch.

MISSION PIE Map p168   American, Bakery $

☎ 415-282-1500; www.missionpie.com; 2901 Mission St; ⊙ 7am-9pm Mon-Thu, 7am-10pm Fri, 8am-10pm Sat, 9am-9pm Sun; 🚍 14, 26, 48; ⊚ 24th St Mission

Like mom used to make, only better: from savory quiche to all-American apple, all pie purchases here support a nonprofit sustainable farm where city kids find out where their food comes from, and learn about nutrition and cooking.

SOMA

BOULEVARD Map p160   Californian $$$

☎ 415-543-6084; www.boulevardrestaurant .com; 1 Mission St; ⊙ lunch & dinner Mon-Fri, dinner Sat-Sun; 🚍 F, J, K, L, M, N; 🚍 & ⊚ Embarcadero

The 1889 belle-epoque styling of the quake-surviving Audiffred Building is a fitting locale for Boulevard, which remains one of San Francisco's most consistently creative and widely respected restaurants. Chef Nancy Oakes has a light, easy touch with juicy pork chops, enough local soft-shell crab to satisfy a sailor and chocolate ganache cake with housemade bourbon ice cream.

SALT HOUSE Map p160   Californian $$$

☎ 415-543-8900; www.salthousesf.com; 545 Mission St; ⊙ 11am-10pm Mon-Fri, 5:30-11pm Sat, 5:30-9pm Sun; 🚍 6, 10, 14, 21, 31, 71, F, J, K, L, M, N; 🚍 & ⊚ Montgomery St

For a business lunch that feels more like a spa getaway, take your choice of light fare such as duck confit or yellowfin tuna with beets. Service is leisurely, so order that carrot cake with cream-cheese ice cream now.

WATERBAR Map p160   Seafood $$$

☎ 415-284-9922; 399 The Embarcadero; ⊙ 11:30am-9:30pm Sun-Tue, to 10pm Wed-Sat; 🚍 F, N, T; 🚍 & ⊚ Embarcadero

Leave the dining room to Silicon Valley strivers trying hard to impress dates and investors, and make a beeline for the oval bar, where the plates and prices are smaller, and oyster shells and corks are popping to keep pace with orders of local mollusks with shallot/wine mignonette and local champagne by the glass.

SENTINEL Map p160   Sandwiches $

☎ 415-284-9960; www.thesentinelsf.com; 37 New Montgomery St; ⊙ 7:30am-2:30pm

RICK GERHARTER

Salt House

Mon-Fri; 🚌 6, 10, 14, 21, 31, 71, F, J, K, L, M, N; 🚌 & Ⓜ Montgomery St

Rebel SF chef Dennis Leary is out to revolutionize lunchtime take-out, taking on the classics with top-notch seasonal ingredients. Tuna salad gets radical with chipotle mayo and the snap of crisp summer vegetables, and roast beef does an about-face with horseradish cream cheese. Menus change daily; come prepared for about a 10-minute wait, since every sandwich is made to order.

TROPISUEÑO Map p160   Mexican $
☎ 415-243-0299; www.tropisueno.com; 75 Yerba Buena Lane; 🕐 11am-10:30pm; 🚌 6, 10, 14, 21, 31, 71, F, J, K, L, M, N; 🚌 & Ⓜ Powell St

Last time you enjoyed casual Mexican dining this much, there were probably balmy ocean breezes and hammocks involved. Instead, you're steps away from SFMOMA, savoring an *al pastor* (marinated pork) burrito with mesquite salsa and grilled pineapple, and sipping a margarita with a chili-salted rim.

BUTLER & THE CHEF Map p160 French $
☎ 415-896-2075; www.thebutlerandthechef bistro.com; 155a South Park St; 🕐 8am-3pm Tue-Sat, 10am-3pm Sun; 🚌 12, N, T

All the French classics you'd never expect to find among SoMa warehouses are here, from the *croque monsieur* with Niman Ranch ham, Emmenthal cheese and béchamel on organic bread, all the way through to light, flaky-crusted quiche Lorraine studded with crisp Niman Ranch bacon.

RAINBOW GROCERY Map p160   Groceries $
☎ 415-863-0620; www.rainbowgrocery.org; 1745 Folsom St; 🕐 9am-9pm; 🚌 12

The legendary cooperative attracts masses to buy eco/organic/fair-trade products in bulk, drool over the bounty of local cheeses, and flirt in the hemp-based skincare aisle. To have your questions about where to find what in the Byzantine bulk section answered, ask a fellow shopper – staff can be elusive.

TU LAN Map p160 Vietnamese $
☎ 415-626-0927; 8 6th St; ⏰ 11am-9:30pm Mon-Sat; 🚌 5, 6, 21, 31, F, J, K, L, M, N; 🚇 & ⓥ Civic Center
Sidewalks don't get skankier than the one you'll be waiting on, but try complaining after your heap of velvety Vietnamese chicken curry or tangy tomato-onion prawns. One dish under $10 easily fills two starving artists.

THE CASTRO & NOE VALLEY

CATCH Map p168 Seafood $$
☎ 415-431-5000; www.catchsf.com; 2362 Market St; ⏰ lunch Mon-Fri, dinner nightly, brunch Sat & Sun; 🚌 24, 33, F, K, L, M, Castro St
As in, 'of the day' – Dungeness crab, oysters, sole – not necessarily a reference to that silver fox by the fireplace. The crowd consists almost entirely of men in turtlenecks and leather jackets accessorized with same, but, like the menu, you may find that the conversation gets unexpectedly saucy.

HOME Map p160 American $$
☎ 415-503-0333; www.home-sf.com; 2100 Market St; ⏰ 11am-midnight daily, brunch Sat & Sun; 🚌 22, 33, 37, F, J, K, L, M, Church St; ⓥ ♿
There's no place like it, especially if you enjoy your comfort food fireside with a gaggle of gym-fresh men and a $4 Homegirl (aka Cosmo plus champagne) or margarita during the 4pm to 7pm happy hour.

SUSHI TIME Map p168 Japanese, Sushi $
☎ 415-552-2280; www.sushitime-sf.com; 2275 Market St; ⏰ 5:30-10:30pm Mon-Sat; 🚌 22, 24, 37, F, J, K, L, M, N, Castro St; ⓥ
Barbie, GI Joe and Hello Kitty make cameos on the *maki* (sushi roll) menu at this surreal sushi spot downstairs from a bookstore and gym, Tokyo-style. Devour sashimi in the tiny glassed-in patio like a shark in an aquarium, and notice how your munching mysteriously synchronizes with the J-pop on the stereo and exercise bikers pumping away upstairs.

SABRINA DALBESIO

Medjool Sky Terrace

HOT COOKIE Map p168   Bakery $

☎ 415-621-2350; 407 Castro St; ☽ 11am-11pm Mon-Thu, to 1am Fri & Sat, to 11:30pm Sun; 🚍 24, 33, F, K, L, M, Castro St

After a couple of adult film scenes were shot here, Hot Cookie became the place to be seen and photographed for porn stars – hence the wall of signed Hot Cookie underwear, and customers eating chocolate chip cookies with a certain gusto.

DRINKING
THE MISSION

ZEITGEIST Map p160   Bar

☎ 415-255-7505; 199 Valencia St; ☽ 9am-2am; 🚍 26; ◉ 16th St Mission

You've got two seconds flat to order from tough-gal barkeeps who are used to putting macho bikers in their place. When it's warm, regulars head straight to the bar's huge graveled back patio to sit at long picnic tables and smoke out.

ELIXIR Map p168   Bar

☎ 415-552-1633; www.elixirsf.com; 3200 16th St; ☽ 3pm-2am Mon-Fri, noon-2am Sat & Sun; ◉ 16th St Mission

SF's first certified-green bar uses organic spirits and fresh fruits to mix knockout drinks for an always appreciative, unpretentious crowd of Bacchanalian revelers, who throng this cozy, vintage-1907 saloon – some bring their dogs. Great habanero-chili cosmos.

MEDJOOL SKY TERRACE
Map p168   Bar

☎ 415-550-9055; www.medjoolsf.com; 2522 Mission St; ☽ 5-11pm Sun-Thu, to 2am Fri & Sat; 🚍 14, 26; ◉ 24th St Mission

SF's only open-air rooftop bar has knockout views, a party crowd, Mediterranean small plates and tasty (cash-only) cocktails.

DOC'S CLOCK Map p168   Bar

☎ 415-824-3627; www.docsclock.com; 2575 Mission St; ☽ 6pm-2am Mon-Sat, 8pm-midnight Sun; 🚍 14, 49

Dig the dazzling neon sign at this happy-mellow, green-certified dive that's always good for a few pints, shuffleboard and conversation. Every second and fourth Tuesday is local-filmmaker night, with screenings of indie shorts and $2 draft PBR.

FARLEY'S Map p160   Cafe

☎ 415-648-1545; www.farleyscoffee.com; 1315 18th St; ☽ 6:30am-10pm Mon-Fri, 7:30am-10pm Sat, 8am-10pm Sun; 🚍 22; 🛜

Retro-Americana down to the whitewashed slat-board walls and soda-shop-style counter, Farley's is Potrero Hill's unofficial gathering place, and has a big community newsboard and stellar magazine selection.

RITUAL COFFEE ROASTERS
Map p168   Cafe

☎ 415-641-1024; www.ritualroasters.com; 1026 Valencia St; ☽ 6am-10pm Mon-Fri, 7am-10pm Sat, 7am-9pm Sun; 🚍 14, 26; ◉ 24th St Mission; 🛜

Blue Bottle and Ritual Roasters are the two big names in SF's 'Third Wave' coffee movement, which esteems coffee as highly as fine chocolate and grand cru wine. We love bringing our laptop to Ritual's to get jacked and eavesdrop on tattooed bikers, internet pros and coffee aficionados.

SOMA

BLOODHOUND Map p160   Bar

☎ 415-863-2840; www.bloodhoundsf.com; 1145 Folsom St; ☽ 4pm-2am; 🚍 12, 19, 27, 47

Our favorite SoMa bar feels vaguely Nordic, with white wood, antler chandeliers and fantastic art, including a murder of crows painted on the ceiling. Top-shelf ingredients, but no drink is over-intellectualized. Killer jukebox.

⬈ WOMEN: OUT & ABOUT IN THE MISSION

Ladies who love ladies love the Mission, especially these neighborhood institutions:

- **Wild Side West** (Map p160; ☎ 415-647-3099; 424 Cortland Ave; ◷ 1pm-2am Mon-Sat, to midnight Sun; 🚊 14, 24, 67) A noisy saloon bar with pin-up-girl art where straight friends are welcome. Crafty grrrls flirt at the sewing-machine table by the fireplace and make out in the overgrown garden.
- **Femina Potens** (Map p160; ☎ 415-864-1558; www.feminapotens.org; 2199 Market St; ◷ noon-6pm Thu-Sun; 🚊 F, Church St) A tiny storefront gallery by day, and night-time venue for performance and workshops ranging from Crafty Bitches, a knitting and crafts night, to seminars on BDSM for queers and trans.
- **Lexington Club** (Map p168; ☎ 415-863-2052; 3464 19th St; ◷ 3pm-2am; 🚊 14, 26, 33, 49) Lexington can be cliquish at first, so be strategic: compliment someone on her skirt (she made it herself) or tattoo (she designed it herself) and casually mention you're undefeated at pinball, pool or thumb-wrestling. When she wins (because she's no stranger to the Lex) pout just a little, and maybe she'll buy you a $4 beer.
- **Brava Theater** (Map p160; ☎ 415-641-7657; www.brava.org; 2781 24th St; 🚊 9, 27, 33, 48) Brava has been producing women-run theater for 20 years, and it's the nation's only company whose sole purpose is to produce original works by women of color and lesbians.

BUTTER Map p160   Bar
☎ 415-863-5964; www.smoothasbutter.com; 354 11th St; ◷ 6pm-2am Tue-Sun; 🚊 47
Butter satirizes trailer trash – think cocktails mixed with Tang – providing a refreshing contrast to the VIP clubs across the street. Best of all, you'll never pay $10 for a drink at this tiny, always-jumpin' bar, leaving you extra cash for Tater Tots and Spaghettios – cooked, of course, in a microwave.

BRAINWASH Map p160   Cafe
☎ 415-431-9274; www.brainwash.com; 1122 Folsom St; ◷ 7am-10pm Mon-Thu, 7am-11pm Fri & Sat, 8am-10pm Sun; 🚊 12, 19; 📶
The coolest place to do laundry is also a happening cafe with coffee, beer and live performances most nights. Last wash is at 8:30pm.

THE CASTRO & NOE VALLEY

SAMOVAR TEA LOUNGE
Map p168   Cafe
☎ 415-626-4700; www.samovartea.com; 498 Sanchez St; ◷ 10am-10pm; 🚊 24, 33, F, K, L, M
Samovar's sunny Castro location specializes in organic, fair-trade teas, and provides a cozy alternative to the neighborhood's ubiquitous bars. *Bento* boxes, cheese plates and tea cookies give reason to linger.

ENTERTAINMENT & ACTIVITIES
THE MISSION
EL RIO Map p160   Clubbing
☎ 415-282-3325; www.elriosf.com; 3158 Mission St; admission $3-8; ◷ 5pm-2am Mon-Thu, 3pm-2am Fri-Sun; 🚊 14, 26; 🚊 & Ⓜ 24th St Mission

El Rio likes its music and patrons eclectic and mixed, funky and pansexual. The club rightly boasts about the back garden, its 'Totally Fabulous Happy Hour' from 4pm to 9pm Tuesday to Friday, and free oysters on the half shell on Fridays at 5:30pm.

OBERLIN DANCE COLLECTIVE

Map p160   Dance

☎ 415-863-9834; www.odctheater.org; 3153 17th St; ⊕ 16th St Mission

The ODC's season runs from September through to December, and its stage presents year-round shows, which feature local and international artists. Its Dance Commons is a hub and hangout for the dance community and offers 200 classes a week; all ages and levels are welcome.

ROXIE CINEMA Map p168   Film

☎ 415-863-1087; www.roxie.com; 3117 16th St; admission prices vary, generally around $10; 🚌 14, 22, 33, 49; ⊕ 16th St Mission

The Roxie carries major clout with cinemaniacs for helping distribute and launch Hong Kong films Stateside, and for showing controversial films and documentaries banned elsewhere in the US. Matt Groenig may show up to introduce a Simpsons film festival, and the audience will likely throw popcorn during the screening of the Academy Awards.

RED POPPY

ART HOUSE Map p160   Jazz, Blues & Funk

☎ 415-826-2402; www.redpoppyarthouse.org; 2698 Folsom St; suggested donation $12-15; 🕙 generally Thu-Sun; ⊕ 24th St Mission

By day an open artists studio, by night an all-volunteer-artist-run intimate coffeehouse featuring local jazz talent.

MISSION CULTURAL CENTER
FOR LATINO ARTS

Map p168   Other Activities

☎ 415-643-2785; www.missionculturalcenter .org; 2868 Mission St; 🕙 10am-5pm Tue-Sat; 🚌 14, 26, 48, 49; ⊕ 24th St Mission; ♿

Join a class in flamenco, salsa or Latin bellydancing; make arts and crafts with the kids; or create a poster at the printmaking studio at this happening cultural center.

ARTWORKS FROM LEFT: WORKS IN PROGRESS, FERNANDO DIAZ, 2010; DESERT HOLES, TODD T BROWN, 2004. PHOTO BY SABRINA DALBESIO

Red Poppy Art House

↘ CRUISING THE CASTRO

No GLBT circuit is complete without visits to these Castro institutions:

- **Twin Peaks Tavern** (Map p168; ☎ 415-864-9470; www.twinpeakstavern.com; 401 Castro St; ☽ noon-2am Mon-Fri, 8am-2am Sat & Sun; 🚌 24, 33, F, Castro St) This was the first gay bar in the world with windows opening to the street. The jovial crowd skews over-40, but it's everyone's favorite for tête-à-têtes after films at the Castro and Judy Garland sing-a-longs.

- **QBar** (Map p168; ☎ 415-864-2877; www.qbarsf.com; 456 Castro St; ☽ 4pm-2am Mon-Fri, 2pm-2am Sat & Sun; 🚌 24, 35, F, Castro St) QBar packs in 20-something twinks on a tiny dance floor; smokers pack the front room. Occasional go-go boys add spice; Wednesday's Booty Call is a staple.

- **Gold's Gym** (Map p168; ☎ 415-626-4488; www.goldsgym.com; 2301 Market St; admission $15; ☽ 5am-midnight Mon-Thu, 5am-11pm Fri, 7am-9pm Sat, 7am-8pm Sun; 🚌 24, 33, F, K, L, M, Castro St) Gold's draws a neighborhood crowd of chatty muscle-Marys with a full selection of equipment, a dance studio, yoga classes and notorious steam room.

- **Human Rights Campaign Action Center & Store** (Map p168; ☎ 415-431-2200; www.hrc.org; 600 Castro St;h10am-7pm; 🚌 24, 33, F, K, L, M, Castro St) This is where hopeful romantics go to sign marriage-equality petitions, buy Marc Jacobs–designed HRC tees, and pop the question with rings inscribed with *Aequalitas* (Equality).

- **Blackbird** (Map p160; ☎ 415-503-0630; www.blackbirdbar.com; 2124 Market St; ☽ 3pm-2am Mon-Fri, noon-2am Sat & Sun; 🚌 22, F, J, K, L, M, N, Church St) Sleek but not overstyled; the cocktails are strong, and there's a good selection of wines and craft beers by the glass for Castro hunks and their platonic gal-pals.

- **Lookout** (Map p168; ☎ 415-431-0306; www.lookoutsf.com; 3600 16th St; ☽ 3:30pm-2am Mon-Fri, 12:30pm-2am Sat & Sun; 🚌 F, Castro St) Hosts crossover crowds for raucous fundraisers, hot rugby players at Sunday afternoon's Jock, and hip chicas Thursday nights for Les Ladiez ($2).

- **A Different Light Bookstore** (Map p168; ☎ 415-431-0891; www.adlbooks.com; 489 Castro St; ☽ 10am-11pm; 🚌 24, 33, F, Castro St) Specializes in GLBT titles and authors; check the bulletin board for upcoming readings.

- **440 Castro** (Map p168; ☎ 415-621-8732; www.the440.com; 440 Castro St; ☽ noon-2am; 🚌 Castro St) The most happening bar on Castro, drawing bearded 30-something dudes and Peter Pans for Monday's underwear night.

- **Cafe Flore** (Map p168; ☎ 415-621-8579; www.cafeflore.com; 2298 Market St; ☽ 7am-midnight Sun-Thu, to 2am Fri & Sat; 🚌 24, 33, F, Castro St; 🛜) Where the neighborhood converges to lollygag on the sun-drenched patio; wi-fi is available weekdays.

MAKE-OUT ROOM Map p168   Rock

☎ 415-647-2888; www.makeoutroom.com; 3225 22nd St; live music cover $5-10; 🕑 6pm-2am; 🚍 14, 26, 48, 49; 🚇 24th St Mission

Velvet curtains and round booths add dusty swank to the evening's entertainment, which ranges from improv to punk-rock fiddle to occasional minor celebs – sometimes on the same night. For lovers of indie, the Make-Out's a must.

BOTTOM OF THE HILL Map p160   Rock

☎ 415-621-4455; www.bottomofthehill.com; 1233 17th St; admission $5-12; 🕑 shows after 8:30pm Tue-Sat, other nights vary; 🚍 19, 22

Top of the list for seeing fun local bands, such as punk-polka Polkacide and goth-psychedelic Bellavista, Bottom of the Hill is out of the way – literally at the bottom of Potrero Hill – but worth the trek for indie-rockers.

ELBO ROOM Map p168   Rock

☎ 415-552-7788; www.elbo.com; 647 Valencia St; admission $5-20; 🕑 5pm-2am; 🚍 14, 26, 33, 49; 🚇 16th St Mission

The Elbo Room draws a diverse indie crowd and showcases diverse acts in its upstairs black-box performance space, including rockabilly, salsa and reggae, with emphasis on funk and soul.

MARSH Map p168   Theater

☎ 415-641-0235; www.themarsh.org; 1062 Valencia St; tickets $8-35; 🕑 8pm Thu-Sun; 🚍 14, 26, 49

One-acts and one-off stagings of works-in-progress involve the audience in the creative process. This is San Francisco theater at its most exciting. A sliding-scale pricing structure allows all to participate.

YOGA TREE Map p168   Yoga

☎ 415-647-9707; www.yogatreesf.com; 1234 Valencia St; drop-in classes $17; 🕑 10am-10pm; 🚇 24th St Mission

Yoga-lovers will find instant community in this clean, warm, colorful studio, which has personable, high-quality instructors, great deals on introductory classes (three sessions for $20) and drop-in classes, primarily in Hatha yoga.

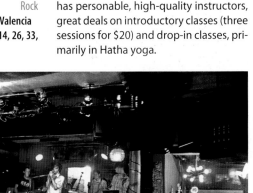

SABRINA DALBESIO

Bottom of the Hill

MISSION, SOMA & CASTRO

ENTERTAINMENT & ACTIVITIES

SOMA

MEZZANINE Map p160   Clubbing

☎ 415-625-8880; www.mezzaninesf.com; 444 Jessie St; admission $10-40; ☼ call for details; 🚌 5, 26

With possibly the best sound system in SF, behemoth Mezzanine hosts electro-funk disco, house, hip-hop, classic alt bands such as the Psychedelic Furs and electronic shows by the likes of Wyclef Jean, to keep you dancing all night inside its awesome brick-walled former-industrial space.

ENDUP Map p160   Clubbing

☎ 415-646-0999; www.theendup.com; 401 6th St; admission $5-20; ☼ 10pm-4am Mon-Thu, 11pm-11am Fri (into Sat), 10pm Sat-10pm Sun; 🚌 12, 27, 47

Anyone left on the streets of San Francisco after 2am on weekends is subject to the magnetic force of the EndUp's marathon dance sessions. It's the only club with a 24-hour license and remains best known for its Sunday tea dances, in full force since 1973, though the club has branched out with reggae and other changing parties (check the web).

MIGHTY Map p160   Clubbing

☎ 415-626-7001; www.mighty119.com; 119 Utah St; admission $10-20; ☼ 10pm-4am Fri, Sat & occasional weeknights; 🚌 9

In a former warehouse sequestered in a no-man's land between SoMa, the Mission and Potrero Hill, Mighty packs a no-bullshit wallop with its awesome sound system, underground dance music, urban vibe, graffiti-esque art, and cool local crowd that doesn't fuss about dress codes.

PARADISE LOUNGE Map p160   Clubbing

☎ 415-252-5018; www.paradisesf.com; 1501 Folsom St; admission $5-25; ☼ 9pm-4am Fri & Sat, to 2am Sun; 🚌 19, 27

The stalwart Paradise is good on Fridays and Saturdays when you're wandering around 11th St undecided about where to go. Sound is good on both dance floors, and the upstairs-downstairs layout is fun for running around. The GLBT crowd hits

---

↘ DANCIN' THE NIGHT AWAY

SF was at the forefront of the swing revival, and salsa and tango remain perennial favorites. The following host dance nights; admission ranges from $5 to $25 when live bands play.

- **Cheryl Burke Dance Center** (Map p160; ☎ 415-252-9000; www.cherylburkedance.com; 1830 17th St; ☼ 1-9pm Mon-Thu, 1-11pm Fri, 11am-7pm Sat, 10am-4pm Sun; 🚌 22) This has one of the largest floors in the city, with classes daily and dances nightly. No need for a partner in most classes; there are same-sex events, too.
- **Verdi Club** (Map p160; ☎ 415-861-9199; www.verdiclub.net; 2424 Mariposa St; ☼ hours vary; 🚌 33) Verdi sizzles Thursday nights, with *bandoneón* (free-reed instrument) players and tango dancers circling the floor to *milonga* (Spanish dance). Lindy-hoppers take over Tuesday nights; other nights vary.
- **Roccapulco Supper Club** (Map p160; ☎ 415-648-6611; www.roccapulco.com; 3140 Mission St; admission $10-15; ☼ 8pm-2am; 🚌 14, 26; ◎ 24th St Mission) A stadium-sized salsa palace that books fantastic Latin touring acts such as El Grupo Niche.

the dance floor here some Sundays at **Honey Soundsystem** (☎ 415-252-5018; www.honeysoundsystem.com).

TEMPLE Map p160   Clubbing
☎ 415-978-8853; www.templesf.com; 540 Howard St; admission $20; ☽ 10pm-3am Fri & Sat, sometimes weeknights; ☐ 10, 14; ☐ & Ⓜ Montgomery St

The city's greenest club is a restaurant before 10pm, when it turns into a nightclub, serving drinks in biodegradable cups. Occasional big-name DJs spin the gamut from house to trance to techno; Fridays are consistently good for house. It's $5 before 11pm if you're on the guestlist.

DNA LOUNGE Map p160   Clubbing
☎ 415-626-1409; www.dnalounge.com; 375 11th St; admission $5-25; ☽ 9pm-late Fri & Sat, other nights vary; ☐ 12, 47, F, J

One of SF's last mega clubs hosts live bands and big-name DJs. Second-and-fourth Saturdays are Bootie, the kick-ass original mashup party (now franchised worldwide); Monday's 18-and-over night is goth.

YERBA BUENA CENTER FOR THE ARTS Map p160   Dance
☎ 415-978-2787; www.ybca.org; 700 Howard St; tickets $15-50; ☐ 30, 45; ☐ & Ⓜ Powell St

Rock stars regularly have their thunder stolen by YBCA openings, which draw hipper crowds willing to brave lines and coat-check their skateboards for contemporary art by the likes of filmmaker Isaac Julien and cartoonist R Crumb. The center also fosters fresh local talent that has mounted everything from an aerial circus to a dance piece set entirely on bicycles.

AMC LOEWS METREON 16 Map p160   Film
☎ 415-369-6201; www.amctheatres.com; 101 4th St; adult/child/senior & matinee $10.50/7.50/8.50; ☐ 30, 45; ☐ & Ⓜ Powell St

Housed in a mega-entertainment complex, the 16-screen Metreon has stadium reclining seats, digital projection screens and an IMAX theater.

RICK GERHARTER

El Rio (p182)

YERBA BUENA CENTER ICE SKATING & BOWLING

Map p160   Ice-Skating & Bowling

☎ 415-820-3532; www.skatebowl.com; 750 Folsom St; skating adult/child/senior $8/5.50/6.25 plus skate rental $3, bowling per game $4.50-6, per hr $25-35; ⊙ bowling 10am-10pm Sun-Thu, to midnight Fri & Sat, check website or call for skating times; ⊜ & ⊕ Powell St; ⊛

Built on the rooftop of the Moscone Convention Center, the ice and bowling centers are a huge draw for families. Unlike most rinks, this one is bright and naturally lit with walls of windows; the bowling alley is small but serves beer.

111 MINNA Map p160   Lounges

☎ 415-974-1719; www.111minnagallery.com; 111 Minna St; admission $5-15, Tue free; ⊙ hours vary; ⊜ 10, 14; ⊜ & ⊕ Montgomery St

Marsh (p185)

SABRINA DALBESIO

Window-lined gallery by day, rockin' lounge space and bar by night, 111 Minna hosts a wild array of events, from monthly free Sketch Tuesdays, when artists make work for sale to the audience, to SF's best techno-dance party Qoöl, to live acoustic performances and disco-house nights.

CITY KAYAK Map p160   Other Activities

☎ 415-357-1010; http://citykayak.com; South Beach Harbor; kayak rentals per hr $14-26, 3hr lesson & rental package $49, tours $59-69; ⊜ N, T

If you're new to paddling, it's best to stick to the waters near the Bay Bridge; if you've some experience, opt for a trip to the choppy waters beneath the Golden Gate Bridge, or for a moonlight tour. Adventurers can set out alone with all-inclusive rentals; aspiring newbies can take lessons and get their sea arms, then head out alone or with an escorted tour – check the website for details.

SLIM'S Map p160   Rock

☎ 415-255-0333; www.slims-sf.com; 333 11th St; tickets $11-28; ⊙ 5pm-2am; ⊜ 9, 12, 47, F, J

Big acts such as Prince and Elvis Costello have played this midsized club owned by R & B star Boz Skaggs, and usually you'll find damn good touring and local bands. Shows are all-ages, though shorties may have a hard time seeing from the floor. Come early for burgers and fries.

HOTEL UTAH Map p160   Rock

☎ 415-546-6300; www.hotelutah.com; 500 4th St; bar admission free, shows $7-12; ⊙ 11:30am-2am Mon-Fri, 6pm-2am Sat & Sun; ⊜ 27, 30, 45, N

Whoopi Goldberg and Robin Williams broke in the stage on the ground floor of a Victorian residence hotel in the '70s, and now it's a sure bet for indie-label favorites and acts you may only see in SF. The nonconformist streak goes deep here: back in

⇖ SOMA LIKE IT HOT: GAY CLUBS

The bathhouses may be gone, but SOMA is still the place to go for action, especially at these gay-centric clubs:

- **Eagle Tavern** (Map p160; ☎ 415-626-0880; www.sfeagle.com; 398 12th St; ☽ noon-2am; ▣ 9, 12, 47) Gay SF's destination of choice on Sundays, with all-you-can-drink beer ($10) from 3pm to 6pm. The enormous open-air back patio gets packed with a mishmash of biker-daddies, hipsters, art boys, shirtless drunks, bears, gay softball teams and the occasional politician working the pack (SF's version of kissing babies).

- **Blow Buddies** (Map p160; ☎ 415-777-HEAD; www.blowbuddies.com; 933 Harrison St; admission $12, plus $8 membership fee; ☽ Thu-Sun nights, call about Wed-night fetish parties; ▣ 27, 47) Blow Buddies was originally owned by a Disney fetishist who set out to recreate, with exacting detail, Disneyland-like attractions, with mazes and specialty-fetish rooms spread over 6000 sq ft of indoor-outdoor warehouse space. Note: no cologne, or they won't let you in.

- **Stud** (Map p160; ☎ 415-252-7883; www.studsf.com; 399 9th St; admission $5-8; ☽ 5pm-3am; ▣ 12, 19, 47) Stud has rocked the gay scene for more than 40 years, and continues the tradition at gender-twisted Friday drag shows and Pink Slip dance parties.

the '50s the bartender graciously served Beats, grifters and Marilyn Monroe, but snipped the ties of businessmen when they leaned across the bar.

SPINNAKER SAILING Map p160   Sailing
☎ 415-543-7333; www.spinnaker-sailing.com; Pier 40; lessons $375; ☽ 10am-5pm; ▣ N, T
Do luff, cringle and helms-a-lee mean anything to you? If yes, captain a boat from Spinnaker and sail into the sunset. If no, charter a skippered vessel, or take classes and learn to talk like a sailor – in a good way.

BAKAR FITNESS & RECREATION CENTER
Map p160   Swimming
☎ 415-514-4545; http://mbfitness.ucsf.edu; 1675 Owens & 16th Sts; day pass $15; ☽ 5:30am-10pm Mon-Fri, 7:30am-8pm Sat & Sun; ▣ 22, T
As outdoor pools go, the view from the dizzyingly high 25yd rooftop pool is enough

to make you forget you came here to swim. A second pool offers exercise classes.

EMBARCADERO YMCA
Map p160   Swimming
☎ 415-957-9622; www.ymcasf.org/embarcadero; 169 Steuart St; day pass $15; ☽ 5:30am-9:45pm Mon-Fri, 8am-7:45pm Sat, 9am-5:45pm Sun; ▣ & ⬤ Embarcadero
Downtown professionals flock to this clean, modern YMCA, with complete gym equipment, swimming pool, basketball court and massage services.

CASTRO & NOE VALLEY
CAFÉ DU NORD/SWEDISH AMERICAN HALL
Map p160   Live Music & Comedy
☎ 415-861-5016; www.cafedunord.com; 2170 Market St; admission price varies; ☽ 7pm or 8pm-2am; ▣ 22, 37, J, K, L, M
You never know what's doing at Café du Nord, a former basement speakeasy, with

bar and showroom. Rockers, chanteuses, comedians, raconteurs and burlesque acts perform nightly, and the joint still looks like it must've in the '30s. The hall upstairs features bigger acts, balcony seating and Scandinavian woodworking, but no booze.

SHOPPING
SOMA

JEREMY'S Map p160   Clothing & Accessories
☎ 415-882-4929; www.jeremys.com; 2 S Park St; ⏲ 11am-6pm Mon-Sat, to 5pm Sun; 🚌 10, 15, 30, 76, N, T

Runway modelling, window displays and department store customer returns translate to jaw-dropping bargains on major designers for men and women. Men's stuff gets picked over faster, but you could score a skinny Jil Sander suit at half off if you work fast.

ISDA & CO
Map p160   Clothing & Accessories, Local Designer
☎ 415-512-1610; www.isda-and-co.com; 21 S Park Ave; ⏲ 10am-6pm Mon-Sat; 🚌 10, 15, 30, 76, N, T

Sharp SF urban professionals aren't born into casual Friday elegance – they probably clawed their way up through racks of pin-tucked jackets and tie-front cardigans at this local designer outlet. Colors are mostly variations on a charcoal-gray theme, but the lean silhouette is shamelessly flattering.

ROLO GARAGE
Map p160   Clothing & Accessories
☎ 415-355-1122; www.rolo.com; 1235 Howard St; ⏲ 11am-7pm Mon-Sat, noon-6pm Sun; 🚌 12,19, F, J, K, L, M, N; 🚇 & ⊕ Civic Center

You'd go out tonight, but you haven't got a stitch to wear? Rolo Garage fixes that old excuse at 30% to 60% off retail price for club-ready menswear, including artfully distressed G-Star jeans, a French military jacket by SF's own Nice Collective, a stag shirt so everyone is clear on your single status, and sunglasses for tomorrow morning.

MADAME S & MR S LEATHER
Map p160   Costumes & Fetish Wear
☎ 800-746-7677; www.madame-s.com; 385 8th St; ⏲ 11am-7pm; 🚌 12, 19, F, J, K, L, M, N; 🚇 & ⊕ Civic Center

Only in San Francisco would an S&M superstore outsize Home Depot, with such musts as suspension stirrups, latex hoods and, for that special someone, a chrome-plated codpiece. If you've been a very bad puppy, there's an entire department catering to you, and gluttons for punishment will find inspiration in Dungeon Furniture.

SAN FRANCISCO FLOWER MART
Map p160   Flowers & Gardens
☎ 415-781-8410; www.sfflmart.com; 640 Brannan St; ⏲ 10am-3pm Mon-Sat; 🚌 27, 42, N

When you're in San Francisco, in love, and in the doghouse, do what the locals do: bring armloads of relentlessly cheerful sunflowers, bask in forgiveness and never let on that you got them cheap at the Flower Mart. Many of the flower and plant vendors offer seasonal flowers grown locally, so you can enjoy your greenery the green way.

THE MISSION
GOOD VIBRATIONS
Map p160   Adult Toys
☎ 415-522-5460; www.goodvibes.com; 603 Valencia St; ⏲ noon-7pm Mon-Wed, noon-8pm Thu, noon-9pm Fri, 11am-9pm Sat, 11am-7pm Sun; 🚌 14, 22, 33, 49; ⊕ 16th St Mission

'Wait, I'm supposed to put that where?' The understanding salespeople in this worker-owned cooperative are used to giving rather, um, explicit instructions, so don't hesitate to ask – Margaret Cho is on the board, so you know they're not shy. Check out the antique vibrators, and imagine getting up close and personal with the one that looks like a floor waxer – then thank your stars for modern technology.

ADOBE BOOKS & BACKROOM GALLERY
Map p160   Books, Art
☎ 415-864-3936; 3166 16th St; ☼ 11am-midnight; ☐ 14, 22, 33, 49; ◉ 16th St Mission
Come here for every book you never knew you needed. But first you'll have to navigate the obstacle course of sofas, cats and art books. Head to the gallery in back to discover emerging artists.

DEMA
Map p168   Clothing & Accessories, Local Designer
☎ 415-206-0500; www.godemago.com; 1038 Valencia St; ☼ 11am-7pm Mon-Fri, noon-7pm Sat, noon-6pm Sun; ☐ 14, 22, 26, 33, 49; ◉ 24th St Mission
BART from Downtown lunches to Mission art openings in vintage-inspired chic by San Francisco's own Dema Grimm. Like any original designer, Dema's not dirt-cheap, but you get what you pay for here in squealed compliments; check bins and sales racks for deals up to 80% off.

MISSION SKATEBOARDS
Map p160 Clothing & Accessories, Sporting Goods
☎ 415-647-7888; www.missionsk8boards.com; 3045 24th St; ☼ 11am-7pm; ☐ 14, 26, 33, 49; ◉ 24th St Mission
Street creds come easy with locally designed decks, tees to kick-flip over, and Toms canvas shoes, where for every pair sold, one is gifted to kids in need (140,000 pairs donated to date).

MISSION STATEMENT
Map p168   Clothing & Accessories, Local Designer
☎ 415-255-7457; www.missionstatementsf.com; 3458 18th St; ☼ noon-8pm; ☐ 14, 22, 33, 49; ◉ 16th St Mission
Finally: locally designed, fashion-forward clothing and accessories that keep real people, real bodies and real budgets in mind. Sofie Ølgaard's drop-waisted silk

SABRINA DALBESIO

Dema

RICK GERHARTER

Paxton Gate

sheaths are drop-dead gorgeous, Vanessa Gade's circle-chain necklaces bring a touch of infinity to your neckline, and Estrella Tadao's reconstructed '70s men's jackets revive radical-chic Maoist placket pockets.

SUNHEE MOON
Map p168   Clothing & Accessories, Local Designer
☎ 415-355-1800; www.sunheemoon.com; 3167 16th St; ☻ noon-7pm Mon-Fri, to 6pm Sat & Sun; ☒ 14, 22, 33, 49; ⊕ 16th St Mission
Minding your girlish figure so you don't have to, Sunhee Moon creates svelte shirtdresses and flattering tree-print tunics to make those curves work for you. You'll never need to wait for a sale, since there's always a rack with 20% to 50% off – yet another excuse to splurge on locally designed, free-form hoop earrings.

NEEDLES &
PENS Map p168   DIY, Local Designer
☎ 415-255-1534; www.needles-pens.com; 3253 16th St; ☻ noon-7pm; ☒ 14, 22, 33, 49; ⊕ 16th St Mission

Do it yourself or DIY trying: this scrappy zine/craft/how-to/art gallery delivers the inspiration to create your own magazines, rehabbed T-shirts or album covers. Nab Sara Thustra's silkscreened zines with drawings of every household purchase for a year, Maria Forde's 'advice portraits' of neighbors and their wisdom (eg 'don't wax on what you can't wax off') and re-cycled T-shirts screen-printed with portraits of famous suffragists.

PAXTON GATE
Map p168   Gifts, Flowers & Gardens
☎ 415-824-1872; www.paxton-gate.com; 824 Valencia St; ☻ noon-7pm Mon-Fri, 11am-7pm Sat & Sun; ☒ 14, 22, 33, 49; ⊕ 16th St Mission
What with puppets made with animal skulls, a stuffed mouse dressed like the Pope, a vast selection of pruning shears and lollipops with actual worms in them, this place is beyond surreal. The new kids' shop down the street is worthy of Lemony Snickett, with volcano-making kits, sea-monster mobiles and solar-powered dollhouses.

DISCOLANDIA Map p160   Music
☎ 415-826-9446; 2964 24th St; ⏰ 11:30am-6:30pm Mon-Sat, noon-4pm Sun; 🚌 48; ⓣ 24th St Mission
The oldest Latin-music store in the Bay Area and as funky as ever, making passersby step in time with merengue, salsa and Tejano blasting out the door. Get yours on CD or vintage vinyl, and stock up on Spanish-language mags, adult comics and pulp fiction.

THE CASTRO & NOE VALLEY

OMNIVORE Map p160   Books
☎ 415-282-4712; www.omnivorebooks.com; 3885a Cesar Chavez St; ⏰ 11am-6pm Mon-Sat, noon-5pm Sun; 🚌 24, 48, J
Salivate over signed cookbooks by chef-legend Alice Waters, A16's James Beard Rising Star Chef Nate Appelbaum, and signed copies of *Omnivore's Dilemma* by Michael Pollan. Check the in-store events calendar for standing-room-only events with star chefs, and don't miss the collection of vintage cookbooks and such rarities as a Civil War–era recipe-book, written longhand.

AMBIANCE Map p168   Clothing & Accessories
☎ 415-647-7144/5800; www.ambiancesf.com; 3985 & 3989 24th St; ⏰ 11am-7pm Mon-Fri, 10am-7pm Sat, 11am-7pm Sun; 🚌 24, 48, J
The splashy prints reel you in, and the sales pitch works every time: 'Oh. My. God. That looks so *key-oot* on you!' The shoe-and-sale store next door encourages you to keep the retail rush going, while the sister store at 1458 Haight St features teen-appropriate prom dresses, and 1858 Union St in the Marina offers cocktail attire.

SUI GENERIS
Map p160   Clothing & Accessories
☎ 415-436-9661; www.myspace.com/sui generis_sfo; 2265 Market St; ⏰ noon-7pm Wed & Thu, to 8pm Fri & Sat, to 4pm Sun; 🚌 24, F, K, L, M, Castro St
Even guys who thought they'd never go back in the closet crowd into this walk-in wardrobe of a boutique, with its stream-lined Costume National jackets and crisp,

SABRINA DALBESIO

Sunhee Moon

Needles & Pens (p192)

SABRINA DALBESIO

slim-fit Filippa K shirts in front and rock tees in back. The selection is best for men who fit runway-model sizes, yet have relatively fat wallets – think of them as collectibles, and auction them off on eBay next year.

CLIFF'S VARIETY

Map p168   DIY, Housewares

☎ 415-431-5365; www.cliffsvariety.com; 479 Castro St; ☻ 8:30am-8pm Mon-Fri, 9:30am-8pm Sat, 11am-6pm Sun; ⊜ 24, 33, F, K, L, M, Castro St

None of the hardware maestros at Cliff's will raise an eyebrow if you express a dire need for a 4x4 beam, a jar of rubber nuns, nontoxic silver paint and more cocktail toothpicks than anyone can safely use in a lifetime, though they might angle for an invitation. The window displays at Cliff's, a community institution since 1936, are a local landmark.

UNDER ONE ROOF

Map p168   Gifts, Housewares

☎ 415-503-2300; www.underoneroof.org; 518a Castro St; ☻ 10am-9pm; ⊜ 24, 33, F, K, L, M, Castro St

All the fabulous gift ideas under this roof are donated by local designers and businesses, so AIDS service organizations get 100% of the proceeds from your indispensable elephant tape dispenser, etched San Francisco skyline martini glasses and adorable Jonathan Adler vase. Those sweet sales clerks are volunteers, so show them some love for raising $11 million to date.

GLOBAL EXCHANGE FAIR TRADE CRAFT CENTER

Map p168   Gifts, Housewares

☎ 415-648-8068; www.globalexchangestore. org; 4018 24th St; ☻ 11am-6pm Sun-Thu, 11am-7pm Fri, 10am-7pm Sat; ⊜ 24, 48, J

Consumerism with a heart of gold: wild splurges on splashy Rwandan laptop bags, fair-trade chocolate, sweatshop-free sneakers from Pakistan and crates of organic-Egyptian-cotton carrots seem noble, since the proceeds go right back to the community cooperatives that made them via nonprofit Global Exchange.

THE HAIGHT & HAYES VALLEY

A   **B**   **C**   **D**

INFORMATION
Davies Medical Center......................**1** E4
Haight Ashbury Free Clinic **2** B4

SIGHTS
Alamo Square....................................**3** E2
Buena Vista Park...............................**4** D4
Grateful Dead House........................**5** B4
Haight Ashbury Food
   Program **6** B4
Zen Center...**7** G3

SLEEPING
Belvedere House **8** B6
Chateau Tivoli...................................**9** E1
Edwardian San Francisco
   Hotel..**10** H3
Hayes Valley Inn............................**11** H2
Inn 1890..**12** A4
Metro Hotel.....................................**13** D3
Red Victorian Bed, Breakfast
   & Art..**14** A4
Sleep Over Sauce...........................**15** H2
Stanyan Park Hotel **16** A4

EATING
Axum Cafe **17** E3
Bar Crudo...**18** D2

Bar Jules...**19** G2
Cole Valley Cafe **20** A4
Escape from New York Pizza........**21** A4
Little Chihuahua.............................**22** E3
Little Star Pizza...............................**23** D2
Magnolia Brewpub.........................**24** C4
Paulette Macarons.........................**25** H2
Rosamunde Sausage Grill.............**26** F3
Stacks..**27** G2
Suppenküche....................................**28** G2
Uva Enoteca.....................................**29** D3
Ziryab...**30** D3
Zuni Cafe..**31** H3

DRINKING
Alembic...(see 23)
Aub Zam Zam.................................**32** B4
Cav Wine Bar...................................**33** H3
Coffee to the People......................**34** C4
Hôtel Biron......................................**35** H3
Madrone..**36** D3
Mint...**37** G4
Momi Toby's Revolution Café.......**38** G2
Noc Noc..**39** F3
Sugar Lounge...................................**40** H2
Toronado..**41** F3

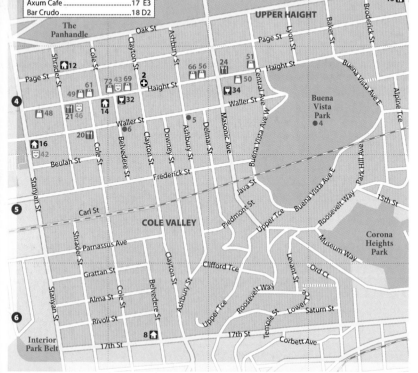

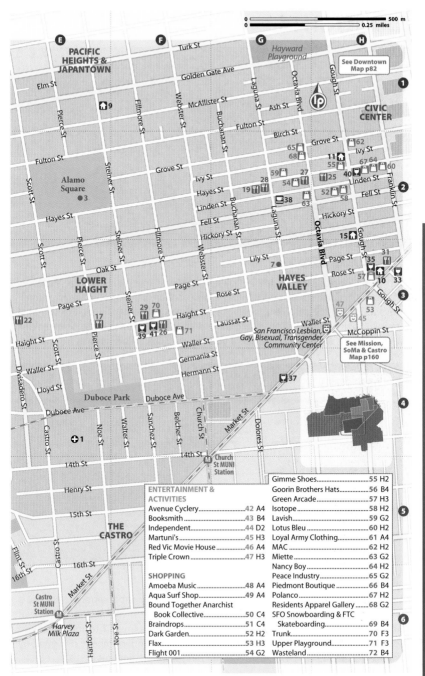

ENTERTAINMENT &
ACTIVITIES
Avenue Cyclery.............................42 A4
Booksmith...................................43 B4
Independent.................................44 D2
Martuni's......................................45 A4
Red Vic Movie House.................46 A4
Triple Crown................................47 H3

SHOPPING
Amoeba Music...............................48 A4
Aqua Surf Shop.............................49 A4
Bound Together Anarchist
  Book Collective..........................50 C4
Braindrops.....................................51 C4
Dark Garden..................................52 H2
Flax..53 H3
Flight 001......................................54 G2

Gimme Shoes................................55 H2
Goorin Brothers Hats.................56 B4
Green Arcade................................57 H3
Isotope...58 H2
Lavish..59 G2
Lotus Bleu......................................60 H2
Loyal Army Clothing...................61 A4
MAC...62 H2
Miette...63 G2
Nancy Boy.....................................64 H2
Peace Industry.............................65 G2
Piedmont Boutique.....................66 B4
Polanco..67 H2
Residents Apparel Gallery........68 G2
SFO Snowboarding & FTC
  Skateboarding...........................69 B4
Trunk..70 F3
Upper Playground.......................71 F3
Wasteland......................................72 B4

HIGHLIGHTS

1

↘ ALAMO SQUARE

Did these **Painted Ladies** (p204) make a deal with the devil? They're survivors of the 1906 earthquake and fire, yet Alamo Square's ageless Victorians are always ready for their close-ups in vacation shots of Postcard Row. For the best table in town, nab a hilltop picnic table with views Downtown, past mansions with turrets and cupola – and see if you can tell your Queen Annes from Sticks.

2

↘ ZEN CENTER

Those saffron robes you see gliding past Hayes Valley shop windows are not a passing fashion statement – that's the garb of Buddhist monks in residence at America's oldest **Zen retreat** (p204). Newcomers are invited to join weekend seated meditation and visit the 1922 courtyard building, originally designed by architect Julia Morgan as a residence for single working women.

THE HAIGHT & HAYES VALLEY

HIGHLIGHTS

⬎ RED VIC MOVIE HOUSE

The calendar at this co-op **cinema** (p213) is packed with cult classics, short-film festivals and virtually every surf and rock documentary ever made. The padded church pews are more comfortable than the busted sofas but, really, where else are you going to catch a late show of *The Muppet Movie* with a mug of gourmet cocoa in hand?

⬎ HAYES VALLEY BOUTIQUES

The attack of the killer sales rack begins innocently enough. Perhaps you came to Hayes Valley for some other reason, like a macaron or pre-Symphony cocktail – but once these clever Victorian **boutiques** (p215) pull you in, suddenly you're knee-deep in ankle boots, corsetry, carpets and luggage.

⬎ TORONADO

Request a pint of mead or a light Serbian summer brew, and you'd get laughed out of most bars – but at **Toronado** (p210), they thought you'd never ask. If the international selection of more than 100 craft beers, seasonal ales and house-brewed mead leaves you craving ever more obscure fermented drink, don't miss its annual Barleywine Festival.

1 DIANA MAYFIELD; 2 RYAN FOX; 3 SABRINA DALBESIO; 4 SABRINA DALBESIO; 5 EMILY RIDDELL

WALKING TOUR: HAIGHT FLASHBACKS

This tour covers more than 100 years of Haight history, starting in the 1860s at Buena Vista Park and meandering aimlessly right through the Summer of Love – all in a matter of 1.3 miles and under an hour and a half.

❶ BUENA VISTA PARK

Start your trip back in time with panoramic city views that inspired Victorians to make scandalously bold romantic moves c 1867, and that moved surviving San Franciscans to tears after the fire of 1906.

❷ MAGNOLIA BREWPUB

Heading west on Haight St, you can't miss this corner microbrewery and organic eatery named after a Grateful Dead song, which hippies may dimly recognize as the site of the infamous Drogstore Café. Pull up a seat at the communal table for a bite and/or a sampler of beer – with any luck, Arrogant Bastard will be on tap.

❸ BOUND TOGETHER ANARCHIST BOOK COLLECTIVE

Across Haight St, you may recognize Emma Goldman and Sacco and Vanzetti in the *Anarchists of Americas* mural – if you don't, staff can provide you with some biographical comics by way of introduction.

❹ 1235 MASONIC AVE

You might once have glimpsed the Simbionese Liberation Army in disguise at this address, where the SLA is believed to have held Patty Hearst, the kidnapped heiress turned revolutionary bank robber.

❺ 32 DELMAR ST

Turning right off Masonic Ave onto Waller St, you'll notice a narrow lane leading uphill. No 32 was the site of the 1978 Sid Vicious overdose that finally broke up the Sex Pistols. Under new ownership, this building betrays no trace of its rock 'n' roll past.

❻ GRATEFUL DEAD HOUSE

Pay your respects to the former flophouse of Jerry Garcia, Bob Weir and Pigpen, plus sundry Deadheads, at 710 Ashbury St. In October 1967, antidrug cops raided the house and arrested everyone in it (Garcia wasn't home).

❼ 635 ASHBURY ST

Down the block from the house of the Dead, this is one of many known San Francisco addresses for Janis Joplin, who had a hard time hang-

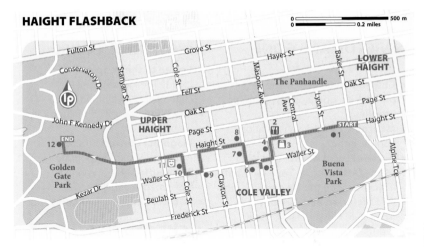

ing onto leases in the 1960s – but, as she sang in her rendition of Kris Kristofferson and Fred Foster's 'Me & Bobby McGee,' 'Freedom's just another word for nothin' left to lose.'

❽ 4:20 CLOCK
At the corner of Haight and Ashbury, you'll notice that the clock overhead always reads 4:20, better known in 'Hashbury' as International Bong Hit Time.

❾ HAIGHT ASHBURY FOOD PROGRAM
Back on Waller St, swing by the nonprofit that serves up hot meals and fresh starts to anyone in need. With a helping hand or modest donation, visitors can help the Food Program keep the spirit of the Summer of Love alive.

❿ 635 COLE ST
Another innocuous-looking building with a dark past, this apartment building once housed Charles Manson, the cult leader behind the 'Helter Skelter' murder of Sharon Tate – but on the corner, the rainbow *Evolution* mural serves to lighten the mood.

⓫ RED VIC MOVIE HOUSE
Check out the schedule of this movie house, which regularly screens cult classics, surf documentaries and premieres by local filmmakers.

⓬ HIPPIE HILL IN GOLDEN GATE PARK
Follow the erratic beat of the drum circle to 'Hippie Hill,' where free spirits have gathered since the '60s to tune in, turn on and attempt to hit a danceable groove.

BEST...

➘ VICTORIANS GONE WILD

- **Chateau Tivoli** (p205) The haunt of Victorian opera divas…perhaps literally.
- **Madrone** (p211) Art installations and absinthe.
- **Grateful Dead House** (opposite) As the Dead sang in 'Truckin,' What a long, strange trip it's been…'
- **Red Victorian Bed, Breakfast & Art** (p205) Flower-child theme rooms with psychedelic art.

➘ COLLECTIVE EFFORTS

- **Bound Together Anarchist Book Collective** (p213) It's anarchy inside this bookstore – well organized, too.
- **Haight Ashbury Food Program** (opposite) Free meals and second chances.
- **Red Vic Movie House** (p213) Worker-owned independent cinema.
- **Residents Apparel Gallery** (p217) Let the resident designers outfit you.

➘ POWERFUL DRINK

- **Coffee to the People** (p211) The Flower Power: chai+espresso+almond milk.
- **Cav Wine Bar** (p212) Malbec wine flights.
- **Magnolia Brewpub** (p208) Arrogant Bastard Strong Ale.
- **Alembic** (p211) Bourbon Old-Fashioned cocktails.
- **Aub Zam Zam** (p211) Martini, up.

➘ CHEAP DATES

- **Little Chihuahua** (p209) Sustainable steak tacos for two.
- **Rosamunde Sausage Grill** (p209) Piled with condiments, best with beer.
- **Axum Cafe** (p209) Lip-tingling spicy lentils.
- **Cole Valley Cafe** (p209) Hearty gourmet sandwiches.
- **Escape from New York Pizza** (p209) Potato pesto slices big enough to share.

ANTHONY PIDGEON

Red Victorian Bed, Breakfast & Art (p205)

DISCOVER THE HAIGHT & HAYES VALLEY

Whether you're a hippie born too late, punk born too early, or a weirdo who passes as normal, the Haight is here to claim you as its own. Since its '60s Summer of Love heyday, the Upper Haight has specialized in skateboarding, street musicians, potent coffee, radical literature and retail therapy for rebels. Though neighboring Cole Valley was once the haunt of Hunter S Thompson, Sid Vicious and Charles Manson (see Walking Tour, p200), the biggest excitements here nowadays are bistro openings and baby-stroller traffic jams. Savvy eateries rebranded Divisadero St south of Geary Blvd as 'NoPa,' attempting to attract a hip, foodie crowd that can afford to leave a decent tip. East of Divisidero, the Lower Haight has better bars, candy-colored mansions ringing Alamo Square, and a pot-club kind of mellow only occasionally disrupted by gang activity northeast of Fillmore and Haight Sts. Downhill from Alamo Square lies creative-chic Hayes Valley, where resident Zen monks wander past Victorian storefronts showcasing cutting-edge local designers and upstart chefs.

SIGHTS

BUENA VISTA PARK

Haight St btwn Central Ave & Baker St; 🚌 6, 24, 33, 71

True to its name, this park founded in 1867 offers sweeping views of the city beyond century-old cypresses to the bay and even Marin County, depending how far you're prepared to hike up the steep hill. When SF went up in flames in 1906, this was the safe spot where San Franciscans found refuge, and watched the town smolder; on your way downhill, take Buena Vista Ave West to spot Victorian mansions that date from that era.

GRATEFUL DEAD HOUSE

710 Ashbury St; 🚌 6, 33, 37, 71

Like most of the members of the Grateful Dead, this Victorian sports more than just a touch of gray – but back in the 1960s this was the candy-colored flophouse where Jerry Garcia and bandmates blew minds, amps and brain cells. The mom-and-pop flower shop up the block has done brisk business selling bouquets left on the steps here ever since Jerry's membership in the Dead took a turn for the literal, but the new owners would be most Grateful if you paid your respects to the great man with a donation to the Haight Ashbury Food Program.

HAIGHT ASHBURY FOOD PROGRAM

☎ 415-566-0366; www.thefoodprogram.org; 1525 Waller St; 🚌 6, 33, 37, 43, 71, N

Flower children who arrived in the '60s to a free hot meal in the Haight are now returning the favor at Haight Ashbury Food Program. Hippie idealism meets 21st-century street smarts here, where everyone gets a healthy meal and a second chance through retraining. If you volunteer to serve a meal or contribute

'Painted Ladies,' Alamo Square

ANTHONY PIDGEON

↘ ALAMO SQUARE

The finest restaurants in town can't provide views as spectacular as the picnic tables atop Alamo Square Park facing Steiner St's **Postcard Row**, a row of pastel Victorian 'Painted Lady' houses with gingerbread detailing and frosting flourishes that may leave you craving dessert. The city skyline looms in the background, and from the corner of Steiner and Fulton Sts you can glimpse City Hall. On the crest of the hill, check out the old shoes creatively reused as planters. On foggy days, you may want to wear a parka – as you can guess from the wind-sculpted pines, it can get a tad blustery up here.

Things you need to know: Hayes & Scott Sts; 🚌 21, 22, 24

to job training programs, you'll help them prove the Summer of Love isn't over yet.

ZEN CENTER

☎ 415-863-3136; www.sfzc.org; 300 Page St; ⏰ 9:30am-12:30pm & 1:30-5pm Mon-Fri, 8:30am-noon Sat; 🚌 6, 21, 22, 71

No, this isn't a spa, but rather an active spiritual retreat since 1969 for the largest Buddhist community outside Asia. The graceful landmark building was designed by Julia Morgan, California's first licensed female architect, who earned her reputation as a savvy cross-cultural architect with the Spanish-Greek Hearst Castle and the Chinatown YWCA (now the Chinese Historical Society of America Museum;

see p118). The center is open to the public for visits, meditation (see website for meditation schedule) and workshops, and also offers overnight stays by prior arrangement for intensive meditation retreats.

SLEEPING
THE HAIGHT
STANYAN PARK HOTEL   Historic Hotel $$

☎ 415-751-1000; www.stanyanpark.com; 750 Stanyan St; r $135-225, ste $275-350, incl breakfast; 🚌 71; 🛜

On the eastern edge of Golden Gate Park, a block from Haight St, this stately

Victorian hotel is completely up-to-date, with nary a drafty window or creaky floor. There's nothing risky about the traditional American decor – Queen Anne and Chippendale-style chairs, floral-print wallpaper and dusty-green and pale-pink color schemes – but that's also its charm: soothing familiarity and timelessness.

BELVEDERE HOUSE   B&B $$

☎ 415-731-6654, 877-226-3273; www.belvedere house.com; 598 Belvedere St; r incl breakfast $130-190; 🚌 6, 33, 37, N; 🛜

Six cozy rooms have eclectic art and vintage chandeliers, and the living room is packed with treasures from the owner's world travels. Though primarily for gay guests, all are welcome – kids get child-sized bathrobes.

CHATEAU TIVOLI   Historic Inn $$

☎ 415-776-5462; www.chateautivoli.com; 1057 Steiner St; r $140-170, r without bathroom $100-130, ste $250-290; 🚌 5, 22; 🛜

This imposing, glorious chateau on a secondary thoroughfare near Alamo Square has somewhat faded since the time when Isadora Duncan and Mark Twain were guests. The guestrooms are modest, with no TVs, but the place is full of soul, character and, rumor has it, the ghost of a Victorian opera diva.

RED VICTORIAN BED, BREAKFAST & ART   B&B $$

☎ 415-864-1978; www.redvic.net; 1665 Haight St; r $149-229, without bathroom $89-129, incl breakfast; 🚌 43; 🛜

The year 1968 lives on at the tripped-out Red Vic. Each individually decorated room in the 1904 landmark building pays tribute to peace, ecology and global friendship, with themes such as Sunshine, Flower Children and, of course, the Summer of Love. Only four of the 18 rooms have bathrooms; all come with breakfast in the (naturally) organic Peace Café.

METRO HOTEL   Hotel $

☎ 415-861-5364; www.metrohotelsf.com; 319 Divisadero St; r $76-120; 🚌 24; 🛜

On a thoroughfare bisecting the Upper and Lower Haight districts, this straightforward no-frills hotel provides cheap, clean rooms with private bathroom and an outdoor garden patio. Its location is largely residential, but you can easily walk to the Haight's bars and restaurants.

INN 1890   Historic Inn $

☎ 415-386-0486; www.inn1890.com; 1890 Page St; r $129, r without bathroom $99-119, ste $169; 🚌 33; 🛜

This stately 16-bedroom Victorian mansion sits on a residential street just one block from the action on Haight St. Every room

---

↘ TRANSPORTATION: HAYES VALLEY

BART Civic Center BART is four blocks east of Hayes Valley.

Bus The number 21 heads from Downtown along Hayes St to Golden Gate Park, and the 49 runs up Van Ness Ave along the eastern edge of Hayes Valley. Market St buses 6 and 71 stop along the south end of Hayes Valley, while bus 5 passes along the north side.

Streetcar The N and J lines stop at Van Ness station on Market St.

Parking Street parking is usually available, and there's a public lot underneath the City Hall plaza.

is different, with eclectic furniture and nothing frou-frou to get in your way. Most rooms only have a shower, but all have robes, slippers and down comforters. You can reserve one of the four parking spaces.

HAYES VALLEY

EDWARDIAN SAN FRANCISCO HOTEL   Hotel $$

☎ 415-864-1271, 888-864-8070; www.edwardiansfhotel.com; 1668 Market St; r $119-189; 🚐 F, Van Ness; 🛜

An unassuming brick-faced inn, the Edwardian has an ideal middle-of-the-city location between the Castro/Mission and Downtown, close to the symphony and opera. The excellent **Cav Wine Bar** (p212) is downstairs, and **Zuni Cafe** (p210) and the **Hôtel Biron** (p212) are nearby.

SLEEP OVER SAUCE   B&B $

☎ 415-252-1423; www.sleepsf.com; 135 Gough St; r $110-185; 🚐 21; 🛜

We like the homey vibe of this vintage 1906 inn, set upstairs from Sauce, a pretty-good dinner house. In late 2009 new owners renovated the former Albion House Inn, determined to remove all the little-old-lady furnishings left by the previous owners. Some rooms have baths across the halls; ask when you book if yours has en-suite facilities.

HAYES VALLEY INN   Inn $

☎ 415-431-9131; www.hayesvalleyinn.com; 417 Gough St; s $76-94, d $84-105, incl breakfast; 🚐 21; 🛜

Like a European pension, this amazingly reasonable find is surrounded by Hayes

---

↘ MAKING QUEEN VICTORIA BLUSH

The city's signature architectural style is usually called 'Victorian,' but demure Queen Victoria would surely blush to see the eccentric architecture perpetrated in her name in San Francisco. True Victorians tend to be drab, stately, earth-toned structures – nothing like San Franciscan **'Painted Ladies'** with candy-jar color palates, lavish gingerbread woodworking dripping off steeply peaked roofs, and gilded stucco garlands swagging huge, look-at-me bay windows. Of the 19th-century buildings that survived the 1906 fire and earthquake, many belong to other architectural categories.

- **Italianate** (1860s–1880s): around Jackson Sq, you can still see original Italianate brick buildings with elevated false facades capped with jutting cornices, a straight roofline and graceful arches over tall windows.
- **Stick** (1880s): in the Lower Haight and Pacific Heights, you'll notice some squared-off Victorians built to fit side-by-side in narrow lots, usually with flat fronts and long, narrow windows.
- **Queen Anne** (1880s–1910): Alamo Square has several exuberant examples built in wood with fish-scale shingle decoration, rounded corner towers and decorative bands to lift the eye skyward.
- **Edwardian** (1901–1914): most of the 'Victorians' you'll see in San Francisco are actually from the postfire Edwardian era, and art nouveau, Asian-inspired, and Arts and Crafts details are the giveaway. You'll notice the stained-glass windows and false gables in homes in the inner Richmond and Castro.

SABRINA DALBESIO

Chateau Tivoli (p205)

Valley shops and has simple, small rooms with shared bathrooms, a cocker spaniel panting in the parlor and staff who want to mother you. Many guests are long-term, repeat visitors.

EATING
THE HAIGHT

The Upper and Lower Haight have mural-covered eateries that are easy on the wallet and great for people-watching, but Divisadero St between Fell and Fulton Sts offers more trendy, sexy options for hot dates. When the folks are in town and in the mood for upscale dining, try Cole Valley.

BAR CRUDO   Seafood $$
☎ 415-409-0679; www.barcrudo.com; 655 Divisadero St; ⏲ 5-11pm Tue-Sat, 5-10pm Sun; 🚌 5, 21, 24
An international idea that's pure California: choice morsels of local seafood served raw Italian-style, with pan-Asian condiments and Belgian beers. Stick to

the pilsners with delicate raw Hawaiian kampachi served with Asian pear and mustard oil, and graduate to darker ales with gingery yellow-fin tuna served with Thai fish sauce and spring onion.

> ## ↘ TRANSPORTATION: THE HAIGHT
>
> **Bus** The 6 and 71 lines all connect the Haight with Downtown along Market St. Bus 43 connects the Upper Haight with the Presidio and the Marina, and 33 runs through the Upper Haight en route between the Richmond and the Mission. The 22 links the Lower Haight to the Mission and Potrero Hill to the south, and Japantown, Pacific Heights and the Marina to the north.
>
> **Streetcar** The N heads from Downtown all the way to Ocean Beach, with stops at Duboce Park in the Lower Haight and at Carl and Cole Sts in Cole Valley.

UVA ENOTECA   Californian, Italian $$

☎ 415-829-2024; www.uvaenoteca.com; 568 Haight St; ⏱ 5-11pm Mon-Thu, 5-11:30pm Fri, 11am-2:30pm & 5-11:30pm Sat, 11am-2:30pm & 5-10pm Sun; 🚌 6, 22, 71

Boys with shags and girls with bangs discover the joys of Bardolino and Barbera by the tasting glass, served with inventive small plates of local veggies, cheese and charcuterie boards by a sassy staff of tattooed Lower Haight hotties.

ZIRYAB   Middle Eastern $$

☎ 415-522-0800; www.ziryabgrill.com; 528 Divisadero St; ⏱ 5-11:30pm Mon-Thu, 11:45am-11:30pm Fri, 9am-11:30pm Sat, 10am-3pm Sun, brunch Sat & Sun; 🚌 5, 6, 21, 24, 71

Banish all traumatic memories of dry chicken *shwarmas* with this succulent, organic poultry rolled in flatbread and sealed by hummus with a tantalizing whiff of curry. The lentil soup is so robust it'll make your voice drop an octave, and the hookahs on the front porch provide solace to smokers rendered furtive by SF's antismoking laws.

LITTLE STAR PIZZA   Italian $$

☎ 415-441-1118; www.littlestarpizza.com; 846 Divisadero St; ⏱ 5-10pm Tue-Thu, 5-11pm Fri, 3-11pm Sat, 3-10pm Sun; 🚌 5, 21, 24; Ⓥ 🚳

Midwest weather patterns reveal that Chicago's thunder has been stolen by Little Star's deep-dish pie, with California additions of cornmeal crust, fresh local veggies and just the right amount of cheese. The all-meat pizza is a Chicago stockyard's worth of meat – not for the faint of heart.

MAGNOLIA BREWPUB   Californian, American $

☎ 415-864-7468; www.magnoliapub.com; 1398 Haight St; ⏱ noon-midnight Mon-Thu, noon-1am Fri, 10am-1am Sat, 10am-midnight Sun; 🚌 6, 33, 37, 43, 71; Ⓥ

Organic pub grub and samplers of home-brews keep the conversation flowing at communal tables, while grass-fed Prather Ranch burgers satisfy stoner appetites in the side booths – it's like the Summer of Love all over again, only with better food. Magnolia smells vaguely like a brewery

Bar Jules (p210)

SABRINA DALBESIO

because it is one, which can be a problem at brunch but is definitely an asset otherwise, with seasonal microbrew ales and wheat beers you won't find elsewhere.

AXUM CAFE
Ethiopian $

☎ 415-252-7912; www.axumcafe.com; 698 Haight St; ☽ dinner; 🚌 6, 22, 71, N; Ⓥ
When you've got a hot date with a vegan, the hunger of an athlete, and/or the salary of an activist, Axum's vegetarian platter for two with spongy *injera* bread is your saving grace. Dig in with your bare hands, and try not to hog the lip-tingling red lentils and mellow yellow chick peas.

LITTLE CHIHUAHUA
Mexican $

☎ 415-255-8225; www.thelittlechihuahua.com; 292 Divisadero St; ☽ 11am-10pm Mon-Wed, 11am-11pm Thu & Fri, 10am-11pm Sat, 10am-10pm Sun; 🚌 6, 24, 71
Who says sustainable, organic food has to be chichi and French? Charbroiled tomatillos, sustainable fish, Niman Ranch meats and organic veggies add up to sensational fresh flavor, packed into $4 tacos and $6 burritos.

ROSAMUNDE SAUSAGE GRILL
Sausages $

☎ 415-437-6851; 545 Haight St; ☽ 11:30am-10pm; 🚌 6, 22, 71, N
Impress a dinner date with $10: load up classic Brats or duck-fig links with complimentary roasted peppers, grilled onions, whole-grain mustard and mango chutney, and enjoy with your choice of 100 beers at **Toronado** (p210) next door.

COLE VALLEY CAFE
Cafe $

☎ 415-668-5282; www.colevalleycafe.com; 701 Cole St; ☽ 6:30am-8pm Mon-Fri, 7am-8:30pm Sat & Sun; 🚌 6, 33, 37, 43, 71, N; 🛜 Ⓥ ♿
Powerful coffee, free wi-fi, and hot gourmet sandwiches that are a bargain at

SABRINA DALBESIO

Coffee to the People (p211)

any price – let alone $6 for lipsmacking thyme-marinated chicken with lemony avocado spread, or the smoky roasted eggplant with goat cheese and sundried tomatoes. Chef-owner Jawad knows the entire neighborhood by name and lunch order, and has a kind word for everyone.

ESCAPE FROM NEW YORK PIZZA
Pizza $

☎ 415-668-5577; www.escapefromnewyork pizza.com; 1737 Haight St; ☽ 11:30am-midnight Sun-Thu, to 2am Fri & Sat; 🚌 6, 33, 37, 43, 71, N; Ⓥ ♿
The Haight's obligatory midbender stop for a hot slice. Pesto with roasted garlic and potato will send you blissfully off to carbo-loaded sleep, but the sundried tomato with goat cheese, artichoke hearts

and spinach will recharge you to go another round.

HAYES VALLEY

Shoe-shoppers and Sunday brunchers
throng Hayes Valley at weekends, but
during the week you might have your
choice of tables – at least until the opera
or symphony let out. The blocks of Market
St between Van Ness Ave and Octavia Blvd
are included in this section as well.

ZUNI CAFE   Californian $$$
☎ 415-552-2522; www.zunicafe.com; 1658
Market St; ☼ 11:30am-11pm Tue-Thu, 11:30am-
midnight Fri & Sat, 11am-11pm Sun; ☒ 6, 71, F
Reservations and fat wallets are necessary, but the see-and-be-seen seating is
a kick and the food is beyond reproach:
organic-beef burgers on focaccia, Caesar
salad with house-cured anchovies, crispy
roasted free-range chicken with horseradish mashed potatoes, and impeccable
chocolate pudding.

BAR JULES   Californian $$
☎ 415-621-5482; www.barjules.com; 609 Hayes
St; ☼ dinner Tue-Sat, lunch Wed-Sat, brunch
Sun; ☒ 5, 21
Small, local and succulent is the credo at
this corridor of a neighborhood bistro.
The short daily menu thinks big with
flavor-rich, sustainably minded pairings
such as local duck breast with farro, an
abbreviated but apt local wine selection
and the dark, sinister 'chocolate nemesis.'

PAULETTE MACARONS   Dessert $
☎ 415-864-2400; www.paulettemacarons.com;
437 Hayes St; ☼ 11am-7pm Tue-Sat, noon-6pm
Sun & Mon; ☒ 5, 21
Sorry, Oreo: the competition for the
ultimate sandwich cookie is down to
Paulette's Sicilian pistachio and passion-
fruit French macarons. Declare a winner

from your seat on a macaron-shaped
pouf, or go for a second championship
round: caramel *fleur-de-sel* salt and violet
cassis.

SUPPENKÜCHE   German $
☎ 415-252-9289; www.suppenkuche.com; 525
Laguna St; ☼ dinner daily, brunch Sun; ☒ 6,
21, 71
Feast on housemade Bratwurst sausages
and spaetzle oozing with cheese, and
toast your new friends at the unvar-
nished communal table with a 2L glass
boot of draft beer – then come back tomorrow to cure inevitable hangovers with
Sunday brunches of inch-thick 'Emperor's
Pancakes' studded with brandied raisins.

STACKS   American $
☎ 415-241-9011; www.stacksrestaurant.
com; 501 Hayes St; ☼ 7am-2:30pm Mon-Fri, to
3:30pm Sat & Sun; ☒ 6, 21, 71
The kitschy urns of artificial flowers and
faux-garden decor are more Branson-
Missouri motel than Cali cafe, but the
fluffy-crispy wheat-germ pancakes and
crepes stuffed with pesto, portobello and
roast chicken are fresh California takes on
brunch.

DRINKING
THE HAIGHT
TORONADO   Bar
☎ 415-863-2276; www.toronado.com; 547
Haight St; ☼ 11:30am-2am; ☒ 6, 22, 71
Glory hallelujah, beer-lovers: your prayers
have been heard. Be humbled before the
chalkboard altar listing 50-plus beers on
tap and hundreds more bottled, including
spectacular seasonal microbrews. Bring
cash, come early and stay late, with a
sausage from **Rosamunde** (p209) next
door to accompany ale made by Trappist
monks.

ALEMBIC   Bar

☎ 415-666-0822; www.alembicbar.com; 1725 Haight St; ⏰ noon-2am; 🚌 6, 7

Haight St's spiffiest bar has hammered tin ceilings, rough-hewn wood floors and an impressive array of whiskeys and mixology drinks, appealing to bon-vivant 30-somethings who jam the space every night. If you're not ordering dinner, expect to stand shoulder to shoulder. Great bar nibbles include za'atar potato chips.

AUB ZAM ZAM   Bar

☎ 415-861-2545; 1633 Haight St; ⏰ 3pm-2am; 🚌 6, 7

Arabesque arches, a gorgeous *Arabian Nights*–style mural, blues on the jukebox and top-shelf cocktails at low-shelf prices keep poets and musicians happy for the night at this Haight St mainstay. Ask about Bruno, the legendary now-deceased owner, who'd throw you out for ordering a vodka martini. Seriously.

MADRONE   Bar

☎ 415-611-6838; www.madronelounge.com; 500 Divisadero St; ⏰ 6pm-2am Tue-Sat, to midnight Sun & Mon; 🚌 5, 21, 24

A changing roster of DJs and giggling cuties come as a surprise in a goth-Victorian bar decorated with animal skulls, creepy murals of uprooted madrone trees and art suggesting untimely demises, but nothing surprises us as much as the jaw-dropping mashups at the Saturday-monthly Prince vs Michael Jackson party, when the place packs.

NOC NOC   Bar

☎ 415-861-5811; www.nocnocs.com; 557 Haight St; ⏰ 5pm-2am; 🚌 6, 22, 71

Who's there? Nearsighted graffiti artists, anarchist bike messengers moonlighting as electronica DJs, and other characters straight out of an R Crumb comic, that's who. The sake cocktails will knock you off your stool.

COFFEE TO THE PEOPLE   Cafe

☎ 415-626-2435; www.coffeetothepeople.com; 1206 Masonic Ave; ⏰ 6am-9pm Mon-Fri, 7am-9pm Sat & Sun; 🚌 6, 7; 📶

This utopian coffee shop hosts folksy Tuesday open-mic, and serves enough fair-trade coffee to revive the Sandinista movement. Five percent of your purchase

RICK GERHARTER

Zuni Cafe

goes to support community organizations, and baristas donate 3% of their tips to send children in coffee-growing regions to school.

HAYES VALLEY

CAV WINE BAR
Bar

☎ 415-437-1770; www.cavwinebar.com; 1666 Market St; ☉ 5pm-midnight Mon-Sat; ☐ 5, 6, F

Cav serves 40 wines by the glass (most under $10), available in flights or 2.5oz pours, in a concrete-and-metal industrial space. Tasty small plates keep your palate zinging.

HÔTEL BIRON
Bar

☎ 415-703-0403; www.hotelbiron.com; 45 Rose St; ☉ 5pm-2am; ☐ 5, 6, F

The vibe is French underground, with cool art, moody lighting and little nooks, but it's hard to score a table. Once you do, barkeeps let you keep tasting until you find what you like. Great cheese plates.

MINT
Bar

☎ 415-626-4726; www.themint.net; 1942 Market St; ☉ noon-2am; ☐ 22, F, J

Die-hard singers comb through giant books for the perfect song at this mixed-straight-gay karaoke bar, where show tunes are serious stuff. Best with a big posse.

SUGAR LOUNGE
Bar

☎ 415-255-7144; www.sugarloungesf.com; 377 Hayes St; ☉ 4-11:30pm Mon-Thu, to 2am Fri & Sat; ☐ 21

Cozy low-slung velvet snugs, chill downtempo beats, red lights and rock-candy-like wall sconces set a sexy mood at this tiny Hayes Valley bar, ideal after the symphony or opera, or for catching a buzz after shopping for strappy sandals up the street.

MOMI TOBY'S REVOLUTION CAFÉ
Cafe

☎ 415-626-1508; 528 Laguna St; ☉ 7:30am-10pm Mon-Thu, 7:30am-11pm Fri, 8am-10pm Sat & Sun; ☐ 6, 21, 71

For once, a cafe that's not an internet port. Dig the boho scene, with artists on both sides of the counter, swilling coffee and wine. Take sun at outdoor tables, or snag a window seat inside and meet the locals.

SABRINA DALBESIO

Momi Toby's Revolution Café

ENTERTAINMENT & ACTIVITIES
THE HAIGHT

AVENUE CYCLERY — Cycling
☎ 415-387-3155; www.avenuecyclery.com; 756 Stanyan St; bikes per hr/day $8/30; ☽ 10am-7pm Mon-Sat, to 6pm Sun; 🚌 21, 33; ♿

In one of the more bike-friendly parts of the city, Avenue has an extensive selection of bikes for rent and for sale. It also does repairs, fittings and cycle clinics. Rental includes a helmet.

RED VIC MOVIE HOUSE — Film
☎ 415-668-3994; www.redvicmoviehouse.com; 1727 Haight St; adult/senior & child/matinee & Tue night $9/6/7; 🚌 6, 33, 37, 43, 71, N

Collectively owned and operated for decades, the Red Vic has preserved a funky '70s vibe right down to the dilapidated couch seating and popcorn served in faux-wood snack bowls with optional brewer's yeast. Surfer flicks, punk rockumentaries and movies by local filmmakers pack the place, so get in line if you hope to avoid the too-deep seats with busted springs.

BOOKSMITH — Readings
☎ 415-863-8688; www.booksmith.com; 1644 Haight St; ☽ 10am-10pm Mon-Sat, to 8pm Sun; 🚌 6, 33, 37, 43, 71

SF is one of the country's top book markets, and authors often swing through town on tours. Past readings have included the likes of Kazuo Ishiguro, Ursula Le Guin and Jeanette Winterson.

INDEPENDENT — Rock
☎ 415-771-1421; www.theindependentsf.com; 628 Divisadero St; tickets $15-100; ☽ box office 11am-6pm Mon-Fri, to 9:30pm show nights, doors 7:30pm or 8:30pm; 🚌 5, 21, 24

One of the city's coolest live-music venues, the Independent showcases damn-good up-and-coming acts, big names such as Green Day, old bands such as Erasure, and wacky events such as the US Air Guitar Championships.

HAYES VALLEY

TRIPLE CROWN — Lounge
☎ 415-863-3516; www.triplecrownsf.com; 1760 Market St; admission varies; ☽ 5:30pm-2am; 🚌 F

A storefront bar with adjoining black-box rooms – one with glittering chandeliers, another with a disco-ball dance floor – Triple Crown hosts DJs spinning everything from '60s-soul and '80s-pop to down-tempo funk and hip-hop. Tuesdays are gay; call ahead or check the website to confirm opening times.

MARTUNI'S — Lounge
☎ 415-241-0205; www.martunis.citysearch.com; 4 Valencia St; ☽ 2pm-2am; 🚌 F

Slip behind the velvet curtains to see who's tickling the ivories at the city's last piano bar, where gay and straight graying regulars seem to have committed the *Great American Songbook* to memory.

SHOPPING
THE HAIGHT

BOUND TOGETHER ANARCHIST BOOK COLLECTIVE — Books
☎ 415-431-8355; www.boundtogetherbooks.com; 1369 Haight St; ☽ 11:30am-7:30pm; 🚌 6, 33, 37, 43, 71

Since 1976, this volunteer-run, nonprofit bookstore has kept free thinkers supplied with organic farming manuals, prison literature and radical comics, while coordinating the Anarchist Book Fair and restoring its *Anarchists of the Americas* storefront mural – makes us tools of the state look like slackers.

AQUA SURF
SHOP   Clothing & Accessories, Sporting Goods

☎ 415-876-2780; www.aquasurfshop.com; 1742 Haight St; 🕑 11am-7pm; rental per day board/ wetsuit $25/15; 🚌 6, 33, 37, 43, 71

No locals-only attitude here: this laid-back, tiki-themed surf shop has sex wax for your board, Bantu's fair-trade African-print bikinis and signature hoodies to brave chilly Ocean Beach. Even kooks (newbies) become mavericks with Aqua's wetsuit rentals, tide updates and lesson referrals.

LOYAL ARMY CLOTHING
Clothing & Accessories, Local Designer

☎ 415-221-6200; www.loyalarmy.com; 1728 Haight St; 🕑 10am-8pm Mon-Sat, 11am-7pm Sun; 🚌 6, 33, 37, 43, 71

Food with high self-esteem is a recurring theme on this San Francisco designer's cartoon-cute tees, totes and baby clothes: California rolls brag to nigiri sushi, 'That's how we roll!,' smiling custard declares 'Girls just wanna have flan!' and a grumpy bran muffin surrounded by uber-adorable pink cupcakes protests, 'Muffins are cute on the inside.'

UPPER PLAYGROUND
Clothing & Accessories, Local Designer

☎ 415-861-1960; www.upperplayground.com; 220 Fillmore St; 🕑 noon-7pm Mon-Fri, 11am-7pm Sat & Sun; 🚌 6, 22, 71, N

Blend into the SF scenery with locally de-signed Fillmore neighborhood hoodies, Barbary Coast pirate tees and knit Muni caps. Men's gear dominates the main store, but there's an even more impres-sive selection of locally designed tees in the women's annex, and slick graffiti art in Fifty24SF Gallery next door.

GOORIN
BROTHERS HATS   Millinery, Local Designer

☎ 415-436-9450; www.goorin.com; 1446 Haight St; 🕑 11am-7pm Sun-Fri, to 8pm Sat; 🚌 6, 33, 43, 71

Peacock feathers, high crowns and lo-cally designed embellishments make it easy for SF hipsters to withstand the fog while standing out in a crowd. Straw fe-

Amoeba Music

SABRINA DALBESIO

doras with striped tie-silk bands bring the shade in style, and flat-brim baseball caps go high-culture with embroidery of Sumerian hero Gilgamesh destroying the demon Humbaba.

AMOEBA MUSIC
Music

☎ 415-831-1200; 1855 Haight St; ⏲ 10:30am-10pm Mon-Sat, 11am-9pm Sun; 🚌 6, 33, 37, 43, 71

Enticements are hardly necessary to lure the masses to the West Coast's most eclectic collection of new and used music and video, but Amoeba offers listening stations, a free music zine with uncannily accurate reviews, a free concert series that recently starred Elvis Costello and the Breeders, and a foundation that's saved more than 950 acres of rainforest.

SFO SNOWBOARDING & FTC SKATEBOARDING
Sporting Goods, Local Maker

☎ 415-626-1141; www.sfosnow.com; 1630 Haight St; ⏲ 11am-7pm; 🚌 6, 33, 37, 43, 71

Show some San Franciscan style as you grab air on a Western Edition deck tricked out with drawings of Fillmore jazz greats and ramshackle Victorian houses, or hit the slopes with Tahoe-tested gear. Check the website for upcoming SF street games and current Tahoe snow conditions.

WASTELAND
Vintage Clothing & Accessories

☎ 415-863-3150; www.wastelandclothing.com; 1660 Haight St; ⏲ 11am-8pm Mon-Sat, noon-7pm Sun; 🚌 71

The catwalk of thrifting, this vintage superstore adds instant style with funky bell-sleeved Custo shirts, Pucci maxi-skirts and a steady supply of go-go boots. Hip occasionally verges on hideous with acrylic sweaters and patchwork suede

jackets, but at these prices, you can afford to take fashion risks.

HAYES VALLEY

FLAX
Art Supplies, DIY

☎ 415-552-2355; www.flaxart.com; 1699 Market St; ⏲ 9:30am-7pm Mon-Sat; 🚌 6, 71, J, K, L, M, N; ♿

People who swear they lack artistic flair suddenly find it at Flax, where an entire room of specialty papers, racks of plump paint tubes in luscious colors, and a wonderland of hot glue guns practically make the collage for you. Kid-art projects start here, and the vast selections of pens and notebooks are novels waiting to happen.

POLANCO
Arts & Crafts

☎ 415-252-5753; 393 Hayes St; ⏲ 11am-7pm Tue-Sat, 1-6pm Sun; 🚌 6, 21, 71

Contemporary folk art by Mexican and Chicano artists mix traditional techniques and new ideas at Polanco, from Artemio Rodriguez' woodcuts of Day of the Dead skeletons sporting Mohawks to a traditional ex-voto painting on tin showing before and after portraits of a transgendered friend by Fernando Guevara. Don't miss the Oaxacan devil masks embedded with actual goat's horns and teeth, or the Frida Kahlo–esque earrings of silver hands cupping tiny hearts.

NANCY BOY
Beauty Products, Local Maker

☎ 415-552-3802; www.nancyboy.com; 347 Hayes St; ⏲ 11am-7pm Mon-Fri, to 6pm Sat & Sun; 🚌 5, 21, 42, 47, 49

All you closet pomaders and after-sun balmers: wear those products with pride, without feeling like the dupe of some cosmetics conglomerate. Clever Nancy Boy knows you'd rather pay for the product than for advertising campaigns featuring the starlet du jour, and delivers locally made products with effective

↘ IF YOU LIKE...

If you like scoring original fashion statements at **Wasteland** (p215), check out these other sources for SF alternative fashion:

- **Piedmont Boutique** (☎ 415-864-8075; www.piedmontsf.com; 1452 Haight St; ☉ 11am-7pm; ☐ 6, 7, 33, 37, 43, 71) The costumer of choice for cross-dressers, cabaret singers, strippers and people who take Halloween dead seriously. All the getups are custom-designed in-house and built to last – so, like certain escorts, honey, they're not as cheap as they look.

- **Trunk** (☎ 415-861-5310; www.trunksf.com; 544 Haight St; ☉ 11am-8pm Wed-Mon; ☐ 6, 7, 22, 71, N) A cooperative local-designer boutique that keeps the Burning Man aesthetic alive year-round, mixing Miranda Caroligne's radically reconstructed patchwork sweaters, mesmerizing Dida glass-globe earrings and high-drama flower fascinators with veils.

- **Dark Garden** (☎ 415-431-7684; www.darkgarden.com; 321 Linden St; ☉ 11am-5pm Sun-Tue, to 6pm Wed-Sat; ☐ 6, 7, 21, 71) Makes Victorian-theme weddings and Marilyn Manson tribute band performances a cinch with made-to-measure corsets in silk jacquard or va-va-voom velvet.

- **Braindrops** (☎ 415-621-4162; www.braindrops.net; 1324 Haight St; ☉ noon-7pm Sun-Thu, to 8pm Fri & Sat; ☐ 6, 7, 33, 37, 43, 71) The SF tattoo shop of choice for the visiting artists from New York and Berlin. Piercings are done here gently without a gun, with body jewelry ranging from pop-star opal belly-button studs to mondo jade ear spools.

plant oils that are tested on boyfriends, never animals.

ISOTOPE   Books
☎ 415-621-6543; www.isotopecomics.com; 326 Fell St; ☉ 11am-7pm Tue-Fri, to 6pm Sat & Sun; ☐ 6, 21, 71; ♿

The toilet seats signed by famous cartoonists over the front counter show just how seriously Isotope takes comics. Newbies tentatively flip through Daniel Clowes and Chris Ware, while fanboys load up on Berkeley's Adrian Tomine or the latest from SF's Last Gasp Publishing and head upstairs to lounge with local cartoonists.

GREEN ARCADE   Books
☎ 415-431-6800; www.thegreenarcade.com; 1680 Market St; ☉ 11am-7pm Tue-Sun; ☐ 6, 21, 71

Everything you always wanted to know about foraging for mushrooms, composting with worms and running for office on an environmental platform, but were afraid to ask. This bookstore emphasizes helpful how-to books over eco-apocalypse treatises, so you'll leave with a rosier outlook on how you can make the world a greener place.

MAC   Clothing & Accessories
☎ 415-863-3011; 387 Grove St; ☉ 11am-7pm Mon-Sat, noon-6pm Sun; ☐ 5, 21, 42, 47, 49

'Modern Appealing Clothing' is what it promises, and what it delivers with structured looks from Belgian minimalist Dries Van Noten, pop-art patterns from Van Beirendonck and silk dresses with midnight-blue forest silhouettes by Tsumori Chisato. The staff are on your side, rooting for you to rock these designs, steering you away from looks that don't quite click and enjoying the contact retail high when you find something from the 40%-to-75%-off sales rack.

RESIDENTS APPAREL GALLERY

Clothing & Accessories, Local Designer
☎ 415-621-7718; www.ragsf.com; 541 Octavia Blvd; ◷ noon-7pm Mon-Sat, to 6pm Sun; ᗑ 6, 21, 71
Local designers at design-school prices make eclectic SF chic easy at this certified-green cooperative boutique. Take your pick of limited-edition screen-printed tees; locally made designer dark denims (no sweatshops here, thank you); clever reconstructed vintage dresses and de-signer jewelry in silver; gemstones; and recycled comics.

MIETTE

Food & Drink
☎ 415-626-6221; www.miettecakes.com; 449 Octavia Blvd; ◷ 11am-7pm; ᗑ 6, 21, 71, F
Pure candy heaven: racks of licorice twists, a table of artisan chocolate bars and a fully stocked cupcake counter. Tots load up on Pixie Stix and chocolate fire trucks, while adults ogle salty French caramels and dark chocolates spiked with chili. Ask for help first, so that you don't get caught with your hand in the candy jar.

LAVISH

Gifts, Clothing & Accessories
☎ 415-565-0540; www.shoplavish.com; 508 Hayes St; ◷ 11am-7pm Mon-Sat, to 6pm Sun; ᗑ 6, 21, 71, F
Baby shower gifts are a done deal here with teensy superhero capes, eensy uni-sex pink dumptruck onesies and weensy moon boots. Splurge on your favorite mom while you're at it, with pin-tucked Plume organic peasant tops and screen-printed hipster hoodies that look nothing like standard-issue momswear.

LOTUS BLEU

Housewares, Local Designer
☎ 415-861-2700; www.lotusbleudesign.com; 327 Hayes St; ◷ 11am-6pm Tue-Fri, to 7pm Sat, noon-5pm Sun; ᗑ 5, 21, 42, 47, 49
French whimsy, Vietnamese design and a San Franciscan love of splashy color keeps eyes open wide in this tiny design boutique packed from basement to rafters

SABRINA DALBESIO
Green Arcade

RICK GERHARTER

Miette (p217)

with linen pillows with psychedelic blooms, French striped canvas totes and pop-art lacquer breakfast trays.

PEACE INDUSTRY
Housewares, Local Designer

☎ 415-255-9940; www.peaceindustry.com; 539 Octavia Blvd; ⊙ 10am-6pm Mon-Fri, 11am-6pm Sat, 11am-5pm Sun; 🚌 6, 21, 71

Persian carpets usually take credit for grand entrances, but Peace Industry's cooperative-made Iranian felted wool rugs offer graphic appeal and a deliciously spongy, ticklish texture. Get back to nature with a dewdrop pattern in off-white and brown wool, go arty with Ruth Asawa–inspired orbs, or opt for a single flower underfoot.

GIMME SHOES
Shoes

☎ 415-864-0691; www.gimmeshoes.com; 416 Hayes St; ⊙ 11am-7pm Mon-Sat, noon-6pm Sun; 🚌 6, 21, 71

Don't let SF hills become your arch-rivals: head to Gimme Shoes and kick up those high-end heels. Bide your time and those coral Dries Van Noten kitten heels might hit the 40%-to-60%-off rack alongside Chie Mihara acid-yellow-and-eggplant slingbacks. Men have their pick of pewter Converse by Varvatos.

FLIGHT 001
Travel Accessories

☎ 415-487-1001; www.flight001.com; 525 Hayes St; ⊙ 11am-7pm Mon-Sat, to 6pm Sun; 🚌 6, 21, 71

Having a nice flight in the zero-legroom era is actually a possibility with the in-flight assistance of Flight 001. Clever carry-ons built to fit international size regulations come with just the right number of pockets for rubber alarm clocks, travel Scrabble sets and the first-class Jet Comfort Kit with earplugs, sleep mask, booties, neck rest, candy and cards.

GOLDEN GATE PARK & THE AVENUES

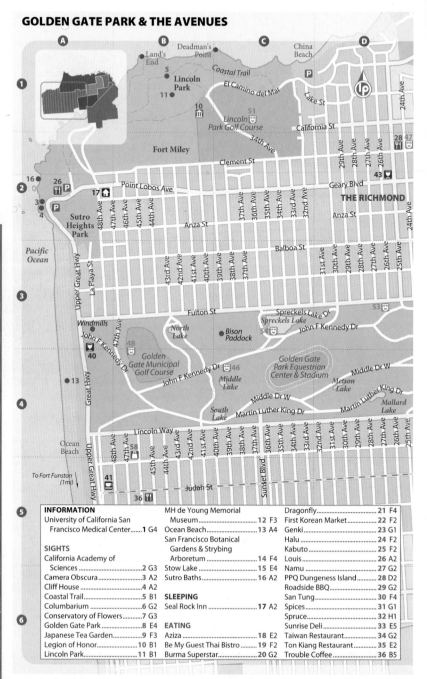

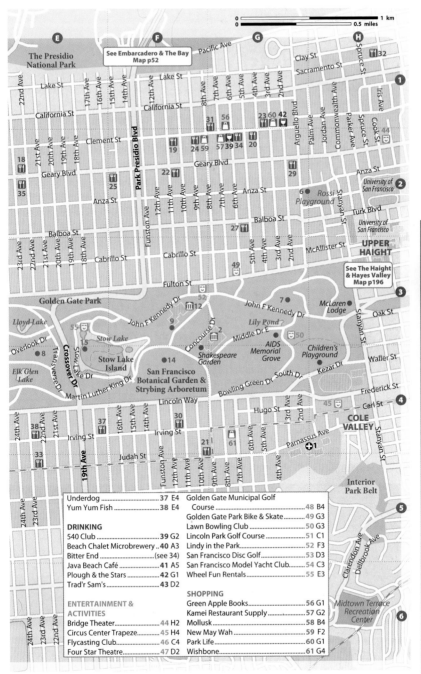

See Embarcadero & The Bay
Map p52

See The Haight
& Hayes Valley
Map p196

HIGHLIGHTS

1 GOLDEN GATE PARK

Wild schemes have unfolded in Golden Gate Park ever since its approval by San Francisco voters in 1865, including camel-riding, igloos, casinos and roller derbys. Luckily, its most enduring characteristic is a stretch of greenery so ruggedly romantic an 1886 newspaper editorial cautioned that its park benches inspired 'excess hugging.' Windbreakers and willpower come in handy as you approach the western end of the park, where quixotic bison run toward windmills, and urban hikers are rewarded with microbrews and historic murals at the Beach Chalet.

⇘ OUR DON'T MISS LIST

❶ CALIFORNIA ACADEMY OF SCIENCES
Mad scientists would surely approve, from the basement electric-eel forest to the solar-paneled wildflower meadow on the roof. The Academy's tradition of weird science dates from 1853, and it houses thousands of live animals and 46 scientists under one roof.

❷ MH DE YOUNG MUSEUM
The sleek, copper-clad de Young is oxidizing green to match the park, but its eclectic, globe-trotting collection is a standout, including Beat collage, international textiles and Oceanic art dating from the museum's 1894 origins.

❸ SAN FRANCISCO BOTANICAL GARDEN & STRYBING ARBORETUM
This botanical wonderland confounds all geography: South African cape grasses sway near the California redwood grove, not far from the Japanese Moon-Viewing garden. Almost anything

Clockwise from top: Japanese Tea Garden (p232); View from MH de Young Museum (p231)

CLOCKWISE FROM TOP: RICHARD CUMMINS; STEPHEN SAKS

thrives in Golden Gate Park's peculiar temperate climate, with 8000 varieties of plants and no need for a greenhouse.

❹ JAPANESE TEA GARDEN
A signature attraction since 1894, this tiny garden erupts into cherry blossoms in spring and turns flaming red with maple leaves in fall. Pagoda pa-

vilions and miniature waterfalls offer a photo-op at every turn.

❺ CONSERVATORY OF FLOWERS
The prim and proper 1878 greenhouse has a definite flair for the exotic, from Amazonian waterlilies to the fanged Dracula orchid and the occasional giant corpse flower.

- ❶ California Academy of Sciences
- ❷ MH de Young Fine Arts Museum
- ❸ San Francisco Botanical Garden & Strybing Arboretum
- ❹ Japanese Tea Garden
- ❺ Conservatory of Flowers

0 —— 500 m
0 —— 0.25 miles

❧ THINGS YOU NEED TO KNOW

Car-free weekends JFK Dr is closed weekends and holidays from Stanyan St to 19th Ave **Free concerts** Check out Sharon Meadow or Polo Fields on weekends, especially September and October **Transportation** Take the N Judah to 9th or buses 5, 21 or 71 **For full Golden Gate Park details, see p229**

HIGHLIGHTS

⬊ LEGION OF HONOR

Inside this marble-clad replica of Paris' Legion d'Honneur is a **world-class collection of arts and crafts** (p227), from Monet waterlilies to John Cage soundscapes, ancient Iraqi ivories to R Crumb comics. Rodin's 'The Kiss' is the star of the legacy of Legion benefactor 'Big Alma' de Bretteville Spreckels – except at 4pm on weekends, when pipe organ recitals steal the show in the Rodin gallery.

⬊ COASTAL TRAIL

Bundle up and bring your binoculars: this 9-mile **trek** (p227) along San Francisco's windswept Pacific Coast leads from abandoned missile silos haunted by hawks and hang gliders to smooch-inspiring sculpture at a war-memorial museum. But wait, there's more: this trail is an essential link in a planned 1200-mile coastal hiking trail from Mexico to Oregon.

4

⬆ NON-OLYMPIC SPORTS

Atypical athletes find their niches in Golden Gate Park, which gives unsung **sports** (p239) their due with fly-casting pools, the lawn bowling club, a model-yacht marina, 18 holes of disc golf, a big-band shell for Lindy-hopping, and blacktop reserved for Sunday roller disco. Or try trapeze and in-line skating in the Avenues.

5

⬆ MULTI-ETHNIC EAT STREETS

When you can sniff **dinner** (p233) underway across three continents, you've arrived in the Avenues. Try Irving, Geary or Clement Sts for all manner of fare: Middle Eastern stuffed grape leaves, organic Moroccan, traditional dim sum, wildly inventive sushi, sizzling-hot Szechuan, Irish pub fare or Burmese ti-leaf salad.

6

⬆ OCEAN BEACH

Toes curl at their first encounter with the frigid Pacific, but they'll be back for more. Beachcombers strike it rich in sand dollars on the south end of the **beach** (p229), while surfers and sea lions brave wicked waves around Seal Rock to the north. By day, puppies and kids have the run of the place; by night, bonfires keep bikers and Beat poetry readers warm.

2 RAY LASKOWITZ; 3 LEE FOSTER; 4 SABRINA DALBESIO; 5 THOMAS WINZ; 6 RICK GERHARTER

2 Sculpture at Legion of Honor (p227); 3 View of Golden Gate Bridge from Coastal Trail (p227); 4 Roller skating, Golden Gate Park; 5 Clement St, the Richmond; 6 Ocean Beach (p229)

BEST...

URBAN NATURE WALKS

- **Golden Gate Park** (p229) Three miles of wilderness and weirdness.
- **Fort Funston** (p229) Hang gliders leap from fortifications.
- **Lincoln Park** (p228) End-of-the-world views.
- **Ocean Beach** (p229) Pacific waves take on sandcastle condos and hardcore surfers.

VICTORIAN CURIOSITIES

- **Conservatory of Flowers** (p233) Venus flytraps in a lacy white greenhouse.
- **Sutro Baths** (p228) Ruins of a wooly-bathing-suit wonderland.
- **Columbarium** (p228) Gorgeously macabre stained-glass crematorium.
- **Camera Obscura** (p228) Pacific seascape projections.

OUTPOSTS OF COOL

- **Park Life** (p240) Indie publisher, art gallery, design showcase.

- **Mollusk** (p242) Surfboard-shapers in residence, and hoodies by Whitney Biennial artists.
- **MH de Young Museum** (p231) Friday nights bring experimental music and Mission muralists.
- **Genki** (p236) Anime fans freak over Japanese candy and super-hero-shade hair dye.
- **Trouble Coffee** (p236) Surfers scarf raisin toast, coffee and whole coconuts.

GOURMET AUTHENTICITY TRIPS

- **Sunrise Deli** (p235) Baba ghanoush just like Middle Eastern mamas make.
- **New May Wah** (p241) Durian, rice wine and other Asian foodie essentials.
- **Ton Kiang Restaurant** (p235) Pork buns cause dim-sum-cart traffic jams.
- **Halu** (p235) Beatles-themed yakitori diner.
- **First Korean Market** (p236) Killer kimchi counter.

LEE FOSTER

Hang glider, Fort Funston (p229)

DISCOVER GOLDEN GATE PARK & THE AVENUES

All those Golden Gate Bridge postcards and talk of Downtown restaurants are diabolical ploys by San Franciscans to direct your attention away from the western stretch of the city, which they'd prefer to keep to themselves. Golden Gate Park is the city's glorious wild streak, with pagan altars, bonsai forests, redwood groves and bison paddocks that make New York's Central Park look entirely too staid. If the park had decent espresso and burritos, locals might never leave.

Populist millionaire and future mayor Adolph Sutro built a public railway in the 1890s to transport residents of cramped Downtown tenements to breezy Ocean Beach. Modest tract homes sprang up along the line in the Richmond District, where transplanted immigrant communities thrived alongside the park's botanical transplants.

South of Golden Gate Park, the Sunset District is a swath of candy-colored stucco homes running from the Haight to Ocean Beach. The neighborhood gets hip around Irving and 9th and Judah and 45th, with top-value ethnic eateries and surf hangouts.

SIGHTS
THE RICHMOND
COASTAL TRAIL
☼ sunrise-sunset; 🚌 28, N

Suit up and hit your stride on the 9-mile Coastal Trail, starting at Fort Funston and wrapping around the Presidio paralleling Lincoln Blvd to end at Fort Mason. The 4 miles of sandy Ocean Beach will definitely work those calves and numb your toes – yep, the water's about that cold year-round. Casual strollers will prefer to pick up the trail near Sutro Baths, head around Land's End for a peek at Golden Gate Bridge, and then duck into the Legion of Honor (below) at Lincoln Park.

LEGION OF HONOR
☎ 415-750-3600; legionofhonor.famsf.org; Lincoln Park; adult/child under 12yr/teen/senior $10/free/6/7, $2 discount with Muni transfer, 1st Tue of month free; ☼ 9:30am-5:15pm Tue-Sun; 🚌 1, 2, 18, 38; ♿

Never doubt the unwavering resolve of a nude model. The Legion was a gift to San Francisco from Alma de Bretteville Spreckels, a sculptor's model who married well and decided to create a fitting artistic tribute to Californians killed in France in WWI. Today, the Legion still 'honors the dead while serving the living' with blockbuster exhibitions, mixing crowd-pleasing shows of Egyptian art and Fabergé eggs with Max Klinger's obscure, macabre 19th-century Waking Dream etchings.

The collection spans medieval to 20th-century European art, including many works by the impressionists and the Achenbach Foundation for Graphic Arts, one of the premier collections of works on paper in the US. In honor of 'Big Alma's' early career, the museum also has a sizable collection of sculpture by Auguste Rodin and Henry Moore.

LINCOLN PARK

☎ 415-221-9911; Clement St; admission free;
☼ sunrise-sunset; 🚌 1, 2, 18, 38
John McLaren took time out from his day job as Golden Gate Park's superintendent for 56 years to establish lovely Lincoln Park. A well-tended walking path covers a surprisingly rugged, bucolic stretch of coast from the Cliff House to the Legion of Honor, part of the 9-mile Coastal Trail. Terrific views of the Golden Gate are a highlight of the half-hour hike from Land's End to the Legion – and it's worth it, fog or no fog. Pick up the trailhead near the remains of the Sutro Baths.

SUTRO BATHS

☼ sunrise-sunset; 🚌 5, 18, 31, 38
In its heyday, Victorian dandies and working stiffs converged here for a bracing bath and workout in itchy wool rental swimsuits. Mining magnate and populist mayor Adolph Sutro built hot and cold indoor pools to accommodate 25,000 frolicking unwashed masses in 1896, but the masses apparently preferred dirt, and the place was finally closed in 1952. Follow the path through the sea-cave archway at low tide for an end-of-the-world view of Marin.

CLIFF HOUSE

☎ 415-386-3330; www.cliffhouse.com; 1090 Point Lobos Ave; admission free; 🚌 18
Populist millionaire Adolph Sutro imagined this place as a working-man's paradise, and in 1863 it already provided a much-needed escape from the tenements and tawdriness of Downtown. It miraculously survived the 1906 earthquake, only to be destroyed by fire the following year. The 1909 replacement didn't match the original, and was mostly popular for its bar and restaurant. The latest attempt to reclaim former glory was in 2004, when a $19 million facelift turned the Cliff House into an upscale (read: overpriced) restaurant with all the charm of a fast-food outlet. Sutro would not be pleased, though two of the area's popular attractions remain: views of sea lions blithely frolicking among the seagull guano on Seal Rock, and the **Camera Obscura** (☎ 415-750-0415; www.giantcamera.com; 1090 Point Lobos Ave; admission $3; ☼ 11am-sunset), a Victorian invention that projects the sea view outside onto a parabolic screen inside a small building.

COLUMBARIUM

☎ 415-771-0717; 1 Loraine Ct btwn Stanyan St & Arguello Blvd (off Anza St); ☼ 8am-5pm Mon-Fri, 9:30am-3pm Sat & Sun; 🚌 5, 21, 31, 33, 38
The ancient Roman innovation of memorial buildings for cremated remains came in handy in San Francisco in 1898, when real estate was already hitting a

---

↘ TRANSPORTATION: GOLDEN GATE PARK & THE AVENUES

Bus Numbers 1 and 38 run from Downtown to the Richmond. Buses 5 and 21 head from Downtown along the north edge of Golden Gate Park. Bus 71 hooks around Golden Gate Park on the Sunset side, while number 2 runs the length of Clement St from Arguello Blvd past the Legion of Honor.

Streetcar The N train runs from Downtown, through the Sunset to Ocean Beach.

Parking There's a small lot near the MH de Young Memorial Museum in Golden Gate Park; otherwise, curb-side parking is available in the park.

STEPHEN SAKS

Ruins of Sutro Baths

premium on the seven-by-seven peninsula. The neoclassical Columbarium was abandoned to raccoons and mushrooms from 1934 until 1979, when it was rescued by the Neptune Society, a cremation advocacy group. The restored, resplendent domed Columbarium is lined with art nouveau stained-glass windows and more than 5000 niches, honoring dearly beloved friends, dogs and rabbits.

THE SUNSET
OCEAN BEACH
☎ 415-556-8371; ☼ sunrise-sunset; 🚌 5, 23, 31, 38, 48, 71, N

Bikinis, Elvis sing-alongs and clambakes are not the scene here – think more along the lines of wetsuits, pagan rituals and s'mores (toasted marshmallow treats). Bonfires are permitted in the artist-designed fire pits, but be sure to follow park rules about fire maintenance and alcohol (not allowed) or you could get fined. On rare sunny days the waters may beckon, but only hardcore surfers and sea lions should brave these riptides.

FORT FUNSTON
☎ 415-561-5505; Skyline Blvd; ☼ 6am-9pm

The grassy dunes of Fort Funston give you some idea what the Sunset looked like before it was paved over in the early 20th century. The fort is protected as part of the Golden Gate National Recreation Area, and it attracts butterflies and migrating birds. The park is a defunct military installation, and you can still see a WWII gun battery where 146-ton guns point out to sea, and remains of Nike missile silos near where the parking lot is now. One of the most thrilling aspects of the park is that **hang gliders** launch and land from here.

GOLDEN GATE PARK
GOLDEN GATE PARK
☎ 415-831-2700; McLaren Lodge park headquarters, cnr Fell & Stanyan Sts; admission free; ☼ 24hr; 🚌 5, 7, 21, 31, 33, 71, N

When San Franciscans refer to 'the park,' there's only one that gets the definite article: Golden Gate Park. Everything San Franciscans hold dear is here: free spirits, free music, redwoods, Frisbee, protests, fine art, bonsai and buffalo. Check out the range of attractions (see p222), or just follow your bliss from east to west.

Mayor Frank McCoppin's wild idea for a park was ahead of its time in 1866, when western sand dunes seemed utterly uninteresting compared with the gold and silver mines in the mountains to the east. Even Frederick Law Olmstead, the celebrated architect of New York's Central Park, was daunted by the prospect of transforming 1017 acres of dune into park. Instead, San Francisco's green scheme fell to a young but surprisingly tenacious civil engineer William Hammond Hall, who steered the project to completion. Instead of hotels and casinos, Hammond Hall insisted on botanical gardens, the **Japanese Tea Garden** (p232) and boating on scenic **Stow Lake** (p233).

The park does have its outlandish attractions, including carnivorous plants and outer-space orchids in the 1879 **Conservatory of Flowers** (p233). But even in Hammond's wildest dreams, he might not have imagined the park's newest attractions: architect Renzo Piano's **California Academy of Sciences** (opposite) with an indoor rainforest and California wildflowers sprouting from the roof, and Herzog & de Meuron's sleek, copper-clad **MH de Young Museum** (opposite).

To accommodate the masses that descend on the park any given Sunday, John F Kennedy Dr is closed to motor vehicles east of Crossover Dr (around 8th Ave), where the skateboarders, in-line skaters and unicyclists come out in force. Saturdays from June to October the park is also closed to traffic along John F Kennedy Dr.

To plan a picnic, protest or some other event in the park and get detailed park maps, check in at **McLaren Lodge** (cnr Fell & Stanyan Sts; ⏰ 8am-5pm Mon-Fri) at the eastern entrance of the park, under the splendid cypress that's the city's official tree. For information about free park walking tours, call **Friends of Recreation & Parks** (☎ 415-263-0991).

MH de Young Memorial Museum

MH DE YOUNG MEMORIAL MUSEUM

☎ 415-750-3600; http://deyoung.famsf.org; 50 Hagiwara Tea Garden Dr; adult/child under 12yr/college student & child 13-17yr/senior $10/free/6/7, $2 discount with Muni transfer, 1st Tue of month free; ⏰ 9:30am-5:15pm Tue-Sun, until 8:45pm Fri mid-Jan–Nov; 🚌 5, 21, 44, 71, N; ♿ You'd think the art would be upstaged by Swiss architects Herzog & de Meuron (of Tate Modern fame) and their sleek building, with its copper cladding oxidizing green to become part of the scenery, the facade perforated in a seemingly abstract pattern drawn from aerial photography of the park. But this landmark collection of arts and fine crafts from around the world puts California's own artistic pursuits into global perspective, and hides a surprise around every corner – don't miss 19th-century Oceanic ceremonial masks and stunning Central Asian rugs from the 11,000-plus textile collection. Blockbuster temporary shows range from Tutankhamen's treasures to Dale Chihuly's bombastic glass sculpture, but the real gems here are rotating-collection highlights such as a coffin shaped like a cocoa pod by Ghanian artist Kane Kwei, and Masami Teraoka's 1977 wry commentary on globalization: a geisha eating Baskin & Robbins vanilla ice cream. Special collections are downstairs, and the museum shop offers two floors of shopping temptation.

The 144ft twisting medieval-style armored tower is the one feature of the building that seems incongruous with the park setting, but though you might expect to see vats of oil boiling on the top floor, instead there are spectacular views on clear days to the Pacific and Golden Gate Bridge, and yes, another bookstore. Access to the tower viewing room is free, and worth the wait for the elevator by Ruth Asawa's mesmerizing filigreed pods.

SABRINA DALBESIO

California Academy of Sciences

CALIFORNIA ACADEMY OF SCIENCES

☎ 415-379-8000; www.calacademy.org; 55 Music Concourse Dr; adult/child under 4yr/child 4-11yr/senior, child 12-17yr & student $29.95/free/19.95/24.94; ⏰ 9:30am-5pm Mon-Sat, 11am-5pm Sun; 🚌 5, 21, 44, 71, N

Finally the California Academy of Sciences has a museum suited to its fascinating collection of 38,000 natural wonders and the occasional freak of nature. Under the wildflower-covered 'living roof' of Renzo Piano's LEED-certified green building, butterflies flutter through a four-storey glass rainforest dome, a rare white alligator stalks a swamp, and Pierre the Penguin paddles his massive new tank in the African Hall. In the basement aquarium, kids duck inside a glass bubble to enter

Japanese Tea Garden

LEE FOSTER

an eel forest, find Nemos in the tropical-fish tanks and squeal to pet starfish in an aquatic petting zoo. The views here are sublime: you can glimpse into infinity in the Planetarium or ride the elevator to the roof for panoramas over Golden Gate Park. Displays throughout the main floor explain conservation issues affecting California's ecosystem, and you can actually eat those words – the cafeteria sells treats made with local, organically grown ingredients. For an even wilder scene, check the schedule for Thursday evenings when the academy is open late and cocktails are served.

SAN FRANCISCO BOTANICAL GARDEN & STRYBING ARBORETUM

☎ 415-661-1316; www.strybing.org; Martin Luther King Dr; non-San Francisco resident adult/12-17yr, senior & student/5-11yr/under 5yr/family $7/5/2/free/15; ⏱ 8am-4:30pm Mon-Fri, 10am-5pm Sat, Sun & holidays; 🚌 5, 21, 44, 71, N There's always something blooming in these 70-acre gardens, which cover a world of vegetation from South African savanna

to New Zealand cloud forest. The Garden of Fragrance is designed for appeal to the visually impaired, and the California native-plant section explodes with color when the wildflowers bloom in early spring, right off the redwood trail. Free arboretum tours take place daily.

JAPANESE TEA GARDEN

☎ 415-831-2700; japaneseteagardensf.com; Hagiwara Tea Garden Dr; non-San Francisco resident adult/senior & 12-17yr/5-11yr/under 5yr $7/5/2/free; ⏱ 9am-6pm, to 4:45pm Nov-Feb; 🚌 5, 21, 44, 71, N; ♿

Have your moment of Zen in the Zen Garden, or while enjoying green tea under a pagoda, watching kids ogle doll-sized bonsais that are pushing 100 years. These bonsai are a credit to the dedicated gardeners of the Hagiwara family, who returned from WWII Japanese American internment camps to discover their prized bonsai had been sold. The Hagiwaras spent the next two decades tracking down the trees, and returned the bonsai grove to its rightful home.

CONSERVATORY OF FLOWERS

☎ 415-666-7001; www.conservatoryofflowers. org; Conservatory Dr West; adult/senior & 12-17yr/5-11yr/under 5yr $7/5/2/free; ☼ 10am-4pm Tue-Sun; 🚌 5, 21, 33, 71; ♿

Flower power is alive and well inside this grand Victorian greenhouse, where orchids sprawl out like bohemian divas, lilies float contemplatively in ponds and carnivorous plants give off odors that smell exactly like insect belches. The 1878 structure is newly restored and the plants are thriving.

STOW LAKE

☎ 415-752-0347; ☼ sunrise-sunset; 🚌 28, 44

The miniresort in the center of the park is Stow Lake, with a picturesque island called Strawberry Hill for short but steep and sweaty hikes. Huntington Falls tumble down the hill into the lake, near a romantic Chinese pavilion. Pedal boats, row boats and electric motor boats are available at the **boathouse** (☎ 415-752-0347; per hr paddleboats/canoes/rowboats $24/20/19, surrey bikes $20-35, tandem bikes $12, bikes $6-8; ☼ rentals 10am-4pm). Boats must have at least one person 16 or older aboard, and you can bring dogs on rowboats.

SLEEPING

SEAL ROCK INN   Inn $$

☎ 415-752-8000, 888-732-5762; www.sealrock inn.com; 545 Point Lobos Ave; s $110-142, d $120-152; 🚌 38; 📶 📺 ♿

Hunter S Thompson used to stay at this vintage-1950s ocean-side motel to listen to the seals. Rooms need updating (think 1970s rumpus-room style), but they're big and most sleep up to four people. All have refrigerators; some have kitchens. It's good for families who want to spend time at the beach and hiking the coastal trails. Reserve way ahead for the upgraded 3rd-floor fireplace rooms. A heated pool (summer only)

and Ping-Pong keep the kids from getting antsy. There's wi-fi in the lobby.

EATING

The best value for authentic ethnic foods and intriguing California variations on them is found out in the Avenues. Key foodie destinations include Clement St east of Park Presidio for Taiwanese, French, Thai and more, and Geary Blvd west of Park Presidio for Cal-Moroccan, dim sum, sushi, Polish delis and then some. The Sunset District has budget ethnic eating places along Irving St from 5th Ave all the way to 25th Ave, and along the last blocks of Judah St near the Ocean Beach. Come early if you want a spot, since service often winds down by 9pm.

SPRUCE   Californian $$$

☎ 415-931-5100; www.sprucesf.com; 3640 Sacramento St; ☼ 11:30am-2:30pm Mon-Fri, 5-10pm Mon-Sun, bar & lounge 11:30am-10pm Mon-Fri; 🚌 1, 2, 4, 33

VIP all the way, with studded ostrich-leather chairs, mahogany walls and your choice of 1000 wines. Expense-accounters forget business and feast on pork tenderloin with crispy pork belly, and ladies who lunch dispense with polite conversation and tear into lavish salads of warm duck confit, plums, and greens grown on the restaurant's own organic farm.

PPQ DUNGENESS
ISLAND   Seafood $$$

☎ 415-386-8266; 2332 Clement St; ☼ 11am-10pm Wed-Mon; 🚌 1, 2, 29, 38; ♿

Dungeness crab season lasts most of the year in San Francisco, which means now is a fine time to enjoy one whole atop garlic noodles or dredged in peppercorn-laced flour and lightly fried, for a typical market price of about $20 per person (depending on weight and season). Ignore everything else on the menu, and put that bib to work.

KABUTO　　　　　Californian, Sushi $$
☎ 415-752-5652; www.kabutosushi.com; 5121 Geary Blvd; ⏲ lunch Tue-Sat, dinner Tue-Sun; 🚌 38

Even doubting sushi-traditionalists and Japanese-food agnostics find themselves worshipping at the sushi bar of Kabuto, a former hot-dog place that's become a temple of sushi innovation. Every night there's a line out the door to witness sushi chef Eric top nori-wrapped sushi rice with foie gras and ollalieberry reduction, *ono* (Hawaiian wahoo fish) with grapefruit and crème fraîche, and the most religious experience of all: the 49er oyster with sea urchin, caviar, a quail's egg and gold leaf, chased with rare sake.

NAMU　　　　　Korean, Californian $$
☎ 415-386-8332; www.namusf.com; 439 Balboa St; ⏲ 6pm-midnight Wed-Sun, 6-10:30pm Sun-Tue, 10am-3pm Sat-Sun; 🚌 5, 21, 31, 38

SF's unfair culinary advantages – top-notch organic ingredients, Silicon Valley inventiveness and deep roots in Pacific Rim cuisine – are elegantly showcased in Korean-inspired small plates ($9 to $15) of buttery kampachi fish with chili oil and *fleur de sel*, bacon-wrapped enoki mushrooms, and Niman Ranch Kobe beef and organic vegetables in a sizzling stone pot.

AZIZA　　　　　Moroccan, Californian $$
☎ 415-752-2222; www.aziza-sf.com; 5800 Geary Blvd; ⏲ dinner Wed-Mon; 🚌 2, 29, 38; Ⓥ

Mourad Lahlou's inspiration is Moroccan and his produce organic Californian, but his flavors are out of this world: quail is a major sensation with huckleberries and cumin-orange glaze, and the prawn *tagine* with Meyer lemons is pizzazz in a pot. Glitz is kept to a minimum and lighting low, so as not to distract from desserts of pecan tartlets with sea-salt caramel ice cream.

DRAGONFLY　　　　　Vietnamese $$
☎ 415-661-7755; www.dragonfly420.com; 420 Judah St; ⏲ lunch & dinner Tue-Sun; 🚌 44, 66, 71, N; ♿

RACHAEL NUSBAUM

Namu

You'd think this place was high-end from the sunken dining room, garlic noodles with lavish heapings of Dungeness crab, and shaking beef that threatens to steal the crown from **Slanted Door's** (p73) version – but prices and service are plenty friendly. Desserts and starter pâté aren't standouts, so load up on mains served family-style.

HALU   Japanese $$
☎ 415-221-9165; 312 8th Ave; ☼ 5-10pm Tue-Sat; ◻ 2, 38, 44
Entering Halu is like wandering into a scene from Yellow Submarine: rare Beatles memorabilia plasters this five-table yakitori joint, where the ramen is reliably toothsome and your choice of chicken parts comes skewered on a stick.

TON KIANG RESTAURANT   Chinese, Dim Sum $$
☎ 415-387-8273; www.tonkiang.net; 5821 Geary Blvd; ☼ 10am-9pm Mon-Thu, 10am-9:30pm Fri, 9:30am-9:30pm Sat, 9am-9pm Sun; ◻ 2, 29, 38; ♿
The reigning champion of dim sum runs laps around the competition, pushing trolleys laden with fragrant, steaming bamboo baskets. Don't bother asking for an explanation: choose some on aroma alone, and ask for the gao choy gat (shrimp and chive dumplings), dao miu gao (pea tendril and shrimp dumplings) and jin doy (sesame balls) by name. A running tally is kept at your table, so you could conceivably quit while you're ahead of the $20 mark – but wait, here comes another cart…

BURMA SUPERSTAR   Burmese $$
☎ 415-387-2147; www.burmasuperstar.com; 309 Clement St; ☼ lunch & dinner; ◻ 1, 2, 38, 44
Yes, there's a wait, but do you see anyone walking away? Blame it on creamy,

fragrant catfish curries and la pat, a traditional Burmese green-tea salad tarted up with lime and dried shrimp. Reservations aren't accepted, so ask the host to call you at the cafe across the street, and enjoy a glass of wine while you wait.

SUNRISE DELI   Middle Eastern $
☎ 415-664-8210; 2115 Irving St; ☼ 9am-9pm; ◻ 71, N; ⓥ
A hidden gem in the fog belt, Sunrise dishes up what is arguably the city's best smoky baba ghanoush, mujeddrah (lentil-rice with crispy onions), garlicky foul (fava bean spread) and crispy falafel, either to go or to enjoy in the old-school cafe atmosphere. Local Arab American hipsters confess to passing off the Sunrise's specialties as their own home cooking to older relatives.

SPICES   Szechuan, Chinese $
☎ 415-752-8884; 294 8th Ave; ☼ 11am-11pm; ◻ 1, 2, 28, 38, 44
The menu reads like an oddly dubbed Hong Kong action flick, with dishes labeled 'explosive!!' and 'stinky!' But the chefs can call zesty pickled Napa cabbage with chili oil, silky ma-po tofu and brain-curdling spicy chicken whatever they want – it's definitely worthy of exclamation. When you head towards the kitchen for the bathroom, the chili aroma will make your eyes well up – or maybe that's just gratitude. Cash only.

SAN TUNG   Chinese, Dim Sum $
☎ 415-242-0828; 1031 Irving St; ☼ 11am-9:30pm Thu-Tue; ◻ 29, 44, 71, N
When you arrive at 5:30pm on a Sunday and already the place is packed, you might think you've hit a family dinner rush – but no, it's this crowded all the time. Blame it on the dry braised chicken wings – tender, moist morsels that defy the very

name – and the housemade dumplings and noodles. You'll be smacking your lips with the memory when the bill comes: a three-course meal for two for $20. Next time you'll be in line by 5pm.

GENKI   Dessert, Groceries $
☎ 415-379-6414; www.genkicrepes.com; 330 Clement St; ⏰ 10:30am-10:30pm Sun & Tue-Thu, 2-10:30pm Mon, to 11:30pm Fri-Sat; 🚌 1, 2, 33, 38, 44

Life is always sweet at Genki, with aisles of packaged Japanese gummy candies nonsensically boasting of flavors 'shining in the cheeks of a snow-country child,' a dozen tropical fruit variations on tapioca bubble tea, and French crepes by way of Tokyo with green-tea ice cream and Nutella. Stock up in the beauty supply and Pocky aisle to satisfy sudden snack or hair-dye whims.

BE MY GUEST THAI BISTRO   Thai $
☎ 415-386-1942; www.bemyguestthaibistro. com; 951 Clement St; ⏰ lunch & dinner Tue-Sun, dinner Mon; 🚌 1, 2, 28, 38, 44; Ⓥ ♿

For mod orange and white decor, a full cocktail bar and clever variations of Thai themes, there's only one thing to say: Be My Guest. The marinated Volcano Chicken is served flaming and melts in your mouth, while Mango Tango Prawns and Sea Bass Edamame bring surf to California turf with tangy, earthy flavors.

YUM YUM FISH   Japanese, Sushi $
☎ 415-566-6433; www.yumyumfishsushi.com; 2181 Irving St; ⏰ 10:30am-7:30pm; 🚌 71, N; Ⓥ

Watch and learn as Yum Yum's sushi chef lovingly slices generous hunks of fresh sashimi, preparing a platter to order with your special *maki* needs in mind. Rolls can be made specially for vegans for as little as a dollar per order, and if you want sustainable sushi, bring your Seafood Watch Card and order accordingly.

TROUBLE COFFEE   Cafe $
☎ 415-682-4732; www.troublecoffee.com; 4033 Judah St; ⏰ 7am-7pm; 🚌 N

Coconuts are an unlikely find by blustery Ocean Beach, but Trouble Coffee happens to like unlikelihood. Hence the 'Build Your Own Damn House' breakfast special: coffee, thick-cut cinnamon-laced toast and an entire young coconut. Surfers, stoners and surrealists in need of a snack, then you must be looking for Trouble.

FIRST KOREAN MARKET   Korean $
☎ 415-221-2565; 4625 Geary Blvd; ⏰ 9am-8pm; 🚌 1, 2, 33, 38, 44

Kimchi and *kimbap* cravings are well and truly satisfied at First Korean, where you'll find entire rows of the spicy fermented veggies (better than pickles) and sesame-oil-laced Korean seaweed, vegetable and rice rolls (not to be confused with sushi) at bargain prices.

UNDERDOG   Sausages $
☎ 415-665-8881; 1634 Irving St; ⏰ 11am-9pm; 🚌 28, 29, 44, 71, 91, N; Ⓥ ♿

For $4 to $5 organic meals on the run in a bun, Underdog is the clear winner. The roasted garlic and Italian pork sausages are United States Department of Agriculture-certified-organic, and the smoky veggie chipotle hot dog could make dedicated carnivores into fans of fake meat.

ROADSIDE BBQ   American $
☎ 415-221-7427; www.roadside-bbq.com; 3751 Geary Blvd; ⏰ 11:30am-10pm Sun-Thu, to 11pm Fri & Sat; 🚌 2, 33, 38

Generous $8 pulled-pork sandwiches and $10 racks of ribs are slow-cooked in a smoker, and its baked beans, sweet-potato fries and coleslaw 'roadsides' are made fresh from scratch – diets are definitely roadkill here.

LOUIS
American $

☎ 415-387-6330; 902 Point Lobos Ave;
6:30am-4:30pm Mon-Fri, to 6pm Sat & Sun,
to 8pm in summer; 5, 18, 31

The newfangled and sadly soulless Cliff House can't compare to old-school Louis just up the street, with its Pacific views, '70s brown-and-orange decor, and hearty diner fare confidently slapped down in front of you by waitstaff who know you'll be back for more. At brunch on weekends, get your name on the list, then explore Sutro Baths until your 20-minute wait is up.

TAIWAN RESTAURANT
Chinese, Taiwanese $

☎ 415-387-1789; 445 Clement St; 11am-9:30pm Mon-Fri, 10am-10pm Sat & Sun; 1, 2, 33, 38, 44; V

Feast for days on heaping, housemade, sesame hot-sauce noodles, dumplings made fresh to order, smoky dry braised green beans and feisty black bean chicken. The pink and chrome '80s decor just goes to show that the Taiwan is single-minded in its pursuit of the most lavish banquet for four you'll ever get this cheap.

DRINKING

BEACH CHALET MICROBREWERY
Bar

☎ 415-386-8439; www.beachchalet.com; 1000 Great Hwy; 9am-10pm Sun-Thu, to 11pm Fri & Sat; 5, 18, 31, 38, N

Gaze over the Pacific with microbrewed beer at the Beach Chalet. There's always a long wait here, but that's OK because it gives you time to admire the downstairs 1930s Works Project Administration (WPA) frescoes, showing a condensed history of San Francisco and the development of Golden Gate Park.

BITTER END
Bar

☎ 415-421-7033; 441 Clement St; 4pm-2am Mon-Fri, 11am-2am Sat & Sun; 1, 2, 33, 38, 44

Tuesday-night trivia is big at this beat-up pub with worn wood floors, big tables for six, two pool tables and an overlit dart

Beach Chalet Microbrewery

ROBERTO GEROMETTA

Lincoln Park Golf Course

ROBERTO GEROMETTA

board. Pretty good pub grub makes it a good spot to start the night.

540 CLUB
Bar

☎ 415-752-7276; www.540-club.com; 540 Clement St; ⏰ 11am-2am; 🚌 2, 44

Regulars love to party at this neighborhood bar inside a former bank with two-story-high coffered ceilings, dusty red velvet curtains and cool pop art. Bartenders pull 12 brews on tap, and everyone seems to know each other – you will too after a couple of games of darts.

PLOUGH & THE STARS
Bar

☎ 415-751-1122; www.theploughandstars.com; 116 Clement St; ⏰ 3pm-2am Mon-Thu, 2pm-2am Fri-Sun; 🚌 1, 2, 33, 38

Rumor has it the owners here are celebrities back in the Emerald Isle, which would explain how they manage to pull in top Celtic talent with little fanfare or advance warning. Other nights, shoot pool, throw darts and make merry with neighborhood locals.

TRAD'R SAM'S
Bar

☎ 415-221-0773; 6150 Geary Blvd; ⏰ 11am-2am; 🚌 2, 29, 38

Snag a rattan island-themed booth at this threadbare faux-tiki gem. Classic-kitsch lovers order the Hurricane, which comes with two straws to share for a reason: drink it by yourself and it'll blow you away.

JAVA BEACH CAFÉ
Cafe

☎ 415-665-5282; www.javabeachcafe.com; 1396 La Playa St; ⏰ 6am-11pm; 🚌 18, N; 📶

Fearless surfers fuel up on coffee and carbs at the last stop on the N Judah, right before the beach. If it's not foggy, score an outdoor table, but we prefer to sit inside and cruise the dudes.

ENTERTAINMENT & ACTIVITIES

BRIDGE THEATER
Film

☎ 415-267-4893; www.landmarktheatres.com; 3010 Geary Blvd; adult/senior, child & matinee $10.50/8; 🚌 18, 38

One of the city's few remaining single-screen theaters, the Bridge shows an international lineup of independent films. Weekends in summer, at midnight, the Bridge hosts Midnight Mass, featuring camp, horror and B-grade movies, such as *Showgirls* and *Mommie Dearest,* with each screening preceded by a drag show spoofing the film.

FOUR STAR THEATER Film
☎ 415-666-3488; www.hkinsf.com/4star; 2200 Clement St; single & double feature/matinee $9/7; 🚌 1, 2, 29, 38
Long before John Woo, Ang Li and Wong Kar-wai hit multiplex marquees, they brought down the house in the Four Star's postage-stamp-sized screening rooms. This diminutive cinema is still the audience testing ground for emerging Hong Kong and Taiwan cinema, and also shows double features.

**GOLDEN GATE
MUNICIPAL GOLF COURSE** Golf
☎ 415-751-8987; www.goldengateparkgolf course.com; 47th Ave & Fulton St; Mon-Thu $14, Fri-Sun $19; 🕑 6am-8pm; 🚌 5
Golden Gate Park has a challenging nine-hole, par-27 course with a variety of holes, from 100yd drop-offs to 180yd elevated greens. Peaceful and with some nice views of the Pacific, it's busiest before 9am weekdays and after school. On weekend afternoons, prepare for an hour-long wait. No reservations.

LINCOLN PARK GOLF COURSE Golf
☎ 415-221-9911; www.lincolnparkgc.com; 34th Ave & Clement St; Mon-Thu $34, Fri-Sun $38; 🕑 sunrise-sunset; 🚌 1, 18, 38
For game-sabotaging views, the hilly, 18-hole Lincoln Park course wraps around the Palace of the Legion of Honor and graces the coast west of the Golden Gate

Bridge. This one has the most iconic SF vistas; it's the number-two public course after Harding.

**CIRCUS CENTER
TRAPEZE** Other Activities
☎ 415-759-8123, ext 810 for trapeze enrolment; www.circuscenter.org; 755 Frederick St; 2hr workshop $42; 🚌 71, N; ♿
If you've ever dreamed of running away and joining the circus, indulge your fantasy at this serious circus-arts school, where students learn everything from Chinese acrobatics to the flying trapeze. Neophytes can arrange one-off courses in trapeze, but be warned: if you fall in love, you may end up enrolling in the school's Clown Conservatory – the only clown-training school in the US.

FLYCASTING CLUB Other Activities
www.ggacc.org; McLaren Anglers' Lodge & Casting Pools, John F Kennedy Dr, Golden Gate Park; 🚌 5, 9
Across from the buffalo paddock in Golden Gate Park, sheltered from the breeze by tall cypress and eucalyptus trees, there's an impressive set of casting pools, complete with targets, for the general public to use. You can stroll in and watch fly casters out in their waders, gracefully setting a fly from a thin line that looks about a mile long. Check the website for dates and times of free casting lessons.

LAWN BOWLING CLUB Other Activities
☎ 415-487-8787; http://sflb.filesforfriends.com; Bowling Green Dr, Golden Gate Park; 🚌 44, N
Pins seem ungainly and bowling shirts unthinkable once you've stepped onto Golden Gate Park's spongy lawn-bowling green in your classic sweater-and-slacks combo. Free lessons are available on Wednesday at noon, Wednesday evenings in summer or by appointment. Flat-

soled shoes are mandatory, as is all-white clothing at its social events.

LINDY IN THE PARK   Other Activities
www.lindyinthepark.com; John F Kennedy Dr btwn 8th & 10th Aves, Golden Gate Park; admission free; ☻ 11am-2pm Sun, weather permitting; ➔ 5, 38, 44; ♿

Start your Sunday right with swing-dancing in Golden Gate Park. In the classic SF tradition, this party is open to everyone: the point is to have fun. You'll spot amazing dancers as well as giggling first-timers, so no need to worry if you've two left feet. Free half-hour lessons begin at noon. Or just come watch. If you can't make it Sunday, there's a monthly Wednesday party at Union Square from May to October.

SAN FRANCISCO DISC GOLF   Other Activities
www.sfdiscgolf.org; Marx Meadow Dr at Fulton St btwn 25th & 30th Aves; admission free; ➔ 5, 28, 29, 31

If you love to throw Frisbees, head to the tranquil woods of Golden Gate Park to find a permanent 18-hole disc-golf course, enjoyed by cultish veterans and reckless beginners. You can rent a bag of flying saucers at **Golden Gate Park Bike & Skate** (right). Tournaments happen Sundays from 8:30am to 10am.

SAN FRANCISCO MODEL YACHT CLUB   Other Activities
☎ 415-386-1037; www.sfmyc.org; Spreckels Lake, Golden Gate Park; ➔ 5; ♿

Kids go nuts for the impeccable scale-model yachts that sail on little Spreckels Lake. The parade of tiny ships is serious business for collectors, who lovingly build and maintain their crafts in the adjacent clubhouse, and occasionally throw miniature regattas (check the website). While

you're here, look for tortoises on shore: Spreckels Lake is where many locals dump their unwanted turtles.

GOLDEN GATE PARK BIKE & SKATE   Skating
☎ 415-668-1117; 3038 Fulton St; skates per hr/day $6/24, bikes $5/25, discs $5/20; ☻ 10am-6pm (closed when raining); ➔ 5

In addition to bikes and skates (both quad-wheeled and in-line), this little rental shop just outside the park also rents saucer-shaped putters and drivers for the nearby free disc-golf course. Call ahead to confirm it's open if the weather looks iffy.

WHEEL FUN RENTALS   Skating
☎ 415-668-6699; www.wheelfunrentals.com; 50 Stow Lake Dr; skates per hr/day $6/20, bikes $8/25; ☻ 9am-7pm; ➔ 44

Achy feet slowing you down? Problem solved at this rental shop in the heart of Golden Gate Park. Dip into the Sunset (the neighborhood to the south), roll westward to Ocean Beach's promenade for a glimpse of the kiteboarders, or just glide around the park. Cheaper cruiser bikes cost the same price as skate rentals. If you want to hit Stow Lake, hop aboard a surrey (tandem paddleboat) with a baguette and feed the geese.

SHOPPING

PARK LIFE   Art, Books
☎ 415-386-7275; www.parklifestore.com; 220 Clement St; ☻ noon-8pm Mon-Thu, 11am-9pm Fri & Sat, 11am-7pm Sun; ➔ 1, 2, 33, 38, 44; ♿

Is Park Life a design store, an art gallery or an indie publisher? All of the above, with limited-edition scores that include flashlight-shaped candles, Styrofoam coffee cups recast in sustainable ceramic, and Park Life's own publications on graffiti artist Andrew Schoultz. The back gallery shows rising art stars such as Alexis McKenzie, whose surreal collages show animals spelling out the words 'Never Be Sad.'

GREEN APPLE BOOKS — Books

☎ 415-387-2272; 506 Clement St; ⏰ 10am-10:30pm Sun-Thu, to 11:30pm Fri & Sat; 🚌 1, 2, 33, 38, 44; ♿

Blissed-out booklovers emerge blinking into the sunset after an entire day browsing three floors of new releases, used titles and staff picks more reliable than *New York Times* reviews. Local favorites are easy to spot in the local interest section – look for the local author tag. You can sell your books here, but be prepared for rejection – they can afford to be picky. Don't miss the annex two doors down.

NEW MAY WAH — Food & Drink

☎ 415-221-9826; 719 Clement St; ⏰ 7:30am-7pm; 🚌 1, 2, 28, 38, 44

No truly adventurous eater should leave town without a trip here. Flavored tapioca tea kits and stinky, acquired-taste durian are just the beginning: sharpen your stir-fry-tasting skills with an array of fish sauce and bean pastes, and work your way through the shelves of chili sauce and *soju* (Korean rice wine) if you dare.

WISHBONE — Gifts

☎ 415-242-5540; www.wishbonesf.com; 601 Irving St; ⏰ 11:30am-7pm Mon-Sat, to 6pm Sun; 🚌 N, 44, 71; ♿

Certain gifts never fail to please: explode-in-your-mouth Pop Rocks candy, smiling toast coin purses, candy-colored jewelry and a stuffed toy called 'Yes, a Cat Named Marty Cohen.' Baby gear here is bound to please hipster parents, from baby Ramones T-shirts to Tiny Tyrant striped ensembles.

KAMEI RESTAURANT SUPPLY — Housewares

☎ 415-666-3699; 547 Clement St; ⏰ 9am-7pm; 🚌 1, 2, 28, 38, 44

The human brain was not built to comprehend this broad a selection of ceramics, with three precariously stacked aisles ranging from basic geometric white to

RICK GERHARTER

Park Life

GOLDEN GATE PARK & THE AVENUES

SHOPPING

THOMAS WINZ

Green Apple Books (p241)

spectacular high-end raku platters that would make fried eggs look gourmet. But wait, there's more: enough industrial steel pots to open 50 restaurants simultaneously, and scouring pads to suit the most discerning dishwashers – all at bargain-basement prices.

MOLLUSK   Sporting Goods, Local Designer
☎ 415-564-6300; www.mollusksurfshop.com; 4500 Irving St; 🕙 10am-6:30pm; 🚌 N

The high-impact store sign by renowned artist Tauba Auerbach is the first hint that this is the source of West Coast surfer cool. Visits by celebrity shapers (surfboard makers) yield limited-edition boards, and the signature Mollusk T-shirts and hoodies by local artists buy you nods of surfer recognition. Surf books and sculpture installations by the likes of the Society of Driftwood Enthusiasts give nonsurfers vicarious surf-subculture thrills.

↘ DAY TRIPS

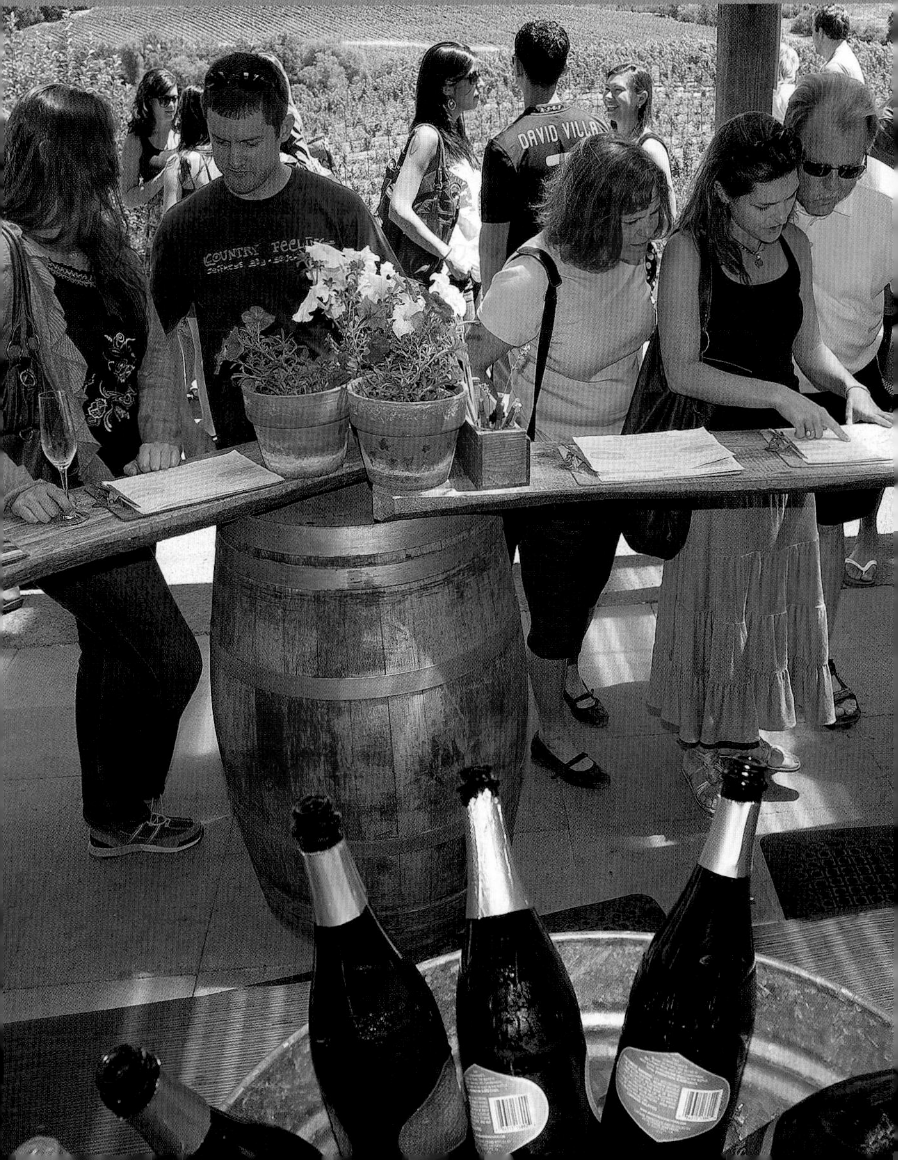

DAY TRIPS

Within a 90-minute drive of San Francisco, you'll discover primordial redwood groves, long rocky beaches and sweeping hilltop vistas of the Pacific Ocean – plus America's most celebrated wining and dining. To explore Wine Country, you'll need one full day, but we recommend staying at least one night to immerse yourself in the local culture and drink with nary a care about the 90-minute drive back to SF. For a quick dose of stunning Northern California scenery, most visitors head over the Golden Gate Bridge to Marin Headlands bluffs, bayside Sausalito, and especially Muir Woods, an old-growth redwood stand on the Marin coast, 30 minutes north of the Golden Gate. Hwy 1 over Mt Tamalpais is winding and slow, but if you love woods, you'll hardly notice. If you've a day to explore, continue north to Point Reyes National Seashore. The beaches at Half Moon Bay are good for family excursions.

WINE COUNTRY

For 150 years the West has gone wild for the spas, the gourmet grub and the almighty grape in the patchwork of vineyards stretching from sunny Napa to coastal Sonoma. Napa has art-filled tasting rooms by big-name architects with prices to match; in down-to-earth Sonoma, you'll drink in sheds and probably meet the vintner's dog.

ORIENTATION

Wine Country is about 90 minutes north of San Francisco by car via Hwy 101 or I-80, or via Vallejo ferry (p297). Skinny Napa Valley stretches from Carneros in the southwest to Howell Mountain in the northeast; most wineries are clustered along Hwy 29 and Silverado Trail. Sonoma County sprawls from Sonoma Valley along Hwy 12 north to Healdsburg and Dry Creek Valley and west to Russian River Valley.

NAPA VALLEY

Brace your senses for impact: Napa awaits with 220 standard-setting wineries, a con-

stellation of star chefs and sleek new spa-hotels. When Napa wines took top honors at a 1976 blind tasting in Paris, the wine-drinking world was shocked – except Napa, which has been growing grapes since the Gold Rush.

INFORMATION

Napa Valley Visitors Bureau (☎ 707-226-7459; www.napavalley.com; 1310 Napa Town Center; ☽ 9am-5pm) Spa deals, wine-tasting passes and the free *Preiser Key to Napa Valley*, which has comprehensive winery maps.

WINERIES

Ditch the car and mellow out in downtown Napa at the **Vintners' Collective** (☎ 707-255-7150; www.vintnerscollective.com; 1245 Main St; tastings $25; ☽ 11am-6pm) with a sampling of six wines from 20 boutique wineries in a 19th-century brothel, then discover affordable pinot blends in the spiffy mural-lined tasting room of **Ceja** (☎ 707-226-6445; www.cejavineyards.com; 1248 First St; tastings $10; ☽ 11am-6pm Sun-Wed, to 9pm Thu-Sat). Head northeast of

WINE COUNTRY

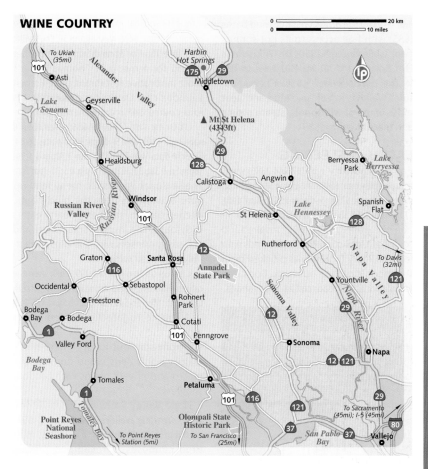

downtown Napa for boutique wineries along the **Silverado Trail**, starting with super-Tuscan-style Sangiovese at **Luna Vineyards** (☎ 707-255-5862; www.lunavineyards.com; 2921 Silverado Trail; ⏱ 10:30am-5pm). Try top-of-the-line Napa cult wines off Silverado at **Joseph Phelps** (☎ 800-707-5789; www.jpvwines.com; 200 Taplin Rd, off Silverado Trail; tastings $25; ⏱ 10am-3:30pm Mon-Fri, to 2:30pm Sat & Sun), makers of complex, highly collectible Insignia, the reigning Napa Meritage red blend reinvented every year since 1974 with a simple recipe: 'five grapes, no rules.'

SIGHTS & ACTIVITIES

When you notice scrap-metal sheep grazing Carneros vineyards, you've spotted **di Rosa Art + Nature Preserve** (☎ 707-226-5991; www.dirosapreserve.org; 5200 Carneros Hwy 121; ⏱ gallery 9:30am-3pm Wed-Fri, tours depart 10am, 11am, 1pm Wed-Fri, 10am, 11am, noon Sat). Reserve ahead for tours covering everything from Tony Oursler's grimacing video projections in the wine cellar to million-dollar Robert Bechtel abstracts hung on the living-room ceiling.

Indian Springs (☎ 707-942-4913; www.indianspringscalistoga.com; 1712 Lincoln

Ave; ☺ 9am-8pm) offers volcanic mud baths ($85) with free access to its hot-springs pool, while vintage-1950s **Dr Wilkinson's Hot Springs** (☎ 707-942-4102; www.drwilkinson.com; 1507 Lincoln Ave; ☺ 8:30am-3:45pm) features wallows in volcanic mud and peat moss, mineral whirlpools, steam rooms and blanket wraps ($89).

EATING & SLEEPING

French Laundry (☎ 707-944-2380; www.frenchlaundry.com; 6640 Washington St, Yountville; fixed-price menu $250; ☺ dinner 5:30-9.30pm daily, 11am-1pm Sat & Sun by reservation) The definition of California fine dining: inspired and seasonal, setting international trends with extraordinary ingredients plucked from the organic garden out back. Book one to six months ahead; call at 10am sharp.

Russian River Valley vineyards

Ad Hoc (☎ 707-944-2487; www.adhocrestaurant.com; 6476 Washington St, Yountville; ☺ 5-10pm Thu-Mon & brunch Sun) Don't bother asking for a menu at Thomas Keller's most innovative restaurant since French Laundry: chef Dave Cruz dreams up his four-course, $48 market menu daily.

Ubuntu (☎ 707-251-5656; www.ubuntunapa.com; 1140 Main St, Napa; small plates $6-14; ☺ 5:30-9pm Mon-Thu, 11:30am-2:30pm & 5:30-10pm Fri & Sat, 11:30am-2:30pm & 5:30-9pm Sun) The seasonal, vegetarian menu features natural wonders from the biodynamic kitchen garden, satisfying hearty eaters with four to five inspired small plates and eco-savvy drinkers with 100-plus sustainably produced wines.

Carneros Inn (☎ 707-299-4900; www.thecarnerosinn.com; 4048 Sonoma Hwy (Hwy 121/12), Carneros; r Mon-Fri $435-595, Sat & Sun $475-655; ☻) The corrugated-metal buildings among the vineyards look like a winery from afar, but luxury guest-sheds feature kingly beds, wood-burning fireplaces and private patios with outdoor showers.

Napa Valley Railway Inn (☎ 707-944-2000; www.napavalleyrailwayinn.com; 6523 Washington St, Yountville; r $125-210) Rest tired cabooses in revamped railcars with cushy beds, skylights, flat-screen TVs and gym access, right in downtown Yountville.

SONOMA VALLEY

Sonoma belonged to Mexico in 1846, when American settlers of varying sobriety declared an independent 'California Republc' [sic] with a homemade flag featuring a blotchy, porcine bear. Today, Sonoma showcases its independent thinking in adventurous farm-to-table menus, pioneering green wineries, and 'vinotherapy' spa treatments.

INFORMATION

Sonoma Valley Visitors Bureau (☎ 707-996-1090; www.sonomavalley.com; 453 1st St E; ☽ 9am-5pm) Arranges accommodations (no fee) and offers walking-tour maps and festival and event info.

WINERIES

Down a country road from downtown, **Gundlach-Bundschu** (☎ 707-938-5277; www.gunbun.com; 2000 Denmark St, Sonoma) is a solar-powered castle perched above a reclaimed-water lake producing legendary tempranillo. Another maverick is Demeter-certified biodynamic behemoth **Benziger** (☎ 800-989-8890; www.benziger.com; 1883 London Ranch Rd, Glen Ellen; tastings $10-15, tram tour adult incl tasting/under 21yr $15/5; ☽ 10am-5pm; ⛟), where educational tram tours explain environmentally savvy, esoteric winegrowing methods that yield sensational truffled-cranberry cabs. West off Hwy 12, many of Sonoma Valley's best buys await at **Wellington** (☎ 800-816-9463; www.wellingtonvineyards.com; 11600 Dunbar Rd, Glen Ellen; tastings $5; ☽ 10am-5pm), where under $30 gets you hazelnutty white port or award-winning, white-peppery zins produced by 100-year-old vines that miraculously survived Prohibition.

SIGHTS & ACTIVITIES

Obey the call of the wild up Hwy 12 at **Jack London State Historic Park** (☎ 707-938-5216; www.jacklondonpark.com; 2400 London Ranch Rd; ☽ 10am-5pm Oct-Apr, 9:30am-7pm May-Sep), where adventure-novelist Jack London brought Sonoma's slashed-and-burned hillsides back to life. Hike to the lake to overlook London's pristine 129-acre farmstead or ride through fragrant redwood groves with **Triple Creek Horse Outfit** (☎ 707-887-8700; www.triplecreek horseoutfit.com; 2400 London Ranch Rd; group rides 1/2/3hr with lunch $60/90/250; ☽ by reservation).

EATING & SLEEPING

Vineyards Inn Bar & Grill (☎ 707-833-4500; www.vineyardsinn.com; 8445 Sonoma Hwy 12, Sonoma; mains $8-20; ☽ 11:30am-9:30pm Wed-Mon) Seafood is fresh, wild and line-caught, and most produce comes from chef Esteban's certified-organic and bio-dynamic Rose Ranch.

Fig Cafe (☎ 707-938-2130; www.thefigcafe. com; 13690 Arnold Dr, Glen Ellen; mains $15-20; ☽ 5:30-9pm daily, 10am-2:30pm Sat & Sun) Sonoma's take on comfort food: organic salads, Sonoma duck cassoulet and free corkage on Sonoma wines, served in a converted living room.

Beltane Ranch (☎ 707-996-6501; www.bel taneranch.com; 11775 Hwy 12; r incl breakfast $150-220; ℗ ☏) Guests enjoy ranch-raised meals and can hike trails, play tennis and sit on the porch swing and watch horses graze.

Gaige House Inn (☎ 707-935-0237, 800-935-0237; www.gaige.com; 13540 Arnold Dr, Glen Ellen; r $229-289, ste $359-459; ☏) Sonoma's sleekest inn, with Zen-chic rooms in the historic main house and spa suites with hewn-granite tubs and pebbled meditation courtyards near the pool.

RUSSIAN RIVER VALLEY

The West preserves its wild ways in Russian River, two hours north of San Francisco (via Hwys 101 and 116) in western Sonoma County. Here ancient redwoods tower over independent wineries, and the aptly named 10-mile **Bohemian Highway** is lined with resorts for rebels, hippie craft galleries and gay-friendly honky-tonks.

INFORMATION

Sebastopol Area Chamber of Commerce & Visitors Center (☎ 707-823-3032, 877-828-4748; www.sebastopol.org; 265 S Main St, Sebastopol; ☽ 10am-noon & 1-5pm Mon-Fri) Provides maps and the free

Sonoma County Farm Trails Guide (www.farmtrails.org), which lists Sonoma farms open to visitors.

WINERIES

At organic, certified-biodynamic **Porter Creek Vineyards** (☎ 707-433-6321; www.portercreekvineyards.com; 8735 Westside Rd; tastings free; 🕙 10:30am-4:30pm), woodsy pinot noir is served in a shed on a bar made from a bowling alley lane. Near the coast, **Freestone** (☎ 707-874-1010; www.freestonevineyards.com; 12747 El Camino Bodega, Freestone; 🕙 11am-5pm Thu-Mon) grows grapes biodynamically and interferes minimally to yield pomegranate-bright Fogdog pinot noir. For sparkling wines served to US presidents, head 15 minutes south of Guerneville to the splendid outdoor hilltop tasting bar at **Iron Horse Vineyards** (☎ 707-887-1507; www.ironhorse vineyards.com; 9786 Ross Station Rd; tastings $10-15; 🕙 10am-4:30pm).

SIGHTS & ACTIVITIES

Paddle down winding Russian River past herons and otters in **Burke's Canoes** (☎ 707-887-1222; www.burkescanoetrips.com; 8600 River Rd, Forestville; canoes $60; 🕙 9am-6pm May-Oct).

Towering old-growth redwoods at 805-acre **Armstrong Redwoods State Reserve** (☎ 707-869-2015; www.parks.ca.gov; 17000 Armstrong Woods Rd; parking $6, overnight camping $20; 🕙 8am-sunset) were saved by lumber baron Colonel James Boydston Armstrong, who bought these woods in 1874 and saved them from the axe, including the 308ft, 1400-year-old Colonel Armstrong tree.

Get buried up to your neck in warm wood chips at **Osmosis** (☎ 707-823-8231; www.osmosis.com; 209 Bohemian Hwy, Freestone; 🕙 by appointment 9am-8pm), where redwood tubs filled with soft, slow-fermenting cedar and rice bran soothe weary muscles ($85 for 45 minutes).

EATING & SLEEPING

Zazu (☎ 707-523-4814; www.zazurestaurant.com; 3535 Guerneville Rd; dishes $19-26; 🕙 dinner Wed-Mon & brunch Sun) Get fresh over farm-to-table feasts with housemade salumi, organic ingredients from the garden out back, delicate Liberty duck or whole roasted pig, and warm, honey-drizzled Sonoma cheese for dessert.

Dawn Ranch (☎ 707-869-0656; www.dawn ranch.com; 16467 River Rd; d incl breakfast $99-120; 🏊) Take your pick of vintage cabins with woodstoves among the redwoods or poolside cabanas, and don't miss the historic roadhouse for killer cocktails and organic dining.

Boon Hotel & Spa (☎ 707-869-2721; www.boonhotels.com; 14711 Armstrong Woods Rd; d $185-205, tr $225-250; 🏊) Guerneville's chic new eco-retreat has sleek cork-floored and solar-heated cabanas alongside the chlorine-free pool.

HEALDSBURG & DRY CREEK VALLEY

More than 90 wineries are located within a 30-mile radius of Healdsburg, where upscale eateries, wine-tasting rooms and stylish inns ring the Spanish-style plaza. Just over Hwy 101 from downtown Healdsburg is Dry Creek, a dreamscape of lazily grazing sheep, fish leaping from glistening creeks, and gnarled old vineyards blooming with organic ground cover.

INFORMATION

Healdsburg Visitors Center (☎ 707-433-6935, 800-648-9922; www.healdsburg.org; 217 Healdsburg Ave; 🕙 9am-5pm Mon-Fri, 9am-3pm Sat, 10am-2pm Sun) Handy for tasting passes, maps and info.

WINERIES

Natural beauty gets bottled in Dry Creek, beginning with zins served in caves at Bella Vineyards (☎ 707-473-9171, 866-572-3552; www.bellawinery.com; 9711 W Dry Creek Rd; tasting $5; ⏰ 11am-4pm). Mosey over to the 19th-century homestead at Preston Vineyards (☎ 707-433-3327, 800-305-9707; www.prestonvineyards.com; 9282 W Dry Creek Rd; tastings $5, refundable with purchase; ⏰ 11am-4:30pm) for picnics of certified organically grown Barbera and Viognier with home-baked bread, organic fruit and Pug's Leap goat cheese, plus marathon bocce ball games. Pristine biodynamic field blends are served inside a fluorescent-lit garage at Unti (☎ 707-433-5590; www.untivineyards.com; 4202 Dry Creek Rd; ⏰ Sat & Sun, by appointment Mon-Fri), but even under harsh lighting, everyone looks gorgeous after a glass of bodacious Brunello-style Sangiovese and the voluptuous Syrah.

EATING & SLEEPING

Cyrus (☎ 707-433-3311; www.cyrusrestaurant.com; 29 North St, Healdsburg; fixed-price menu $102-130; ⏰ 5:30-9:30pm Thu-Mon, lunch Sat) Critics rave about the decadent truffle-laced dishes, but the local secret is the bar, where dishes are served à la carte with mad-scientist cocktails.

Bovolo (☎ 707-431-2962; www.bovolorestaurant.com; 106 Matheson St, Healdsburg; dishes $6-14; ⏰ 9am-6pm Thu, Fri, Mon, Tue, to 9pm Sat & Sun) Fast food gets a slow-food spin at this bistro in the back of a bookstore, with locally grown salads, farm-fresh egg breakfasts and pizza topped with meats cured in-house.

Healdsburg Inn on the Plaza (☎ 707-433-6991, 800-431-8663; www.healdsburginn.com; 110 Matheson St, Healdsburg; Mon-Fri $200-250, Sat & Sun $220-325) Renovated in 2005 with a nod to Tuscany, sunny, high-ceilinged guestrooms have fine linens and gas fire-places; hang out in the solarium or the cushy living room over full breakfasts, afternoon wine, cheese and cookies.

Hotel Healdsburg (☎ 707-431-2800, 800-889-7188; www.hotelhealdsburg.com; 25 Matheson St, Healdsburg; r incl breakfast $260-790; 🏊) Smack on the plaza, this polished-concrete chic hotel has soothing earth-toned guestrooms with vast beds, some with soaking tubs; leave rested and gleaming from a Crushed Zinfandel Body Polish ($115 for 50 minutes) in the garden spa.

MARIN COUNTY

Majestic redwoods cling to coastal bluffs while the thundering surf bludgeons new shapes into the cliffs. Woodsy-chic Marin County is home to some of the Bay Area's loveliest towns, but you'll need a car to

Canoeing on Russian River

JERRY ALEXANDER

reach the further-flung villages of West Marin, such as Point Reyes Station and Stinson Beach.

ORIENTATION

Busy Hwy 101 heads north across the Golden Gate Bridge ($6 toll, southbound only), connecting the well-to-do communities of Sausalito, Larkspur and San Rafael. Bucolic Hwy 1 twists through sparsely populated West Marin, passing beauty spots such as Muir Woods and Stinson Beach on its way to Point Reyes.

INFORMATION

Marin County Convention & Visitors Bureau (☎ 866-925-2060, 415-925-2060; www.visitmarin.org; Suite B, 1 Mitchell Blvd, San Rafael; ⏱ 9am-5pm Mon-Fri) Handles tourist information for the entire county.

MARIN HEADLANDS

Immediately northwest of the Golden Gate Bridge, the rugged natural beauty of the Marin Headlands stands in stark contrast to Downtown San Francisco's towers, visible across the bay. Pick up trail maps, field guides and historical information at the **Marin Headlands Visitors Center** (☎ 415-331-1540; www.nps.gov/goga; Bldg 948, Fort Barry; ⏱ 9:30am-4:30pm).

Every fall, migratory birds and raptors – including hawks, falcons and eagles – soar overhead at **Hawk Hill** (www.ggro.org; Conzelman Rd; admission free). Go 1.8 miles up Conzelman Rd, park along the road and walk up the west side of the hill; for a map and details on which birds are there now, see www.ggro.org. Near the end of Conzelman Rd the still-operating 1855 **Point Bonita Lighthouse** (⏱ 12:30-3:30pm Sat-Mon, free tours at 12:30pm), is a breathtaking half-mile path from the parking area, ending at a suspension footbridge above the churning surf (acrophobes: beware).

Marine Mammal Center (☎ 415-289-7325; www.tmmc.org; 4 Bunker Rd; admission free, donation suggested; ⏱ 10am-5pm), on the hill above Rodeo Lagoon, is the largest marine mammal hospital in the world. In 2009 the center opened its all-green, solar-powered hospital, with observation decks for visitors to get close to the recovering patients (mostly seals and sea lions) before they're released back into the wild. At the end of Bunker Rd sits black-sand **Rodeo Beach** (ro-*day*-oh), protected from the wind by cliffs.

SAUSALITO

Sausalito is the first town you hit after crossing the Golden Gate. Perched above Richardson Bay, it's known for galleries, window-shopping and its **houseboat community**, one of the world's largest and most diverse, ranging from mansions to hippie hovels. At Fort Baker, the **Bay Area Discovery Museum** (☎ 415-339-3900; www.baykidsmuseum.org; 557 McReynolds Rd, Sausalito; adult/child to 17yr $10/8; ⏱ 9am-4pm Tue-Fri, 10am-5pm Sat & Sun) is cool for kids, with hands-on science exhibits, musical instruments, festivals and camps.

EATING & SLEEPING

Fish (☎ 415-331-3474; 350 Harbor Dr, Sausalito; mains $12-30; ⏱ 11:30am-8:30pm; ♿) This kid-friendly dockside joint at the end of Harbor Dr hooks locals with sustainable, line-caught fish – some from their own boats – and down-home details, such as picnic-table seating and Mason-jar glasses. No credit cards.

Gables Inn (☎ 415-289-1100, 800-966-1554; www.gablesinnsausalito.com; 62 Princess St, Sausalito; r $155-495; 🛜) All nine cozy B&B rooms in this swank historic home have massive baths; the more expensive have Jacuzzis, fireplaces and balconies with spectacular views.

MUIR WOODS

Coastal redwoods are the tallest living things on earth, and you can explore a glorious old-growth stand at **Muir Woods National Monument** (☎ 415-388-2595; adult/child under 16 $5/free; ☽ 8am-sunset, call ahead), 12 miles north of the Golden Gate Bridge.

The 1-mile **Main Trail Loop** is easy, leading alongside Redwood Creek to 1000-year-old trees at **Cathedral Grove**; it returns via **Bohemian Grove**, where the park's tallest tree stands at 254ft. The **Dipsea Trail** is a strenuous 2-mile hike to the top of aptly named **Cardiac Hill**, but it's possibly the most beautiful hike for views – a half-mile steep grade through lush, fern-fringed forest leads from the canyon to an exposed ridge, from which you can see Mt Tamalpais, the Pacific and San Francisco.

The turnoff to **Muir Beach** from Hwy 1 is marked by the north coast's longest row of mailboxes (Mile 5.7, just before Pelican Inn). The oh-so-English Tudor-style **Pelican Inn** (☎ 415-383-6000; www.pelicaninn.com; 10 Pacific Way; lunch $10-17, dinner $15-29) is Muir Beach's only commercial establishment. Hikers, cyclists and families come for pub lunches inside its timbered restaurant and cozy bar, perfect for a pint, a game of darts and warming up beside the open fire. Upstairs are seven luxe rooms (from $190), each individually decorated in Tudor style, with cushy half-canopy beds.

To get to Muir Woods, drive north on Hwy 101, exit at Hwy 1 and continue north along Hwy 1/Shoreline Hwy to the Panoramic Hwy (a right-hand fork). Continue for about 1 mile to Four Corners, where you turn left onto Muir Woods Rd (look for signs). In summer, Golden Gate Transit offers a daily **shuttle service** (adult/youth & senior $3/1) from the ferry in Sausalito to Muir Woods;

Muir Woods

THOMAS WINZ

DAY TRIPS

MARIN COUNTY

purchase tickets at the SF ferry ticket booth before boarding the Sausalito-bound ferry.

MT TAMALPAIS

The 6300 hill-and-dale acres of **Mt Tamalpais State Park** (☎ 415-388-2070; www.mttam.net; 801 Panoramic Hwy) were formed in 1928 from land donated by naturalist William Kent; deer, foxes and bobcats rustle deep in the trees and scurry over the trails. Get information and pick up the free park map at **Pantoll Station** (☎ 415-388-2070; 801 Panoramic Hwy), the state park's headquarters, just past Mt Home Inn and Bootjack on Panoramic Hwy (watch carefully or you'll miss the turnoff). You can day-hike from here – it's a beautiful 8.5-mile climb to East Peak Summit and back – or drive 4.2 miles along Ridgecrest Blvd to the East Peak Summit Visitors

DAY TRIPS

MARIN COUNTY

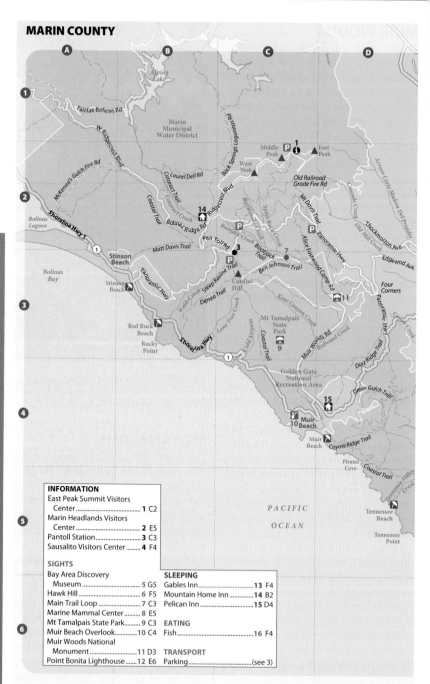

MARIN COUNTY

PACIFIC
OCEAN

INFORMATION

East Peak Summit Visitors Center	**1** C2
Marin Headlands Visitors Center	**2** E5
Pantoll Station	**3** C3
Sausalito Visitors Center	**4** F4

SIGHTS

Bay Area Discovery Museum	**5** G5
Hawk Hill	**6** F5
Main Trail Loop	**7** C3
Marine Mammal Center	**8** E5
Mt Tamalpais State Park	**9** C3
Muir Beach Overlook	**10** C4
Muir Woods National Monument	**11** D3
Point Bonita Lighthouse	**12** E6

SLEEPING

Gables Inn	**13** F4
Mountain Home Inn	**14** B2
Pelican Inn	**15** D4

EATING

Fish	**16** F4

TRANSPORT

Parking	(see 3)

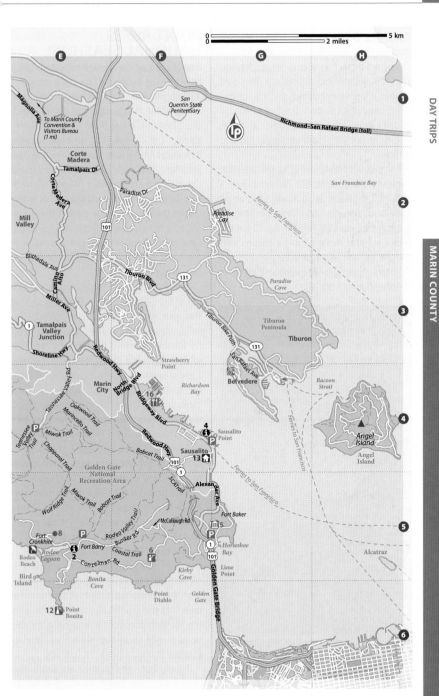

0   5 km
0   2 miles

E   F   G   H

San Quentin State Penitentiary

Richmond–San Rafael Bridge (toll)

San Francisco Bay

Magnolia Ave

To Marin County Convention & Visitors Bureau (1 mi)

Corte Madera
Tamalpais Dr

Corte Madera Ave

Paradise Dr

Paradise Cay

Ferries to San Francisco

Mill Valley

Camino Alto

Blithedale Ave

Tiburon Blvd

131

Paradise Cove

Miller Ave

1   Tamalpais Valley Junction

Tiburon Bike Path

Tiburon Peninsula

Tiburon

Shoreline Hwy

Redwood Hwy

131

Strawberry Point

San Rafael Ave

Belvedere

Racoon Strait

North Bridge Blvd

Marin City

Bridgeway Blvd

16

Richardson Bay

Ferries to San Francisco

Angel Island

4

Tennessee Valley Rd

Oakwood Trail

Marincello Trail

Redwood Hwy

Bobcat Trail

4
1   Sausalito Point

P

Angel Island

Tennessee Valley Trail

P

Miwok Trail

Chaparral Trail

Sausalito

13

101

SCA Trail

1

Golden Gate National Recreation Area

Wolf Ridge Trail

Miwok Trail

Bobcat Trail

Rodeo Valley Rd

Alexan der Ave

Ferries to San Francisco

5

McCollough Rd

Fort Baker

Fort Cronkhite

8

P

Fort Barry

Bunker Rd

Coastal Trail

6

5

P

1   Horseshoe Bay

Alcatraz

Rodeo Beach

Rodeo Lagoon

1

2

Conzelman Rd

Kirby Cove

101

Lime Point

Bird Island

Bonita Cove

Point Diablo

Golden Gate

Golden Gate Bridge

12   Point Bonita

6

Center (parking $6), then climb the remaining quarter-mile to the summit.

From Pantoll Station, Steep Ravine Trail follows a wooded creek to the coast (about 2.1 miles each way). For a longer hike, veer right after 1.5 miles onto the Dipsea Trail, which meanders through woods for a mile before ending at Stinson Beach.

Mountain Home Inn (☎ 415-381-9000; www.mtnhomeinn.com; 810 Panoramic Hwy; r $195-345; 🛜) is set atop a ridgeline amid redwood, spruce and pines, perfect for a romantic, woodsy retreat. All 10 rooms face east and most have balconies and fireplaces. Its restaurant serves brunch ($10 to 20) and dinner (prix fixe $38) from Wednesday to Sunday.

THOMAS WINZ
Highway 1 near Montara

POINT REYES NATIONAL SEASHORE

Established by President Kennedy in 1963, Point Reyes National Seashore includes 110 sq miles of pristine ocean beaches, wind-tousled ridgetops and diverse wildlife. Start out at the **Bear Valley Visitors Center** (☎ 415-464-5100; www.nps.gov/pore; Bear Valley Rd; 🕑 9am-5pm Mon-Fri, 8am-5pm Sat & Sun), the park's headquarters (near Olema), which provides maps, information and worthwhile exhibits. This is the major trailhead for the park – the longest trail is **Palomarin Trail** at 11.5 miles. One of the coolest interpretive walks is the **Earthquake Walk**, smack-dab on the San Andreas Fault.

The **Point Reyes Lighthouse** (☎ 415-669-1534; 🕑 10am-4:30pm Thu-Mon) sits at the end of Sir Francis Drake Blvd. The wild, steep terrain here gets buffeted by ferocious winds, and offers the best whale-watching along the coast. Nearby **Chimney Rock** makes a lovely short hike, especially in spring when wildflowers are blossoming. On weekends during good weather, from 9am to 5:30pm in late December through mid-April, the road to Chimney Rock and the lighthouse is closed to private vehicles. Instead, you must take a **shuttle** (adult/child under 16yr $5/free) from Drakes Beach. Shuttles run every 20 minutes from 9:30am to 3:30pm, weather permitting; for daily updates call ☎ 415-464-5100, ext 2, then press 1.

McClures Beach, near the north end, is a gem of a beach, with white sand, forceful surf and excellent tidepools at low tide. Start the steep half-mile trail down to the beach at the end of Pierce Point Rd, also the starting point of the stunning, mostly level 3-mile bluff-top walk to **Tomales Point** – through herds of Tule elk.

To explore the peninsula from the water, contact **Point Reyes Outdoors**

(☎ 415-663-8192; www.pointreyesoutdoors. com; 11401 Hwy 1, Point Reyes Station; guided trips $85-110); or Blue Waters Kayaking (☎ 415-669-2600; www.bwkayak.com; rentals $40-120, guided trips $68-98), which has two locations, one in Inverness, the other in Marshall.

EATING & SLEEPING

Nick's Cove & Cottages (☎ 415-663-1033; http://nickscove.com; 23240 Hwy 1, Marshall; mains $14-30; ☺ 8am-9pm) Celeb SF chef Mark Franz runs the kitchen at Point Reyes' only destination restaurant, a vintage-1930s roadhouse perched over Tomales Bay (20 minutes north of Point Reyes Station), with trophy heads mounted on knotty pine walls and a roaring fireplace. The adjoining cottages are expensive ($355 to $700), but oh-so romantic.

Tomales Bay Foods (☎ 415-663-9335; www.cowgirlcreamery.com; ☺ 10am-6pm Wed-Sun) Home of the famous Cowgirl Creamery cheese-makers (tours Friday mornings at 11:30am; reservations recommended), here you can gather stellar picnic fixings – fruit, bread and gooey-delicious cheese.

Hog Island Oyster Company (☎ 415-663-9218, ext 208; www.hogislandoysters.com; 20215 Hwy 1, Marshall; picnic fee Mon-Fri $5, Sat & Sun $8, 12 oysters $10-15, 50 oysters $32-52, 100 oysters $60-90; ☺ 9am-5pm) Picnic on fresh local oysters in a bayside cove at this renowned oyster farm, which provides tables, barbecues, lemons, hot sauce, trays of ice, shucking knives and instruction. Bring wine, beer and other food items. Make reservations.

Motel Inverness (☎ 866-453-3839, 415-236-1967; www.motelinverness.com; 12718 Sir Francis Drake Blvd, Inverness; r $100-150; ☎) This upmarket motel has wonderful service and spiffy rooms with good beds.

SF TO HALF MOON BAY

The coastal road south of San Francisco is lined with craggy beaches, windswept coastal plains, grassy prairies and small towns straight out of a Norman Rockwell painting. Lovely Gray Whale Cove State Beach is the most popular clothing-optional strand; bring a sweater. Montara State Beach is a half-mile south and the local favorite for pristine sand. South of the Montara lighthouse, Fitzgerald Marine Reserve (☎ 650-363-4020; www.fitz geraldreserve.org) at Moss Beach has exquisite tidepools. When the wintertime surf rages, climb the dunes from Pillar Point Harbor to Mavericks, and watch death-defying surfers ride 40ft-plus swells past rocky cliffs.

The town of Half Moon Bay is an old Victorian beach resort and the main coastal town between SF and Santa Cruz. If you're here on a weekend, don't miss the Bach Dancing & Dynamite Society (☎ 650-726-4143; www.bachddsoc.org; 311 Mirada Rd, Half Moon Bay; admission $25-35) and its stellar salon-style jazz, classical and world-music concerts at Douglas Beach House.

EATING & SLEEPING

Sam's Chowder House (☎ 650-712-0245; www.samschowderhouse.com; 4210 North Cabrillo Hwy, Half Moon Bay; dishes $12-32; ☺ 11:30am-9pm) In the tradition of big Cape Cod waterside fish houses, Sam's makes a mean bowl of chowder, whole steamed crab (in season), traditional lobster-clambake with all the fixings, and a knockout lobster roll – to find better, fly to Maine.

Old Thyme Inn (☎ 650-726-1616, 800-720-4277; www.oldthymeinn.com; 779 Main St, Half Moon Bay; r $139-299; ☎) This 1898 inn has cheerful B&B rooms, some with Jacuzzis and fireplaces. Full breakfast.

ARCHITECTURE

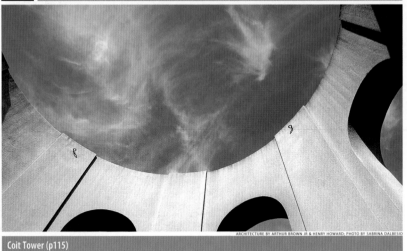

ARCHITECTURE BY ARTHUR BROWN JR & HENRY HOWARD; PHOTO BY SABRINA DALBESIO

Coit Tower (p115)

Superman wouldn't be especially impressive in San Francisco, where most buildings are low enough for even a middling superhero to leap in a single bound. The Transamerica Pyramid and Ferry Building clocktower are helpful pointers to orient newcomers, and Coit Tower adds emphatic punctuation to the city skyline – but San Francisco's low-profile buildings are its highlights. A trip across town will bring you face to facade with the region's Spanish and Mexican heritage, East Asian influences, and Victoriana, California Arts and Crafts and high modernist architecture.

MISSION & MAKESHIFT SF

Not much is left of San Francisco's original Ohlone style, beyond the grass memorial hut you'll see in the graveyard of the Spanish Mission Dolores (p167) and the wall of the original presidio (military post; p68), both built in adobe with conscripted Ohlone labor. During the Gold Rush, buildings were slapped together from ready-made sawn timber components, sometimes shipped from the East Coast or Australia. In those Barbary Coast days, City Hall wasn't much to look at, at least from outside: it was housed in the bawdy Jenny Lind Theater in Portsmouth Square (p119).

VICTORIANA

As San Francisco boomed, rows of Victorian houses were built with a similar underlying floor plan, but eye-catching embellishments and paint jobs. Some proved surprisingly sturdy: several upstanding Victorian row-houses remain in Pacific Heights. San

Franciscans incorporated designs from great civilizations such as ancient Rome, Egypt and the Italian Renaissance into their houses, giving fresh-out-of-the-box San Francisco a certain instant culture. With their rococo-cosmopolitan flourishes, Nob Hill mansions and waterfront bordellos shared a common design sensibility.

The 1906 earthquake and fire destroyed many of the city's 19th-century treasures and much of its kitschy excess. But Victorian-era styles can still be spotted around the city: long-windowed brick Italianates, gabled Gothic Revivals and exuberant Queen Annes, lavished with balconies, towers, turrets, chimneys, bay windows and gables. Bodacious Queen Annes survive around Alamo Square Park (p204) and Pacific Heights, including the Haas-Lilienthal House (p146). Postquake Edwardian homes are more square and less showy; the Mission and Castro have some well-preserved examples. Some Victorian mansions are now B&Bs, so you too can live large in swanky San Francisco digs of yore; see Sleeping options in the Haight (p204), Pacific Heights (p148) and the Mission and Castro (p176).

PACIFIC POLYGLOT ARCHITECTURE

This Pacific Rim city also felt a pull in other stylistic directions. Mission St movie-palace facades and Sansome St banks incorporated Spanish and Aztec design influences from Mexico. The 1920s also brought the mission revival style, a nostalgic look back at the state's Hispanic heritage.

Julia Morgan became the first licensed female architect in California, and rose to fame with precocious postmodern landmarks incorporating wildly different cultural traditions, from her over-the-top Spanish-Gothic-Greek Hearst Castle to her tastefully restrained pagoda-topped brick Chinese Historical Society of America Museum (p118). Distinctive Chinatown deco became a cornerstone of Chinatown's redevelopment initiative after the 1906 quake, when a forward-thinking group of merchants led by Look Tin Eli consulted with a cross-section of architects and rudimentary focus groups to produce a crowd-pleasing, modern chinoiserie look that would attract tourists. (It worked.)

Meanwhile, Berkeley-based architect Bernard Maybeck reinvented England's Arts and Crafts movement with the down-to-earth California bungalow, a small, simple, single-story design derived from summer homes favored by British officers serving in India. California Arts and Crafts style can be spotted in Berkeley Craftsman cottages and earthy ecclesiastical structures such as San Francisco's Swedenborgian Church (p70).

> **THE BEST**

ROBERTO GEROMETTA

MH de Young Museum (p231)

↘ **LOW-PROFILE SF LANDMARKS**

- **California Academy of Sciences** (p231)
- **Zen Center** (p204)
- **MH de Young Museum** (p231)
- **AP Hotaling Warehouse** (p90)
- **Chinese Historical Society of America Museum** (p118)

RICHARD I'ANSON

Transamerica Pyramid (p87)

MODERN SKYLINE

Once steel-frame buildings stood the test of the 1906 earthquake, San Francisco began to think big with its buildings. Willis Polk was among the city's busiest architects, defining downtown with his Hallidie Building at the Powell St cable car turnaround. The city hoped to rival the capitols of Europe, and commissioned architect Daniel Burnham to build a grand City Hall (p89) in the classicizing beaux arts or 'city beautiful' style.

San Francisco became a forward-thinking port city in the 1930s, with Streamline Moderne apartment buildings that looked like ocean liners and its signature art deco Golden Gate Bridge (p65). But except for Coit Tower (p115), most new buildings kept a low profile. Until the 1960s, San Francisco was called 'the white city' because of its low, unbroken swaths of white stucco.

As engineers figured out how to retrofit and reinforce buildings for earthquakes, the Financial District became a forest of glass boxes, with the pointed exception of the Transamerica Pyramid (p87). Recent high-rise construction has sprung up in South of Market (SoMa), as San Francisco braces itself for booms in biotech and social media. Amid Victorian-prefab row houses in San Francisco neighborhoods, you might also spot some of the sleek, architect-designed eco-prefab homes innovated in the Bay Area during the 1990s. Detractors debate the clash in styles, but this is San Francisco: eclectic is what we do here.

↱ ARTS

SABRINA DALBESIO

A mariachi band poses on Valencia St

Between its skyscrapers and Victorians, San Francisco is held together by fog and creativity. Is it something in the water? Back during the Summer of Love, definitely. But a lot has happened since then that defies explanation, and makes psychedelic drugs seem redundant. Since 1970, diminutive San Francisco has consistently been rated one of the top five US cities for the caliber and number of fine artists, musicians, dancers and independent filmmakers. Everyone's an artist, or plays at being one on weekends and at Burning Man arts festival.

MUSIC

If San Francisco history had a soundtrack, it would start with opera and bluegrass, then segue into cool West Coast jazz: Dave Brubeck with Paul Desmond on saxophone. Spoken-word jazz splinters off into folk – think Bob Dylan and Joan Baez during their West Coast affair. Next thing you know, amps are blown by Jimi Hendrix, Janis Joplin wails herself hoarse and Grace Slick hits ear-splitting notes to clear the air. The song remains the same with the Grateful Dead for decades, until the Dead Kennedys wage aural anarchy and the Sex Pistols split up onstage in Japantown. The reverb of '70s funk meets Mission salsa and disco in the Castro, until synthesizers take over; '80s anthems ensue. Grunge trickles down from Seattle in the '90s and stomps power pop. Now you'll hear remixes, with jazz-inflected hip-hop and pop punk.

Here's where to find your groove of choice:

Classical Music & Opera The San Francisco Symphony (p102) has been rated among the finest interpreters of classical music since conductor Michael Tilson

Thomas was wooed away from the London Symphony Orchestra to take up the baton here in 1995. While New York's Metropolitan Opera is larger in size and reputation, San Francisco Opera (p101) takes big, bold risks with avant-garde productions such as *Dangerous Liaisons, Harvey Milk* and *Dead Man Walking*. New York critics grouse that their city's music scene now seems comparatively staid, and they're right – on the bright side, they can always score Grammy-winning SF symphonies and arias at Amoeba Music (p215).

Funk & Hip-Hop The '60s were summed up by freaky-funky, racially integrated San Francisco supergroup Sly and the Family Stone in their 1969 number-one hit: 'Thank You (Falettinme Be Mice Elf Agin).' That psychedelic San Francisco Sound entered the DNA of the Bay Area hip-hop scene, including jazz-inflected Charlie Hunter Trio, Michael Franti's pop-political grooves, and chart-topping Blackalicious and the Blackeyed Peas. San Francisco rapper San Quinn got his start opening for Oakland's Tupac Shakur, but takes a less hard line than the fallen gangsta rapper: in his 'San Francisco Anthem,' he remixes the 1967 hit 'San Francisco (Be Sure to Wear Flowers in Your Hair).'

Jazz Ever since house bands pounded out ragtime to distract Barbary Coast audiences from bar-room brawls and gunshots, San Francisco has had a romance with jazz. Today, the SF Jazz Festival (p48) attracts leading talents, and such is the continued devotion to the work of John Coltrane that he's revered as a saint at the African Orthodox Church of St John Coltrane (p146). At the legendary Yoshi's (p154), tempos shift from Latin jazz to klezmer, acid jazz to swing – and at the holidays, everyone hums along to SF composer Vince Guaraldi's song for *A Charlie Brown Christmas*.

Punk London was possibly more political and Los Angeles more hardcore, but San Francisco's take on punk was weirder. Dead Kennedys frontman Jello Biafra

RICK GERHARTER

Museum of Craft and Folk Art (p172)

ran for mayor in 1979 with a platform written on the back of a bar napkin: ban cars, set official rates for bribery and force businesspeople to dress as clowns. (His endorsement is still highly prized in SF mayoral races.) In the 1990s, the East Bay's one-two punch of ska-inflected Rancid and Berkeley's Green Day brought punk into the media spotlight. But SF punk is not dead, thanks to queercore Pansy Division, the brass-ballsiness of Latin-punk La Plebe, and unpredictable NOFX – whose impressively degenerate show at Slim's (p188) became the album *They've Actually Gotten Worse Live!*

Rock Fire up those lighters, but don't call for 'Freebird' as an encore: at Mission, Potrero and Polk Gulch venues, and the free concerts at Amoeba Music (p215), alt-rock rules. Still, there's always room on the bill at the Warfield (p100) or Great American Music Hall (p101) for sentimental-favorite local rockers, ranging from hard-rocking Metallica and anthem-wailers Journey and Santana to gruff honkytonk poet Tom Waits and whispery folksters Peggy Honeywell and Joanna Newsom. Jam bands continue the legacy of the Grateful Dead, while the Dead still occasionally perform minus guitarist Jerry Garcia – who survived decades beyond any medically explicable life expectancy, only to die in rehab in 1995.

PERFORMING ARTS

If you don't see it here, you might not catch it anywhere: SF's independent cinemas and theaters specialize in sleeper hits, strangely captivating one-offs and cult classics. Check for half-price theater tickets at the Union Square kiosk, or last-minute tickets to film festivals and dance performances on Craigslist (www.craigslist.org) – but if you can't score a seat, there's always the street theater of San Francisco's street fairs, protests and parades.

THEATER

Before San Francisco was a foodie town, or a tech town, or even much of a town at all, it was the West Coast's home for theater. Major productions destined for Broadway and London open at the American Conservatory Theater (p100), with breakthrough productions by Tony Kushner *(Angels in America),* Robert Wilson and William S Burroughs *(Black Rider),* Tom Stoppard *(Arcadia)* and David Mamet *(Oleanna, November).* For better or for worse, depending on how likely a tune is to haunt you, San Francisco is the proving ground for musicals such as *Rent* and *Phantom of the Opera.*

In city parks, you'll find free Shakespeare (see p48) and political satires by the San Francisco Mime Troupe (www.sfmt.org). Troupe founder RG Davis won a free-speech case back in 1962 and ever since, the Troupe has been gleefully trying (sometimes successfully) to get arrested and get audiences on their feet, whichever happens first.

DANCE

Never afraid of kicking up its heels and showing off its knickers, San Francisco has danced since its Barbary Coast days – notwithstanding a failed attempt to ban dance just after the 1906 earthquake, targeted at bawdy entertainment venues. From burlesque to ballet and all shades of modern, San Francisco's gotta dance – especially at the Dance-Along Nutcracker (p49).

The city is home to the nation's oldest professional ballet company, the San Francisco Ballet (p101) was formed in 1933 with George Ballanchine setting the tone, and produced the nation's first full-length productions of *Nutcracker Suite* and *Swan Lake*. Widely credited with originating modern dance, Isadora Duncan (1877–1927) was born west of Union Square, and an alley off Taylor St between Post and Geary Sts today bears her name. Today, Oberlin Dance Collective (p183) combines raw, Western physicality with modern San Francisco ingenuity.

VISUAL ARTS

While global art trends are making many art scenes look eerily alike, SF continues its homegrown tradition of rough-and-readymade '50s Beat collage, '60s psychedelic Fillmore posters, earthy '70s funk and beautiful-mess punk, and '80s graffiti culture; today, street artists and graduates from SF's distinguished art schools fill risk-taking arts venues downtown and in the Mission. Art collectors stock up in SF, where world-class collections such as di Rosa Art + Nature Preserve (p245) have surprisingly affordable works from local galleries.

Here's what to look for and where:

⬎ THE BEST

STEPHEN SAKS

Club Fugazi, venue of Beach Blanket Babylon (p128)

⬎ WAY-OFF BROADWAY THEATER

- **Magic Theatre** (p77)
- **Marsh** (p185)
- **Beach Blanket Babylon** (p128)
- **BATS Improv** (p77)

Women's Building (p170)

⚓ OUR FAVE 'HOLLYWOOD NORTH' DIRECTORS

- **Francis Ford Coppola** *The Godfather* auteur's American Zoetrope head-quarters is North Beach's Columbus Tower.
- **George Lucas** Never mind the Presidio-based director's *Star Wars* prequels – *American Graffiti* (1973), *Star Wars* (1977) and *Raiders of the Lost Ark* (1981) were hugely influential.
- **Sean Penn** The director and Academy Award–winning actor (for 2008's *Milk*) is a sometime Columbus Tower tenant.
- **Sofia Coppola** Produces variable films with consistent dreamlike qualities, including *Virgin Suicides* (1999) and *Lost in Translation* (2003).
- **Wayne Wang** Indie director of *Chan is Missing (*1982), *Smoke (*1995) and *Because of Winn Dixie (*2006); also headquartered in Columbus Tower.

Conceptual craft Skill becomes a mind-altering substance in meticulously crafted works such as Ruth Asawa's light-shattering wire cocoons at the MH de Young Memorial Museum (p231) and Clare Rojas' ominous fairytale installations for the Museum of Craft and Folk Art (p172).

Murals Inspired by the mural at Diego Rivera Gallery (p142), Depression-era artists painted Works Progress Administration (WPA) murals across town, including at Coit Tower (p115). *Muralistas* from the 1970s to today have filled Mission alleys with more than 300 murals, as seen in Clarion and Balmy Alleys, and on muralist-led Precita Eyes tours (p294).

New Media SF loves experiments taken to extremes: Tom Marioni drinking beer as performance art at Yerba Buena Center for the Arts (p187); Jim Campbell's mother-boards programmed to misbehave at Hosfelt Gallery (p173); and Matthew Barney's breakthrough Vaseline-smeared *Cremaster Cycle* videos at San Francisco Museum of Modern Art (SFMOMA; p170), where they debuted.

Painting & Printmaking Postwar abstraction left a lasting impression on San Francisco, from Richard Diebenkorn's elemental works to current minimalism in yarn, Bic pen and feathers at 49 Geary (p87), 77 Geary (p88), Ratio 3 (p173) and Hosfelt Gallery (p173) Wayne Thiebaud's gumball machines brought pop art to SF in the 1960s, but pop gets political in Enrique Chagoya's post-financial-bailout take on Warhol's Campbell's Soup: 'Mergers, Acquisitions and Lentils' soup at Electric Works (p173).

Photography San Francisco is a photogenic city with an outstanding photography tradition to prove it, from Pirkle Jones and Ansel Adams' definitive California landscapes to high-concept works such as Larry Sultan's porn-set smoke breaks and Todd Hido's creepy ranch houses – all in the collections of SFMOMA (p170) and occasionally shown at 49 Geary (p87).

FAMILY TRAVEL

LEE FOSTER

Musée Mécanique (p63)

The rumors are true: there really are more pets than children in San Francisco. Census data reveals that San Francisco has the least number of children per capita of any US city, while, according to SF/SPCA data, there are about 19,000 more dogs than children living here. Yet San Francisco is packed with attractions designed for kids, from neighborhood playgrounds to claymation seminars. A lot of people around here – including Pixar animators and video-game designers – actually make a living from entertaining children, so if anything, kids risk overstimulation in San Francisco.

FUN FOR ALL AGES

Adults think San Francisco is meant for them, but kids know better. There's a certain storybook quality to this city that kids can relate to: wild parrots squawking indignantly at passersby on Telegraph Hill (p115), murals in hidden alleys awaiting discovery, slumbering sea lions nudging one other off the docks and into the water at Pier 39 (p63) with a comical *sploosh!* Golden Gate Park is basically the world's weirdest playground, with a butterfly-filled rainforest dome and penguins at the California Academy of Sciences (p231), miniature forests at the Japanese Tea Garden (p232), and paddleboats and tandem bikes at Stow Lake (p233).

CHILD-FRIENDLY ATTRACTIONS

To kids, San Francisco is one big carnival ride. Uphill journeys become big adventures on cable cars and a ferry ride can make a grand day out. Alcatraz (p61) fascinates and creeps out kids, and keeps them on their best behavior for hours. When spirits and feet begin to drag, there's plenty of ice cream and kid-friendly meals to pick them back up, plus toy stores to bribe them up that last hill – look for the ⛄ symbol throughout this book. Except for a few swanky restaurants that toddlers probably wouldn't appreciate anyway, the admiration is mutual between San Francisco and kids.

For entertainment aimed specifically at kids, make a beeline to the waterfront. In the Marina, kids squeal their way through the Tactile Dome at the Exploratorium (p66) and fly kites at Crissy Field (p66). For vacation photo-ops, check out the charming old carousel at Pier 39 (p64), historic ships and 19th-century arcade games at Musée Mécanique (p63). San Francisco has the high-tech Zeum (p172), where kids can make their own music videos, and the Cartoon Art Museum (p172), with original Spiderman cover drawings.

Educational opportunities abound Downtown for kids with a scientific or artistic bent, including at the Asian Art Museum (p82), Legion of Honor (p227), MH de Young Museum (p231) and Museum of the African Diaspora (p172). All are free to kids under 12.

> ↘ **THE NITTY GRITTY**
>
> - **Babysitting** Available at high-end hotels or American Child Care (p292)
> - **Change facilities** Best public facilities are in Westfield Center (p103) and SF Main Library (p90)
> - **Diapers & formula** Available at Walgreens pharmacies citywide (p294)
> - **Emergency care** San Francisco General Hospital (p293)
> - **Kiddie menus** Mostly in cafes and downtown diners; call ahead about dietary restrictions
> - **Strollers & car seats** Bring your own

KID HANGOUTS

Kids who'd like some company their own age can make friends in the plethora of neighborhood parks, especially Portsmouth Square (p119), St Mary's Square (p120) and Mission Dolores Park (p169). For teens:

Clement St Genki (p236) and Park Life (p240).

Haight St SFO Snowboarding & FTC Skateboarding (p215), Amoeba Music (p215) and Loyal Army Clothing (p214).

Japantown Kinokuniya Books & Stationery (p156), Super7 (p156), and Sundance Kabuki Cinema (p153).

Valencia St 826 Valencia (p167), Needles & Pens (p192) and Ritual Coffee Roasters (p181).

FOOD & DRINK

Ferry Building (p62)

EMILY RIDDELL

San Francisco cuisine has been called a lot of names lately – organic, locavore, seasonal, sustainable, Pacific Rim fusion. While local farmers, chefs and winemakers work hard to supply food and drink that lives up to those weighty titles, San Francisco fare still answers to the same name it has been called for 160 years: *damn tasty*.

KEY INGREDIENTS

During the Gold Rush, two secret ingredients transformed this backwater almost overnight into a global culinary capitol: competition and dirt. Miners from around the world craved the flavors of home, and fortunes were made and lost speculating on local tastes for specialties such as Japanese rice and Australian wines. Imports took months to arrive by ship, so chefs increasingly looked to local sources. Turns out that almost anything can and does grow in California's fertile Central Valley to the south of San Francisco; rocky, sandy coastal pastures to the north are prime grazing territory for livestock; and rocky hillsides and volcanic terroir yield fine wines in nearby Sonoma and Napa counties.

SF CUISINE

Clever SF chefs are making the most of the city's three distinct advantages: its Pacific Rim location, a population of adventurous eaters and its local produce. In 1971, Berkeley chef Alice Waters pioneered California cuisine, making the most of the Bay Area's seasonal, sustainably produced bounty. Within 200 miles of San Francisco, chefs can now find premium organic produce, free-range meats, hormone-free dairy products and sublime wines. The city's signature fresh flavors come from raw ingredients that don't lose flavor or nutrients during weeks (or months) of transit and warehousing. Add local, sustainably harvested seafood to the mix, and it seems like a no-fail recipe for success.

But what a chef does with those ingredients can make or break a restaurant in San Francisco, where there is one restaurant for every 28 people – that's 10 times as many restaurants per capita as any other city in North America. Stiff competition has created a culture of picky eaters who demand both consistency and innovation – not to mention value for their money. For even a $10 meal, San Franciscan diners expect inventive combinations of fresh, seasonal ingredients; for $50, they expect to know where the organic dry-farmed tomatoes were grown, when the fish was caught, and everything but the pet nickname of the cow. Menus at even low-end San Francisco restaurants are meticulously detailed and heavily footnoted, sharing credit with the farms that grew key ingredients and noting which ingredients are organic and sustainably sourced. Mock if you must, but people have been known to move here for the food.

SPECIALTIES

When San Franciscans idly discuss moving to New York or London for a change of pace, inevitably the objection is raised: 'Yeah, but where would you find decent Mexican, dim sum, oysters, salami, vegetarian food, sourdough bread and artisan ice cream – all within walking distance?' Point taken. Instead of booking ahead for your SF feast, you can just head to a major culinary strip and take your pick of restaurants offering local specialties. Here's what you'll find where:

Burritos, vegetarian and artisan ice cream Follow your nose to taquerias around 16th and Valencia and 24th and Mission. Tucked in among the Mexican mainstays between 16th and 30th streets you'll find artisan ice creameries and inspired Indian, Middle Eastern, and Californian vegetarian options.

JUDY BELLAH

Dishes at Boulette's Larder (p73)

Dim sum and then some Venture beyond Chinatown to the Richmond and inner Sunset, especially upper Geary between 15th and 30th Avenues for traditional dim sum and organic Moroccan, and around 9th and Irving for dim sum, bakeries and curry. For more eclectic dining choices, Clement St in the Richmond offers standout Burmese, Szechuan and Vietnamese options; in the Sunset at Irving around 19th, the choices range from Middle Eastern to Japanese, and Judah around 48th offers organic California cuisine.

Fresh sourdough bread and seafood Head for the Embarcadero and the Piers, especially in and around the Ferry Building.

Italian specialties For spicy salami, fresh focaccia, seafood cioppino (stew) and gelato, hit North Beach along upper Grant and around Washington Square Park.

OPENING HOURS

Most places to eat are open seven days a week in San Francisco, though some close Sunday and/or Monday night. To feed caffeine needs, cafes open as early as 6am or 7am and tend to stay open until 8pm. Lunch starts at noon and runs until 3pm. Evening dining starts around 7pm, with restaurants opening for happy hour around 5:30pm; last service is usually 9:30pm on weekdays and 10pm on weekends.

RESERVATIONS

Most restaurants take reservations for both lunch and dinner, so call ahead if you can – even if it's the same day. You also could just show up and try your luck – many restaurants that take reservations also set seats aside for walk-ins, or offer meals at the bar. Restaurants that don't take reservations frequently subject customers to a long wait (20 minutes or more), so get your name on the waiting list and make yourself comfy at the bar.

Unless you're hoping for a prime table on Valentine's Day, you should be able to get reservations at most restaurants with a couple of days notice. A few restaurants require reservations well in advance – namely Restaurant Michael Mina (p95), Gary Danko (p71), Slanted Door (p73), Kabuto (p234), or anywhere in Napa (p246).

THE BILL

Even if it's hard to tell in the rebounding tech-based economy of the Bay Area, there's still a recession on in the US, so the bulk of San Francisco's meal tabs are on the low end of the spectrum (between $3 and $100). For dinner celebrations on a budget, bringing

⚓ FAVORITE SAN FRANCISCO TREATS

- **Artisan ice cream** Thai curry peanut butter ice cream at Humphry Slocombe (p178)
- **Burritos** Carnitas, no rice, spicy pickles at La Taqueria (p177)
- **Dim sum** Leek and shrimp dumplings at City View (p126)
- **Seafood** Sustainable sushi at Tataki (p151)
- **Vegetarian fare** Organic black bean chili at Greens (p74)

JERRY ALEXANDER

Anchor Steam Beer

in your own bottle of bubbly and/or cake is often allowed if you call ahead – but a $10 to $20 corkage charge and a cake-cutting fee of $2 to $4 per plate may apply.

As elsewhere in the USA, tipping is customary in restaurants. Servers expect at least 15% of the check total before tax, unless something went horribly wrong with the service, and diners give up to 10% more if the service is exceptional. Keep in mind that servers get paid minimal wages, and tips are what make their wages livable. Many restaurants add an automatic 18% service charge for parties of six or more, so if you're traveling with an entourage, check before you tip. Tipping is optional at coffee bars and places where you order at the counter, but a tip (50¢ to $1 per coffee) is appreciated by busy baristas.

Lately some restaurants have started tacking on a 4% surcharge to cover city-mandated employee healthcare, passing onto patrons a basic cost of doing business. If you're offended by the surcharge, take it up with the management in writing or on an online review site – don't take it out of the tip, which only hurts the server.

WASH IT DOWN

So how do you wash down a bite of bliss? You're spoiled for pairing suggestions in San Francisco, where your server might recommend cocktails custom-muddled by the resident mixologist, seasonal Anchor Steam microbrews, or dusty-boots cowboy cabernets from Napa Valley. Tips are expected: $1 per beer and $1 to $2 for wine or a cocktail, even when your bartender seems curt. San Franciscans don't mind bossy bartenders, as long as the pours are generous.

BEER

Blowing off steam took on a new meaning during the Gold Rush, when entrepreneurs, trying to keep up with the demand, started brewing beer faster at higher temperatures.

When a keg was tapped, an effervescent mist was released – hence the name of San Francisco brewery Anchor Steam, which brews its signature amber ale locally using vintage 1896 copper distillery equipment. Local microbrews remain the drink of choice at many bars and restaurants, but the best selection can be found on tap at Toronado (p210) and Zeitgeist (p181).

⇘ CLASSIC SF COCKTAILS

- **Basil gimlet** Rye, Downtown (p199)
- **Caffé corretto** Tosca Cafe, North Beach (p127)
- **Habañero-chili cosmos** Elixir, the Mission (p181)
- **Mint julep** Alembic, Haight (p211)
- **Pisco sour** La Mar Cebicherià, Embarcadero (p73)

COCKTAILS

San Franciscans are hardly traditionalists, except when it comes to cocktails. Flashy flaming drinks and vodka martinis fizzled out with the dot-com boom: now local boozehounds prefer their cocktails hand-muddled and seasonal, with obscure Kentucky bourbons or gin from San Francisco distilleries Junipero and 209 Gin. Restaurants offer cocktail pairing suggestions from resident mixologists (don't call them bartenders) who pore over recipes from 1930s speakeasies for inspiration.

Thanks to SF's resident research historians of drink, you can now get a gin martini served with a twist and a dash of bitters, in a nod to its 19th century origins. Legend has it that the martini was invented in San Francisco when a local lush needed a drink to tide him over on a trip across the bay to Martinez. (A likely story…but hey, we'll drink to that.) *Caffé corretto* (coffee 'corrected' with liquor) is another beloved tradition in foggy North Beach, while classic margaritas (tequila, lime, Cointreau, ice and salt) come in seasonal fruit variations ideal for balmy Mission nights.

Across the bay, Hangar vodka and Berkeley-produced Takara sake provide raw materials for cosmos and sake-tinis innovative enough to satisfy Silicon Valley thirsts. Listen closely during SF cocktail hour and you may hear the next round of social media and biotech start-ups being founded over drinks.

WINE

San Francisco wine lists weren't always so extensive. Grapes have been grown around San Francisco since its Mission days, producing sacramental wine and swill for soldiers – which turned out to be a strategic military error. On one wine-soaked Sonoma night in 1846, a group of frontier rabble-rousers decided to seize the state government from Mexican authorities. To everyone's surprise, they succeeded, and California history was made along with Sonoma's Wine Country reputation. Some 130 years later, neighboring Napa Valley kicked off another revolution at the 1976 Paris Tasting, aka the 'World Cup of Wine,' when Stag's Leap cabernet sauvignon and Chateau Montelena chardonnay beat home-terroir French favorites.

⬊ GAY/LESBIAN/BI/TRANS

HOLGER LEUE

Halloween revellers, the Castro

It doesn't matter where you're from, who you love or who's your daddy: if you're here and queer, you're home. San Francisco is the mothership of gay culture, America's pinkest city and the easiest place in the US to be out of the closet. Singling out the best places to be out and about in San Francisco is almost redundant.

WHERE TO BE GAY IN THE BAY

The Castro is awash in rainbow flags, SoMa loves its leather daddies, and the Mission is a lesbian and transgender magnet, but the entire city is indisputably the center of the known GLBT world – hence the number of out elected representatives, rainbow flags flying year-round and city-wide, and Pride celebrations that last the entire month of June. To get the latest on the GLBT scene, check the *Bay Area Reporter* (aka BAR; www.ebar.com) for news and listings, and pick up the *San Francisco Bay Times* (www. sfbaytimes.com), which also has good resources for transsexuals.

NIGHTLIFE

New York Marys may call SF the retirement home of the young – indeed, the sidewalks roll up early – but when it comes to sexual outlaws and underground weirdness, SF kicks New York's ass. Back in the pre-1960s bad old days of police raids, bars would euphemistically designate Sunday afternoons as 'tea dances,' appealing to gay crowds to make money at an otherwise slow time. The tradition makes Sunday one of the busiest times for SF's gay bars, though now you can also find your choice of gay bars open any day of the week – and most will accommodate well-behaved straight friends (hint: tip well and don't stare). Drag shows are perennially popular with San Franciscans, though this is not a town where you need a professional reason to cross-dress. For the latest, pick up the free rag *Gloss Magazine* and community newspapers *Bay Area Reporter* and *Bay Times* at kiosks, bars and A Different Light Bookstore (p184).

MEN

Party boys cruise Castro by day and SoMa by night (see listings on p184 and p189). The intersection of 18th and Castro Sts is the heart of the gay scene, and there are bars a go-go, but most are predictably middlebrow. Dancing queens and slutty boys head South of Market (SoMa), the location of most thump-thump clubs and sex venues. Juanita More (www.juanitamore.com) throws fierce parties (especially during Gay Pride), and they're always attended by sexy-hot boys. Fresh (http://freshsf.com) at Ruby Skye (p99) is the monthly Sunday-night circuit party, and there's *caliente* (hot) gay salsa and dance lessons at Cheryl Burke Dance Center (p186). At clubs with outdoor patios, expect clouds of pot smoke: SF is stoner central. Weeknights, it's trickier to find the party – most guys stay home, and the main cruising action is online.

WOMEN

So where are all the hot chicks into hot chicks? They're busy scamming on their exes' exes at the Lexington Club (p182), screening documentaries at the Roxie (p183), or raising kids in Noe Valley and Bernal Heights. To join parties already in progress, scan our Mission listings (p182) or just head to Valencia St – the funkier outer fringe where Castro hits the Mission, and the preferred 'hood of bad-ass dykes, alt-chicks and cute femmes. Hipster chicas pack Stay Gold the last Wednesday of the month at the Make-Out Room (p185); 3pm to 9pm the fourth Saturday of the month is blazing hot Mango at El Rio (p182); and femme fatales should hit the Lexington Club (p182) and inquire about the roving party Flourish, when dykes dress up.

Many gay bars host regular ladies' nights: expect grrrls galore at Les Ladiez Thursday night at the Lookout (p184), Friday at the Stud (p189) and Saturday at the EndUp (p186). For more options, check Get Your Girl On (http://goget yourgirlon.com) for concerts and parties; plug into the A-list for power lesbians, Betty's List (www.bettyslist.com); or go to Craigslist (www.craigslist.org) and click on women-seeking-women to search for monthly parties or post a query.

THE BEST

Women's Building (p170)

⚐ MUST-SEE GLBT SITES

- Women's Building (p170)
- Human Rights Campaign Action Center & Store (p184)
- Castro Theatre (p174)
- Under One Roof (p194)
- Femina Potens (p182)
- Hot Cookie (p181)

RICK GERHARTER

Pride (p47)

GAY BY DAY

Hop the refurbished antique streetcar of your desire: whether you prefer the orange Milan model Castro-bound, a green Bostonian headed straight Downtown, or might consider going both ways, this is one city where your orientation can always be accommodated. In the Castro, it's all gay, all day: gay restaurants, gay dry cleaners, gay CPAs, and a gay Gold's Gym (p184). On sunny days, Speedo-clad gay boys colonize the grassy hill at 20th and Church Sts, in Mission Dolores Park (p169) overlooking Downtown. If you're on girls' gaydar and in the Mission, you can flirt the day away in cafes, thrift shops, bookstores and arts venues.

At most SF hotels, it doesn't matter how vigorously you wave your rainbow flag, as long as your cash is green – but most places in the Castro and Mission go out of their way to make same-sex couples welcome. Accommodations in these neighborhoods can be hard to find and way more expensive during June, aka Pride month – but for the chance to tumble out of bed and into a parade, it's worth it.

SAN FRANCISCO IN FOCUS

HISTORY

HISTORY

JOHN ELK III

Fort Point (p68)

Before gold changed everything, San Francisco was a hapless Spanish mission. Without immunity to European diseases, many native Californians who had been conscripted to build the 1776 mission didn't survive to see the end result – some 5000 Ohlone and Miwok are buried under Mission Dolores. The mission settlement never really prospered: the sandy fields were difficult to farm, 20 soldiers manning San Francisco's Presidio (military post) made more trouble than they prevented, and fleas were a constant irritation. Spain stopped sending supplies long before the colony was lost to Mexico, who promptly surrendered the troublesome backwater to the US.

GOLD FEVER

Mexico could not have had worse timing: within days of signing away California in the Treaty of Guadalupe Hidalgo, gold was discovered in the Sacramento River. San Francisco ballooned from a population of 800 to 100,000, due to the influx of prospectors from South America, China, Europe and Mexico between 1847 and 1849, and

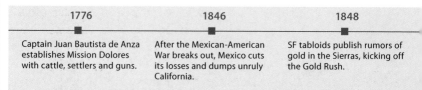

1776	1846	1848
Captain Juan Bautista de Anza establishes Mission Dolores with cattle, settlers and guns.	After the Mexican-American War breaks out, Mexico cuts its losses and dumps unruly California.	SF tabloids publish rumors of gold in the Sierras, kicking off the Gold Rush.

California was fast-tracked for statehood in 1850. But nominal rule of law didn't change San Francisco saloons, where a dollar would procure whiskey, opium, opera tickets, or one of the women frolicking on swings rigged from saloon ceilings – publicly revealing they weren't wearing bloomers 150 years before Britney Spears. The lawless harbor known as the 'Barbary Coast' soon filled with ships abandoned by crews with gold fever.

Early arrivals panned for gold side by side and returned to San Francisco with fortunes to splurge on Chinese takeout, French food and Australian-imported wines. In 1848, each prospector earned an annual average of about $300,000 in today's terms, but by 1865 that mining income had dipped to $35,000. Surface gold became harder to find, and the real money was made by San Francisco's robber-barons, who hoarded the machinery for deep-mining operations.

Panic ensued after gold was discovered in Australia, and irrational resentment turned on Australians and Chinese dockworkers. Ordinances restricted housing and employment for anyone born in China in 1870, and the 1882 US Chinese Exclusion Act barred Chinese from immigration and citizenship until 1943. Anti-Asian sentiment was a windfall for San Francisco's robber-barons, who recruited Chinese San Franciscans on the cheap to do the dangerous, dirty work of dynamiting through the Sierras and building railways to mining claims.

UP FROM THE ASHES

Anxious to distract attention from waterfront fleshpots and attract legitimate business interests, San Francisco built a beaux-arts Civic Center in the early 20th century. These grand plans were destroyed in under a minute on April 18, 1906, when an earthquake estimated at a terrifying 7.8 to 8.3 on today's Richter scale struck. For 47 seconds, the city emitted unholy groans as streets buckled, windows popped and brick buildings keeled over. Fire-fighters couldn't pass through rubble-choked streets to put out blazes, and fires raged for three days. When the smoke lifted, the devastation was clear: as many as 3000 people were dead or missing, and 100,000 were left homeless.

Some survivors fled San Francisco, but those who stayed rebuilt the city at an astounding rate of 15 buildings per day. All but one of San Francisco's 20 theaters were destroyed, so theater tents were set up while the city still smoldered, and opera divas performed for free to boost morale. A city plan was concocted to relocate Chinatown to less desirable real estate in Hunter's Point, but was dropped after the Chinese consulate, Waverly Place temples and several gun-toting Chinatown merchants refused to vacate. With the mysterious, highly flammable exception of the AP Hotaling whiskey warehouse (p90), most of the Barbary Coast had burned, and the city rebuilt the ragged pirate piers into a major port.

1873	1882	1906
When a nervous driver backs out, Andrew Hallidie successfully steers the first SF cable car downhill.	US Exclusion Act suspends immigration from China; Canada, Australia and New Zealand enact similar measures.	A massive earthquake levels entire blocks of SF; fires finish off most of what's left.

ROCKING THE BOAT

Longshoremen pulling long hours unloading heavy cargo for scant pay didn't see the upside of San Francisco's new port. In 1934, a coordinated strike among 35,000 workers along the coast lasted 83 days, while shipments spoiled dockside. Finally police and the National Guard intervened, killing 34 strikers and wounding 40 sympathizers. The strategy backfired: public sympathy helped force concessions from the shipping magnates, and Works Projects Administration murals in Coit Tower (p115) capture the 1930s proworker sentiment that swept the city.

WWII brought a shipbuilding boom, fueled largely by African Americans and women working the assembly lines. But not everyone benefited from wartime expansion. Two months after the Japanese attack on Pearl Harbor, President Franklin Delano Roosevelt signed Executive Order 9066, ordering 120,000 Japanese Americans to internment camps. The San Francisco–based Japanese American Citizens League challenged the measure, and after a historic 40-year effort, won reparations and a formal letter of apology signed by President George HW Bush in 1988 – and along the way, set key precedents for the Civil Rights movement.

WWII sailors discharged in San Francisco for insubordination and homosexuality soon found themselves at home among the bohemian coffeehouses and anarchic alleyways of North Beach. When the rest of the country took a sharp right turn with

RICK GERHARTER

Pride (p47)

1910	1915	1937
Angel Island immigration station opens, subjecting 175,000 Asian arrivals to interrogation, deprivation and imprisonment.	As host of Panama-Pacific International Exposition, SF becomes a showplace for new technology, art and ideas.	After four years of labor in treacherous Pacific tides, the Golden Gate Bridge is complete.

McCarthyism in the 1950s, rebels and romantics headed for the Left Coast, where jazz broke down barriers in de-segregated clubs and José Sarria led gay bar-patrons in nightly choruses of 'God Save Us Nelly Queens.' San Francisco became America's home of free speech and free spirits, and soon everyone who was anyone was getting arrested: Beat poet Lawrence Ferlinghetti for publishing Allen Ginsberg's epic poem *Howl*, African American Jewish anarchist Bob Kaufman for taunting police in rhyme, comedian Lenny Bruce for uttering the F word onstage, and burlesque dancer Carol Doda for going topless.

FLOWER POWER

But it wasn't ribald jokes, striptease, gay bars, or even uncompromising poetry that would pop the last button of conventional morality in San Francisco – no, this would be a job for the CIA. The federal agency inadvertently kicked off the psychedelic era when a CIA operation tested psychoactive drugs – intended to create the ultimate soldier – on writer Ken Kesey, who promptly introduced LSD to the masses at the legendary 1966 San Francisco Acid Tests. At the January 14, 1967 Human Be-In event in Golden Gate Park, tripmaster Timothy Leary urged a crowd of 20,000 hippies to dream a new American dream, and 'turn on, tune in, drop out.'

For weeks, months, even a year or two, depending on who you talk to and how stoned they were at the time, San Francisco was the place where it seemed possible to make love, not war. There were draft-card-burning protests in Golden Gate Park and free food, love and music in the Haight until 1969, when the assassinations of Bobby Kennedy and Martin Luther King, Jr brought a sudden chill to the Summer of Love.

PRIDE

As the fog settled in over the Haight, San Francisco gays ditched hetero hippie communes for sunny Victorians in the Castro, and proceeded to make history to a funky disco beat. The Castro was triumphant when local entrepreneur Harvey Milk became

THE BEST

Buena Vista Park (p203)

RICK GERHARTER

1906 QUAKE SURVIVORS

- **Postcard Row, Alamo Square** (p204)
- **Tien Hou Temple** (p118)
- **AP Hotaling Warehouse** (p90)
- **Old St Mary's Catherdral** (p120)
- **Buena Vista Park** (p203)

1940s	1957	1967
WWII soldiers discharged in San Francisco because of their homosexuality find themselves at home in bohemian North Beach.	City Lights Bookstore wins a landmark case for free speech over Allen Ginsberg's *Howl and Other Poems*.	The Summer of Love begins with the burning of draft cards, Human Be-In and Allen Ginsberg streaking.

the nation's first openly gay elected official in 1977, but the news sent washed-up politician Dan White on a Hostess Twinkie binge and down to City Hall, where he shot Milk and then-mayor George Moscone. The charge was reduced to manslaughter due to the infamous 'Twinkie Defense,' faulting the high-sugar snacks; White committed suicide a year after his 1984 release.

By then the city was preoccupied with a strange illness appearing in local hospitals. The gay community was hit hard by the virus initially referred to as GRID (Gay-Related Immune Deficiency). A social stigma became attached to the virus, compounding a grim prognosis with patient isolation. But San Francisco healthcare providers and gay activists rallied to establish standards for care and prevention of the pandemic (now known as HIV/AIDS), and vital early interventions made possible through local fundraisers saved untold lives around the world.

Another item on the community's political agenda is same-sex marriage, authorized by San Francisco Mayor Newsom in time for Valentine's Day, 2004. In 2008, California voters voided 4037 same-sex marriages with Proposition 8, which limited marriage rights to heterosexual couples. Outspoken opponents of the measure included Amnesty International, *San Francisco Chronicle,* Apple, Google and a wide majority of SF voters.

DIANA MAYFIELD

Atrium of San Francisco Museum of Modern Art (SFMOMA; p170)

1969	1977	1989
Native American activists claim Alcatraz as reparation for broken treaties; the protest lasts 19 months.	Harvey Milk fatefully says: 'If a bullet should enter my brain, let that bullet destroy every closet door.'	The Loma Prieta earthquake hits 6.9 on the Richter scale in 15 seconds, killing 41.

Prop 8 was judged unconstitutional in 2010; unless the decision is overturned on appeal to the US Supreme Court, same-sex couples may again be permitted to marry in California in 2011.

GEEKING OUT

Industry dwindled steadily in San Francisco after WWII, but the brains of military-industrial operations found work in Silicon Valley. At San Francisco's first West Coast Computer Faire in 1977, 21-year-old Steve Jobs and Steve Wozniak introduced the Apple II, the first personal computer with a then-staggering 4 KB of RAM, 1 MHz microprocessor, and a retail price of US$1298 (about $4300 today), and networking capabilities. Skeptics were stumped: what would consumers do with a computer network?

By the mid-1990s, a modest computer network had grown into a World Wide Web selling vegan dog food, art by the

THE BEST

SABRINA DALBESIO

Musée Mécanique (p63)

🔄 PLACES TO SEE REALLY WEIRD TECHNOLOGY

- **Exploratorium** (p66)
- **Musée Mécanique** (p63)
- **Green Festival** (p149)
- **Zeum** (p172)
- **San Francisco Museum of Modern Art** (SFMOMA; p170)

yard and extra socks – until venture capital funding dried up in 2000, and multi-million-dollar dot-coms shrank into online oblivion. Yet San Francisco managed to retain its talent pool, and still has more entrepreneurs with advanced degrees than any other US city. It's a self-selecting community that can live with the risk of earthquakes and a volatile economy based on technology and tourism, but more people keep opting in each year. Today there are new booms in the works: biotech in Mission Bay, and Web 2.0 social media ventures in former dot-com headquarters.

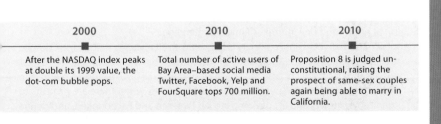

2000	2010	2010
After the NASDAQ index peaks at double its 1999 value, the dot-com bubble pops.	Total number of active users of Bay Area–based social media Twitter, Facebook, Yelp and FourSquare tops 700 million.	Proposition 8 is judged un-constitutional, raising the prospect of same-sex couples again being able to marry in California.

SAN FRANCISCO IN FOCUS

LIFESTYLE

↘ LIFESTYLE

SABRINA DALBESIO

A native San Franciscan spends some time in the sun

Conversation is easy to strike up in San Francisco: just ask locals to recommend a restaurant or political candidate. But ask them to describe a day in the life of a typical San Franciscan and they'll claim they can't help you, because no San Franciscan likes to be considered typical. Praise them as innovators or deride them as total slackers, and they'll gleefully contradict you. San Franciscans are highly educated and hold the most patents per capita in the US, yet also frequent the most medical marijuana clubs per capita in the US.

ICONOCLASM GOES MAINSTREAM

It's been decades since the Summer of Love, and San Franciscans are weary of being characterized as hippies. They prefer to think of themselves as forward-thinking ideal-ists, and to that end support some 2000 local nonprofits.

So how do you recognize a San Franciscan when you encounter one? Just listen: true to California surfer stereotypes, you'll probably overhear 'right on,' 'hella' and even 'gnarly' uttered with no trace of irony. Other than dudespeak, there is no dominant language in San Francsico, where half the population speaks a language other than English at home, and one in three claim Asian heritage.

Look around and you'll notice the city is blessed with an uncanny metabolism: despite an obsession with food and thousands of restaurants, San Francisco has the lowest body-mass index of any US city. Still, gym-ripped abs raise suspicion as being 'too LA.' Really, who has time to spend all day doing crunches when there are protests to be organized, concerts and art openings to be Tweeted and Facebooked, and online

⚓ MOVIES SET IN SF

- **Bullitt** (1968) Watch Steve McQueen's Ford Mustang fly over Nob Hill and land in SoMa – hence that editing Oscar.
- **Chan Is Missing** (1982) When Chan disappears with their $4000, two cabbies realize they don't really know Chan, Chinatown, or themselves.
- **Escape from Alcatraz** (1979) Clint Eastwood plots the ultimate jailbreak, using only a spoon and his wits.
- **Milk** (2008) Sean Penn stars as the camera-store owner determined to become America's first openly gay elected official.
- **Tales of the City** (1993) Laura Linney unravels a mystery involving a pot-growing landlady, closeted Nob Hill socialites, and the swinging '70s disco scene.

avatars that need redesigning? And honey, those parade costumes aren't going to make themselves.

All this earnest endeavor can be endearing, and almost always over the top. After a couple of days in San Francisco, you may begin to doubt how many of the latest Web 2.0 technologies are all that revolutionary; how tattoos and drag can still be transgressive when they're so ubiquitous; if graffiti artists who sell their work for five figures in galleries still qualify as graffiti artists; and whether the umpteenth documentary about San Francisco subcultures can still be described as 'shattering stereotypes.' San Franciscans will take any opportunity to prove reality wrong, and that contrarian streak could itself become predictable, but for some truly astonishing breakthroughs: Beat poetry, free speech, gay liberation, locavore cuisine, new media art, green architecture, and Folsom Street Fair getups that may permanently impair your ability to blush. Never mind, you won't be needing those inhibitions anyway – you're in San Francisco now.

SABRINA DALBESIO

Local residents out and about

LITERATURE

SABRINA DALBESIO

Vesuvio (p127)

If San Francisco didn't exist, writers would have to make it up. Set an unlikely story in San Francisco and somehow it seems believable. Where else could poetry fight the law and win? Yet when Beat poet Lawrence Ferlinghetti and bookseller Shig Murao were arrested for 'wilfully and lewdly' publishing Allen Ginsberg's incendiary *Howl and Other Poems*, they won a landmark 1957 free-speech court case for City Lights. Without poetic will and, let's be honest, a certain amount of lewdness, Bay Area bookstores would look mighty barren – or worse, boring.

BOOKISH CROWDS

Today you can hardly throw a pebble in this town without hitting a writer, though it might get you cursed in verse. San Francisco has more writers per capita than any other US city, buys more books per capita than any other North American burg, and hoards three times the national average of library books. Despite pronouncements of their imminent demise in the internet age, books remain wildly popular here in the capital of new technology.

FICTION

Many San Franciscans seem like characters in a novel, and the reverse is also true. After a few days here, you might feel like you've seen Armistead Maupin's bright-eyed, corn-fed Castro newbies, Dashiell Hammet's mysterious redheads, and Amy Tan's American-born daughters explaining slang to their Chinese-speaking moms. Ambrose Bierce and Mark

Twain set the San Francisco standard for sardonic wit early on, but recently, Bay Area graphic novelists such as Daniel Clowes have added a twist to this tradition with finely drawn, deadpan behavioral studies.

For fiction inspired by San Francisco's bizarre reality, check out these books:

Martin Eden by Jack London – semi-autobiographical 1909 account of San Francisco's first literary star, who got by on his wits in the illicit oyster trade.

The Man in the High Castle by Philip K Dick – the bestselling Berkeley sci-fi writer imagines San Francisco c 1962 if Japan and Nazi Germany had won WWII.

Tales of the City by Armistead Maupin – this 1976 romp follows San Francisco characters you might still recognize around town: pot-growing landladies, love-struck Castro clubgoers and socialites gone radical.

Ghost World by Daniel Clowes – this celebrated graphic novel about hipsters seeking direction and drifting apart takes visual cues from SF's Avenues.

NONFICTION

People-watching rivals reading as a preferred San Francisco pastime, and close observation of antics that would seem bizarre elsewhere pays off in stranger-than-fiction nonfiction – hence Hunter S Thompson's gonzo journalism and Joan Didion's core-shaking truth-telling. For weird stories closely observed and the occasional rant, check out SF's nonfiction standbys:

On the Road by Jack Kerouac – the book Kerouac banged out on one long scroll of paper in a San Francisco attic over a couple of sleepless months in 1951 made postwar America restless.

Hell's Angels: A Strange and Terrible Saga by Hunter S Thompson – this gonzo account of the outlaw Bay Area motorcycle club disturbed the deluded peace of America in the early '60s.

Slouching Towards Bethlehem by Joan Didion – Didion's 1968 essays burn right through the hippie haze to reveal glassy-eyed teenage revolutionaries adrift in the Summer of Love.

The Electric Kool-Aid Acid Test by Tom Wolfe – follow Ken Kesey, the Merry Pranksters, the Grateful Dead and Hell's Angels as they tune in, turn on, and drop out.

San Francisco Stories: Great Writers on the City edited by John Miller – 150 years of San Francisco impressions, including Jack London's 1906 earthquake reports, Jack Kerouac's attempts to hold a day job and Anne Lamott's send-up of pretentious cafes.

POETRY

So what's everyone reading? Any self-respecting SF bookshelf or e-reader should be well stocked with poetry (Beat authors obligatory); some satire; a graphic novel; a noir, nonfiction collection of essays about the San Francisco scene; and at least one novel by a Bay Area author. San Francisco's Kenneth Rexroth popularized haiku here back in the 1950s, and San Franciscans still enjoy nothing more than a few well-chosen words – the fog seems to lift with a few solar syllables supplied by Berkeley-based US poet laureate Robert Hass.

To wax poetic in City Lights' designated Poet's Chair (p130), turn to these titles for inspiration:

A Coney Island of the Mind by Lawrence Ferlinghetti – an indispensable doorstop for the imagination by SF's poet laureate.

Howl and Other Poems by Allen Ginsberg – an ecstatic improvised mantra chronicling the waking dreams of a generation that rejected postwar suburban complacency.

Time and Materials by Robert Hass – in the latest collection by the Berkeley-based poet and winner of the 2008 Pulitzer Prize for Literature, every word is as essential as a rivet in the Golden Gate Bridge.

THE BEST

RICK GERHARTER

Cartoon Art Museum (p171)

SF LITERARY SCENES

- **LitQuake** (p148)
- **Edinburgh Castle** (p199)
- **Make-Out Room** (p185)
- **Cartoon Art Museum** (p171)

'ZINES

San Francisco's literary scene isn't confined to books and iPads. The local 'zine scene has supplied notes from the underground since the 1970s brought punk and V Vale's *RE/Search* to San Francisco, and you can read the latest word at San Francisco Main Library (p90), Needles & Pens (p192) and Bound Together Anarchist Book Collective (p213). The most successful local 'zine of all, *McSweeney's,* is masterminded by Dave Eggers, who used the proceeds from his memoir *A Heartbreaking Work of Staggering Genius* to start McSweeney's publishing and 826 Valencia (p167), a nonprofit writing program for teens. *McSweeney's* also publishes an excellent map of literary San Francisco, so you can get out there and walk the talk.

⤵ SHOPPING

SABRINA DALBESIO

Boutique shopping, the Haight (p213)

Though it's been weaned off most of the harder stuff since the '60s, San Francisco still has one serious habit: shopping. San Franciscans like to think they've got more important things to worry about than following New York or Los Angeles retail trends – such as protesting wars, attaining enlightenment and finishing that documentary film. But though SF favors easy, eclectic style, that casual flair comes from scouring Hayes Valley and Fillmore St boutiques, Haight and Mission vintage stores, Downtown art galleries, Ferry Building gourmet retailers and Sunset surf shops. Not that you'll mind: potent SF retail highs last for hours.

LOCAL SPECIALTIES

Although you'll find the usual malls around Union Square, San Franciscans love to hate chain stores, even ones based locally, such as the Gap or American Apparel. Naysayers cite political reasons (support local designers, the economy, fellow workers of the world etc), but there's also SF's individualist self-image at stake: many San Franciscans would rather spend Friday night at home than be caught at a party in the same T-shirt as three other people. Not coincidentally, a surprising number of smaller SF-based stores are surviving the recession, successfully catering to SF's retail rebels with specialties that appeal to local passions for food, design, surf/skate culture and out-there oddities.

SAN FRANCISCO IN FOCUS

SHOPPING

FASHION

Dressing off the rack is only for the fashion-impaired in San Francisco, where DIY is the dominant ethic. Vintage shops, local boutiques and indie designers are the preferred style sources, and the savvy regularly trawl the sales racks on SF's key fashion streets: Haight, Valencia, Hayes, upper Grant, Fillmore, Union and upper Polk.

LOCAL & INDEPENDENT DESIGNERS

Some things are worth splashing out for, especially local designers – no one wants to miss out on the next local sensation to follow Derek Lam, Peter Som and a reunion special's worth of SF *Project Runway* contestants. San Francisco dotes on its homegrown designers, including Delilah Crown (p130), Loyal Army Clothing (p214), Dema (p191), Isda & Co (p190) and Sunhee Moon (p192). Residents Apparel

> ## ⬒ ALL DRESSED UP... WHERE TO GO?
>
> Natural, low-maintenance beauty is the norm, or at least the goal – San Franciscans prefer to conserve their effort for drag, Burning Man and promising dates. The most double-take-inducing, original looks are spotted by night, especially at Mission bars and SoMa clubs. Few SF clubs have actual dress codes, velvet ropes, or bouncers that need to be impressed for admittance – just call ahead to get on the guest list, and wear whatever puts you in a party mood. For maximum mileage by day, strut your fashion-forward finery on Valencia St or Haight St, at SFMOMA or in cutting-edge galleries.

Gallery (p217) and Mission Statement (p191) are collectives of local designers cutting out the middleman to offer standout style and value, while Mingle (p79), Eco Citizen (p154), Studio (p154) and Velvet da Vinci (p155) offer a tantalizing range of clothes and accessories by local and indie designers.

SF STYLE

The ultimate SF fashionista compliment isn't on your choice of accessories, but on your sense of style – the more individual, the better, even in office settings. In other cities, tattoos and muscle tees are the native dress of bar bouncers; in SF they're standard getup for startup software engineers. Yet there's no designated underground-culture uniform here: trucker hats, ironic T-shirts, white belts and skinny jeans are far too mass-marketed for SF's sub-subcultures.

If San Francisco had its own unisex national costume besides drag, here's what it would include: fly kicks or funky low-heeled shoes to manage those hills; jeans of course, invented here by Levi Strauss 150 years ago and getting more overpriced by the minute; a whimsical silkscreened T-shirt, or possibly a vintage Western shirt or '80s secretary blouse, worn ironically; a sweater and/or coat of some kind, which remains inexplicably unbuttoned even in the chilliest fog; and a backpack, handbag or man-bag to hold big books and exceedingly small techno-gadgets.

This is one city where men are expected to have fashion sense, and must try even harder than women to get noticed. You'll spot San Francisco's peacocks working looks that range from Sui Generis vintage (p193) to MAC chic (p216), and wearing everything from dapper Goorin Brothers fedoras (p214) to Upper Playground streetwear (p214), Madame S & Mr S leather (p190) and Piedmont drag (p216).

SUSTAINABLE TRAVEL

SABRINA DALBESIO

Butterfly, California Academy of Sciences (p231)

Nature has been kind to San Francisco, lavishing the city with gardens, parks, and top-notch produce – and the city does its best to repay the favor, with mandatory composting citywide and thoughtful conservation measures every day. This is one town where you can eat, sleep and cavort sustainably.

GREEN INITIATIVES

All around you in San Francisco, you'll notice pioneering green ideas in action, with support ranging from local businesses to the Green Party (a power player in city politics). San Francisco has pioneered curbside recycling and composting programs, and its claim to fame as the US capital of creative reuse dates from 1950s Beat artists' scavenged collages and assemblages. All these measures have helped make San Francisco a livable, breathable city – that city-shut-in sensation you get surrounded by New York skyscrapers or Los Angeles freeways isn't a problem here.

Not bad for a city that started out with rotting ships, slapdash buildings and plenty of muck. The city wasn't exactly planned, with sailors abandoning their ships in the harbor as they swarmed ashore during the Gold Rush. But among the early arrivals were naturalist and Muir Woods founder John Muir and Golden Gate Park champion William Hammond Hall, who saw beauty and not just gold in these hills. Today virtually every hilltop in San Francisco has a precious green toupee it wouldn't be seen without, including scenic Telegraph Hill (p115), Buena Vista Park (p203) and Sterling Park (p141). Architects working with the local landscape have created organic landmarks, including Nagao Sakurai's 1951 Zen Garden at the Japanese Tea Garden (p232) and Renzo Piano's flower-capped 2008 California Academy of Sciences (p231).

⇘ GREEN IDEAS

- **Drink organically** Cheers to wine made with organically grown grapes in Sonoma (p247) and seasonal, organic cocktails at Elixir (p181).
- **Eat locally grown, sustainable food** After grazing tasty local produce at the Ferry Building (p62), you'll recognize farm names on menus across town – and know the good stuff.
- **Enjoy a green night at the movies** Your reserved, recycled-fiber seat awaits at Sundance Kabuki Cinema (p153).
- **Plant an urban garden** Find gardening inspiration atop the 'living roof' of LEED-certified California Academy of Sciences (p231).
- **Renew, recycle, retail** Fashion-forward SF designers use recycled materials and/or source responsibly at Eco Citizen (p154).
- **Snore sustainably** Sleep at Orchard Garden Hotel (p92), SF's first LEED-certified green hotel.

PARKS & RECREATION

As local real-estate prices remain among the highest in the US, there's always the fear that San Francisco's outdoor living-room spaces will be swallowed up by private development. But San Francisco's motley coalition of neighborhood councils, dog walkers, parrot-feeders, parents, kite-flyers, conservationists and lollygaggers has kept a watchful eye on urban green spaces for a century. San Franciscans successfully lobbied for the preservation of Golden Gate Park in the 19th century, and recently convinced the US military to hand over the Presidio military base, including Baker Beach and Crissy Field, for use as public parkland.

Inspired ideas are continuing to change the local scenery. In 2009, local art group REBAR repurposed a decrepit fountain in front of City Hall to grow organic vegetables for community nonprofits, gaining support from Slow Food San Francisco and kicking off an urban farming movement. Rooftop vegetable gardens have taken off, and defunct freeway ramps have been converted into city-center farms. There's also a buzz about public beekeeping, to encourage healthy cross-pollination in urban plantlife. Don't laugh just yet: as you can see from the plentiful greenery, wild ideas tend to take root in San Francisco.

⬎ DIRECTORY & TRANSPORTATION

DIRECTORY

ACCOMMODATIONS

If you can't find a room, the **Visitor Information Center** (☎ 800-637-5196, 415-391-2000; www.onlyinsanfrancisco.com) helps with reservations. Ask about parking: it's rarely included (when it is, we've noted it with a ⓟ). The rates we quote are for high season (summer); you can sometimes do better, unless there's a convention in town.

BUSINESS HOURS

Banks 9am-4:30pm or 5pm Monday to Friday (occasionally 9am to noon Saturday)

Offices 8:30am to 5:30pm Monday to Friday

Restaurants Breakfast 8am to noon, lunch noon to 3pm, dinner 5:30pm to 10pm; Saturday and Sunday brunch 10am to 2pm

Shops 10am or 11am to 6pm or 7pm Monday to Saturday and noon to 6pm Sunday

CHILDREN

To find the best places for children, just look for the ⍟ symbol, and see Family Travel (p266). Licensed childcare can be found through **American Child Care** (Map p107; ☎ 415-285-2300; www.americanchildcare.com; Suite 1600, 580 California St; ⓐ California) for $20 per hour plus gratuity, and a four-hour minimum.

CLIMATE

EMBASSIES & CONSULATES

Australia (Map p160; ☎ 415-536-1970; www.australiaconsulate.org; Suite 200, 625 Market St, SoMa; ☽ 8:45am-1pm & 2-4:30pm Mon-Fri; ⓐ 6, 7, 71, F, J, K, L, M, N, T; ⓐ & ⊕ Embarcadero)

Canada (Map p107; ☎ 415-834-3180; www.sanfrancisco.gc.ca; 580 California St, 14th fl, Chinatown; ☽ 8:30am-4:30pm Mon-Fri; ⓐ & ⊕ Embarcadero) For legal emergencies or visa questions call the Operations Centre toll-free ☎ 1-800-267-6788; outside Canada, call collect ☎ 613-996-8885.

France (Map p82; ☎ 415-397-4330; www.consulfrance-sanfrancisco.org; 540 Bush St, Downtown; ☽ 9am-12:30pm Mon-Fri; ⓐ & ⊕ Embarcadero)

Germany (Map p134; ☎ 415-353-0300; www.germanyinfo.org; 1960 Jackson St, Japantown; ☽ 9am-noon Mon-Fri; ⓐ 1, 38)

Ireland (Map p82; ☎ 415-392-4214; 33rd fl, 100 Pine St, Downtown; ☽ 10am-noon & 2-3:30pm Mon-Fri; ⓐ & ⊕ Montgomery St)

Japan (Map p160; ☎ 415-777-3533; www.cgjsf.org; Suite 2300, 50 Fremont St, SoMa; ☽ 9am-5pm Mon-Fri; ⓐ & ⊕ Embarcadero)

Mexico (Map p160; ☎ 415-354-1700; www.consulmexsf.com; 532 Folsom St, Downtown; ☽ 7:30am-1:30pm Mon-Fri; ⓐ & ⊕ Powell St)

Netherlands (☎ 650-403-0073; www.ncla.org; 901 Mariners Isl Blvd, San Mateo; ☽ by appointment)

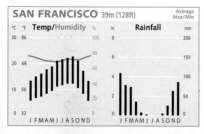

SAN FRANCISCO 39m (128ft)   Average Max/Min

Temp/Humidity   Rainfall

New Zealand (Map p82; ☎ 415-399-1255; www.mft.govt.nz; Suite 700, 1 Maritime Plaza, Downtown; ☺ by appointment; 🚌 & ⓜ Embarcadero)

UK (Map p82; ☎ 415-617-1361; www.ukinusa.fco.gov.uk; Suite 850, 1 Sansome St, Downtown; ☺ 8:30am-1pm & 2-5pm Mon-Fri; 🚌 & ⓜ Embarcadero)

HOLIDAYS

New Year's Day January 1

Martin Luther King Jr Day Third Monday in January

Presidents' Day Third Monday in February

Easter Sunday (and Good Friday and Easter Monday) in March or April

Memorial Day Last Monday in May

Independence Day July 4

Labor Day First Monday in September

Columbus Day Second Monday in October

Veterans Day November 11

Thanksgiving Fourth Thursday in November

Christmas Day December 25

INTERNET ACCESS

Places listed in this guide that offer wi-fi have a 🛜 symbol. Those traveling without laptops can surf the internet for free at almost any public library, or the Downtown Apple Store (Map p82; ☎ 415-392-0202; www.apple.com; 1 Stockton St; ☺ 10am-9pm Mon-Sat, 11am-7pm Sun; 🚌 & ⓜ Powell St; 🛜), which has high-speed wi-fi access and internet terminals. The San Francisco Main Library (Map p82) has 160 terminals, including some available to non-library-card-holding visitors on the 1st floor; internet access is available on a 15-minute basis, and there's spotty wi-fi access. Brainwash laundromat (p182) offers internet as well as food, coffee, beer and occasional live music.

LEGAL MATTERS

Americans are eligible to vote at 18, the legal age of consent is 17, and driver's licenses can be obtained by passing the necessary tests at age 16. Visitors old enough to drink back home might not be here, where the legal drinking age is 21. Drinking alcoholic beverages outdoors is not officially allowed, though drinking beer and wine is often permissible at street fairs and other outdoor events.

MEDICAL SERVICES

Overseas visitors should acquire travel insurance that covers medical situations in the US, where nonemergency care for uninsured patients can be very expensive. For nonemergency appointments at hospitals, you'll need proof of insurance or cash.

CLINICS

Haight Ashbury Free Clinic (Map p196; ☎ 415-746-1950; 558 Clayton St; ☺ call for appointment; 🚌 6, 24, 66, 71, N) Services offered by appointment only, but once you're in, a doctor will see you for free and will offer advice if further medical attention is needed.

Lyon-Martin Women's Health Services (Map p160; ☎ 415-565-7667; www.lyon-martin.org; Suite 201, 1748 Market St; ☺ 11am-7pm Mon & Wed, 9am-5pm Tue & Fri, noon-5pm Thu; 🚌 6, 66, 71, F) Relatively affordable health services are available at this women's clinic; lesbian-friendly.

EMERGENCY ROOMS

Davies Medical Center (Map p196; ☎ 415-565-6000; Noe St; ☺ 24hr; 🚌 6, 24, 71, J, N) Has 24-hour emergency services.

San Francisco General Hospital (Map p160; ☎ emergency room 415-206-8111, main hospital 415-206-8000; www.sfdph.org; 1001 Potrero Ave; ☺ 24hr; 🚌 9) Provides care to uninsured patients; no documentation required beyond ID.

University of California San Francisco Medical Center (Map p220; ☎ 415-476-1000; www.ucsfhealth.org; 505 Parnassus Ave; ☼ 24hr; ☒ 6, 24, 71, J, N) At the vanguard of medical advances.

PHARMACIES

Walgreens (Map p168; ☎ 415-861-3136; www.walgreens.com; 498 Castro St at 18th St; ☼ 24hr; ☒ 24, 35, F, Castro St) Pharmacy and over-the-counter meds; dozens of locations citywide (see website).

MONEY

CREDIT CARDS

Following is a list of phone numbers to report lost or stolen credit cards.

American Express (☎ 800-992-3404)
MasterCard (☎ 800-622-7747)
Visa (☎ 800-847-2911)

EXCHANGE

American Express (AmEx; Map p160; ☎ 415-536-2600; www.americanexpress.com/travel; 455 Market St; ☼ 8:30am-5:30pm Mon-Fri, 9:30am-3:30pm Sat; ☒ 21, 71, F, J, K, L, M, N, T; ☒ & ☺ Embarcadero)

Bank of America (Map p82; ☎ 415-837-1394; www.bankamerica.com; downstairs, 1 Powell St; ☼ 9am-6pm Mon-Fri, to 2pm Sat; ☒ 5, 6, 721, 31, 71 F, J, K, L, M, N; ☒ & ☺ Powell St)

NEWSPAPERS & MAGAZINES

San Francisco Bay Guardian (www.sfbg.com) Free weekly; alternative news and entertainment listings.

San Francisco Chronicle (www.sfgate.com) Main daily newspaper; news, entertainment and event listings online (no registration required).

SF Weekly (www.sfweekly.com) Free weekly; local gossip and entertainment.

ORGANIZED TOURS

Chinatown Alleyway Tours (☎ 415-984-1478; www.chinatownalleywaytours.org; adult/child 6-9yr/student $18/5/12; ☼ 11am-1pm Sat or by appointment) Teens who grew up here lead two-hour tours offering an up-close-and-personal peek into Chinatown's past.

Precita Eyes Mission Mural Tours (☎ 415-285-2287; www.precitaeyes.org; adult $10-12, child under 17yr $5; ☼ 11am & 1:30pm Sat & Sun) Offers two-hour walking tours by local artists covering 60-plus murals in a six-block radius of mural-covered Balmy Alley.

Public Library City Guides (☎ 415-557-4266; www.sfcityguides.org; public tours free, donations accepted) Local historians lead one-to-two-hour tours by neighborhood and theme: Art Deco Marina, Gold Rush Downtown, and Summer of Love Treasure Hunt in the Haight.

Transported SF (☎ 415-424-1058; www.transportedsf.com) The journey is the destination with these DJ-equipped buses bound for organic Sonoma wineries, East Bay foraging expeditions, and nowhere in particular in the Mission.

TAXES

SF's 9.5% sales tax is added to virtually everything, including meals, accommodations and car rentals. There's also a 14% hotel room tax to take into consideration when booking a hotel room.

TELEPHONE

The US country code is ☎ 1, and San Francisco's city code is ☎ 415. To make an international call from the Bay Area, call ☎ 011 + country code + area code + number. When dialing another area code, the code must be preceded by a ☎ 1.

AREA CODES IN THE BAY AREA

East Bay ☎ 510
Marin County ☎ 415

Peninsula ☎ 650
San Francisco ☎ 415
San Jose ☎ 408
Santa Cruz ☎ 831
Wine Country ☎ 707

OPERATOR SERVICES
International operator (☎ 00)
Local directory (☎ 411)
Long-distance directory information
(☎ 1 + area code + 555-1212)
Operator (☎ 0)
Toll-free number information (☎ 800-
555-1212)

TOURIST INFORMATION
The helpful, centrally located **San Francisco Visitor Information Center** (Map p82; ☎ 415-391-2000, events hotline 415-391-2001; www.onlyinsanfrancisco.com; lower level, Hallidie Plaza, Market & Powell Sts; ☺ 9am-5pm Mon-Fri, to 3pm Sat & Sun, closed Sun Nov-Apr; ☐ & ⓟ Powell St) provides practical information for tourists, publishes glossy tourist-oriented booklets and runs a 24-hour events hotline.

TRAVELERS WITH DISABILITIES
The *San Francisco Bay Area Regional Transit Guide* (http://tripplanner.transit.511.org) covers accessibility for people with disabilities. For further information about wheelchair accessibility on public transit and in hotels and other facilities, contact the **Independent Living Resource Center of San Francisco** (☎ 415-543-6222; www.ilrcsf. org; ☺ 9am-4:30pm Mon-Thu, to 4pm Fri).

VISAS
The USA Visa Waiver Program (VWP) allows nationals from 27 countries to enter the US without a visa, provided they are carrying a machine-readable passport. Citizens of VWP countries need to regis-ter with the government online (http://esta.cbp.dhs.gov/) three days before their visit. For the updated list of countries included in the program and current requirements, see the website of the **US Department of State** (http://travel.state. gov/visa).

TRANSPORTATION
AIR
Flights and rail tickets can be booked online at www.lonelyplanet.com/travel_services.

AIRPORTS
SAN FRANCISCO INTERNATIONAL AIRPORT
One of the busiest airports in the country, **San Francisco International Airport** (SFO; ☎ 650-821-8211; www.flysfo.com) serves over 40 million passengers annually on 45 airlines. There are **information booths** (☺ 8am-1:30am) and white **courtesy phones** (☎ information 7-0018) on the lower (arrivals) level of all three terminals, **Traveler's Aid information booths** (☺ 9am- 9pm) on the upper levels, and an **airport ground transportation hotline** (☎ 800-736-2008; ☺ 7:30am-5pm Mon-Fri). All terminals have ATMs, and there is a currency exchange in the International terminal. SFO is on the bayside of the peninsula, 14 miles south of Downtown San Francisco. Highway 101 connects the airport directly to Downtown.

OAKLAND INTERNATIONAL AIRPORT
Travelers arriving at **Oakland International Airport** (OAK; ☎ 510-563-3300; www.oaklandairport.com), 15 miles east of Downtown, will have a little further to go to reach San Francisco. The least expensive way from the Oakland airport is via BART train and the **AirBART shuttle**

(☎ 510-569-8310; adult/child & senior $3/1; ⏱ 5am-midnight Mon-Sat, 8am-midnight Sun). The AirBART shuttle leaves both terminals every 10 to 20 minutes for the BART Coliseum Station; buy your AirBART shuttle ticket from the ticket machine before exiting the airport.

NORMAN Y MINETA SAN JOSE INTERNATIONAL AIRPORT

Fifty miles south of Downtown San Francisco, Norman Y Mineta San Jose International Airport (SJC; ☎ 408-501-0979; www.sjc.org) is a straight shot into the city by car via Highway 101. The VTA Airport Flyer (bus 10; tickets $1.75, from 5am to midnight) makes a continuous run between the Santa Clara Caltrain station (Railroad Ave and Franklin St) and the airport terminals, departing every 10 to 15 minutes. From Santa Clara station, Caltrain (one-way $7.75, 80 minutes) runs several trains every day to the terminal at 4th and King Sts in SF.

BOAT

Blue & Gold Fleet Ferries (Map p52; ☎ 415-705-8200; www.blueandgoldfleet.com) operates ferries from the Ferry Building, Pier 39 and Pier 41 at Fisherman's Wharf to Jack London Sq in Oakland (one-way $7.75), Tiburon or Sausalito (one-way $11) and Angel Island. Ticket booths are located at the Ferry Building and Piers 39 and 41 (Map p52).

⤵ GETTING INTO TOWN

- **BART (Bay Area Rapid Transit;** ☎ 415-989-2278; www.bart.gov; ⏱ 6am-11pm) BART offers a cheap, direct 30-minute ride from the San Francisco airport to Downtown San Francisco for $8.10 one-way, and connects to the Oakland airport via the AirBART shuttle (p295). The SFO BART station is connected to the international terminal; tickets can be purchased from machines inside the station entrance.
- **Door-to-door shuttle vans** Shuttles pick up and drop off from any San Francisco location to/from SFO, and usually take some time circulating to different hotels to pick up more passengers. Companies include Super Shuttle (☎ 415-558-8500; www.supershuttle.com), Lorrie's (☎ 415-334-9000), Quake City (☎ 415-255-4899; www.quakecityshuttle.com) and American Airporter Shuttle (☎ 415-202-0733, 800-282-7758). Fares range from $15 to $17 one-way.
- **SFO Airporter** (☎ 650-246-2775; www.sfoairporter.com/pickups.htm; one-way/round-trip $15/22) This bus departs every 30 minutes from the baggage claim areas and stops at major hotels.
- **SamTrans** (☎ 800-660-4287) express bus KX ($4.50, 30 minutes) and the slightly slower local SamTrans bus 292 ($1.75) leave from the BART station at SFO, and drop you at San Francisco's Transbay Terminal, near Downtown in the South of Market area.
- **Taxis** Taxis from SFO to Downtown cost $30 to $45, plus tip, departing from the yellow zone on the lower level. Taxis at Oakland International Airport leave curbside and cost $60 to $70 to Downtown SF.

⇘ CLIMATE CHANGE & TRAVEL

Travel – especially air travel – is a significant contributor to global climate change. At Lonely Planet, we believe that all who travel have a responsibility to limit their personal impact. As a result, we have teamed with Rough Guides and other concerned industry partners to support Climate Care, which allows people to offset the greenhouse gases they are responsible for with contributions to energy-saving projects and other climate-friendly initiatives in the developing world. Lonely Planet offsets all staff and author travel.

For more information, turn to the responsible travel pages on www.lonely planet.com. For details on offsetting your carbon emissions and a carbon calculator, go to www.climatecare.org.

Golden Gate Transit Ferries (Map p52; ☎ 415-455-2000; www.goldengateferry. org; ☾ 6am-9:30pm Mon-Fri, 10am-6pm Sat & Sun) runs regular ferry services from the Ferry Building to Larkspur and Sausalito (one-way adult/child under five years/ senior and youth six to 18 years $7.85/ free/3.90).

Get to Napa car-free via **Vallejo Ferry** (Map p52; ☎ 877-643-3779; www.baylink ferry.com; adult/child under 6yr/senior & child over 6yr $13/free/6.50) with departures from Ferry Building docks about every hour from 6:30am to 7pm weekdays and every two hours from 11am to 7:30pm on weekends; bikes are permitted. From the Vallejo Ferry Terminal, take Napa Valley Vine bus 10 to downtown Napa, Yountville, St Helena or Calistoga.

BUS, CABLE CAR & STREETCAR

The city's principal public transportation system, **Muni** (☎ 415-701-2311; www.sfmuni. com; adult/child under 4yr/senior & child 5-17yr $2/ free/75¢; ☾ 5am-late Mon-Fri, reduced schedules Sat & Sun) operates nearly 100 bus lines, the streetcar system, and the city's signature cable cars. Buses and streetcars are referred to interchangeably as Muni and marked in this book with 🚌 , while cable cars are marked with 🚠 . For fastest routes and the most exact departure times, consult http://transit.511.org.

Tickets can be bought on board buses and streetcars, or at Muni stations for the underground streetcars. On most Muni lines, free transfer tickets are available at the start of your journey and you can then use them for two connecting Muni trips within 90 minutes or so (but not BART or cable cars). Hang onto your ticket or transfer even if you're not planning to use it again: if you're caught without one by the transit police, you're subject to a $75 fine (repeat offenders may soon be fined up to $500).

DISCOUNTS & PASSES

One-day Muni Passport good for unlimited travel on buses, streetcars and cable cars $11
Three-day Passport $18
Week-long Passport $24
10-ride ticket book $20

Ticket books and Passports can be purchased at the Muni kiosk at the Powell St cable car turnaround on Market St, at Montgomery station ticket booth, the half-price ticket kiosk on Union Square, and from a number of hotels.

BUS

The main hub connecting San Francisco to points across the bay and beyond is the **Transbay Terminal** (Map p160; **425 Mission St**); this is the SF terminus for Greyhound.

WITHIN SF

Muni buses display their route number and final destination on the front and side. The major bus routes:

5 Fulton From the Transbay Terminal, along Market and McAllister Sts to Fulton St, along the north side of Golden Gate Park to the ocean.

15 Kearny From 3rd St in SoMa, through the Financial District on Kearny St, through North Beach on Columbus Ave, then along Powell St to the Fisherman's Wharf area.

22 Fillmore From Dogpatch (Potrero Hill), through the Mission on 16th St, along Fillmore St past Japantown to Pacific Heights and the Marina.

33 Stanyan From San Francisco General Hospital, through the Mission, Castro and Haight, past Golden Gate Park to Clement St.

BUS SERVICES TO/FROM SF

Golden Gate Transit (Map p160; ☎ 415-455-2000; www.goldengatetransit.org), the main public transit company serving Marin and Sonoma counties, connects to San Francisco, but be advised that service can be slow and erratic. Bus 70/80 runs from San Francisco to Petaluma ($8) and to Santa Rosa ($8.80); catch it at 1st and Mission Sts, across from the Transbay Terminal.

Greyhound (☎ 800-231-2222; www.greyhound.com; **425 Mission St**) provides nationwide bus service from the Transbay Terminal and somewhat more limited service from its terminal in downtown Oakland (2103 San Pablo Ave). Regular services operate from San Francisco to Los Angeles ($39 and up, from eight hours) and Santa Rosa ($21 to $26); transfer for local buses.

Samtrans (☎ 800-660-4287; www.samtrans.com) runs buses up and down the peninsula between San Francisco and the South Bay, including two bus services to/from SFO. Buses pick up/drop off from the Transbay Terminal and other marked bus stops within the city; see the website for the transit map.

CABLE CAR

Cable cars cost $10 to ride all day or $5 for a single trip (no transfers); kids under four years old ride free. Tickets can be purchased on board or at the Muni kiosks at Powell and Market Sts or Hyde St at Beach. Cable cars run from approximately 6am to 12:30am daily.

CABLE CAR LINES

California Runs east–west along California St, from the Downtown terminus at Market and Davis Sts through Chinatown and Nob Hill to Van Ness Ave.

Powell-Mason Runs from the Powell St cable car turnaround past Union Square, turns west along Jackson St, and descends north down Mason St, Columbus Ave and Taylor St towards Fisherman's Wharf. On the return trip it takes Washington St instead of Jackson St.

Powell-Hyde Follows the same route as Powell-Mason until Jackson St, where it turns down Hyde St to terminate at Aquatic Park; coming back it takes Washington St.

STREETCAR

Muni Metro streetcars run both above and below ground, from 5am to midnight on weekdays, with limited schedules on weekends.

F Fisherman's Wharf and Embarcadero to Castro
J Downtown to Mission/Castro
K, L, M Downtown to Castro
N Caltrain to Haight and Ocean Beach
T Embarcadero to Caltrain, China Basin and Bayview

CAR & MOTORCYCLE

If you can, avoid driving in San Francisco: traffic is a given, street parking is harder to find than true love, and meter readers are ruthless. Before heading to any bridge, airport or other traffic choke-point, call ☎ 511 toll-free for a traffic update. Members of the **American Automobile Association** (AAA; Map p82; ☎ 415-773-1900, 800-222-4357; www.aaa.com; 160 Sutter St; ☽ 8:30am-5:30pm Mon-Fri) can call the 800 number any time for emergency road service and towing.

CAR SHARE

Zipcar (☎ 866-494-7227; www.zipcar.com) rents Prius Hybrids and Minis by the hour for flat rates starting at $8.33 per hour, including gas and insurance, or by day for $62.10; a $25 application fee and $50 prepaid usage are required in advance. Drivers without a US driver's license should follow instructions at www.zipcar.com/apply/foreign-drivers. Once approved, cars can be reserved at www.zipcar.com or at 866-4ZIPCAR. Check the website for pick-up/drop-off locations.

PARKING

The most convenient Downtown parking lots are at the Embarcadero Center, at 5th and Mission Sts, under Union Square, and at Sutter and Stockton Sts; for more public parking garages, see www.sfmta.com. Desperate motorists often resort to double-parking or parking in red zones or on sidewalks, but parking authorities

are quick to tow cars. If this should happen to you, you'll have to retrieve your car at **Autoreturn** (Map p160; ☎ 415-865-8200; www.autoreturn.com; 450 7th St; ☽ 24hr; 🚍 27, 42).

RENTALS

Alamo Rent-a-Car (Map p134; ☎ 415-693-0191, 800-327-9633; www.alamo.com; 750 Bush St; ☽ 7am-7pm; 🚍 2, 3, 4, 76; 🚋 Powell-Mason, Powell-Hyde)
Avis (Map p82; ☎ 415-929-2555, 800-831-2847; www.avis.com; 675 Post St; ☽ 6am-6pm; 🚍 2, 3, 4, 76)
Budget (Map p82; ☎ 415-292-8981, 800-527-0700; www.budget.com; 321 Mason St; ☽ 6am-6pm; 🚍 2, 3, 4, 38)
Dollar (Map p82; ☎ 800-800-5252; www.dollarcar.com; 364 O'Farrell St; ☽ 7am-7pm; 🚍 2, 3, 4, 38)
Hertz (Map p82; ☎ 415-771-2200, 800-654-3131; www.hertz.com; 325 Mason St; ☽ 6am-6pm Mon-Thu, to 8pm Fri & Sat; 🚍 2, 3, 4, 38)
Thrifty (Map p82; ☎ 415-788-6906, 800-367-2277; www.thrifty.com; 350 O'Farrell St; ☽ 7am-7pm; 🚍 2, 3, 4, 38)

TAXI

Fares start at $3.50 at the flag drop and run about $2.25 per mile. The following taxi companies have 24-hour dispatches.
Arrow Taxicab (☎ 415-648-3181)
DeSoto Cab (☎ 415-970-1300)
Green Cab (☎ 415-626-4733; www.greencab.com) Fuel-efficient hybrids; worker-owned collective.
Luxor Cab (☎ 415-282-4141)
Yellow Cab (☎ 415-333-3333)

TRAIN

Throughout this book, venues readily accessible by **BART** (Bay Area Rapid Transit; ☎ 415-989-2278; www.bart.gov; ☽ 4am-midnight Mon-Fri, 6am-midnight Sat, 8am-midnight Sun) are denoted by ⊖ followed by the name of the nearest BART station. The fastest link between Downtown and the Mission District also offers transit to SF airport, Oakland and Berkeley. Within SF, one-way fares start at $1.75. BART tickets are sold in machines in BART stations, and you'll need your ticket to enter and exit.

From the depot at 4th and King Sts in San Francisco, Caltrain (☎ 800-660-4287; www.caltrain.com) heads south to Millbrae (connecting to BART and SFO, 30 minutes), Palo Alto (one hour) and San Jose (1½ hours).

The train routes Amtrak (☎ 800-872-7245; www.amtrakcalifornia.com) runs with government support through the San Francisco Bay are some of the most scenic in the USA, so take advantage while government subsidies last. Amtrak runs free shuttle buses to San Francisco's Ferry Building and Caltrain station from its terminals in Emeryville and Oakland's Jack London Sq.

⬎ BEHIND THE SCENES

THE AUTHORS

ALISON BING
Coordinating author

Over 15 years in San Francisco, Alison has done everything you're supposed to do in the city and many things you're not, including falling in love on the 71 Haight-Noriega bus and gorging on Mission burritos before Berlioz symphonies. Alison holds degrees in art history and international diplomacy – respectable diplomatic credentials she regularly undermines with opinionated culture commentary for radio, newspapers, foodie magazines, and books, including Lonely Planet's *California, USA, Coastal California, California Trips, San Francisco* and *San Francisco Encounter*.

Author thanks Many thanks and crushing California bear hugs to editorial superhero Suki Gear; Lonely Planet *San Francisco* city guide coauthor John Vlahides, delightful raconteur and major contributor to this book; fearless leaders Brice Gosnell and Heather Dickson at Lonely Planet; editor Katie O'Connell; managing editor Sasha Baskett; the Sanchez Writers' Grotto for steady inspiration; cartographer Alison Lyall; and above all to Marco Flavio Marinucci, whose powerful kindness and bracing espresso make anything possible, including romance on a skeevy Muni bus.

JOHN A VLAHIDES

John Vlahides lives in San Francisco. He's a former luxury-hotel concierge and member of the prestigious Les Clefs d'Or, the international union of the world's elite concierges. He is cofounder of the travel site 71miles.com, and appears regularly on television and radio; watch some of his travel videos on lonelyplanet.tv. John spends his free time singing with the San Francisco Symphony, sunning on the beach beneath the Golden Gate Bridge, skiing the Sierra Nevada and touring California on his motorcycle.

THE PHOTOGRAPHER

San Francisco-based photographer Sabrina Dalbesio grew up in Santa Cruz, California. A constant desire to travel combined with her love for both art and the natural world have kept her inspired to get out and capture moments of life in images. She enjoys creating both traditional photography and alternative art works that begin with a photographic image.

THIS BOOK

This 1st edition of *Discover San Francisco* was coordinated by Alison Bing, and researched and written by Alison and John A Vlahides. This guidebook was commissioned in Lonely Planet's Oakland office, and produced by the following:

Commissioning Editor Suki Gear
Coordinating Editor Katie O'Connell
Coordinating Cartographer Jolyon Philcox
Coordinating Layout Designer Jim Hsu
Managing Editors Sasha Baskett, Liz Heynes
Managing Cartographers Alison Lyall, Herman So
Managing Layout Designers Indra Kilfoyle, Celia Wood
Assisting Editors Kate Evans, Martine Power
Assisting Cartographer Hunor Csutoros
Cover Research Sabrina Dalbesio
Internal Image Research Sabrina Dalbesio, Jane Hart
Thanks to Glenn Beanland, Heather Dickson, Joshua Geoghegan, Chris Girdler, Michelle Glynn, Brice Gosnell, Wayne Murphy, Darren O'Connell, Rebecca Skinner, Juan Winata

Internal photographs p4 Alcatraz ruins, Rhonda Gutenberg; p10 Cable car on Hyde St, Sabrina Dalbesio; p12 Castro trolley car, Christina Lease; p31 Amazon Flooded Forest display at California Academy of Sciences, Sabrina Dalbesio; p39 Transamerica Pyramid and Francis Ford Coppola Building, Sabrina Dalbesio; p3, p50 Golden Gate Bridge at dusk, Orien Harvey; p3, p81 Cable car on California St, Angus Oborn; p3, p105 Bike taxi driver in Chinatown, Sabrina Dalbesio; p3, p133 Coit Tower and North Beach from Russian Hill, Sabrina Dalbesio; p3, p159 Maestra-Peace©1994 & 2000 by Juana Alicia, Miranda Bergman, Edyth Boone, Susan Cervantes, Meera Desai, Yvonne Littleton & Irene Perez, all rights reserved, photo by Sabrina Dalbesio; p3, p195 Haight St, Shania Shegedyn; p3, p219 California Academy of Sciences, Sabrina Dalbesio; p3, p243 Iron Horse Vineyards, Judy Bellah; p256 Mural in Castro district, Richard I'Anson; p291 Ferry Building, Lee Foster.

SEND US YOUR FEEDBACK

We love to hear from travelers – your comments keep us on our toes and help make our books better. Our well-traveled team reads every word on what you loved or loathed about this book. Although we cannot reply individually to postal submissions, we always guarantee that your feedback goes straight to the appropriate authors, in time for the next edition. Each person who sends us information is thanked in the next edition, and the most useful submissions are rewarded with a free book.

Visit lonelyplanet.com to submit your updates and suggestions or to ask for help. Our award-winning website also features inspirational travel stories, news and discussions.

Note: We may edit, reproduce and incorporate your comments in Lonely Planet products such as guidebooks, websites and digital products, so let us know if you don't want your comments reproduced or your name acknowledged. For a copy of our privacy policy visit lonelyplanet.com/privacy.

↘ INDEX

See also separate indexes for Drinking (p305), Eating (p305), Entertainment & Activities (p307), Shopping (p308), Sights (p309) and Sleeping (p311).

INDEX

ENTERTAINMENT & ACTIVITIES

INDEX

SHOPPING

INDEX

SIGHTS

000 Map pages
000 Photograph pages

INDEX
SLEEPING

MAP LEGEND

ROUTES

Tollway	One-Way Street
Freeway	Mall/Steps
Primary	Tunnel
Secondary	Pedestrian Overpass
Tertiary	Walking Tour
Lane	Walking Tour Detour
Under Construction	Walking Path
Unsealed Road	Track

TRANSPORT

Ferry	Rail/Underground
Metro	Tram
Monorail	Cable Car, Funicular

HYDROGRAPHY

River, Creek	Canal
Intermittent River	Water
Swamp/Mangrove	Dry Lake/Salt Lake
Reef	Glacier

BOUNDARIES

International	Regional, Suburb
State, Provincial	Marine Park
Disputed	Cliff/Ancient Wall

AREA FEATURES

Area of Interest	Forest
Beach, Desert	Mall/Market
Building/Urban Area	Park
Cemetery, Christian	Restricted Area
Cemetery, Other	Sports

POPULATION

✪ **CAPITAL (NATIONAL)**	◉	**CAPITAL (STATE)**	
●	**LARGE CITY**	●	**Medium City**
●	Small City	●	Town, Village

SYMBOLS

Sights/Activities

	Buddhist		Sento (Public Hot Baths)
	Canoeing, Kayaking		Shinto
	Castle, Fortress		Sikh
	Christian		Skiing
	Confucian		Surfing, Surf Beach
	Diving		Taoist
	Hindu		Trail Head
	Islamic		Winery, Vineyard
	Jain		Zoo, Bird Sanctuary
	Jewish		
	Monument		
	Museum, Gallery		
●	Point of Interest		
	Pool		
	Ruin		

Information

Bank, ATM
Embassy/Consulate
Hospital, Medical
Information
Internet Facilities
Police Station
Post Office, GPO
Telephone
Toilets
Wheelchair Access

Eating

Eating

Drinking

Cafe
Drinking

Entertainment

Entertainment

Shopping

Shopping

Sleeping

Camping
Sleeping

Transport

Airport, Airfield
Border Crossing
Bus Station
Bicycle Path/Cycling
FFCC (Barcelona)
Metro (Barcelona)
Parking Area
Petrol Station
S-Bahn
Taxi Rank
Tube Station
U-Bahn

Geographic

Beach
Lighthouse
Lookout
Mountain, Volcano
National Park
Pass, Canyon
Picnic Area
River Flow
Shelter, Hut
Waterfall

LONELY PLANET OFFICES

Australia
Head Office
Locked Bag 1, Footscray, Victoria 3011
☎ 03 8379 8000, fax 03 8379 8111

USA
150 Linden St, Oakland, CA 94607
☎ 510 250 6400, toll free 800 275 8555,
fax 510 893 8572

UK
2nd fl, 186 City Rd,
London EC1V 2NT
☎ 020 7106 2100, fax 020 7106 2101

Contact
talk2us@lonelyplanet.com
lonelyplanet.com/contact

Published by Lonely Planet Publications Pty Ltd
ABN 36 005 607 983

Printed through Colorcraft Ltd, Hong Kong
Printed in China

MIX
Paper from
responsible sources
FSC™ C021741
www.fsc.org